The Public Budgeting and Finance Primer

The Public Budgeting and Finance Primer

Key Concepts in Fiscal Choice

Jay Eungha Ryu

M.E.Sharpe
Armonk, New York
London, England

The EuroSlavic fonts used to create this work are © 1986–2014 Payne Loving Trust.
EuroSlavic is available from Linguist's Software, Inc.,
www.linguistsoftware.com, P.O. Box 580, Edmonds, WA 98020-0580 USA
tel (425) 775-1130.

Library of Congress Cataloging-in-Publication Data

Ryu, Jay Eungha.
  The public budgeting and finance primer : key concepts in fiscal choice / by Jay Eungha Ryu.
    pages cm
Includes bibliographical references and index.
ISBN 978-0-7656-3796-3 (cloth : alk. paper)—ISBN 978-0-7656-3797-0 (pbk. : alk. paper)
1. Budget— United States. 2. Budget process—United States. 3. United States—
Appropriations and expenditures. I. Title.

HJ2051.R983 2014
352.4'80973—dc23   2013018762

Printed in the United States of America

Contents

PART IV. PUBLIC CHOICE AND TAXATION

PART V. INTERGOVERNMENTAL FISCAL RELATIONS

PART VI. MACROBUDGETING

PART VII. NEW APPROACHES TO BUDGET AND FINANCE

Preface

The main purpose of this book is to shed light on what factors affect decisions on resource allocation. This book summarizes key concepts in fiscal choice in the public sector for both practitioners and scholars of public budgeting and finance, from a perspective of choice between politics and economics in completely stand-alone chapters for each concept. In short, public-budget decision makers attempt to be rational in allocating scarce resources but find that there are numerous obstacles to their rational attempts. Politics, institutions, and most of all human beings' endless quest for resources are the most decisive drivers of fiscal choice in the public sector.

Part I introduces budget institutions and processes at various levels of government. Public budgets are not formed through arbitrary decisions by random individuals. For instance, an individual cannot decide to spend a certain amount of his or her state's sales tax revenue to renovate state highway systems. There are highly institutionalized procedures for making fiscal choices, especially at the national and state levels. Centrally coordinated budget preparation in both executive and legislative branches constitutes a substantial portion of U.S. budget processes. Other rules and requirements strongly augment or restrict the discretion of budget decision makers. Sometimes, court decisions mandate executive agencies to redress the condition of litigated service. In addition, partisan configurations over budget processes almost always influence how much of the budget should be spent on what programs.

Part II introduces various techniques of budget allocation that are expected to improve efficiency and effectiveness of public goods and services. Budget decision makers have attempted to maximize utility from public budget expenses by adopting rationality-based budget-allocation techniques, but their implementation is often stymied by budget institutions and is heavily swayed by partisan politics. However, rational approaches to budget allocation have recently come back into the field of public budget allocation. This part summarizes these rationality-based resource-allocation techniques that various public and private organizations have adopted in their budget decision-making processes. These techniques borrow fundamental ideas from welfare economics. This part discusses strengths and limits of rational budget-allocation techniques.

Part III introduces theories explaining how budget decision makers prepare budgets under institutional settings. Whereas Part I introduces real-life budget institutions and processes, Part III describes budget theories that have been developed for the past several decades to explain the aspiration and behaviors of budget decision makers under such institutions and processes. Capacity limits and institutional conflicts are two buzzwords that characterize the aspiration and behaviors. They also result in highly predictable and stable interactions among such main budget actors as executive agencies, chief executive officers, and legislators. In addition, the capacity limits and institutional conflicts typically cause incremental budget changes across years. Some recent theories have attempted to explain sudden, dramatic budget changes, but the limits and conflicts explain such dramatic budget changes very well. An economics-based framework sometimes presents observations of the aspiration and behaviors of budget decision makers and nicely explains budget expansion.

Part IV slightly differs from the first three parts in that it basically introduces economics-based analyses of public goods and services. Public finance scholars have developed a field known as public choice, mostly focused on local jurisdictions. Its main framework is demand-and-supply schedules, typically found in microeconomics. This part also introduces the principles of taxation, such as revenue collection, efficiency, and equity. What are the best conditions for revenue maximization? Various tax breaks threaten the bases of governmental taxes, thus jeopardizing governmental revenue collection. Sound tax principles suggest that no taxation can distort the private market economy. In many cases, however, tax cuts are provided as a way to induce businesses to locate in governmental jurisdictions or to stimulate sagging economies. At the same time, taxation should treat taxpayers with different abilities to pay differently while guaranteeing that taxpayers with equal capacities shoulder equal tax burdens. Efficiency and equity are heavily driven by partisan politics. Another important dimension in fiscal choice is how to gauge the fiscal capacity of governmental jurisdictions. Since the amount of intergovernmental grants is often decided based on recipient governments' fiscal capacity, measures of fiscal capacity and stress will be useful for practitioners as well as scholars.

Part V presents rationales, types, and fiscal impacts of intergovernmental (IGR) grants. Higher-level governments typically distribute IGR grants to lower-level governments to account for, or internalize, spillover benefits or costs generated by delivering public services. IGR grants are distributed to lower-level governments to address a mismatch between the benefit- and cost-spillover range and the service-provision range, which might cause resource misallocation. Higher-level governments also rely on IGR grants as tools to improve fiscal equalization across lower-level governments. Sometimes, IGR grants are used as a way to continue cooperative tax administration between lower-level and higher-level governments. Different types of IGR grants have different fiscal impacts on recipient governments' fiscal choice. Part V summarizes theoretical and empirical observations of the fiscal impacts of diverse IGR grants.

Part VI introduces main topics pertaining to macroeconomic theories and policies. Many topics in this part are somewhat technical, and public budget practitioners and scholars might think that they are irrelevant for understanding public budget and finance decisions. However, since the 2008 financial market crisis, both public and private sectors have been converging to the extent that focusing on only one sector does not guarantee an accurate investigation of fiscal choice mechanisms in the two sectors. Without doubt, macroeconomic theories and policies provide us with elaborate frameworks showing how the two sectors are linked. Classical approaches to macroeconomic activities explain the labor market equilibrium, the link of both saving and investment to interest rates, and a theory of price level. Keynesian approaches introduce why aggregate-demand schedules are most important to explain macroeconomic activities. This part then discusses how each of these theories is linked to a specific macroeconomic policy. It also introduces new approaches to describing and prescribing macroeconomic activities. One important caveat regarding macroeconomic policies is that they are subjected to strong congressional budget procedures. Key congressional procedures to decide the federal spending level are summarized as well. Finally, this part discusses the mechanics of debt management by state and local governments. Macroeconomic theories and policies are primarily related to debt-financed governmental expenditures to stimulate the national economy. In contrast, state and local governments tend to borrow monies to finance capital projects. This part shows the structures of state and local bonds and the factors affecting them.

Part VII summarizes emerging or reilluminated budget and finance topics such as participatory budgeting, behavioral economics and finance, and collaborative budgeting.

One advantage of this book is that it combines public budgeting and finance frameworks to have a comprehensive, and thus more accurate, understanding of how public budgets are made. Public budgeting issues are focused somewhat more on fiscal management and institutions, while public finance issues are more centered on public sector economics. The two fields have recently been converging. For instance, after the 2008 financial market crisis, a lot of financial management techniques (which are related to micro-/macroeconomics, banking/finance, etc.) were heavily discussed even in the public budgeting community. Practitioners and scholars of public budgeting cannot fully understand fiscal choices without understanding the economic issues. In contrast, practitioners and scholars of public finance cannot have a complete understanding of such fiscal decisions without learning the budget processes and institutions that are the main topics in public budgeting. As clarified in Parts I, II, and III, budget processes and institutions best explain how public budgets are actually determined. In this sense, practitioners and scholars of public finance are strongly urged to read these three parts. This book fills the gap in the literature by succinctly combining the most relevant topics in public budget and finance into one book.

Another significant feature of this book is the format of its chapters. The budget and finance topics, which are identified as key concepts in fiscal choice, are introduced in completely stand-alone chapters so that readers can read any chapters that interest them first. Readers can freely move around different topics depending on their preferences and study schedules. This is a convenient feature for separate research projects.

This book is mostly the result of my individual summaries of the articles and books that I have prepared during the past ten years. However, I would like to thank my colleagues in the field of public budgeting and finance for their invaluable comments at various stages of this book project. Professor Ken Kriz has provided me with very useful advice on how I can organize book chapters so they can be linked consistently. He has also made numerous comments on what topics should be added and what else had better be cut out. For both the organization of book chapters and expert advice on book contents, I deeply appreciate Professor Kriz. At the early stage of this book project, Professor Bob Kravchuk also offered me very comprehensive ideas on how I could structure the book chapters so that readers could discover what the overarching theme of this book might be. He also gave me specific suggestions on polishing multiple chapters. I also thank Professor Chulho Jung in the Department of Economics, Ohio University, for his useful comments on the general tone of the chapters related to macroeconomics.

I thank many other people who helped me finish this book project. Harry Briggs at M.E. Sharpe has skillfully encouraged me to polish entire chapters, based on his professional experience. Patricia Black provided me with excellent and expert editing help on all the chapters. Roman Suer has also supported me with his research assistance on the earlier draft of this book manuscript. Finally, I would thank my best friend and wife, Jeongwon, and my daughters, Sueyeon and Leah, for their sustained encouragement to write, update, and polish this book. Without any doubt, remaining errors are all mine.

List of Abbreviations

ABC	Activity-based costing
ACIR	U.S. Advisory Commission on Intergovernmental Relations
AE	Aggregate expenditures
AEC	U.S. Atomic Energy Commission
AFDC	Aid to Families with Dependent Children
AFMC	Air Force Material Command
BAA of 1921	Budget and Accounting Act of 1921
BABs	Build America Bonds
BBRs	Balanced budget requirements
BCA of 2011	Budget Control Act of 2011
BCPs	Budget change proposals
BEA of 1990	Budget Enforcement Act of 1990
BIS	Bureau of Industry and Security
BOB	U.S. Bureau of Budget (now the U.S. Office of Management and Budget)
CBA	Cost-benefit analysis
CBA of 1974	Congressional Budget and Impoundment Control Act of 1974
CBO	Congressional Budget Office
CY	Calendar year
DFM	Division of Financial Management (Idaho)
DM	Department of Management
DOC	U.S. Department of Commerce
DOD	U.S. Department of Defense
DOF	Department of Finance (California)
EDA	Economic Development Administration
EGTRRA of 2001	Economic Growth and Tax Relief Reconciliation Act of 2001
EITC	Earned Income Tax Credit

EPA	U.S. Environmental Protection Agency
ESA	Economics and Statistics Administration
EZ	Empowerment Zone
Fannie Mae	Federal National Mortgage Association
FCC	Federal Communications Commission
FGFF	First-generation fiscal federalism
FICO	Financial Assistance Corporation
FOMC	Federal Open Market Committee
FSB	Financial Stability Board
FY	Fiscal year
G&A	General and administrative
GAO	U.S. Government Accountability Office
GASB	Government Accounting Standard Board
GDP	Gross Domestic Product
GO	General Obligation
GOBP	Governor's Office of Budget and Planning (Texas)
GPRA of 1993	Government Performance and Results Act of 1993
GRH	Gramm-Rudman-Hollings Balanced Budget and Emergency Deficit Control Act of 1985
GTB	Guaranteed tax base
HBC	House Budget Committee
IGR	Intergovernmental
ITA	International Trade Administration
JLBC	Joint Legislative Budget Committee (Mississippi)
LBB	Legislative budget board (Texas)
LBO	Legislative budget office (Mississippi)
LIB	Line-item budgeting
LOST	Local-option sales taxes
MBDA	Minority Business Development Agency
MCO	Maintenance of current operations
MPC	Marginal producer cost
MRRPI	Marginal rate of return on private investment
MRTP	Marginal rate of time preference
MSC	Marginal social cost
NAO	Network administrative organization
NASA	National Aeronautics and Space Administration
NASBO	National Association of State Budget Officers
NCSL	National Conference of State Legislatures
NIC	Net interest cost
NIST	National Institute of Standards and Technology
NOAA	National Oceanic and Atmospheric Administration

NPV	Net present value
NRSRO	Nationally recognized statistical rating organizations
NTIA	National Telecommunications and Information Administration
NTIS	National Technical Information Service
OECD	Organization for Economic Cooperation and Development
OIG	Office of Inspector General
OLA	Office of Legislative Analyst
OMB	U.S. Office of Management and Budget
OPEB	Other unfunded postemployment benefits
PART	Program Assessment Rating Tool
PILOTs	Payments in lieu of taxes
PMA	President's Management Agenda
PPB	Planning and performance budgeting
PPBES	Planning, programming, budgeting, and execution system
PPBS	Planning, programming, and budgeting system
PPS	Prospective payment system
PRM	Bureau of Population, Refugees, and Migration
PTO	U.S. Patent and Trademark Office
QE	Quantitative easing
RES	Representative expenditures system
RTS	Representative tax system
SAMHSA	Substance Abuse and Mental Health Services Administration
SBA	U.S. Small Business Administration
SBC	Senate Budget Committee
SBCB	State Budget and Control Board (South Carolina)
SGFF	Second-generation fiscal federalism
SIB	State Infrastructure Bank
STAP	Secure Transportation Asset Program
TABOR	Taxpayer Bill of Rights (Colorado)
TB	Target budgeting
TBB	Target-based budgeting
TBTF	"Too big to fail"
TELs	Tax and expenditure limits
TIC	True interest cost
TTR	Total taxable resources
USF	Universal Service Fund
VAR	Vector autoregression
VERA	Voluntary export restraint agreement
WTP	Willingness-to-pay
ZBB	Zero-based budgeting

PART I

BUDGET PROCESS AND INSTITUTIONS

1 Executive Budgeting System

Under an executive budgeting system, central budget offices on behalf of chief executive officers (e.g., president, governor, or mayor) review budget proposals that executive agencies prepare for upcoming fiscal years. The key point of an executive budgeting system is that central budget offices exert centralized budget coordination over agency budget requests pursuant to the chief executive officers' policy preferences and available budgets. The central budget offices will prepare final, single budget proposals called executive budgets. Executive agencies have been submitting their budget proposals electronically, and citizens can now access these electronic executive budgets. This chapter introduces the following issues crucial for understanding the executive budgeting system, especially centralized budget coordination.

- Why Is an Executive Budgeting System Needed?
- Historical Context of the Executive Budgeting System
- The National Executive Budgeting System: President's Budget
- State Executive Budgeting Systems
- Local Executive Budgeting Systems
- Continuing Debates on the Executive Budgeting System

WHY IS AN EXECUTIVE BUDGETING SYSTEM NEEDED?

When agency bureaucrats prepared budgets, they tended to maximize their parochial interests and agency budgets. This was especially true when there was no centralized budget control over agency budget proposals. According to the Budget and Accounting Act (BAA) of 1921, the central budget office, the Bureau of Budget (BOB, now the Office of Management and Budget [OMB]) in the federal government, was expected to do what chief executives were supposed to do over agency budget requests. Armed with their expert budget information and techniques, and executive supervisory authority, central budget office staffs checked agency budget requests for unnecessary padding and orchestrated agency budget proposals in line with available resources and chief executives' political and policy preferences (Ryu 2011a, 72–73).

HISTORICAL CONTEXT OF THE EXECUTIVE BUDGETING SYSTEM

Around the turn of the twentieth century, there was a movement for governmental budget reforms that could be placed under the rubric of an executive budgeting system. States and localities were the pioneers of executive budgeting. The New York Bureau of Municipal Research, in particular, was in the pioneering group. However, different ideas developed between the principals of executive budgeting: Progressive reformers vs. Taft conservatives.

PROGRESSIVE REFORMERS ON BUDGET REFORMS

Progressive reformers such as Henry Adams and William Allen emphasized efficient democracy with its stress on public education and participation. Up to 1910, the liberal Progressives' ideas dominated. They contended that efficiency of governmental programs would help fund public programs, but the general public could be a driving force for good government to the extent that they were educated on budgeting and accounting (Rubin 1994).

TAFT CONSERVATIVES ON THE EXECUTIVE BUDGETING SYSTEM

Taft conservatives such as Frank Goodnow and Frederick Cleveland generally supported more centralized budget coordination. Although they still retained their trust in the general public, in the 1912 Taft Commission on Economy and Efficiency they emphasized the importance of detailed budget information, such as balance sheets, operation accounts, and cost accounts. Administrative officers were the only ones who knew such technical details of public programs. They understood the conditions needed for efficiency and economy. However, chief executives as representatives of the whole society were assumed to be responsible for reviewing agency budget requests and proposing budgets to legislatures. Therefore, all budget ideas coming up from the departments were to be judged by chief executives. Agencies were generally spendthrift, and chief executives knew more about agency budget requests than legislatures and could cut back fiscally irresponsible requests. Chief executives represented the entire population and, thus, were expected to better prioritize expenditures. This was in contrast to congressional representation of districts (Lee, Johnson, and Joyce 2013, 188; Meyers and Rubin 2011; Rubin 1994). The suggestions made by Taft conservatives ultimately dominated the budget reform movement, and the national and state governments began adopting the executive budgeting system in the 1910s.

ESTABLISHMENT OF THE EXECUTIVE BUDGETING SYSTEM

Maryland was the first state to adopt an executive budgeting system, in 1916, several years earlier than the 1921 BAA. By the 1950s and the 1960s, most states had adopted some form of executive budgeting system (Abney and Lauth 1998). Throughout the late 1960s and into the 1980s, many state legislatures had been more professionalized in terms of session length, staff, and compensation. Legislatures had been more independent from governors, but until very recently state governors had been the dominating budget actors in state budget processes (Rosenthal 1998, 49–55; 2004, 184–205). At the local level, mayors have been at the center of budget decisions despite more diversified power relationships between mayors and city councils (Rubin 2010, 130–41).

Until the enactment of the 1974 Congressional Budget and Impoundment Control Act, the national budget process had been characterized by centralized budget coordination in the executive budgeting system (Schick 2007, 84–117). In the 1921 Budget and Accounting Act that introduced the executive budgeting system in the federal government, the central budget office was the BOB. As the name implies, the BOB primarily dealt with budget issues. However, during the reorganization initiative in the early 1970s, the BOB was renamed the Office of Management and Budget (OMB) and the "M (management)" function was greatly enhanced (Mosher and Stephenson 1982). In addition, policy functions have been gradually incorporated into OMB functions, with a recent example being OMB's supervisory role over the Program Assessment Rating Tool (PART) implementation since 2004 (Gilmour and Lewis 2006). Despite its increased attention to management and policy functions, OMB still maintains tight control over budget proposals made by executive agencies (LeLoup 1977; Schick 2007, 39–117).

THE NATIONAL EXECUTIVE BUDGETING SYSTEM: PRESIDENT'S BUDGET

The national executive budgeting system generates the president's budget. The national executive budget process and the roles of budget actors in the process are somewhat more complicated than those at the state and local levels.

PROCESS OF THE NATIONAL EXECUTIVE BUDGET SYSTEM

Fiscal Year (FY) 2013 for the federal government refers to the period from October in Calendar Year (CY) 2012 to September in CY 2013. Under an executive budgeting system, federal agencies start developing their budget proposals months before the beginning of a certain FY. For instance, during the spring of CY 2011 the OMB issued spring planning guidance to the federal executive agencies on their budget requests for FY 2013. Typically, this guidance is delivered in a letter from the OMB director to heads of the federal agencies. From the spring of CY 2011 to the summer of CY 2011, the OMB and the executive agencies collaborated to discuss and identify major issues for FY 2013 budgets, developed and analyzed options for the upcoming fall budget review, and planned how to deal with future budget issues.

During July in CY 2011, the OMB issued the budget instructions, known as the OMB Circular A-11, to all executive agencies. Typically this circular contains more detailed instructions for budget data and materials. During September, the executive agencies submit their budget requests to the OMB. During October–November, the OMB reviews the agency budget requests. OMB staffs analyze the budget requests in accordance with presidential policy preferences, program performance, and budget-related institutional constraints. The OMB finishes reviewing agency budget proposals and considering overall budget policies during late November. Then, it recommends a complete set of budget requests to the president. From late November of CY 2011 to January of CY 2012, all federal agencies, including legislative and judicial branch agencies, entered computerized budget data and submitted print materials. Once this process is finished, the OMB locks all agencies out of the database. Executive branch agencies may appeal to the OMB and the president during this period. In most cases, the OMB and the agencies collaborate to fix conflicting issues. If they cannot, they work together to get the president's decision. During January of CY 2012, the OMB reviewed congressional budget justifications, i.e., formal agency budget requests, for FY 2013. All agencies prepare the justifications to explain their budget proposals to the responsible congressional subcommittees (Lee, Johnson, and Joyce 2013, 189–93; Schick 2007, 92–99).

ROLES OF BUDGET ACTORS IN THE NATIONAL EXECUTIVE BUDGETING PROCESS

The president's role has varied in the executive budget process. Some presidents, such as Clinton, issued policy guidelines in the early stage of the executive budget process, while others, such as George W. Bush, were not involved in the process until all agencies assembled their budget proposals. In addition, the OMB has become more involved in some form of political gamesmanship between the president and Congress. Although the OMB is a major policy and budget assistance tool for the president, OMB examiners have also been very vigilant about policy preferences of congressional committee members and their staffs (Schick 2007, 92–99). At the same time, however, the OMB has provided the federal agencies with substantial levels of assistance in processing complicated policy and budget information. It has also helped coordinate conflicts across various agencies and agency programs (Ryu 2011, 63–101; Schick 2007, 84–117).

STATE EXECUTIVE BUDGETING SYSTEMS

State executive budget processes have followed patterns quite similar to the national executive budget process (Forsythe 1997). Two examples of state executive budgeting systems illustrate the similarity.

IDAHO EXECUTIVE BUDGETING SYSTEM

The Idaho Division of Financial Management (DFM) distributed central budget guidelines to executive agencies at the beginning of the state budget process throughout the 1970s to the 1990s. Agency budget forms typically include agency goals, objectives, line-item information, and even performance indicators. The DFM functioned as the watchdog for gubernatorial policy preferences. Several budget analysts were assigned to four subdivisions—education, general government, human resources, and natural resources. The budget analysts checked the accuracy within each agency that decided upon the "maintenance of current operations" (MCO) level of appropriations. The MCO level coordinated agency budget requests along with several budget targets. The increases in agency budget requests above the MCO level were tightly reviewed in line with gubernatorial policy preferences, available revenue sources, programmatic considerations, and general policy considerations. The DFM made budget recommendations to the governor, who finalized decisions on agency budget requests. A key part of this centralized budget coordination was the revenue estimate that forecast the available resources for the upcoming fiscal years. Once finalized, the executive budget was passed on to the legislature for approval (Duncombe and Kinney 1991, 63–70).

California Executive Budgeting System

California's budget system is another example of executive dominance over budget preparation. California's executive budgeting system has been gradually developed since the early 1910s. Very similar to Idaho, the California central budget office, the Department of Finance (DOF), develops the executive budget on behalf of the governor. The executive budget document is presented by program categories organized around a line-item base. The DOF circulates budget instructions that include information on forecast population growth and the inflation forecast. The automated budget system in the DOF instantly provides departments and agencies with information on the current budget base and subsequent legislative changes, as well as potential budget changes due to price and demographic changes.

Departments submit Budget Change Proposals (BCPs) to the DOF. BCPs have included changes in workload, need for new technology, court decisions, federal law changes, and new policy directions. During the 1980s, the DOF directed departments and agencies to receive a variety of technical assistance from the DOF. Since then, the DOF has checked the accuracy of program needs and benefits, the sufficiency of documentation for department/agency cost justification, or the relevancy of the assumptions in departmental and agency budget justifications. The DOF has also uploaded model versions of BCPs on its website, which provide substantial informational assistance to departments and agencies (McCaffery 1991, 7–16; 2007, 16–20).

Local Executive Budgeting Systems

At the local level, executive budget systems are not as standardized as those in the national and state executive budget processes. Local budget processes are somewhat different in terms of fiscal choice mechanisms as discussed later in Chapter 17 in Part IV. In addition, local budgets are highly dependent on the budget systems, institutions, and revenue capacities of state governments. However, as mentioned earlier in this chapter, executive budget reform initiatives originated from local governments. During the period 1895 to 1920, characterized as the Progressive Era, the main focus of governmental budgets was how to reconcile activism and efficiency in governmental programs. Executive budget reforms were suggested as a way to enhance both activism and efficiency. Following two world wars, more professional managers have been hired in council-manager forms of local governments. Very recently, mayoral forms of local governments have been on the rise again. Overall, most of the various forms of local governments have employed some form of executive budgeting system (Rubin 2010, 130–41).

CONTINUING DEBATES ON THE EXECUTIVE BUDGETING SYSTEM

Just as there was a controversy between Progressive reformers and Taft conservatives over executive budgeting systems, controversy has been continuously evoked, especially over the effectiveness of centralized budget control. The controversy will not be fixed in a day. Instead, key assertions on each side are more likely to repeat themselves in the budgeting community. It has recently been revived in new forms.

CENTRALIZED BUDGET COORDINATION ENHANCES EFFICIENCY

Some examples evidence the efficiency and effectiveness in governmental budget processes rendered by executive budgeting systems. The enhanced information-processing capacity of central budget offices in executive budgeting systems tended to reduce institutional conflicts between the executive branch and the legislatures, as well as among agencies within the executive branch. The California budget process exemplified this potential. In 1978, an open-access computer information system was adopted statewide. Both the executive branch and the legislature could access agency budgets and even performance data through the system. Centralized budget coordination in the California executive budget system expedited a high level of information sharing between the budget actors (McCaffery 1991, 7–16). During the legislative budget hearings, DOF (Department of Finance) and OLA (Office of Legislative Analyst) budget examiners have been in a somewhat competitive mood. However, such competition minimized errors by bringing budget issues to the surface. In addition, during multiple rounds of hearings, DOF budget examiners served as experienced information processors and reduced potential institutional conflicts (McCaffery 2007, 17, 20–21). Thurmier and Willoughby (2001) shed new light on the role of budget examiners in state central budget offices. These professionals understand budget agenda, interpret budget signals from budget environments, and make judgments on the political feasibility of budget proposals. Most importantly, central budget examiners help align microbudget choices of agencies, governors, and legislatures with macrobudget institutions and constraints. Therefore, central budget examiners are a critically important lynchpin linking microbudget opportunities with macrobudget deliberations.

In a similar vein, Ryu (2011a) empirically tested whether centralized budget coordination in the national and state budget processes facilitates the processing of budget-related information and reduces organizational conflicts among executive agencies or legislative agencies. He found that centralized budget coordination significantly improved information processing and reduced such organizational tensions. However, there was a threshold effect: Up to a certain level of centralized coordination, the effect was evidenced, but beyond that level, centralization stymied information processing and increased organizational conflicts.

CENTRALIZED BUDGET COORDINATION: FUTILE SEARCH FOR EFFICIENCY

In contrast, Meyers and Rubin (2011) dispensed some cautions about centralized budget coordination. In evaluating the national executive budgeting system, they contend that supplemental appropriations (such as emergency supplemental) were not eliminated through centralized budget processing. Budget transparency increased, but citizens are still confused about the basics of governmental finances. The neutrality of the OMB in reflecting political and programmatic priorities is still questionable. Even under executive budgeting, the president and Congress have been involved in political gaming. Most laws are the results of joint products of the two branches.

Meyers and Rubin (2011) introduced some suggestions for better governmental budget processes. Recent recommendations from policy advocacy groups (e.g., the National Academy of Public Administration, the National Research Council, the Committee for a Responsible Federal Budget, the Bipartisan Policy Center, and Our Fiscal Security) made various suggestions. The national debt must be limited to 60 percent of GDP. More rule-based budget-control measures similar to automatic sequestrations or across-the-board-cuts should be adopted. What is common among the proposals is less dependence on executive budget power. Most importantly, more enhanced cooperation between the branches of government is needed. In addition, a better-educated public, which was the goal shared by the early Progressive budget reformers discussed above, should be given priority attention.

CHAPTER SUMMARY

- **Central Budget Offices**

Central budget offices in executive budgeting systems checked for unnecessary budget padding in agency budget requests. They also checked agency budget requests in line with available resources and chief executives' political and policy preferences.

- **History of Executive Budgeting Systems**

States and local governments were the pioneers of executive budgeting systems around the turn of the twentieth century. Principals of the systems had somewhat different ideas on the efficiency and effectiveness of the systems.

Progressive reformers contended that efficiency of governmental programs would help fund public programs but that the general public could be a driving force.

In contrast, Taft conservatives asserted that chief executives should be responsible for controlling agency budget requests because they knew more about the requests than did legislatures.

Maryland was the first state to adopt an executive budgeting system. By the 1960s, most states had adopted some form of executive budgeting system. The national budget process had featured a strong executive budgeting system until the 1974 Congressional Budget and Impoundment Control Act was established. Local governments have budget processes close to executive budgeting systems.

- **Office of Management and Budget (OMB)**

About eighteen months prior to the start of a fiscal year, the OMB issues budget planning guidance to federal executive agencies on their budget proposals. The OMB later issues more specific budget instructions, known as the OMB Circular A-11, to all executive agencies. The OMB is heavily involved in coordinating agency budget requests until it generates the president's budgets.

- **State and Local Executive Budgeting Systems**

State executive budgeting systems are close to the national executive budget process. Central budget offices coordinate agency budget requests pursuant to available resources and chief executives' policy preferences. They also provide agencies with technical analysis assistance. Local budget processes, albeit influenced by state governments, also employ some form of centralized budget coordination.

- **Views on Executive Budgeting Systems**

There are two contrasting views on the effectiveness of the executive budgeting systems.

(1) Central budget offices can expedite a high level of information sharing between budget actors and assist line agencies with processing complex budget information. They also reduce organizational conflicts among executive agencies or legislative agencies.

(2) Critics have contended that the executive budgeting system has not enhanced transparency, so the neutrality of central budget offices in reflecting political and programmatic priorities is still in question. Instead, the critics suggest rule-based budget controls and heightened coordination between executive branches and legislatures.

2 Legislative Budgeting System

Legislatures develop their own budgets separate from budgets that executive branches prepare. There are two key points in understanding legislative budgeting systems. First, a legislative budgeting system is a reflection of legislative initiatives to regain budget control from executive branches. Second, a legislative budgeting system is an effort to control budget padding by legislators and legislative committees through centralized budget coordination, similar to the centralized budget control found in executive budgeting systems. The legislative budgeting system at the national level is called congressional budgeting. This chapter focuses on the following issues:

- Why Was Congressional Budgeting Created?
- Early Observation of Congressional Budgeting
- Revival of Congressional Budgeting
- Legislative Budgeting Systems in States
- Prospect of Legislative Budgeting: The Case of Congressional Budgeting

WHY WAS CONGRESSIONAL BUDGETING CREATED?

Before the Budget and Accounting Act (BAA) of 1921, executive agencies in the federal government were allowed to make their budget requests directly to congressional committees. The dispersal of budget preparation resulted in budget padding by executive agencies and bureaucrats. In numerous ways, the BAA of 1921 established an executive budgeting system to control unnecessary growth in governmental budgets. As noted in the previous chapter, chief executive officers, governors, or presidents were given strong authority to centrally coordinate executive agency budget requests to orchestrate them in line with forecast revenues and policy preferences of the chief executive officers. Up to the enactment of the Congressional Budget and Impoundment Control Act (CBA) of 1974, in the case of the federal government, the president had dominated the budget process. In many ways, executive dominance of the federal budget process first ignited congressional efforts to regain its budget control power, followed by congressional attempts to control dispersed budget review processes in Congress.

Institutional Tension Between the President and Congress

President Nixon was known for his abuse of the executive budget power in refusing to spend what Congress had appropriated. Even before the enactment of the BAA of 1921, presidents could cancel some appropriations for the purpose of savings and efficient management pursuant to the Anti-deficiency Act of 1905, which was further affirmed in the 1950 Omnibus Appropriations Act. President Truman impounded some funds for the Air Force, and President Eisenhower impounded military procurement funds to build a missile system. President Kennedy withheld funds for the production of the B-70 bomber. President Johnson impounded highway funds and some funds for development, education, agriculture, health, and welfare.

In contrast, Nixon abused the power beyond that of his predecessors. He impounded funds for health grants, urban renewal, and Model Cities under the guise of fiscal integrity. By doing this, he was substantially modifying congressional budget priorities because he was simultaneously proposing new spending for defense, space, revenue sharing, and the supersonic transport. He further withheld funds from highway and sewer funds, water pollution control, housing, and agriculture. The Office of Management and Budget (OMB) reported that the total amount of impoundment was about $8 billion, while the actual amount was estimated at around $18 billion (LeLoup 1977, 112–13). In fact, the creation of the CBA was partially congressional response to the presidential abuse of executive budget power and a move to regain budget control power (Schick 2007, 120). The CBA stipulated that the president must get approval from both houses to rescind appropriated funds within forty-five days (Schick 2007, 286–88; Wildavsky and Caiden 2004, 75). It is clear that the president has the burden of getting congressional approval to cancel appropriated funds, one of the key aspects of the congressional budget provided in the CBA.

Uncontrollable U.S. Budgets

Similar to the executive budgeting system, the CBA attempted to regain more centralized budget coordination. Since 1932, one salient aspect of the congressional budget process has been the dispersal of spending power. Congress had been exercising its power of the purse over general fund expenditures through a highly decentralized committee system. In both houses, no single committee was in charge of all general fund expenditure decisions; instead, jurisdiction was divided among multiple committees. In 1932, about 89 percent of general fund expenditures were under the jurisdiction of the Appropriations committees in both houses. In 1992, only about 63 percent were under the jurisdiction of these committees, while committees on energy and commerce, agriculture, and other programs and the Ways and Means Committee obtained jurisdiction over general fund expenditures (Cogan 1994, 22–23).

In addition, other categories of expenditures such as permanent appropriations and borrowing authority completely bypassed the annual appropriation procedures. Spending categories such as appropriated entitlements and contract authority were subject to annual appropriations, but by the time appropriation decisions were made, budget resources had been already committed for appropriated entitlements and contract authority. Overall, the annual appropriation procedures for these programs were regarded as a pro forma decision (Cogan 1994, 22). For instance, some entitlement programs are authorized by permanent or multiyear appropriations in substantive law. Such spending is approved automatically each year, without legislative action by Congress. Examples of such entitlement programs include Medicare, Social Security, and federal employee retirement funds. A portion of entitlement spending, called appropriated entitlements (i.e., general fund entitlements), is funded in annual appropriations acts. Medicaid is such a program. These programs have composed roughly 36 to 38 percent of funding provided in annual appropriations acts. The permanent entitlement programs, along with appropriated entitlements, increased substantially throughout the 1960s. The rapid growth in the entitlement programs was spurred in part in response to the economic emergency of the 1930s and the Great Society initiatives in the 1960s (Cogan 1994, 24–25; Heniff 2010; LeLoup 1977, 53–55).

Also as noted in the previous chapter and in Part III, whenever the locus of budget preparation is dispersed among executive agencies with parochial or special group interests, agencies are likely to be more assertive. As the executive budgeting system was an attempt to control such parochial budget padding, so was the congressional budget initiative. The CBA created a centralized locus of budget coordination through the creation of Budget Committees in both houses (Schick 2007, 118–61).

EARLY OBSERVATION OF CONGRESSIONAL BUDGETING

Cogan (1994, 28–37) showed that the U.S. Congress had already resorted to somewhat centralized budget coordination between 1789 and 1930, long before the establishment of the CBA of 1974. From 1789 to 1865, the House Ways and Means Committee had jurisdiction over all appropriations bills in the House. In 1816, the Senate created its Finance Committee with jurisdiction over appropriations. Since they were and are tax committees, the two committees were in charge of virtually all budget issues. In 1815, appropriations power substantially shifted from the Ways and Means Committee to a newly created House Appropriations Committee. In 1817, the Senate Appropriations Committee was created, shifting appropriations jurisdiction from the Senate Finance Committee. Despite this jurisdictional shift, there were still budget-controlling committees (i.e., Appropriations Committees) in charge of all appropriations for both houses of Congress. This institutional arrangement continued until 1877. Cogan (1994, 28–29) shows that federal budgets had a surplus, except in a few years, during the time period when there were centralized loci on appropriations review covering both houses.

During the next nine years, beginning in 1877, the House stripped the House Appropriations Committee of its jurisdiction over eight of the fourteen appropriations bills. In each case, appropriations authority was shifted to legislative committees with jurisdiction over the programs contained in these bills. By 1885, almost half of all discretionary appropriations were taken away from the Appropriations Committee to substantive legislative committees. The dispersal of spending power in Congress was associated with a rapid increase in spending. From 1881 to 1885, there was a 40 percent surplus, but it turned into a deficit by 1894. This pattern continued between

1900 and 1916 after the Senate also decided to divide appropriations jurisdiction in 1899. As a result of the rapid budget increase, the House divested seven powerful legislative committees of appropriations authority to regain fiscal constraint in 1919. In 1922, the Senate again followed the House ruling that all appropriations bills should be reviewed by one committee. The result was that federal budgets had a surplus in each year from 1920 to 1930 (Cogan 1994, 30–37).

REVIVAL OF CONGRESSIONAL BUDGETING

The CBA of 1974 attempted to control the increase in federal budgets, which was believed to result from the dispersal of spending power in Congress, in a way similar to the executive budgeting system initiated by the Budget and Accounting Act of 1921. The newly created Budget Committees in both houses produced congressional budgets before Appropriations Committees started reviewing appropriations bills. In other words, when Congress received the president's budget, its Budget Committees would develop congressional budgets that defined the budget targets for each fiscal year. These congressional budget targets are specified in budget resolutions that provide possible total revenues, new budget authority, and outlays, deficits, and public debt. Some budget items, revenues, and entitlement spending under existing laws are supposed to be controlled by budget reconciliation procedures. Budget resolutions and reconciliation procedures were at the core of the congressional budgeting system (Schick 2007, 118–61). See Chapter 25 in Part VI (Congressional Macrobudgeting) for details of the two procedures.

LEGISLATIVE BUDGETING SYSTEMS IN STATES

State legislative budgeting systems are not as institutionalized as the congressional budgeting system. In fact, only a few states can be categorized as legislative budgeting states.

TEXAS

In Texas, the legislative budget dominates final budget decisions, although the executive budget is prepared as well. The Legislative Budget Board (LBB) is composed of the lieutenant governor, the Speaker of the House, and eight other legislative members. The LBB prepares a legislative budget that reflects current service levels, while the executive budget reflects only gubernatorial initiatives and policies. Unlike other state executive budgeting systems, the Texas executive budget is less detailed than the legislative budget. Most of all, only the legislative budget functions as a formal and financial working document.

As noted in Part II, performance-based budgeting tends to be initiated by the executive branches. In Texas, it is the state legislature that initiates its planning and performance budgeting (PPB). During the entire phase of PPB implementation, the LBB cooperates with the Governor's Office of Budget and Planning (GOBP). The GOBP and the LBB collaborate to review performance-related agency budget measures. However, the LBB virtually dominates the entire budget process. Congressional budgeting procedures oftentimes conflict with executive budget systems in the federal budget process. One peculiar observation from the Texas legislative system is that the executive and legislative branches are highly collaborative over state budget preparation (Bland and Clarke 2007, 277–84; Cope 1991, 115–24; Texas Governor's Office of Budget and Planning 2003).

MISSISSIPPI AND SOUTH CAROLINA

The Mississippi budget process is another example of a legislative budgeting system. The Joint Legislative Budget Committee (JLBC) prepares a unified state budget used in the legislative review stage. The governor and the JLBC develop budget instructions circulated to executive agencies. However, the Legislative Budget Office (LBO), which supports the JLBC, reviews agency budget proposals. After holding budget hearings, the JLBC submits a legislative budget to the full state legislature, which then triggers subcommittee budget deliberations, and legislators tend to ignore the executive budgets. Similar to Texas's legislative budgeting system, Mississippi legislative budgets include performance measures. The JLBC and its LBO staff actually learned techniques in requiring programmatic budget information by visiting budget officials in Texas in 1993. In 1994, the Mississippi Budget and Performance Strategic Planning Act legally required incorporation of performance indicators in the state legislative budgets (Clynch 2003; 2007, 258).

Another state budget system that can be categorized as a legislative budgeting system is South Carolina's. The State Budget and Control Board (SBCB) is composed of the governor, the Senate Finance Committee chair, the House Ways and Means Committee chair, the state treasurer, and the comptroller general. The SBCB circulates revenue projections and technical budget instructions to agencies, which then submit their budget proposals to the SBCB, not the governor. The SBCB submits the final budget recommendations to the House Ways and Means Committee and the Senate Finance Committee (Graham 2007, 194–95; Whicker 1991, 137–48). Both Mississippi and South Carolina have seen a strong collaboration between their executive budget offices and legislative budget offices, which is somewhat different from the relationship between the executive branch and Congress in the federal government (LeLoup 1977, 145–47).

PROSPECT OF LEGISLATIVE BUDGETING: THE CASE OF CONGRESSIONAL BUDGETING

If one wants to predict the prospects for legislative budgeting systems in general, the experience of the congressional budgeting system offers very relevant lessons. Two issues deserve our attention: politics within Congress and political tension between the president and Congress.

POLITICS WITHIN CONGRESS

In the national budget process, congressional budgeting procedures often created another layer of institutional conflict to the tension between the two branches as noted above. In addition, there have been various sources of potential institutional conflict between the House and Senate Budget Committees. Similar conflicts were also found between the two committees and other congressional committees. LeLoup (1980) offers a succinct yet comprehensive description of how the aspirations and behaviors of the two committees changed after the enactment of the CBA. House Budget Committee (HBC) Republicans were more policy-oriented, while HBC Democrats were focused on the process (LeLoup 1980, 62–67). The difference in goals resulted in different strategies by committee members. Overall, however, HBC members were more concerned about the process contained in budget resolutions and attempted to write budget resolutions that could pass the House. In contrast, the Senate Budget Committee (SBC) was more policy-oriented. SBC Democrats and Republicans were concerned with both fiscal policy and budget control (LeLoup 1977, 72–75, 88, 97).

The differences between the HBC and the SBC were the most salient in terms of the budget environments surrounding their decision structures. Partisan divide in the HBC significantly affected budget resolutions. In addition, the Appropriations Committee was more strongly influenced by budget resolutions because the categorization of federal expenditures was closer to the committee's jurisdiction. Thus, there was a heightened institutional tension between the HBC and the House Appropriations Committee. The SBC generally had a good relationship with the Appropriations Committee, mainly because appropriations bills were not the primary target of SBC opposition (LeLoup 1980, 67–70, 89–94). This tendency remained almost unchanged until recently, but the SBC has changed since the early 1990s. A partisan wedge between SBC Republicans and Democrats has widened (Schick 2007, 136). Therefore, the congressional budget process has been exposed to potential sources of various institutional conflicts even within Congress.

POLITICAL TENSION BETWEEN THE PRESIDENT AND CONGRESS

Regarding the lasting tension between the executive budget/president and the congressional budget/Congress in the federal government, Meyers and Rubin (2011) made some suggestions similar to the collaboration between governors (or central budget offices) and state legislatures (or legislative budget offices) introduced above. A joint budget resolution between the president and Congress, which carries the power of law, would be a good alternative. This would not cede power from Congress to the executive. The 1921 Budget and Accounting Act actually intended to help Congress exercise its budget power more effectively. Centralization in Congress would also facilitate this process. Thus, Meyers and Rubin's idea of a joint budget resolution is another creative suggestion for relieving the institutional tension caused by both congressional budgets and executive budgets.

However, it should also be remembered that the politics inherent in the congressional budget process exerts substantial leverage over final budget choices. As Schick clarifies, if the congressional budget process survives, it is "because the process enables Congress to set the policies and priorities it wants" (2007, 161). Thus, the fundamental question would be how to derive consensus on budget totals that will be included in a joint budget resolution that would transcend partisan division throughout the congressional budget process. This is definitely a question for continued research and practical questions. Ryu (2011a) makes some suggestions. Central budget offices in the two branches of the federal government might help navigate the partisan divide through expedited collaboration on budget-related information. He shows numerous examples of such collaboration in state governments that might give some clues on collaboration between Congress and the executive budget. This will be a meaningful future research topic.

CHAPTER SUMMARY

- **The Congressional Budget and Impoundment Control Act (CBA)**

Congressional budgeting was the result of congressional efforts to regain budget control power from the executive branch. President Nixon was known for impounding, for defense spending, funds appropriated for social domestic programs. The Congressional Budget and Impoundment Control Act (CBA) intended to end such presidential abuse of executive budget authority.

The CBA also attempted to control the dispersed budget process in Congress. Whenever budget review processes are dispersed, there is likely to be more waste. The CBA created Budget Committees as a way to enhance centralized budget coordination and control.

The national budget process experienced how centralized congressional budget coordination affected the federal deficits through the turn of the twentieth century. When appropriations authorities were dispersed among various substantive legislative committees, federal deficits grew rapidly. When single committees in each house regained budget control power over appropriations, the federal deficits were significantly contained. Many scholars contend that the historical experience also provided the rationale for congressional budgeting.

The CBA created Budget Committees in both houses of Congress. These committees set budget targets specified in budget resolutions and budget reconciliations before Appropriations Committees start their annual appropriations review.

- **State Legislative Budgeting Systems**

A few states have adopted legislative budgeting systems:

(1) In Texas, the Legislative Budget Board prepares a legislative budget that reflects current service levels of each executive agency. Unlike the federal experience, there is a high level of coordination between the executive and legislative budget offices.

(2) In Mississippi and South Carolina, central budget offices in state legislatures review executive agency budget requests. As with Texas, there is a strong collaboration between executive and legislative budget offices during their legislative budgeting processes.

- **Budget Committees in Congress**

Creation of Budget Committees in Congress changed the aspirations and behaviors of various committees and their members. House Budget Committee (HBC) Republicans were policy-oriented, but HBC Democrats were more process-oriented.

Senate Budget Committee (SBC) Democrats and Republicans were concerned with fiscal policy and budget control. A partisan divide between SBC Republicans and Democrats has recently widened.

- **How to Achieve Consensus?**

Regarding the lasting tension between executive budgets and congressional budgets, scholars suggest enhanced collaboration through a joint budget resolution between the president and Congress. One lingering question is how they can reach consensus that would transcend any partisan divide throughout the congressional budget process.

3 Line-Item Veto

Unlike U.S. presidents, governors in most states have the authority to strike line items in appropriations bills. Some governors even possess the authority to reduce dollar amounts or delete specific provisos or words in appropriations bills. Gubernatorial line-item veto powers were originally suggested as a way to control legislative pork-barrel spending. When legislatures bundle wasteful spending into appropriations bills, governors' line-item veto power can function as a versatile tool to control it and protect fiscal austerity. However, many empirical findings suggest that line-item vetoes were invoked for policy or partisan reasons rather than fiscal austerity. Although many scholars and practitioners recommended the item-veto power for U.S. presidents as a potential budget tool to curb runaway federal deficits, state experience with such gubernatorial power implies that similar presidential veto power might not function as expected. This chapter discusses the following issues:

- How Does the Line-Item Veto Work?
- Line-Item Veto in Practice
- Fiscal Impacts of the Line-Item Veto
- Implications of the Line-Item Veto for the Federal Government

HOW DOES THE LINE-ITEM VETO WORK?

Since the rise of the Confederate States of America in the nineteenth century, the line-item veto has been supported as a way to enhance fiscal responsibility for governments. Especially in states that usually have appropriations bills covering the entire range of governmental spending, line-item veto power was expected to control pork-barrel politics by state legislatures. Governors can selectively veto specific line items in appropriations bills, which might be included as a way of pork-barrel spending. In some states, governors even have the power to reduce appropriations amount or delete non-germane provisos in appropriations bills. When legislatures attempt to lump items of appropriations, which might nullify item-veto power, the reduction veto is a powerful tool to make the item veto more potent. As legislatures place conditions on how funds will be used in the appropriations bills, the power to delete provisos will also help enhance gubernatorial item-veto power (Abney and Lauth 1985, 1997).

Throughout the 1980s, the Wisconsin state constitution and law allowed the governor to veto appropriations in a spending bill and also bestowed the governor with partial veto of statutory law language within an appropriations bill. Governors could selectively strike even any word or letter within an appropriations bill as long as the appropriation dollar amounts were to be vetoed in their entirety and what remained after veto would be complete and workable law. The veto power accorded to a Wisconsin governor could further be used to eliminate or modify legislative intentions in addition to striking appropriations (Gosling 1986). By way of the so-called Vanna White amendment, the gubernatorial power of partial veto was later prohibited because it would significantly distort original legislative intents. Despite the restriction, Wisconsin governors have enjoyed strong line-item veto power (Conant 2007, 235–41). One merit of such veto power is that governors could item-veto unacceptable legislative initiatives or those fundamentally different from the governors' recommendations in executive budgets (Gosling 1986).

LINE-ITEM VETO IN PRACTICE

As of 2011, ten state governors had item-veto power on all bills. In thirty-four states governors have item-veto power on appropriations only (Council of State Governments 2012, Table 4.4). Overall, the item-veto power has been supposed to allow governors to protect their executive budgets by discouraging unnecessary riders and pork-barrel spending in appropriations bills attempted by state legislatures. The item veto has frequently been regarded as a tool to control the governmental budget total and thereby reduce the size of government (Lauth and Reese 2006). Some governors have the authority to reduce the dollar amounts in appropriations items. As of 2012, in forty-two states, governors have the authority to item-veto appropriations for dollar amounts (Council of State Governments 2012, Table 3.16). This power relieves governors of the burden of making an all-or-nothing choice and thus is deemed a useful opportunity to reduce pork-barrel spending (Lee 2000). In sixteen states governors can item-veto appropriations for specific language or narratives (Council of State Governments 2012, Table 3.16). Although this chapter introduces the categorization of item vetoes reported by the Council of State Governments, there is a significant difficulty distinguishing between line-item veto, reduction veto, and deletion veto. Abney and Lauth (2002) suggest a good discussion of the difficulty.

FISCAL IMPACTS OF THE LINE-ITEM VETO

DOES THE LINE-ITEM VETO ENHANCE FISCAL AUSTERITY?

Unlike the anticipated fiscal impacts of line-item veto powers, some empirical studies do not support governors' veto power as a fiscal constraint. Based on a survey of state legislative officers in the early 1980s, Abney and Lauth (1985) analyzed how governors' line-item veto power had actually affected state budget processes. The authors developed three measures of fiscal restraint. The first was the propensity of legislators to make budget decisions that presumably brought benefits to their districts. In states with legislatures characterized by the high propensity, governors were expected to use the item veto more frequently. The data, however, did not support this expectation: item vetoes were not necessarily cast more often in these states.

The second index was the propensity of state legislatures to increase governors' budget recommendations. It was expected that the item veto might be more frequently invoked as a fiscal constraint when the legislatures tended to increase the governors' budget recommendations. However, the frequency of the item veto was not meaningfully linked to this propensity. A third index measured whether governors dedicated to efficiency improvement would use the item veto more frequently against the less efficiency-oriented state legislatures. Here again, the governors' tendency toward efficiency was not significantly related to the frequency of the item veto. In sum, there was no clear evidence that governors' veto power functions as a fiscal constraint.

PARTISAN CONTINGENCY, BUDGET FORMATS, AND THE LINE-ITEM VETO

Gosling (1986) also investigated the impact of line-item veto power based on the 542 item vetoes in Wisconsin from 1975 to 1985. Data analysis showed that 86 percent of the item vetoes affected statutory or session law. However, 72.1 percent had no fiscal effect. Gosling also reported that partisan contingencies affected the usage of line-item veto power. When the governor's party differed from the majority party in the legislature, item vetoes were more frequently used. Gosling's study also indicated that item vetoes helped increase collaboration between executive and legislative budget decision makers under unified party control. Chapter 7 further details how item vetoes induce forced collaboration between different parties in state legislatures.

In Wisconsin, the governor's budget director and the Joint Finance Committee's member and staff collaborated on budget preparation. Not surprisingly, the data thus indicated that one-third of the item vetoes returned the legislative version of the budget to the original executive budget and another one-fifth restored the Joint Finance Committee's version, which evidences strong collaboration. Additionally, when the governor and the legislature were in the same party, there was likely to be stronger collaboration between the governor and the Joint Finance Committee. Under a divided government, 14.6 percent of item vetoes restored the Joint Finance Committee version, while 23.8 percent did so under the same party rule. In sum, the item veto in Wisconsin was used primarily as a tool of policy and partisan advantage rather than one of fiscal restraint. That is not to suggest, however, that in Wisconsin or elsewhere, item vetoes generally do not reduce the costs of government. For the six biennia included in Gosling's (1986) study, item vetoes collectively saved the state treasury from a low of .006 percent of the state general revenue budget in 1983–85 to a high of nearly 2.5 percent in 1981–83. But the main point was that the amount of budget savings was a very small portion of total state budgets. More significantly, policy and partisan issues were driving factors for gubernatorial item-veto choice.

Reese (1997) conducted a more detailed empirical analysis on the impacts of line-item vetoes in ten southern states from 1973 to 1992. The item-veto power was used more against dollar amounts rather than against language in appropriations bills, in line with earlier findings. Similar to Gosling's (1986) findings, however, vetoed amounts as annual average percentages of state appropriations varied from 0.01 to 1.15 percent of state total budgets. The variation was further mitigated because two states, Florida and Louisiana, drove the average up substantially. In seven of the ten states, the item veto was used primarily for policy or partisan purposes. In addition, only a small portion of vetoes cast were overridden by legislatures.

Reese (1997) also investigated how line-item vetoes were invoked depending on state appropriations processes and political environments. Three states using biennial appropriations were associated with low frequency of use and low dollar effects. Additionally, these states cast the item veto for policy reasons. Budget formats also showed some explanatory power on the veto actions. States with less-itemized budget formats were associated with lower frequency of use and lower dollar effects. States with a large number of appropriations bills were less likely to use the item veto, and dollar effects tied to the veto actions were also low. Readers can imagine that it might be "technically difficult" to veto items if budgets are not itemized enough. In addition, when the number of appropriations bills is small in cases of omnibus appropriations, budget bills could easily bundle some items that governors might otherwise want to delete. Therefore, the need for item veto is stronger for states with a smaller number of appropriations bills or omnibus appropriations. Conversely, there might be no "need" for item veto when the number of appropriations bills is large enough or omnibus appropriations are prohibited.

The findings in Reese (1997) on the relationship between political environments and line-item vetoes were in line with previous studies. Most states with a higher degree of interbranch partisan disparity used the item veto more frequently, albeit with low dollar effects. Even Republican governors used the item-veto power for both policy and fiscal reasons, belying the supposition that Republicans were more likely to be fiscally conservative (Abney and Lauth 1997; Reese 1997).

REDUCTION AND DELETION VETO POWERS AS A POTENTIAL TOOL OF FISCAL RESTRAINT

Partly because of the less clear fiscal impacts of the line-item veto power, recent studies have been more focused on reduction and deletion veto powers. Abney and Lauth (1997) indicated that in terms of fiscal responsibility, governors were more likely to use the item-veto power as a tool to restrain state spending than to control pork-barrel entries or wasteful items (note that earlier studies focused more on whether a line-item veto could control wasteful items bundled into appropriations bills). In particular, governors with reduction veto power were more likely to control state spending. This implies that such veto power might have some potential as a tool to control state spending.

In contrast, the deletion veto was not significantly related to either spending control or efficiency (controlling pork-barrel insertions). This was expected because narratives were typically linked to legal and policy processes rather than to dollar amounts. As such, the deletion veto power was more a tool for policy agenda rather than for budget issues.

Abney and Lauth (2002) reported why state legislatures and governors tend to add narratives or riders in appropriations bills in the first place, even though the convention might deter authorization committees from allowing full policy consideration of policy proposals and appropriation committees from giving careful review of budget dollars. Legislators especially favored these measures and adding riders. Attaching conditions to dollars created more power control over agencies. Additionally, appropriations bills were generally more veto resistant and less swayed by legislative leadership. Finally, when legislation was handled by narratives, policy making might be expedited because the legislative leadership might have more control over the legislative contents rather than going through the lengthy committee system. Governors might also feel that narratives in appropriations bills would expedite the policy-making process.

Data showed that the deletion vetoes were cast more often over narratives than over dollar amounts during the early 1990s, as logically expected above. In contrast, reduction veto has revealed some potential as a fiscal restraint. According to Abney and Lauth (1997), legislative behavior posed several problems with the use of the item veto. First, legislatures attempted to include lump sums in appropriations bills to deter governors from invoking the line-item veto. However, when governors had the reduction veto power, such legislative manipulation was substantially weakened and the line-item veto functioned as a versatile instrument: it allowed the line-item veto power to be a partisan or policy instrument and an instrument for fiscal restraint.

LINE-ITEM VETO POWER AS A TOOL TO PROTECT GUBERNATORIAL POLICY PREFERENCES

Despite some potential of the line-item veto power (especially the reduction veto) as a fiscal constraint, however, a recent study indicates that line-item veto powers have been used more frequently to protect gubernatorial fiscal priorities (Lauth and Reese 2006). The item veto was adopted in Georgia in 1865, and the authors studied use of the item veto from 1963 to 2002 in that state. The current executive budget in Georgia, which simultaneously limited and empowered gubernatorial budget authority, was established by the Budget Act of 1962. During that forty-year period, the item veto controlled only a small portion of state spending, much in line with the literature. Georgia has had somewhat peculiar budget institutions and processes. The General Assembly meets only forty days each year and is highly reliant on the gubernatorial budget agenda. Georgia has a balanced budget requirement, and the governor's official revenue estimates form a constitutionally protected total ceiling for the state budget. Thus, legislative changes occur within the total budget ceiling. As a result, gubernatorial item vetoes have been focused on restoring executive fiscal priorities rather than controlling the size of state spending because of the balanced budget requirement and the governor's formal revenue estimates. In these environments, interbranch conflict has heightened over a small number of legislative initiatives that slightly modified gubernatorial budget priorities.

For instance, Governor Miller vetoed a $479,479 item from the Department of Education section of the 1993 appropriations act with no information provided by his staff or the Office of Planning and Budget. He had found that House members had added a secret budget to fund special projects in local schools. Miller also vetoed more than $36 million in local projects. He believed that the General Assembly added the amount at the expense of his budgets for higher education initiatives. Governor Miller cast item vetoes on eighty-nine community projects in the Department of Community Affairs section of the appropriations act of 1997. He argued that the General Assembly reduced his recommended appropriation for the university system, and he tried to veto an equal amount. Governor Busbee vetoed many capital project fund items and insisted instead on relying on more bond financing in 1977. The controversy developed over a policy issue with some fiscal implications, rather than on budget reduction. Busbee stated that capital outlay "threatened the state's surplus in a time of economic uncertainty. . . . This veto is an example of the line-item veto being used not for budget reduction but to enforce the governor's policy preferences" (Lauth and Reese 2006, 17).

IMPLICATIONS OF THE LINE-ITEM VETO FOR THE FEDERAL GOVERNMENT

For these reasons, many scholars have consistently contended that line-item veto initiatives in the federal budget processes might not be successful as a fiscal constraint.

LINE-ITEM VETO UNDER PARTISAN POLITICS

Just as the general veto is often thwarted by legislative manipulation, so is the item-veto power. As noted earlier, legislatures sometimes lump their preferences and the governor's into one item, thus de facto nullifying the item veto (Abney and Lauth 1985). A presidential item veto might curb the budget, especially when the authority to reduce appropriations would be a flexible budget control for the U.S. president. However, the Wisconsin experience indicates that the president's item-veto power might not result in substantial budget reductions. As noted above, the largest budget reduction was 2.5 percent of budgeted state revenues, with the majority of item vetoes showing no fiscal effect. More importantly, the item veto was primarily adopted as a way to modify unacceptable policy or to further partisan interests. Therefore, an ideologically motivated U.S. president might use the item veto to excise unacceptable riders or appropriations for programs antithetical to the executive policy preferences (Gosling 1986; Reese 1997).

DIFFERENCES IN BUDGET PROCESSES, FORMATS, AND INSTITUTIONS BETWEEN STATES AND THE FEDERAL GOVERNMENT

In the few states where item vetoes were used for fiscal purposes, they were used to fix some procedural anomaly (rather than to function as a fiscal restraint) where states did not have consensually developed, timely revenue estimates. When there was little interbranch disagreement over balanced budgets, there was no strong need for item vetoes even to fix the procedural anomaly. In addition, since many states have balanced-budget requirements, the revenue estimate has been the main source of the interbranch conflict. Many states have recently resolved the conflict by adopting one set of official revenue estimates. At the federal level, however, there has been disagreement between the executive and legislative branches over revenue estimates and how much deficit spending is acceptable. This implies that the interbranch disagreement in the federal government might drive item vetoes to cause political tension over procedural issues rather than to serve as a fiscal restraint. In addition, in states with less-itemized bills, the veto would be less likely to be cast. Since the federal budget is in lump-sum format, although a bit more itemized than state appropriations, the item veto might not be as effective as in the states (Reese 1997).

A final disincentive to use the item veto is that governors are simply not interested in it. They are more interested in other policy initiatives. In addition, if governors have fiscal instruments other than the item veto, it is not very useful. For example, in Hawaii governors have unrestricted impoundment power, thus weakening the necessity to use veto power. In Maryland, the legislature may not appropriate budgets larger than the executive budget, so there is no need for the item veto (Abney and Lauth 1997). In West Virginia, the legislature is limited in adding narratives because it can only increase or decrease items in the executive budget. In Pennsylvania, the governor does not need to use the deletion veto because the constitution prohibits the presence of narratives in appropriations bills. In Arkansas, the deletion veto is not much needed because the constitution prohibits omnibus appropriations bills (Abney and Lauth 2002). Since there are various differences in budget processes, formats, and institutions between states and the federal government, one cannot directly apply state experience with item vetoes to the national level.

LINE-ITEM VETO AND LEGAL CONFLICTS

Governors have invoked numerous court cases regarding line-item vetoes, which are another source for institutional conflicts that will in turn nullify the effectiveness of line-item vetoes as a fiscal constraint (Lee 2000). In general, state constitutions lack a clear definition of an appropriation that opened up controversies over what might or might not be item-vetoed. Another controversial dimension of the item-veto actions was how to define the item. Since most state constitutions did not provide accurate definitions of items, state courts often had to fashion the definition. For instance, in Washington State, the legislature made appropriations to agencies in lump sums. The Washington Supreme Court ruled that the governor could veto provisos in each section for agencies in the lump sum appropriations. If the governor could not veto provisos in each section, then the governor could not help but veto the entire section for a certain agency in the lump sum appropriation, rather than vetoing specific provisos.

There was also a potential for legal conflicts between substantive legislations and appropriations bills. State constitutions typically provided that "any substantive piece of legislation must have only one subject but that appropriation bills may have multiple subjects" (Lee 2000, 272). Since governors might not item-veto general legislation, the constitutional single-subject rule was to prevent the legislature from forcing a governor into a take-it-or-leave-it choice over general legislation. The governors' item veto over appropriations would be effective especially because legislatures were constitutionally allowed to include multiple subjects in appropriations bills. For this reason, legal actions arose when the single-subject provision was violated or a wrong provision was inserted into substantive provisions in appropriations bills.

Another set of legal actions pertained to the governor's veto power to delete language contained in appropriations bills. The Florida Supreme Court held that the legislative provision changing the formula used to fund local school districts in an appropriations bill violated the state constitution by changing a policy through an appropriations bill. The court also ruled that the governor's veto violated the state constitution because the governor did not have the authority to strike words in the appropriations bill. Many state courts disallowed striking language if it might substantially alter or amend the initial legislative intent. For instance, the Iowa Supreme Court held that if taking out a portion of a bill by item veto damaged the legislative intent, then the veto could not be accepted. These cases illustrate that federal line-item veto initiatives might also cause some legal conflicts. As such, they might not be as successful a fiscal constraint as their proponents contend: they might only augment legal conflicts.

CHAPTER SUMMARY

- **Governors' Line-Item Veto Power**

Unlike the U.S. president, governors in most states have the authority to veto line items in appropriations bills. Some governors even have the power to delete provisos or reduce dollar amounts in appropriations. Governors' item-veto power can help reduce legislative pork-barrel spending through bundling or lumping.

- **Reduction Veto Power**

Reduction veto power enhances the effectiveness of line-item vetoes by relieving governors of the burden of an all-or-nothing choice.

- **Fiscal Impact of Line-Item Vetoes**

Empirical findings indicate that line-item vetoes were not invoked as a fiscal constraint.

Governors in the states with higher legislative tendencies toward wasteful spending did not cast line-item vetoes more frequently than did those without the tendencies. In addition, efficiency-oriented governors did not necessarily invoke line-item vetoes either.

Dollar amounts of budget savings from invoking line-item veto were not significant. Instead, policy and partisan issues were driving factors for invoking gubernatorial item vetoes.

Budget formats and political environments also affected how line-item vetoes were used. In states with less-itemized budget formats, line-item vetoes were invoked less frequently and their dollar effects were low. States with a large number of appropriations bills were less likely to invoke the line-item veto, and its dollar effects were low. Interbranch partisan disparity was associated with more frequent use of line-item vetoes.

A governor's reduction veto power has some potential as a tool to control overall state spending, but not necessarily wasteful spending. When governors have reduction veto power, the line-item veto power might function as an instrument for fiscal restraint.

Despite some potential of the line-item veto as a fiscal constraint, recent studies indicate that governors have used it as a tool to protect and restore executive budget preferences.

- **Line-Item Vetoes for Presidents?**
Supporters of gubernatorial line-veto power contend that U.S. presidents need to have the same power to control budget waste. However, an ideologically driven president might exert line-item veto power to excise unacceptable riders or appropriations antithetical to executive preferences.

- **State vs. Federal Government Regarding the Line-Item Veto**
Since there are various differences in budget processes, formats, and institutions between states and the federal government, one cannot directly compare the state experience with the item-veto experience at the national level.

- **Line Item Vetoes Can Create Political Tension**
When governors invoked line-item vetoes, numerous court cases followed, especially over the definition of acceptable line items or governors' ability to strike words in appropriations bills. The court cases intensified political tension between executive and legislative branches. When U.S. presidents have the line-item veto power, one can expect similar political tension.

Balanced Budget Requirements

Most state governments have constitutional or statutory requirements to balance their budgets, known as balanced budget requirements (BBRs). Governors are supposed to submit, legislatures are supposed to pass, and governors are supposed to sign balanced budgets. Some states do not allow year-end deficit carryovers. With the ever-increasing federal deficits, BBRs have been garnering national attention again as a potential deficit-control tool. However, the experience with state BBRs does not necessarily imply that BBRs can function as a fiscal constraint. They do so under very limited conditions. This chapter discusses the following issues:

- Efforts to Control Deficits
- Balanced Budget Requirements (BBRs) in States
- Fiscal Impacts of BBRs
- Why Are BBRs Not Effective as a Fiscal Constraint?
- Recent Empirical Findings on Fiscal Impacts of BBRs
- A New Perspective on BBRs

EFFORTS TO CONTROL DEFICITS

The 2008 financial crisis has aggravated fiscal conditions of various levels of government in the United States. In particular, the federal government has been faced with a record-high deficit due to the multiple rounds of stimulus spending and borrowing through quantitative easing to recover from the economic disaster. After a turbulent political stalemate during the summer of 2011, both parties agreed to control the national deficit by creating a bipartisan supercommittee charged with developing by November 23, 2011, a plan to cut the national deficit by $1.2 trillion over the next ten years. The supercommittee plan would be subjected to a congressional up or down vote. Whether Congress voted to enact the plan or not, it would be linked to considering a balanced budget amendment to the U.S. Constitution (Fessenden et al. 2011). However, similar attempts to institute the balanced budget amendment were faced with numerous hurdles throughout the 1980s and 1990s. Many of its critics were not sure of its effectiveness as a fiscal constraint (Rubin 2010, 205–8).

BALANCED BUDGET REQUIREMENTS (BBRs) IN STATES

In contrast, most state and local governments have balanced budget requirements (BBRs) (Gosling 2009, 5), although their impact as a fiscal constraint is also questionable as will be shown in this chapter. As of the early 1990s, only thirty-six states had any reference to balanced budgets in their state constitutions. Of the remaining fourteen states, all but one, Vermont, had statutory BBRs. Thirty-one state constitutions more specifically required that their legislatures pass balanced budgets (Briffault 1996, 8–10). As of 2008, most states had some form of constitutional or statutory BBR provision. Thirty-three states had constitutional BBRs, and twenty-five states had statutory BBRs that required governors to submit balanced budgets. (Some states had both constitutional and statutory BBRs.) Thirty-four states had constitutional requirements, and seventeen had statutory requirements that state legislatures pass balanced budgets. Thirty-one state governors are constitutionally required to sign balanced budgets, while seventeen state governors are statutorily required to do so. Only seven states were allowed to carry over a deficit, which means that forty-three states must achieve year-end balance in their state budgets (NASBO 2008, Table 1).

FISCAL IMPACTS OF BBRs

Despite constitutional or statutory requirements to balance state budgets, numerous observations have consistently indicated that this might not actually help achieve balanced budgets. Briffault (1996) conducted one of the most comprehensive reviews of the previous observations and generally reported very limited impact of the requirements as a fiscal constraint. Overall, previous empirical studies indicated that there were too many factors other than BBRs, so it was very difficult to carve out the distinct effect of the BBRs. For instance, some studies showed that constitutional BBRs had less impact on spending growth than the presence of executive budgeting systems. Economic, political, institutional, and cultural factors were more significant than BBRs in explaining taxing, spending, and borrowing. Another study, conducted by the U.S. Advisory Commission on Intergovernmental Relations in the early 1980s, reported that constitutional and statutory BBRs together tended to control budget deficits (U.S. Advisory Commission on Intergovernmental Relations 1987). However, the most important factor in explaining state fiscal choice was the level of state wealth measured in terms of state per-capita income (Briffault 1996, 56–58).

WHY ARE BBRs NOT EFFECTIVE AS A FISCAL CONSTRAINT?

Briffault (1996) suggested numerous possible reasons why BBRs cannot achieve fiscal balance, some of which are repeatedly indicated in more recent studies.

OBSCURE FUND TARGETS OF BBRs

The no-deficit-carryover requirement has been regarded as relatively more stringent as a fiscal constraint than are BBRs. The problem is that even this requirement does not apply to all funds. Most states established special accounts such as capital funds to finance public infrastructure projects. In actuality, many special capital funds allowed borrowing by way of issuing revenue bonds. In addition, these funds usually had future revenue sources from running public infrastructures or enterprises. Particular taxes or fees from them were earmarked for the special capital funds. The funds could then further borrow money by pledging the earmarked revenue sources. In many cases, state general funds could borrow from the special funds through interfund transfers and achieve fiscal balance on the accounting books. This was possible because state BBRs often did not specify which funds had to be balanced. Moreover, even when special funds were subjected to the BBRs, many states applied accounting gimmicks. They treated bond proceeds and other obligations as one-time cash revenues, whereas they were obviously future liabilities (Briffault 1996, 11–13).

Fifulco et al. (2012) have recently revisited this gimmick. They show that the level of debt in selected states will be much larger if "borrowing" is more broadly defined than a narrow, legal definition of borrowing. Under a broader definition, borrowing takes places when governments forgo future resources or benefits from public projects in order to acquire resources for current use. One such borrowing technique, which of course obscures the accurate status of debt, is called "fund sweeps." Governments move money from other funds to general funds, leaving future obligation of the latter for the former. In addition, proceeds from long-term borrowing are shifted to special revenue funds that are further transferred to general funds. All in all, these interfund transfers will eventually increase long-term debts for the borrowing entities. Without doubt, these continuing budgetary gimmicks are easy ways around BBRs.

ROSY REVENUE FORECASTING

When state constitutions required governors to submit and legislatures to pass balanced budgets without no-deficit-carryover requirements, budget decision makers frequently relied on optimistic forecasts of economic conditions. Rosy forecasting of revenue collection or federal grants, of course, facilitated satisfaction of the BBRs (Briffault 1996, 19).

MANIPULATING FISCAL YEARS AND ACCOUNTING BASIS

Some states manipulated the fiscal period to achieve balanced budgets on their accounting books. In 1976, Michigan changed its fiscal year from July 1–June 30 to October 1–September 30. The change resulted in an initial fifteen-month fiscal year. The Michigan state government then applied an accrual basis of accounting in recording revenues for the additional three months of the longer fiscal year. In contrast, state grants-in-aid to school districts were scheduled a month later, and the state applied a cash basis of accounting in recording the expenditures. This obviously increased surplus.

Some states deferred payment of Medicaid benefits or salaries. Others reduced contributions to state public employee retirement pension funds to achieve balanced budgets. A common state practice was to overestimate the projected yields on pension trust fund investments, which would thereby reduce its future contribution to the funds. In the case of Michigan, a cash basis of accounting was applied to its public school employee retirement systems. Typically, its payment for retiree health benefits was computed based on so-called baseline budgeting. Under this method, the next year's benefits would be defined based on the next year's forecast liabilities. However, Michigan calculated the benefits based on current-year costs of benefit delivery (i.e., cash basis of cost accounting). Many states also took advantage of the fact that underfunded pension liabilities did not show up on general funds that were more likely to be subjected to BBRs. These gimmicks achieved fiscal balance, but underfunded pension liabilities were merely shifted to future taxpayers (Briffault 1996, 19–21).

Fifulco et al. (2012) have also shown evidence that many states still apply these gimmicks. States continually defer various payments because there is uncertainty about the policies concerning interest payments on delayed payments and their legal enforceability. Backlogs of deferred payments have continuously emerged in many states. There is a strong incentive for states to manipulate underfunded or unfunded pension liabilities. This is partly attributable to the complexity involved in forecasting future cost-and-benefit streams of pension fund programs. For instance, a pension system is considered fully funded if its accumulated employer contributions can cover net present value (NPV: see Chapter 11 in Part II for more details) of future benefit payments. There is a lot of uncertainty regarding turnover rates, future wages, retirement ages, mortality rates, and inflation. In addition, it is very difficult to choose an accurate discount rate for NPV computation. Underfunded pension liabilities are garnering more attention. Other unfunded postemployment benefits (OPEB) reveal stronger uncertainty. These kinds of uncertainty constitute an open invitation for states to manipulate the fund mechanisms as ways around BBRs.

MANIPULATING CAPITAL BUDGETING PROCEDURES

Some states achieved balanced budgets through refinancing their debt obligations. In the short run, interest payments declined and the decrease in interest payments was recorded as expenditure control. In the long run, however, those states refinanced their debt obligations by extending their maturities. Eventually, interest payments increased despite the short-term contribution to fiscal balance.

In addition, some states raised cash revenues through one-time asset sales but at the cost of future income flows from those assets, which were often sold at cheaper prices as well. In some cases the states had to lease those assets at much higher costs. For instance, New York was known for its backdoor financing. The state established a somewhat phantom agency called the Urban Development Corporation. The corporation was a state-created entity and, as such, subject to state political direction, but it was not treated as part of the state budget process. New York sold its Attica Correctional Facility to the corporation probably at a price cheaper than its market value but raised a substantial amount of one-time cash revenue. Though the cash revenue clearly reduced state budget deficits, New York had to make long-term lease payments to use the facility. The problem was that the payments might have covered debt obligations that the corporation presumably incurred. In sum, one-time cash revenues ultimately increased New York's future deficits (Briffault 1996, 22–24). Fifulco et al. (2012) have reported on recent cases in Connecticut, Illinois, and New York that these states have been manipulating debt structuring and refinancing and selling government assets for one-time cash at the cost of increased future debt burden. Again, the states might have achieved phantom budget balances.

MANIPULATING INTERGOVERNMENTAL FISCAL RELATIONS

Briffault (1996, 27–30) also reveals how state governments manipulated intergovernmental fiscal relations as a way around BBRs. Many states received more from the federal government than they distributed to local governments. In addition, they also engaged in some form of fiscal exploitation of Medicaid matching grants. Medicaid matches state expenditures on health care for the economically disadvantaged and on long-term nursing care for the elderly. The federal matching rate ranged from 50 percent of state Medicaid costs to 83 percent during the 1980s. In the late 1980s, many states encouraged health-care providers to make donations to state governments as a "provider tax." The donations were added to state health-care expenditures, and, of course, the federal matching grants increased. Once the states received the grants, they returned the provider tax to the health-care providers. Thus, even under BBRs, state governments were aggressively developing numerous budgetary gimmicks around the requirements. Of course, such temporary measures to increase state revenues were short-lived methods to regain a state's fiscal health or long-term balanced budget.

IMPLICATIONS OF BBRS FOR FEDERAL DEFICIT CONTROL

The federal budget process and institutions are full of potential for such budgetary gimmickry around BBRs, although the requirements have been recently revived as a budget control mechanism. The Gramm-Rudman-Hollings in the 1980s exempted most off-budget items such as Social Security benefit programs. The supercommittee of 2011, as noted above, was supposed to carve out the national deficits. If its measures failed to achieve the deficit control target, an across-the-board cut would be triggered. However, the problem was that the sequester again exempted Social Security and Medicaid (Fessenden et al. 2011). During the 1980s and 1990s, Congress chartered numerous quasi-autonomous corporations such as the Financial Assistance Corporation (FICO), the Federal Financing Bank, and the Federal National Mortgage Association (Fannie Mae). Most of these corporations are off-budget and, thus, obfuscated fiscal conditions of the federal government. This will ultimately weaken the effectiveness of the BBRs, or similar statutory controls, in the federal government (Briffault 1996, 25–27).

RECENT EMPIRICAL FINDINGS ON FISCAL IMPACTS OF BBRS

Fairly consistent with Briffault's observations, recent studies have shown that BBRs were not highly effective in controlling budget growth. Based on a 1998 survey with state agency heads, Ryu et al. (2008) reported that BBRs were not significantly related to state agency appropriations changes. Guo (2011) examined state discretionary tax adjustments from 1988 to 2006 and found that BBRs were not meaningfully associated with the adjustments.

Although overall BBRs did not show any significant impact on budget growth, one of their specific measures, no-deficit-carryover requirements, has been observed to exert some control over state budget expansion. Alt and Lowry (1994) used state fiscal and economic data from 1968 to 1987 to investigate how different partisan configurations reacted to unexpected budget surpluses or deficits. They found that unified governments, where the executive branches and state legislatures were dominated by the same party, reacted to unplanned deficits faster in terms of revenue increase. Split branch governments, where the executive branch faced both chambers in state legislatures dominated by different parties, reacted to the deficits in terms of both revenue increase and spending control. Split legislature governments, where both chambers are dominated by different parties, primarily attempted to control spending. Overall, unified governments made the greatest and fastest efforts to control deficits. More interestingly, Alt and Lowry found that budget control in response to unplanned deficits was much greater where no-deficit-carryover requirements existed (see also Alt and Lowry 2000).

Poterba (1994) reported somewhat contrasting but similar findings using state taxes and spending data during the late 1980s. When governors and lower chambers in state legislatures were from the same party (a configuration defined by Alt and Lowry as split legislature governments), single-party states raised tax revenues and cut spending by greater amounts in response to deficit shocks. This pattern held true even when partisanship was controlled for. Poterba further found that under strict no-deficit-carryover requirements, the single-party states made greater efforts to control deficits, where governors and the lower chambers were dominated by the same party. Hou and Duncombe (2008) studied the impact of overall BBRs on state saving behavior that differed a bit from the target variables used in the previous studies. They found that some provisions of BBRs could raise total state savings as a percentage of general fund expenditures by about 2–3 percent based on state fiscal data from 1979 to 2003.

Primo (2007, 82–104) conducted another comprehensive analysis of how no-deficit-carryover requirements affected spending of forty-seven states from 1969 to 2000. He controlled for various other fiscal institutions and partisan configurations as did the studies introduced above. One peculiar feature of Primo's study is that he controlled for the interaction between elected courts and no-deficit-carryover requirements. Chapter 6 in Part I shows how court-induced mandates define governmental expenditures. Similarly, Primo asserts that elected courts would function as a strong enforcement mechanism for no-deficit-carryover requirements. His empirical findings show that in states with no-deficit-carryover requirements and an elected high court, no-deficit-carryover requirements significantly held down state spending.

A New Perspective on BBRs

While more studies are warranted on the fiscal impacts of BBRs, Hou and Smith (2006) made a very useful and insightful suggestion on the provisions of BBRs. The categorization of BBRs has been based largely on the recommendations made by three institutions: the U.S. Advisory Commission on Intergovernmental Relations (ACIR), the National Association of State Budget Officers (NASBO), and the National Conference of State Legislatures (NCSL). Hou and Smith pointed out some discrepancies among the different categorizations. One potential reason for the discrepancies might be attributable to the fact that as state political processes and legal systems evolved over time, some BBRs might have been inconsistent or even contradictory. In this sense, the BBR provisions, which are technical in their nature, might more accurately reflect the need for balanced budgets. Overall, Hou and Smith provided more detailed categorization of technical provisions of BBRs: own-source revenues must match expenditures, controls are in place on supplementary appropriations, within-fiscal-year controls are in place to avoid year-end deficit, and so on. They further contended that contrary to conventional wisdom, statute-based BBRs might be more effective as a fiscal constraint than constitution-based BBRs. In Florida, the constitution-based requirements ran a total length of 44 words, but the statute-based requirements were 989 words long. Given the high degree of specificity in the latter, one cannot simply imagine that the constitution-based requirements might be a more stringent fiscal constraint. In this sense, more-technical BBRs might have a stronger binding force.

Hou and Smith (2010) later conducted another very insightful study using their new categorization. Scholarly research has frequently employed the categorization of BBRs made by NASBO. One issue with the NASBO categorization is that it is based on surveys of state budget officers. As such, the categorization might reflect what state budget officers have perceived to be legal requirements for balanced budgets. In contrast, Hou and Smith's 2006 study was based on legal research of BBR-related documents.

Hou and Smith (2010) empirically tested how the NASBO categorization and the Hou and Smith categorization (2006) exerted different fiscal impacts on state budget conditions. When informal norms or perceptions (e.g., the NASBO categorization) coincided with formal rules (e.g., the 2006 Hou/Smith categorization), governors-must-submit-balanced-budgets requirements reduced budget surpluses, countering conventional observations. Informal norms as perceived by state budget officers (the NASBO categorization) mostly had no impact on budget surplus, similar to various studies reported above. Legal provisions only, without budget officers' perception (the 2006 Hou/Smith categorization), indicated that governors-must-submit-balanced-budgets requirements somewhat increased budget surplus. Smith and Hou (2013) used the 2006 Hou/Smith categorization (i.e., BBR provisions codified in state statutes or constitutions) to test the effects of BBRs on expenditures in forty eight states from 1950 to 2004. They found that three BBR provisions were effective in controlling state expenditures: governors-must-submit-balanced-budgets requirements, controls on supplemental appropriations, and no-deficit-carryover requirements. Readers need to be cautious that the negative effect of governors-must-submit-balanced-budgets requirements in Smith and Hou (2013) was on state expenditures, while Hou and Smith's 2010 study of the fiscal effect of the requirements was on state balance (i.e., surplus or deficits). Overall, the key point of these studies is that informal norms should be distinguished from formal rules. In addition, these studies cast other perspectives on the controversial debate over whether BBRs can be an effective fiscal constraint.

CHAPTER SUMMARY

- **State Balanced-Budget Requirements**

Most states have constitutional or statutory balanced budget requirements (BBRs). Governors are required to submit, legislatures are supposed to pass, and governors are then required to sign balanced state budgets. Some states further require that year-end budgets not carry over deficits.

- **Factors Influencing Balanced Budgets**

Earlier empirical studies show that legal requirements to balance budgets do not necessarily achieve balanced budgets. Economic, political, institutional, or cultural factors were more decisive factors in states' achieving balanced budgets.

- **Factors Weakening BBRs**

Numerous budget gimmicks nullified the fiscal control of BBRs.

(1) BBRs were not applied to all fund groups. Some special capital funds allowed borrowing. When BBRs controlled deficits in state general funds, the general funds bypassed BBRs by borrowing from the special capital funds.

(2) Rosy forecasting of revenues often satisfied BBRs when budget decision makers were reviewing budget proposals.

(3) Some states achieved balanced budgets on budget documents by manipulating fiscal years or accounting basis.

(4) Some states achieved short-term budget balances by manipulating capital budget processes, which ultimately increased overall borrowing costs.

(5) Some states exploited the matching provisions of federal matching grants. Temporary increases in such revenues did not help regain states' fiscal health.

- **Aspects of BBRs That Function as a Fiscal Constraint**

Some recent empirical findings suggest that specific features of BBRs might function as a fiscal constraint. No-deficit-carryover requirements helped control deficits under unified governments. In addition, general BBRs raised total state savings.

Hou and Smith (2006, 2010) provide very promising aspects of BBRs as a fiscal constraint. More technical, as opposed to political, provisions of BBRs might have a stronger impact as a fiscal constraint. For instance, more technical requirements that own-source revenues match expenditures or that within-year fiscal controls be in place to avoid year-end deficits will exert more effective control over state budgets. In addition, if the provisions of BBRs are explicitly stipulated in legal documents, they are more likely to exert budget control. Smith and Hou (2013) also empirically confirmed these expectations.

5 Tax and Expenditure Limits

States have a variety of statutory control mechanisms over their state and local governments' fiscal choices, including taxation and spending. During recent decades, the fiscal control mechanisms have been more elaborately controlling governmental fiscal decisions. These mechanisms, known as Tax and Expenditure Limits (TELs), have not been highly effective in controlling the levels of taxation and spending in state and local governments. Instead, TELs have shown somewhat unexpected fiscal impacts over state and local governments' fiscal choices. This chapter focuses on the following issues:

- Fiscal Authority of Local Governments
- Historical Context of State's Control Over Local Fiscal Decisions
- Types of State Control Over State and Local Fiscal Decisions
- Why Are Tax and Expenditure Limits (TELs) Adopted?
- Fiscal Impacts of TELs
- Different Perspectives on the Fiscal Impacts of TELs

FISCAL AUTHORITY OF LOCAL GOVERNMENTS

States have had a wide array of regulative power over municipal budgeting, which was developed in the early twentieth century and modified during the Great Depression. These legal frames still influence local budgeting. Because municipalities are legal creatures of the state, state governments regulate their taxing, borrowing, spending, and financial administration (Rubin 1998, 174). This principle is known as Dillon's Rule. If state governments are silent over a local power, it is assumed that the localities lack authority, and therefore the state holds all power in state-local relationships. Recently, there have been home rule movements allowing more discretion to local governments. Even under home rule charter powers, however, many state laws deny local freedom to decide on fiscal affairs. Thus, the general assumption in state-local relationships is that local discretion, especially in the area of fiscal affairs, is highly restricted (Mikesell 2011, 31–32).

HISTORICAL CONTEXT OF STATE'S CONTROL OVER LOCAL FISCAL DECISIONS

Historically, there were five fairly distinctive periods of state regulation over local fiscal decisions. Early attempts to control local budgets during the late 1860s and early 1870s were constitutional or legislative (rigid, across-the-board limitations) rather than administrative. The second period of control covered the Progressive Era (1895–1910). With the advent of home rule movements, states also intensified their monitoring of local fiscal performance, mostly through administrative mechanisms of control. Consistent with the Progressive Era emphasis on democratic accountability, states focused on standardizing financial reporting and accounting. The third, post-Progressive, era of state regulation was a reaction to the rapid spending growth in the Progressive Era, and the high inflation and delayed capital expenditures that resulted from World War I. The focus of control was on keeping taxes down and using enhanced budget examination and revision.

The fourth period of state systems' regulating municipal budgeting occurred during the Great Depression, characterized by two sets of changes. First, states relied more on constitutional amendments and legislation to limit property taxes. This was a return to the earlier rigid, across-the-board regulations. The second feature was to enhance centralized state budget supervision to avoid excessive fiscal stress of localities. The fifth period of concentrated regulation occurred in the 1970s and the early 1980s. By the 1970s, tax resistance combined with a slowing economy accelerated statewide efforts to limit property taxation. Five months after the passage of California's Proposition 13 in 1978, Alabama, Idaho, Michigan, Nevada, and Texas passed legislation or constitutional amendments reducing local government's authority to raise taxes. Massachusetts's Proposition 2½ in 1980 was very restricting of local discretion. Some states did not merely restrict local discretion, but tried to help reduce fiscal stress at the local level. For instance, Florida's constitutional amendment was to prevent unfunded mandates that would impose an additional fiscal burden on localities (Rubin 1998, 176–79).

As shown above, the basic structures of state control of local budget have remained almost intact since the 1930s. As of 1977, thirty-seven states had statutory provisions for monitoring or supervising local budgets, and twenty-four of those had developed uniform budget standards for preparing local budget documents. Thirty-four of the thirty-seven states collected local budgets; most of the states checked whether local budgets conformed to state tax and expenditure limits, and state officials could modify or disapprove local budgets in case of violation. The centralized and statutory controls over municipal budgeting were typically found as at the end of the Great Depression. However, there have been some changes since the end of the Great Depression. Whereas state governments previously stepped in to reduce property taxes by altering local budgets, states now assumed a more legally acceptable role of reviewing local budgets for compliance with statutory provisions. In addition, during the 1970s more states required state approval of local budgets in advance (Rubin 1998, 205–8).

TYPES OF STATE CONTROL OVER STATE AND LOCAL FISCAL DECISIONS

In terms of specific methods of state control over local budgets, the most common form prior to 1970 was an upper limit on the property tax rate. Beginning around 1970, state governments began to impose more diversified tax and expenditure limits (TELs) on local budgets. Around 1980, taxpayers also initiated tax and expenditure limits that affected *both* local and state budgets. California's Proposition 13 in 1978 is considered to have been the start (Fisher 2007, 283).

There have been several typical types of TELs, and property tax rate limits are their most frequent form. If the limits are placed upon overall property tax rates, the rate limits function as the upper ceiling that cannot be bypassed without votes of the electorate in local governments. One caveat is that property tax–rate limits cannot necessarily prevent increases in property tax revenues. In other words, property tax rates are limited, but property tax bases can expand. California's Proposition 13 exemplifies this scenario. Assessed values of local properties were their rollback values in 1976 (e.g., market value as of 1976), subject to an adjustment by an annual inflation rate of 2 percent. The local property tax rate was limited to 1 percent levied on the assessed values. Thus, logically, as the assessed values increase due to adjustment by an inflation rate, property tax revenues can also increase. For this reason, TELs of this type are nonbinding because they can easily be circumvented by altering assessment practices (Fisher 2007, 283–84; Mullins and Joyce 1996; Mullins and Wallin 2004).

Second, some states impose limits on general revenue or expenditure increases in local governments. Revenue limits or levy limits are specified as a maximum percentage increase in certain (mostly property) tax revenues or a maximum proportion of income to be taxed. Restrictions on the maximum level of expenditures are typically set as a maximum annual percentage increase. The limits are often indexed to the inflation rate. Due to the fixed nature of revenues or expenditures, the limits are potentially more binding than the tax rate limits mentioned above (Fisher 2007, 284; Mullins and Joyce 1996; Mullins and Wallin 2004). In addition, revenue limits are more binding than expenditure limits because the latter are usually imposed on general expenditures. This means that state legislatures can bypass expenditure limits by playing between general and special funds (Bae et al. 2012).

A third type of TELs is limits on assessment increases. As noted above, limits on property tax rates are not highly binding as a fiscal constraint if assessed values of properties increase. Once there are limits on assessed property values that might increase either by reassessment or through natural or administrative increases of property values, property tax rate limits become potentially more binding (Mullins and Joyce 1996; Mullins and Wallin 2004).

Fourth, some states further impose limits on state government revenues and expenditures. In some, the annual growth in own-source revenues or expenditures is restricted to the percentage growth rate of state personal income. In some other states the rate is tied to the population growth rate, the general price level, or a fixed percentage (Fisher 2007, 284–85).

Finally, there is another type of TEL. Some states require a certain level of public discussion and legislative vote before tax rates or revenues will be enacted to increase (Mullins and Wallin 2004). For instance, Colorado's TEL, the Taxpayer Bill of Rights (TABOR), was adopted in 1992. TABOR required that the state of Colorado obtain the approval of voters and two-thirds of the state legislature for all types of tax increases. Another aspect of TABOR is worth noting. It also requires the state to immediately refund surplus revenues to taxpayers, although in 2005 the state temporarily suspended this requirement for the subsequent five years due to revenue fluctuations (Bae et al. 2012). The voting and refund requirements might place TABOR in a more binding TEL category.

Maher and Deller (2013) have introduced more recent studies, building on the ones above, with different TEL categorization. The authors indicate that the previous TEL indices are somewhat arbitrary. They introduce a study that constructed a TEL index for local governments based on six characteristics: "the type of TEL, if the TEL is statutory or constitutional, growth restrictions, method of TEL approval, override provisions, and exemptions" (409). The local TEL index for 2005 ranged from 0 for Connecticut, Maine, New Hampshire, and Vermont to the highest of 38 for Colorado with its Taxpayer's Bill of Rights (TABOR) in 1992 (Maher and Deller 2013, 408–11).

There are many obvious reasons TABOR is the strictest form of TEL. It came into being in 1992, when Colorado passed a constitutional amendment limiting the tax revenue growth rate to all taxing districts. It restricted general revenues to the prior year's revenues. It allowed adjustments only for population growth and inflation, not personal income growth. In addition to its general limits over spending and revenue, TABOR specifically limited the annual growth rate of property tax revenues and required local governments to get voter approval for property tax rates. It also required taxing districts to refund excess revenues to taxpayers through temporary tax credits or rate reductions (St. Clair 2012; see Mullins 2010, 201–65, for a thorough and comprehensive review of the nature of TELs).

As of 2008, thirteen states impose overall property tax limits on local fiscal decisions. Thirty-three states impose specific property tax rate limits, thirty states impose property tax levy limits, four states impose general revenue limits, and nine states impose general expenditure limits on local jurisdictions. In addition, fourteen states impose property assessment limits and twenty-two states impose full disclosure limits (Mullins 2010, Tables 9.7 and 9.8). As of 2007, eighteen states impose revenue limits, twenty-seven states impose expenditure limits, and nine states impose both limits on state fiscal decisions (Mullins 2010, Tables 9.9 and 9.10).

WHY ARE TAX AND EXPENDITURE LIMITS (TELs) ADOPTED?

EFFICIENCY GAIN

As introduced above, the goal of TELs has been to restrict the size of governmental revenues and expenditures. However, economists raise one lingering issue—that political processes might already have reflected the public's demands on the adequate size of governmental budgets. Why, then, do we need another procedure? Perhaps TELs might be necessary to address a problem inherent in the political procedures. Governments cannot always accurately reflect the demand. Under the monopoly bureaucrat model, governmental expenditures are likely to be larger than the median voters prefer. In this case, imposing TELs can block the monopolistic bureaucrats' capacity to control fiscal choices proposed to voters. Even under the median voter model (see Chapter 17 in Part IV for more details), imposing TELs might enhance efficiency in terms of consumer surplus depending on the shape of demand curves, tax prices, and the level of TELs (Fisher 2007, 285–87).

PREFERENCES AND SOCIODEMOGRAPHIC CHARACTERISTICS OF VOTERS

There have been numerous studies on what factors drive states to adopt TELs. Studies conducted around 1980 indicated that voters believed they could control governmental efficiency. For instance, Proposition 2½ in Massachusetts attempted to lower tax levels and have a more efficient government rather than just cutting public services. More recent studies also imply that TELs are related to economic rather than political factors. For instance, voters in lower-income municipalities prefer state-imposed local TELs and voters in high property tax communities generally prefer fiscal limitations. Voters in communities run by professional managers prefer eliminating existing TELs, perhaps because the voters might perceive that eliminating TELs could improve governmental efficiency (Grizzle 2011).

Some other studies, however, indicated that sociodemographic characteristics of voters were more crucial factors for the adoption of TELs. For instance, older, less educated, and blue-collar workers were more likely to support TELs (Grizzle 2011). These population groups might have disproportionately higher tax burdens (especially property tax burdens) as discussed in Chapter 19 in Part IV and therefore might support TELs.

FISCAL IMPACTS OF TELS

Without doubt, one of the most important questions regarding TELs is whether they are effective in controlling governmental revenue and expenditure growth or affect economic performance or business climates in the jurisdictions that adopted them in the sense that TELs improve governmental efficiency.

Grizzle (2011) provides a comprehensive summary of somewhat bifurcated empirical findings. Some studies reported that TELs are partially effective as a fiscal restraint. States with expenditure limits borrowed at lower interest rates, while those with tax limits faced higher borrowing costs. A study of Texas school districts under a 1.5 percent property–tax rate ceiling showed that it controlled tax revenues and expenditures, but at the cost of lower education quality. A recent study showed that Proposition 2½ in Massachusetts was fairly successful as a fiscal restraint. It was contended that prudent use of initiatives and overrides by citizens might have been one factor in its effectiveness. A lot of other studies also observed that TELs somewhat controlled government budgets. However, they also found some side effects. States with TELs tended to replace the revenues under limits with other revenue sources such as user fees and service charges. In addition, the states were likely to have high state indebtedness (McCubbins and Moule 2010; Stallmann and Deller 2011).

While more thorough empirical research is warranted on this issue, Chapman and Gorina (2012) call for more methodological caution when we investigate fiscal impacts of TELs on governmental budgets. They contend that both governmental revenues and expenditures are closely linked. For instance, governmental expenditures are driven not by tax rates alone but by overall revenues raised. Intergovernmental aids as well as user fees and charges are also becoming more important for local expenditures. Thus, expenditures should be construed from the perspective of alternative revenue sources. In addition, under a typical process of determining property tax rate, predicted expenditure needs decide revenue amounts. In this sense, there is a strong possibility of two-way causality between revenues and expenditures, thus necessitating the use of simultaneous equation approaches. Chapman and Gorina used data from 378 U.S. cities in forty-four states with populations over 50,000 in 2002. Their key finding, controlling for the two-way causality, shows that localities subjected to a state-imposed property tax limit tend to reduce own-source revenues by about 9.5 percent.

One pattern of TELs' impacts on governmental budgets is worth our further attention. Shadbegian (1999) found, using a panel data set on 2,955 counties from 1962 to 1987, that TELs decreased property and other tax revenues, though they increased the level of other miscellaneous revenues. Thus, TELs shifted the focus of local revenue structure toward miscellaneous revenue sources. In contrast, more stringent TELs reduced such a possibility of revenue shifting. Shadbegian (2003) also reported a similar finding based on panel data on state and local public school budgets from 1966 to 1992. State-level TELs showed some, albeit limited, impact on local public education. However, local TELs controlled local own-source expenditures on public education but simultaneously increased state expenditure on public education. Thus, the fiscal impacts of TELs were placed more on shifting fiscal responsibilities of service delivery among various levels of governments. These findings echo the empirical observations suggested by Mullins and Joyce (1996). Mullins (2010, 253–58) comprehensively summarizes empirical findings on the fiscal impacts of TELs on state and local fiscal choices, which are highly in line with the above findings.

As noted earlier, Maher and Deller (2013) developed a more elaborate index of state-imposed TELs. They also analyzed the impact on the fiscal condition of more than a thousand municipalities in forty-seven states in 2005. They have identified some four measures of local fiscal condition and their change variables: revenues, expenditures, fiscal flexibility, and debt (e.g., future obligations). Overall, the authors hypothesize that TEL severity is expected to aggravate the fiscal condition of localities because TELs are barriers to fiscal flexibility. As hypothesized, TEL severity lowers the level of localities' own-source revenues and general fund expenditures. This finding is in line with the previous findings noted above. Contrary to the hypotheses, however, TEL severity increases localities' unreserved fund balance but decreases overall debt level. "It could be that TELs force communities to more effectively manage their resources by building reserves, funding future obligations better, and controlling debt" (Maher and Deller 2013, 423). TELs therefore achieve their policy goal of restraining revenue and expenditure growth and enhancing fiscal management of local governments, as Maher and Deller stress.

Closely related, TELs are also expected to reduce tax burdens of households and businesses, attract new firms and households, and spur economic growth. Colorado's TABOR has reportedly stimulated higher economic growth. However, there is a contrasting view. Even when TELs can reduce tax levels, it is an open question whether reduced expenditures on public goods due to the decreased revenues might deter economic activities (Bae et al. 2012; Grizzle 2011). Bae et al., based on five-year interval data from 1985 to 2005 in the forty-eight contiguous states, found that state-level TELs had negative impacts on state employment but showed no effects on per capita state personal income. This finding is consistent with other recent studies that showed TELs were not associated with higher levels of economic performance. It was also suggested that states without property tax limitations might have had fewer financial problems during economic downturns (McCubbins and Moule 2010; Stallmann and Deller 2011).

Different Perspectives on Fiscal Impacts of TELs

More recent studies report slightly different findings on the fiscal impacts of TELs on state and local government budgets. Grizzle (2011) used state expenditure data from 1997 to 2006 and reports that TELs controlled state total spending and social sector spending although they increased non–social sector spending. Hou and Duncombe (2008) found that both state-level expenditure limits and biennial budgets were associated with significant increases in total state savings as percent of general fund expenditures by about 2.5 percentage points from 1979 to 2003. More interestingly, Guo (2011) suggests that TELs might function as a fiscal constraint under some specific economic conditions. Shadbegian (1996) reports an interaction effect between TELs and state income levels. In low-income states, TELs controlled per capita expenditures. In high-income states, however, TELs increased per capita state expenditures. Guo applied the findings to a potential interaction effect between state deficits and TELs. He used state discretionary tax adjustments from 1988 to 2006 and found that when states with more stringent TELs face higher deficits, per capita tax revenue in the states is more likely to decrease.

These more recent empirical studies provide a potential for TELs as a fiscal constraint. However, Kioko (2011) offers a much more insightful and creative observation on the potential of TELs as a fiscal constraint. She investigated highly technical aspects of TEL provisions and reports that there are two methods of estimating the appropriation limit. One method "rebases" tax and expenditure limits. Thus, TEL in year t will be actual revenues or expenditures in year $t - 1 \times (1 +$ fiscal growth factor), where fiscal growth factor will be a combination of price level change, population change, and real per capita income change. Another method just "recasts" TEL limits. For instance, TELs in year t will be appropriations limit in year $t - 1 \times (1 +$ fiscal growth factor).

Under the second method, TELs in year t will reflect cumulative changes to the base appropriations in the year TELs were first introduced.

For instance, Florida's constitution "requires the state to estimate its limit on the basis of the limit for the preceding year plus an adjustment for growth that is equal to the personal income growth in the last 20 quarters" (Kioko 2011, 66). This method is an example of recasting TEL bases. The author shows the differential between the revenue target limit created based on the recast method and actual revenue streams from FY 1996 to FY 2011. There are significant gaps between the two lines. For FY 2011, the revenue limit was about $45.77 billion while the actual revenue was about $26.62 billion. With this huge gap between the two values (i.e., the revenue limit target is much higher than the actual revenue), the revenue limit is in fact meaningless or nonbinding. If Florida followed the rebasing method, the revenue limit target and the actual revenue might have been very close. This means that the revenue limit can function as an actual fiscal restraint.

In contrast, Colorado's Taxpayer's Bill of Rights (TABOR) introduced above is one example of rebasing the TEL base. By using actual revenues, Colorado's TABOR achieves a downward ratchet effect. If state revenues in year two declined from those in year one, then the revenue limit in year three will be based on the revenues in year two. This actually imposes a lasting real cut in state revenues, not just a temporary freeze. As of 2011, twelve states rebase their tax limits annually, whereas nineteen states do not rebase their limits. Their limits will trend tightly toward actual revenues in the rebasing states. Of course, in that case, TELs are more likely to constrain spending growth. Kioko (2011) further shows for selective states how much slack (i.e., the gap between the tax limit and actual revenue collection/appropriation, which might mean the extent to which the tax limits are less effective in controlling tax revenues/appropriations) will follow between the two methods. For the non-rebasing states, on average TEL slack as a percent of actual appropriations is about 36 percent. For rebasing states, on average the TEL slack is about 7 percent. In sum, rebasing or recasting does matter in securing the impacts of TELs on governmental revenues and expenditures.

St. Clair (2012) investigated a totally new question on TELs by using Colorado's TABOR: Will TELs increase or decrease revenue volatility? TELs might decrease revenue volatility by imposing an upper limit on revenue totals. There is a different observation. Since most TELs target property taxes, local governments are likely to raise revenues from taxes or fees that are more income-elastic, in which case TELs might increase revenue volatility. Some previous studies introduced reported that TELs resulted in more frequent use of miscellaneous revenue sources such as user charges and fees. St. Clair compared the revenue volatility of 319 local governments in Colorado for the 1986–1992 and 1994–2000 periods. One peculiar aspect of TABOR was that local governments could also vote to override the TABOR limits, known as de-Brucing that was named after Douglas Bruce who sponsored TABOR. Empirical findings indicate that about 52 percent of all districts have shown increased revenue volatility. About 57 percent of the districts that de-Bruced have reported increased revenue volatility, while about 47 percent of the districts that did not (and thus were subject to TABOR) have reported increased revenue volatility. This implies that TELs can increase revenue volatility only when local governments vote to override them. However, regression analyses comparing Colorado with Wyoming, Connecticut, and New Hampshire show that TABOR significantly increases the volatility of both revenues and expenditures. As TABOR provisions specifically limited property tax revenues, local governments might have relied more on income-elastic revenue sources.

CHAPTER SUMMARY

- **Fiscal Control Mechanisms for States**

States have had a wide variety of fiscal control mechanisms over local budgeting decisions since the late nineteenth century. Examples include constitutional or statutory across-the-board limitations over local budgeting decisions or administrative control of local budgeting decisions through standardized financial accounting and reporting.

- **Types of Tax and Expenditure Limits (TELs)**

There are several types of TELs.

(1) Property tax rate limits are the most frequently used form.

(2) Revenue or expenditure increases are sometimes specified as a maximum percentage increase. This has more fiscally binding effects than property tax rate limits.

(3) TELs also limit property value assessment increases. When there is a limit on the assessment of property values, property tax rate limits might be more binding.

(4) Some states tie the annual growth in state revenues and expenditures to a certain percentage growth rate of state personal income or population.

(5) Some states explicitly require public discussions or legislative votes for tax increases.

- **Are TELs Effective in State Government?**

TELs are adopted because they might improve efficiency in governmental fiscal choices or because a certain group of voters prefers them.

TELs have not been effective in controlling revenue or expenditure growth. Many studies indicated that TELs have shifted the focus of local revenue structure toward more miscellaneous revenue sources. TELs have also shifted the fiscal responsibilities of service delivery to state governments.

More recent studies have found that more stringent TELs tend to control tax revenue growth when states with TELs have been experiencing higher deficits. Another recent study indicates that TELs can also increase revenue volatility.

- **More Realistic Functions for TELs**

When TELs rebase annual tax and expenditure limits to actual revenues or expenditures in the immediate previous year, the gap between TELs and expected revenues and expenditures is likely to be minimized. In that case, TELs function as more realistic fiscal targets and are more likely to control revenue and expenditure growth.

6 | Rights-Based Budgeting

Although agencies, governors, and legislatures are the most influential actors in budget processes, courts sometimes affect the strategies and behaviors of the main budget actors. Court decisions based on constitutional rights often stipulate that executive agencies redress unfair or cruel and unusual punishment of individuals. Executive agencies may not decline to comply with the court decisions on the grounds that they do not have adequate resources and as a result, budgets for the litigated programs are expected to grow. But executive agencies do not simply comply with the court decisions as mandated, which interests budget scholars. In fact, the key issue is not whether executive agencies merely comply with court orders or not. Instead, court orders have modified the aspirations and behaviors of budget decision makers in various, subtle ways that early budget scholars did not explain. This observation is widely known as rights-based budgeting. This chapter introduces the following concepts:

- What Do Rights Mean to Budgets?
- Quasi-rights: How Do Court Decisions Affect Budgets?
- Empirical Findings on How Court Decisions Affect Budgets and Administration
- Court Decisions and Budgets: State Education Financing
- Prospects of Rights-Based Budgeting

WHAT DO RIGHTS MEAN TO BUDGETS?

As clarified throughout Part III, incrementalism has been a dominant framework for explaining the budget process. According to incrementalism, budget decision makers have a substantial level of discretion, but they exert it in a way so they distribute fair shares of budget pies among themselves. The result is that annual budget outcomes are likely to follow predictable, stable change patterns as decision makers distribute their fair shares or budgetary bases. Straussman (1988, 101–6) contends, however, that there are significant challenges to this view of budgetary incrementalism. A variety of uncontrollable entitlement programs, such as Aid to Families with Dependent Children, Social Security, Medicare, and Medicaid, render rights based on past legislation and where rights and budgeting are inherently in conflict. The entitlement programs significantly restrict budget decision makers' discretion. Readers can refer to Chapter 2 on legislative budgeting and Chapter 25 on congressional macrobudgeting to see how the entitlement programs reshape the landscape of governmental budget processes. Therefore, this dimension of rights-based budgeting is not the focus of this chapter.

Another source of rights is judicial establishment, defined as quasi-rights. Courts have upheld that overcrowded conditions in state correctional facilities violate the Eighth Amendment's prohibition against cruel and unusual punishment. Another judicially derived due-process right is treatment protection for mentally and physically disabled individuals confined to state institutions. For instance, Arkansas was the first state to experience a court-ordered reform of its penitentiary system. Beginning from *Holt v. Sarver* in 1969, a series of litigations indicated that state penitentiary systems were overcrowded. Court orders also focused on the elimination of the trustee guard system, inmate safety, brutality, racial segregation, and general sanitation levels. In 1978, the U.S. Supreme Court upheld a series of lower court rulings by establishing a maximum inmate population per correctional facility (Axelrod 1989, 48–53; Harriman and Straussman 1983). State agencies (typically defendants) cannot decline to comply with court decisions on the grounds that they do not have enough funds (Straussman 1988, 104–6).

This chapter will focus primarily on the second aspect: how court-induced quasi-rights influence the reactions of legislatures and the behaviors of administrative agencies. The main contribution of this aspect of rights-based budgeting is that it gives us more details on how budget decision makers behave under institutional procedures. Court-induced quasi-rights shed light on how budget decision makers exert their discretion, sometimes more detailed than and different from what incrementalism predicted.

QUASI-RIGHTS: HOW DO COURT DECISIONS AFFECT BUDGETS?

Straussman (1986) develops a very comprehensive theoretical framework to investigate the impacts of court orders on administrators as well as on legislatures. Agency bureaucrats can apply the so-called Wildavsky's crisis techniques. They can publicize and dramatize court decisions and perhaps ask for emergency appropriations to address the problems indicated in those decisions (Wildavsky and Caiden 2004, 66–67). Agency bureaucrats are naturally inclined to expand their budgets and thus are likely to strategically use such litigations for more resources. In that case, court mandates will be good excuses for agency bureaucrats to request more resources to implement court decisions. If so, compliance with court orders and increasing the budgets for litigated programs are likely to be in the interest of agency bureaucrats. In a similar vein, there are some cases where court-mandated litigations have also reinforced the managerial power of the administrators in charge of litigated programs (Bertelli 2004; O'Leary 1989). These observations are not necessarily different from the incrementalist perspective. In fact, they reveal what incrementalism did not explain about the behaviors of budget decision makers. All in all, this scenario implies that budgets for litigated programs are likely to grow but in a manner slightly different from what incrementalism explained.

Court-mandated standards influence budgeting in more subtle ways than merely affecting budget amounts. In many court-mandated budgeting cases, judicial interpretation of satisfactory compliance has been operationalized into more specific measures such as square feet per prisoner in a cell and staffing ratios. As detailed in Part III, budgetary incrementalism suggests that negotiations and strategies among main budget actors typically result in stable, predictable budget changes. The court-mandated standards remove negotiations and budget strategies found in typical incremental budget processes. The debate over fair share, envisioned in incrementalism, is hampered by constitutionally protected rights, and the court-mandated standards substantially restrict budget decision makers' discretion, which also results in heightened competition and turbulence among budget actors (Straussman 1988, 105–6). Another interesting observation from rights-based budgeting is that budget decision makers do not comply with court-ordered standards in a linearly incremental way. Even when they comply with court orders, they are more likely to wait and see how things are developing. This scenario is more likely to develop when budget decision makers do not agree with the policy suggestions in court orders. They wait several years before implementing court orders. These outcomes are what differ from incrementalism.

EMPIRICAL FINDINGS ON HOW COURT DECISIONS AFFECT BUDGETS AND ADMINISTRATION

Empirical findings generally support the above expectations. Sometimes court orders significantly enhance the managerial discretion of agency administrators implementing litigated programs. Agencies also tend to use restrictions in court orders as an excuse to ask for more funds, thereby leading to increased expenditures for litigated programs. At the same time, court decisions significantly restrict agencies' discretion on budget decisions. However, they also show some subtle variation in terms of bureaucratic behavior and discretion: Sometimes they comply with court orders in a strategically delayed manner.

COURT DECISIONS AND ADMINISTRATIVE DECISION PATTERNS

Some findings report how court orders affect budget and management decisions by administrative agencies. In the U.S. Supreme Court's landmark *Missouri v. Jenkins* decision, the Court affirmed a previous court ruling that local property taxes could be increased for Kansas City residents. The tax increase was supposed to be used for desegregation efforts by local school districts. Partly compatible with previous studies, court orders empowered school district bureaucrats and enhanced resources needed for the school system (O'Leary and Wise 1991). However, O'Leary and Wise indicate that federal judges could choose who would have administrative and legislative power at the state and local level. Federal district court judges retained the preeminent power-broker position, thereby weakening the discretion of the district bureaucrats.

Bertelli (2004) presents observations different from those of O'Leary and Wise (1991), based on a comprehensive suit against the child welfare agency in Kansas City, Missouri. Strategic choices by agency bureaucrats during litigation might reinforce their control over the policy-making process. Strong decrees might enhance specific management interests in certain practices with an emphasis on the litigated dimension of operations. O'Leary (1989) also analyzed the impact of federal court decisions on the U.S. Environmental Protection Agency (EPA) based on over 2,000 federal court decisions from 1970 to 1988 in which the EPA was either a plaintiff or defendant. Court-generated issues dominated EPA's policy debates and usually court decisions were at the top of EPA's budget priorities. All other programs dropped to the bottom and were subject to budget cuts. There were also some positive impacts from court orders. Upper-level managers were more willing to listen to the opinions of program staff at the lower level in the EPA hierarchy. As EPA workers collaborated to implement court orders, their morale was greatly enhanced. Thus, court orders can substantially augment the managerial power of the administrators implementing litigated programs.

COURT DECISIONS AND STATE CORRECTIONS EXPENDITURES AND ADMINISTRATION

Harriman and Straussman (1983) investigate fiscal impacts of judicially established rights on state and local expenditures because budgets are necessarily a crucial part of the court decisions. The cost incurred from implementing court decisions regarding state and local correctional facilities ranged from $5 million for some county governments to $1 billion for some state governments. Using spending patterns for corrections in fourteen states that experienced court-mandated reforms, the authors report how the need to pay the costs incurred from implementing court mandates was translated into state corrections expenditures and administration.

Overall empirical findings on the fiscal impact of court-ordered state expenditures for prison systems are somewhat bifurcated. Capital expenditures increased after court rulings. State corrections spending as a percentage of total state budgets increased. In contrast, per-prisoner spending in states that experienced court-mandated reforms was generally lower than in states without such court litigations, so from this early analysis the fiscal impact of court mandates on state corrections expenditures is somewhat unclear.

Harriman and Straussman (1983) also investigated how court mandates influenced the behaviors of agency bureaucrats and state budgetary games. Prison administrators were generally concerned that they could not increase prison spending in real dollar terms, especially when corrections budgets were falling behind the rate of inflation. However, corrections bureaucrats could also find budgetary friends in the judiciary when state legislatures and governors were not likely to campaign for the prison vote. In that case, court orders could serve to maximize corrections bureaucrats' bargaining power to expand their budgets. The mandates also affected state budgetary decision processes. If state funds had to be spent more on prison systems, fewer resources would be available for other state programs. This would intensify the competition for the scarce resources. Therefore, the concept of fair share and the attendant stable budget processes envisioned in incrementalism might not characterize budget processes.

Taggart (1989) reports empirical findings very similar to Harriman and Straussman (1983) and in line with disproportionate information-processing theory introduced in Chapter 15 in Part III. Budget decision makers pay selective attention to a batch of budget information flowing from budget environments. This selective attention, or the so-called indicator lock, results in delayed reactions to environmental budget cues. Using total (capital and operating) state expenditures and operating costs for corrections from 1945 to 1983, Taggart analyzes how court orders regarding prisons, hospitals, and mental health facilities affected state expenditures on those facilities. In general, court orders had a limited but positive impact on "capital" expenditures, similar to Harriman and Straussman's findings. He also suggests that court orders were tempered by the dynamics of state-level budgetary processes, which also supports the assumptions in disproportionate information-processing theory (e.g., bureaucrats' delayed reaction to environmental inputs such as court orders).

COURT DECISIONS AND LOCAL CORRECTIONS EXPENDITURES AND ADMINISTRATION

Straussman and Thurmaier (1989) report local observations very similar to the case of rights-based budgeting at the state level. Rights-based budget allocations restrict the discretion of agency bureaucrats. Paradoxically, however, some bureaucrats tend to be better off because they can protect and defend their budgets. In 1985, a lawsuit was filed against a county government in the northeastern section of the United States for operating a prison that violated the inmates' rights under the first, Fourth, Fifth, Sixth, Eighth, Ninth, and Fourteenth amendments to the U.S. Constitution. The legal arguments of the court decision mirrored the general conditions of prison overcrowding. The county partially implemented the court decision, and in 1987 a judge acknowledged that the county was trying to reduce overcrowding at the prison. The county administrators were not daunted by judicial mandates and generally viewed them as conditions necessitating increased spending for their prison system. This strategy exemplifies the above-mentioned crisis techniques.

However, although the county implemented the court mandate, the overall implementation was a slow process, with several reasons for the delay. It was very difficult to forecast the future prison population. The capacity of the state prison and state mandates might change. It was also difficult to predict revenue streams for needed capital projects. In addition, legislators were generally trying to avoid capital decisions with little or no political benefits. The county, especially legislators, was conducting a kind of cost-benefit analysis over complying with the court mandate. When past court mandates had come and gone without imposing fines, legislators tended to drag their feet. Thus, court orders were not immediately implemented as planned. This behavior of county decision makers is another clear example supporting disproportionate information-processing theory introduced in Chapter 15 in Part III on budget punctuations.

Duncombe and Straussman (1993) also investigated how court orders affect decisions to expand the capacity of local prisons by using a national sample of jails in 1983 and 1988. Their findings indicate that court orders influenced the decisions of the local prisons although there were other jail-related factors that also affected them. For instance, the level of overcrowding and jail age showed much stronger impacts on the decisions than court orders. However, one aspect, much in line with the above cases, showed how budget decision makers modified their budget behaviors. Prison administrators in many jurisdictions tended to plan for capital expansion when they needed it, not when forced by court orders. This implies that budget decision makers filter environmental budget-information inputs, in this case court decisions, according to their own information-processing protocol (e.g., in this case the need for expanding capital facilities) rather than court orders.

COURT DECISIONS AND BUDGETS: STATE EDUCATION FINANCING

In some cases, court-ordered mandates were based on very elaborate policy suggestions. Numerous education-finance litigations illustrate how court orders have intended to improve equity across different school districts by employing much more specific policy provisions. Despite the elaborate policy suggestions in these court orders, their impact on actual budget decisions is still an open question. More importantly, future studies are warranted to improve the framework of rights-based budgeting to explain how education litigations modify the behavior of administrators of litigated education programs.

COURT DECISIONS AND FISCAL EQUALIZATION IN STATE EDUCATION FINANCING

School finance litigation has garnered scholarly attention up to recent years. In the 1971 *Serrano v. Priest* case in California, the highest state court indicated that per-pupil revenue among local school districts ranged from $577 to $1,232. The fiscal disparities were in violation of the equal protection clauses of the federal and state constitutions. In the 1973 *San Antonio Independent School District v. Rodriguez* case from Texas, the U.S. Supreme Court ruled that local school district finance did not violate the equal protection clause in the U.S. Constitution. The confusion in the first wave of school finance litigation was cleared when many court cases appealed more to state equal protection clauses and tried to address fiscal disparities in local school finance, following the 1973 *Robinson v. Cahill* case in New Jersey. Beginning with 1989, the tendency has picked up. For instance, in *Rose v. The Council for Better Education, Inc.* (1989), the Kentucky Supreme Court ruled that fiscal disparities in local school finance violated the state constitution. The state responded to the court order by enacting the Kentucky Education Reform Act (KERA) of 1990. KERA raised the limit of the state's foundation grant and adjusted equalization grants and local property assessments to allow more funds to poor school districts (Axelrod 1989, 55–60; Evans, Murray, and Schwab 1997, and 1999, 72–98). Court orders regarding fiscal disparities encouraged the development of various types of state grants to local

Table 6.1

Comparison of Foundation vs. Guaranteed Tax Base Grants

	Formula	School district A	School district B
Foundation grant	$G_i = F[1 + C_i] - [R^*][V_i]$		
i	Local school district i		
Gi	Per-pupil grant	$4,500	$4,000
F	Per-pupil foundation grant level	$5,000	$5,000
Ci	Cost index	0	0
R^*	Basic property tax rate	1%	1%
Vi	Per-pupil property tax base	$50,000	$100,000
GTB Grant	$G_i = B + (V^* - V_i)R_i$	$2,100	$1,600
B	Basic or foundation grant	$2,000	$2,000
V^*	Guaranteed per-pupil property tax base	$60,000	$60,000
Ri	Property tax rate in district i	1%	1%

governments. Typically, two forms of state educational grants were widely employed to address the fiscal disparities that court orders attempted to correct.

Table 6.1 shows the basic functions of the two main forms of the state grants, foundation grants and guaranteed tax base (GTB) grants, which have been the most frequent forms of state grants to equalize fiscal capacity of local governments. These types of grants are the examples of grants used for the purpose of fiscal equalization introduced in Part V. There were slightly different versions of GTB grants, such as power equalization grants, percentage equalization grants, and wealth neutralization grants (Duncombe and Yinger 1998; Feldstein 1975; Fisher 2007, 505–13; Ladd and Yinger 1994; Reschovsky 1994; U.S. ACIR 1990, 43–50). Readers interested in the details of how foundation grants and GTB grants function are referred to the studies cited above.

Table 6.1 shows a simple simulation result on how the two grants influence fiscal equality of two hypothetical school districts. Assume that the property tax base of school district B is twice that of school district A ($100,000 vs. $50,000). Of course, school district B has more tax revenues if the same property tax rate is imposed by their state government. Under this condition, if an equal amount of per-pupil lump-sum grant, a common type of state educational grants before the litigation started, is distributed to the two districts, it is fairly obvious that school district A might be significantly disadvantaged in terms of total resources available for public education. The various court orders introduced above were efforts to equalize the resources by way of manipulating state grants.

The foundation grant in Table 6.1 was supposed to improve fiscal disparities in local governments (Fisher 2007, 505–6). Rather than distributing lump-sum funds per pupil, state governments set per-pupil foundation grant levels shown in Table 6.1 at $5,000. It is obvious that the per-pupil grant will be inversely related to the property tax base in local school districts: school district A receives $500 more per pupil in state educational grants than school district B. However, it is also notable that unless the basic property tax rate (R^*), which is usually set by state governments, is very high, the power of fiscal equalization is not very strong. For example, if R^* is set at 4 percent, then the per-pupil grant for school district A will be $2,500, while that for B will be zero dollars. There is now a much stronger fiscal equalization (i.e., stronger fiscal assistance to District A that is poorer in terms of property tax base). In fact, beginning in the late 1960s and early 1970s when court litigation started, many states relied on foundation grants with a very low state-set property tax rate (Fisher 2007, 513). Foundation grants with higher property tax rates have been suggested as a way to improve fiscal equalization since the early 1970s.

In practice, many states employed GTB grants shown in Table 6.1 for fiscal equalization as an alternative to foundation grants. The rationale behind GTB grants is that states can thus more directly address the disparity in property tax bases among local governments. State governments can directly assist the property tax bases by allowing "guaranteed" property tax bases (Fisher 2007, 506–8, 513). If state governments guarantee $60,000 as the property tax base for all school districts in Table 6.1, then district A receives $2,100 while B receives $1,600. In a relative proportion, A now receives a relatively higher amount of state grants than it would under foundation grant systems. Fisher (2007, 508–13) conducted a simulation to show potential impacts of the grant types on local educational expenditures. The results indicated that overall local expenditures increased, but unfortunately the fiscal disparity declined only slightly.

EMPIRICAL FINDINGS ON HOW COURT DECISIONS AFFECT STATE EDUCATION FINANCING

Empirical evidence partially supports Fisher's simulation results. Evans et al. (1997, 1999) used local school district data from the early 1970s to the early 1990s and found that resources from state governments increased after court orders. In addition, state grants to the poorest school districts increased, but those to the wealthiest districts remained almost the same. Hyman (2011, 736–38) summarizes other studies conducted during a similar study period. Some empirical studies showed that court-induced fiscal equalization somewhat improved the fiscal inequities across local districts that were delivering public school services. Other studies, however, indicated that court-induced education reforms did not improve educational quality of local districts. In fact, in California some evidence revealed that state financing for local school districts led to a decrease in per-pupil expenditure for local education relative to other states. In addition, there was no evidence that standardized test score differences between wealthy and poor districts were narrowed. Whether fiscal equalization state grants actually improve fiscal disparities is an ongoing research question because, as of 2007, courts in nineteen states declared illegal the property tax systems for local finance (Brunori 2007, 66–67).

Another very important trend in court-mandated education finance is that the rationale for state assistance has shifted from fiscal neutrality to adequacy of education. The key target for state grants has been identified as not just equalizing fiscal capacity, but also guaranteeing adequate amounts of resources necessary for delivering fundamental values and skills to students. In the 1995 *Edgewood Independent School District v. Kirby* case, for instance, the Texas Supreme Court evaluated Texas's standards-based accountability system in terms of constitutional adequacy requirements (Rebell 2002,

236). The adequacy requirements are generally more compatible with foundation grants (Duncombe and Yinger 1998). More recent state grants to local governments have been foundation grants. As of 2001, thirty states were using foundation grant systems, three used GBT grant systems, and eleven used combined GTB and foundation grant systems (Fisher 2007, 514–15). Empirical analysis of grant systems based on the adequacy rationale is highly encouraged as a future research project. In addition, there should be more studies on how education litigations modify the behavior of administrators of education programs. Such studies will significantly improve the framework of rights-based budgeting in areas of education programs.

PROSPECTS OF RIGHTS-BASED BUDGETING

Although there are not many recent studies on the impact of court orders on budget choices, court litigation over prison overcrowding based on the Eighth Amendment is likely to continue in coming years. Over the past three decades, the prison-inmate population in the United States has grown eightfold. Class-action and individual lawsuits filed in Lewisburg, Pennsylvania, indicate that such court litigation might raise questions similar to those discussed above (Emshwiller and Fields 2011). Since the federal prison system inmate population of 216,000 exceeds its capacity by 40 percent, the federal Bureau of Prisons has been relying more and more on for-profit contractors as well as state and local jails. The number of inmates in privately managed security facilities was less than 5,000 in 1990 but increased to above 25,000 by 2012. With such a rapid increase in the number of inmates in private security facilities came increased cases of mistreatment of the inmates. However, the Supreme Court, by an 8–1 vote, recently ruled that the rights-based Eighth Amendment prohibition of cruel and unusual punishment cannot be extended to inmates in private security facilities. Inmates in a privately run federal prison may not sue the prison employees in federal court. The ruling held instead that the state court is the proper venue for such a lawsuit (Bravin 2012). It seems obvious that rights-based budgeting will continue to be a core issue in budget processes in state and local governments.

CHAPTER SUMMARY

- **What Is Rights-Based Budgeting?**

Various entitlement programs limit the discretion of main budget actors. In addition, when court decisions mandate executive agencies to redress unfair and cruel and unusual treatment of individuals, executive agencies are supposed to comply with these decisions. This phenomenon is widely known as rights-based budgeting.

Rights-based budgeting tends to significantly modify the stable and predictable process in budgetary incrementalism.

- **Court Cases Regarding Executive Agency Financing**

Executive agencies frequently take advantage of court decisions to justify their need for increased budgets to comply with court mandates. This is one of the so-called crisis techniques.

(1) Although rights-based budgeting generally enhances the power of judges, executive agencies have also enhanced their control over the policy-making process by emphasizing the litigated dimension of operations.

(2) Empirical findings suggest that state and local correctional expenditures increased slightly after court decisions mandated state corrections agencies to redress unacceptable prison inmate conditions.

(3) In both cases, it took several years for executive agencies or legislatures to increase the budgets of litigated programs. This was primarily due to decision makers' selective attention to budget environmental inputs.

• Court Cases Regarding State Education Financing

More frequent court cases have been reported on the equity of state education financing. The fiscal disparities were in violation of the equal protection clauses of the federal and state constitutions.

(1) Foundation grants attempted to allow state grants to local school districts that are inversely related to the wealth of these districts. Power-equalization grants or similar grant systems were further developed to ease the fiscal disparities that court decisions mandated executive agencies to address.

(2) Empirical findings suggest that court-mandated education reforms did not significantly improve fiscal disparities.

(3) Recent court-mandated education reforms have focused more on adequacy of education than on fiscal neutrality.

• Court Cases Regarding State Security Facilities

Due to the increasing number of inmates in privately managed security facilities, rights-based budgeting has been a controversial issue in recent court decisions. The U.S. Supreme Court tends to hold that the state court is the proper venue for a lawsuit.

7 Divided vs. Unified Governments and Fiscal Choice

Many scholars have observed that the partisan configurations surrounding budget processes significantly affect the behavior of main budget actors. More recent studies have investigated how partisan configurations define the information-processing capacity of main budget actors. In sum, different partisan configurations result in different fiscal choices. When executive branches and legislatures are dominated by the same party, the partisan configuration exemplifies unified governments. For state governments, if the governor's party is the same as the majority party in both chambers of the state legislature, this is called a unified government. When the governor's party faces a different majority party in both chambers (e.g., Republican governor and Democratic majority in both chambers in a state legislature), this partisan configuration is called a split-branch government. When each chamber of a state legislature is dominated by a different party, this partisan configuration is defined as a split-legislature government. This chapter discusses the following topics:

- Divided vs. Unified Governments and Legislative Productivity
- Divided vs. Unified Governments and Fiscal Choice
- Empirical Findings on How Divided vs. Unified Governments Affect Fiscal Choice
- Divided vs. Unified Governments and Information Processing
- Tension From Divided Governments Continues to Cause Budget Conflicts

DIVIDED VS. UNIFIED GOVERNMENTS AND LEGISLATIVE PRODUCTIVITY

Numerous scholarly efforts have investigated how unified or divided party control of government affects the enactment of significant public policies in national and state governments (Bowling and Ferguson 2001; Coleman 1999; Fiorina 2003). The conventional view of party government theorists argues that a divided government invites strategic standoffs between competing party politicians. This leads to gridlock or difficulty in enacting significant public policy (Coleman 1999). According to

Fiorina (2003), some scholars assert that separated institutions buttressed by partisan rivalry pose major obstacles to efficiency and effectiveness in policy formulation and implementation. Mayhew (1991) challenges the conventional wisdom by concluding that significant enactments at the national level are just as frequent under a divided government as under a unified government.

Coleman (1999), however, contended that studies of divided or unified government should more specifically consider the hidden dimension of party responsiveness—the degree to which party politicians are responsive to political environments. With data covering nearly a half century at the national level, Coleman found that under a unified government a more liberal public mood is positively associated with enactment of important legislation. In sum, a unified government contributes to more policy achievements. Coleman's study implies that divided governments are more likely to invite interbranch policy gridlocks and political conflict than unified governments (Fiorina 2003; Poterba 1994). For instance, Rogers (2005) investigated session laws in twenty-three states for selected years from 1981 to 1993. His empirical findings revealed that when two chambers in state legislatures were dominated by different parties, the production of session laws decreased by almost 30 percent.

DIVIDED VS. UNIFIED GOVERNMENTS AND FISCAL CHOICE

However, more subtle dimensions in interbranch partisan power configurations may exist under divided governments. Interbranch partisan configurations differ between split-branch governments (the executive branch facing both houses dominated by a different party) and split-legislature governments (each house under different party control). Previous studies imply that the varying levels of interbranch power configurations will modify the influence of key budget actors on state budget outcomes.

UNIFIED GOVERNMENTS AND FISCAL CHOICE

According to Alt and Lowry (1994, 2000), nothing can prevent unified governments from moving toward their preferred governmental budget levels, namely the "fiscal scale" or the share of income collected as public revenue. Fiscal transitions might be slower due to budgetary inertia or institutional conflicts caused by institutional settings such as entitlements and entrenched constituencies. However, one thing is clear: new budget levels tend to reflect the fiscal scale the majority party pursues. Since most states adopt some form of executive budgeting (Rubin 2010), budget actors in the executive branch, especially governors, are likely to exert the dominant influence on state budget outcomes under unified governments. The majority partisan preference prevails in budget decisions, other things being equal. Therefore, unified governments are likely to adjust quickly to external fiscal changes or shocks.

SPLIT-BRANCH GOVERNMENTS AND FISCAL CHOICE

Under split-branch governments where the executive branch faces both legislative houses dominated by a different party, one can expect observations similar to unified governments: budget choices tend to reflect the fiscal scales the new majority party in legislatures prefers (Alt and Lowry 2000). The literature suggests that the governor's party in legislatures is more likely to be punished for being out of fiscal balance. When governors are faced with veto-induced deficits or unpopular surpluses, they might try to achieve fiscal balance. This tendency is augmented also because veto-induced imbalances generally strengthen the position of opposing legislative parties. Since legislators in governors' parties prefer budget balance to avoid voters' punishment, they press governors to accept the unilateral fiscal preferences of opposing, majority parties in the legislatures. If legislatures are solid enough to override gubernatorial vetoes, they can impose their budget preferences on governors subject to the preference of the last legislative vote needed to override executive vetoes. Even when legislatures are not strong enough on their own, they can impose their preferences based on their appropriation powers (Alt and Lowry 1994, 2000). In sum, split-branch governments are as likely to make rapid fiscal adjustments to external revenue shocks as unified governments are, although legislatures are controlling budget decisions.

SPLIT-LEGISLATURE GOVERNMENTS AND FISCAL CHOICE

Under split-legislature governments where each house is under different partisan control, inter-chamber coordination issues will replace interbranch veto-bargaining problems (Alt and Lowry 1994, 2000). Two different scenarios might apply to fiscal choices under split-legislature governments. One scenario suggests that policy gridlock is more frequent under split-legislature governments. Advantaged partisan actors might be those whose fiscal preferences are closer to reversion budgets that will be adopted when budget decisions are not made in time. Another scenario implies that the chamber whose ideal is closer to the governor's fiscal preferences might be more advantaged. Since governors' parties tend to retain more leveraging power over budgets in conference committees, the result of bargaining between governors and legislatures would be closer to the governor's fiscal preferences. According to Alt and Lowry (2000), at least one thing is clear: budget proposals that satisfy governors' legislative parties also satisfy governors and are less likely to be vetoed. The speed of fiscal adjustment to external fiscal shock under split legislatures is, therefore, somewhat subject to empirical testing.

EMPIRICAL FINDINGS ON HOW DIVIDED VS. UNIFIED GOVERNMENTS AFFECT FISCAL CHOICE

Alt and Lowry (1994) analyzed revenues, spending, and federal fund contributions of the forty-eight contiguous states from 1968 to 1987. Their empirical findings support the hypotheses in their models summarized above. Unified governments increased revenues by 46 cents and expenditures by 1 cent when there was a 1 dollar deficit. Split-branch governments increased revenues by 13 cents and reduced their spending by 12 cents. Split-legislature governments reduced revenues by 7 cents and their spending by 18 cents. In sum, the findings suggest that unified governments make the quickest fiscal responses to external revenue shocks. (Note that Alt and Lowry assume that unified and split-branch governments would adjust revenues more than expenditures.)

Alt and Lowry (2000), in their extremely complicated paper, reported a similar finding. They used general fund revenues for thirty-three non-southern states from 1952 to 1995. Their findings showed that adjustment to revenue gaps was fastest under unified governments. The speed of adjustment for split-branch governments was slower than that for unified governments, but was faster than that for split-legislature governments. Endersby and Towle (1997) used per capita expenditures and debt in fifty states for 1988, 1990, and 1992. They report findings partially similar to Alt and Lowry (1994, 2000). Unified governments were more likely to control deficits. Sheffrin (2004) reported that political adjustments to fiscal shocks take longer under divided governments. Oregon and Connecticut, with especially protracted budget negotiations, had two legislative chambers split between the parties.

Other studies show different findings regarding fiscal choices influenced by different partisan configurations (i.e., divided vs. unified governments). Krause (2000) analyzed U.S. deficit data from 1948 to 1995 and found that the degree of ideological policy divergence among congressional members and political institutions was more significant in explaining the deficits than was divided partisan control. Although Krause used federal budget data, his findings suggest a possibility that factors other than the different partisan configurations might affect fiscal choices. Poterba and Rueben (2001) indicated that limits on state revenues might not matter if there are other institutional contingencies. If a state has a supermajority requirement to pass a state budget, as California does, the state government might not be unified even when one party controls more than half of the state legislature and governorship. As a result, the majority party as in typical unified governments cannot pass budgets by itself (Sheffrin 2004). This study leads researchers to pay more attention to unobserved yet different dimensions within the partisan configurations modeled in Alt and Lowry (1994, 2000).

Poterba's 1994 study raises an issue that is much more significant for budget studies. He constructed measures of unexpected fiscal deficits based on a narrower definition of "unexpected" fiscal shocks than Alt and Lowry (1994) used. He used actual revenues and expenditures from the prior year, forecasts of revenues and expenditures for the current year, and any budget cuts or revenue changes enacted during the current fiscal year. This way, he focused on unexpected fiscal deficits that transpired during the fiscal year. Using data covering the period from 1988 to 1992, he reported that unified governments adjusted to the unexpected fiscal deficits more rapidly than those with divided governments did. At first glance, Poterba's findings seem similar to Alt and Lowry (1994, 2000). However, his definition of unified governments differs from theirs. When a governor and the lower chamber are dominated by the same party, the condition is defined as a single-party state.

Clarke (1998) suggests highly plausible observations of why single-party states can adjust quickly to external fiscal deficits. Under split-legislature governments, governors might find their partisan allies in at least one chamber of the state legislature. Throughout conference committee sessions, the governor's partisans might support his or her budget positions, possibly because they have political positions similar to the governor's fiscal preferences. They might threaten opposition members of the committee that the governor could invoke vetoes over their budget proposals. This would likely force both sides to approve the governor's fiscal positions, and the committee process might result in weaker conflict between branches. Governors can also let legislative leaders and legislators know that if they modify some items in gubernatorial budget recommendations, governors might invoke item-vetoes over specific projects in the legislators' districts. The veto threat would contain potential political conflict over problematic pork projects in advance. Rosenthal (2004, 180) also observes that legislators under split-legislature governments oftentimes conform to gubernatorial policy stances. In that case, governors possess a stronger leveraging power over budget choices under split-legislature governments.

An Illinois case study further illustrates how the gubernatorial item-veto power might explain different results on split-branch governments and split-legislature governments. Governors were likely to invoke gubernatorial item-veto power more frequently under split-branch governments. Under unified governments, there was no need to use the veto power. Under split-legislature governments, however, a lot of budget deals were going on *before* the executive budget was submitted to the legislature. The legislative leadership attempted to control the rank-and-file legislators to ensure that the budget agreement between the governor and the legislature could be approved. The legislative leadership promised and governors awarded the rank and file various state grant-in-aid programs, and capital project funds went to faithful legislators' districts. Under split-legislature governments, negotiations were more likely to thrive between the governor and the legislature. However, it was clear (in addition to the intensified negotiations) that governors utilized gubernatorial item-veto power to enhance legislative support for their own budget recommendation (Snow and Rubin 2006, 103–17). Although more research is warranted, gubernatorial item-veto power might be one of many reasons why split-legislature governments are sometimes quicker to adjust to external fiscal shocks (see also Ryu 2011a, 135–85).

DIVIDED VS. UNIFIED GOVERNMENTS AND INFORMATION PROCESSING

There are a couple of very recent studies on how the partisan configurations affect budget processes in the national and state governments. These studies first analyze how the partisan configurations affect the information-processing capacity of budget decision makers. In Chapter 15 in Part III on budget punctuation, disproportionate information-processing theory will be introduced. This theory suggests that since budget decision makers do not have full information-processing capacity, they are likely to pay selective attention to budget-related information inputs. This phenomenon is called "indicator lock." When budget decision makers pay sudden, selective attention to previously ignored information inputs, these inputs will just as suddenly be incorporated into budget decision outcomes. Thus, there will be a dramatic budget lurch. The indicator-lock feature will be augmented by institutional conflicts caused by numerous institutional procedures and settings. (See Chapter 15 in Part III on budget punctuation for more details.)

Breunig and Koski (2009) investigated how institutional procedures and settings can influence budget processes. Interpartisan squabbles get in the way of smooth programmatic, and hence fiscal, changes. Policymakers in divided governments are less able to make timely policy changes because they are forced to negotiate with other policymakers of different mindsets and different political goals. This leads to higher levels of indicator lock and dramatic budget changes, or budget punctuations. Alt and Lowry's (1994, 2000) studies, introduced above, show that divided governments lead to fiscal hesitation and immobility. These studies point to a fiscal environment in which institutional costs in the form of transaction and decision making are higher in state governments under divided partisan control. Thus, they hypothesize, divided governments are more likely to produce punctuated budgets, due possibly to the weakening information-processing capacity of budget decision makers. Breunig and Koski used financial data for forty-eight states from 1983 to 1999. Unlike their expectations, a divided government did not necessarily increase budget punctuations.

In contrast, Ryu (2011a) indicates that simply analyzing the impacts of divided governments or unified governments cannot reveal how different partisan configurations affect budget decision-making processes and outcomes. He focuses on the key aspects of executive and legislative budgeting systems introduced in Chapters 1 and 2 in Part I. The federal and state budget processes have been featured by executive and, more recently, legislative budgeting systems. Under these systems, central budget offices in the executive and legislative branches function as the central sources of budget-related information. In particular, central budget offices share the informational sources with such line units as departments, agencies, and subdivisions, and they also significantly reduce their computational burden. Bureaucratic centralization through central budget offices was also expected to relieve tensions and conflicts among the line units in bureaucratic organizations.

Ryu (2011a) used several decades of U.S. budget data and state fiscal data. His findings support his expectations. Bureaucratic centralization in the executive branch significantly reduced the probability of budget punctuations that are regarded as symptoms of limited information capacity of decision makers and institutional conflicts. Bureaucratic centralization might have expedited information processing and reduced institutional conflicts. However, the findings were obtained only for unified governments. Under unified governments, political backdrops are fairly compatible with the hierarchical nature of bureaucratic organizations in the executive branch. Therefore, bureaucratic centralization can aptly process budget-related information and reduce inter-unit conflicts when the surrounding political environments are highly conducive to its operations.

Ironically, evidence suggests that bipartisan confrontations are the best conditions for central budget offices in the legislatures, such as the Congressional Budget Office (CBO), to function as efficient and politically neutral information processors. Congress is inherently a decentralized and fragmented institution, allowing various committees and their members to voice their opinions during the congressional budget process. In this sense, decentralization and fragmentation are not necessarily a legislative disorder. Many budget-related measures are simultaneously debated and approved. This practice reinforces the momentum of decentralization and fragmentation.

A single set of congressional committees is least likely to control all budget legislation. Budgetary decentralization and fragmentation have worked reasonably well in forming congressional budgets. In contrast to the Office of Management and Budget, the CBO is supposed to function under the highly decentralized and fragmented organizational conditions where one partisan desire might be pitted against another political preference. Ryu (2011a) found that only under divided governments, where the CBO can secure a safeguard in the middle of political crossfire, does bureaucratic centralization expedite information processing and reduce institutional frictions. Therefore, partisan configurations are again a significant precondition that determines whether bureaucratic centralization affects budget punctuations in the congressional budget process. In sum, Ryu's findings imply that the match between organizational characteristics of central budget offices and their surrounding political environments is the most crucial factor in explaining whether unified or divided governments affect budget processes and outcomes.

TENSION FROM DIVIDED GOVERNMENTS CONTINUES TO CAUSE BUDGET CONFLICTS

As of 2013, the federal government can be defined as a split-legislature government: Democratic president, Democratic Senate majority, and Republican House majority. As hypothesized by Alt and Lowry (1994, 2000), policy gridlock highlights the national budget process. The traditional partisan divide over a debt limit extension between Republicans and Democrats took the United States to the brink of default on August 2, 2011. Congress reached an agreement to create a supercommittee to reduce the U.S. deficit by at least $1.2 trillion. In November 2011, Congress again failed to meet the supercommittee's deadline to strike a deal to control the U.S. deficit (Chaddock 2011). The Democrat-dominated Senate passed a bill to extend the payroll tax cut for another two months in December 2011. The Republican-dominated House was poised to reject the payroll-tax-cut extension initiative. Many rank-and-file Republicans were concerned that the initiative would dampen the revenue flow into the Social Security Trust Fund, which somewhat contrasted with their conventional stance over tax cuts. In contrast, House Republican leaders were concerned about the temporary nature of the initiative and required a yearlong tax cut extension. Ironically, Senate Republicans contended that House Republicans jeopardized potential tax benefits to middle-class families by threatening to reject the Senate bill, which is also somewhat different from typical Republican preferences (Steinhauer and Pear 2011).

These cases illustrate that a split-legislature government might incur additional institutional conflicts and costs when there is a further partisan divide within the same party. As Krause (2000) noted, an ideological partisan divide might have been the main cause for the policy and budget gridlock in these cases. However, the gridlock was obviously intensified by the split-legislature government. One further caveat here is that this case differs from Poterba's (1994) definition of the single-party configuration. In this case, the president's party is the same as the Senate majority party. In the federal and state governments, lower chambers retain primary authority over appropriations issues. These issues will continue to be a good future research topic.

CHAPTER SUMMARY

- **Divided Governments and Fiscal Choice**

Divided governments are more likely to experience higher institutional conflicts and costs. Many studies showed that legislative productivity declines under divided governments.

- **Partisan Configurations and Fiscal Choices**

There are different expectations of fiscal choices under different partisan configurations.

(1) Unified governments are likely to move the fiscal scale or the size of budgets coming from main tax bases in the direction the majority party prefers.

(2) Under split-branch governments, legislators in governors' parties prefer budget balance to avoid punishment by voters over deficits or surpluses. It is highly likely that the legislators attempt to impose their budget preferences on governors and make rapid fiscal adjustments to external fiscal shocks.

(3) Under split-legislature governments, interchamber coordination issues will replace interbranch veto bargaining problems. There are some scholarly controversies, but any budget proposal that satisfies a governor's legislative partisans is likely to satisfy the governor and is less likely to be vetoed.

- **Responses to External Fiscal Shocks**

Empirical findings on how partisan configurations affect fiscal choices overall support the scholarly expectations. Unified governments make the fastest fiscal adjustments to external fiscal shocks. Split-branch governments also make fast fiscal adjustment, but split-legislature governments were slowest in adjusting to fiscal shocks.

- **Split-Legislature Governments and External Fiscal Shocks**

Some other empirical findings suggest that split-legislature governments make the fastest adjustments to external fiscal shocks. Especially when governors and the lower chambers in state legislatures are dominated by the same party, budget decision makers make quicker adjustments to fiscal shocks. One possible reason for this finding is that governors might exert stronger budget coordination power when they have line-item veto power.

- **Partisan Configurations and Information-Processing Capacity**

More recent studies investigated whether and how different partisan configurations affect the information-processing capacity of budget decision makers. When this capacity is limited, scholars anticipate, more frequent cases of sudden, dramatic budget changes, known as budget punctuations, will occur. Some empirical studies revealed that divided governments do not increase the frequency of budget punctuations. Other studies, narrowed down to a specific aspect of executive or legislative budgeting systems, have reported that a certain level of centralization in the executive budgeting systems enhances the information-processing capacity of budget decision makers under unified governments. In contrast, centralization in the legislative budgeting systems tends to do so under divided governments.

Part II

Rational Approaches
to Resource Allocation

8 | Zero-Based Budgeting

Zero-based budgeting (ZBB) is a technique that requires budget decision makers to review all existing programs from scratch or on a zero basis. The fundamental assumption is that all programs will go through an annual review process. Budget decision makers are supposed to estimate costs and benefits of all potential programs and choose the best programmatic alternatives to achieve the goal of their organizations. This chapter investigates the following issues:

- Historical Context of Zero-Based Budgeting
- Mechanisms of Zero-Based Budgeting
- Critiques of Zero-Based Budgeting
- Revival of Zero-Based Budgeting

HISTORICAL CONTEXT OF ZERO-BASED BUDGETING

Under zero-based budgeting (ZBB) systems, budget decision makers are supposed to prepare next year's budgets after reviewing all programs from scratch. They first define what a certain program achieves, usually in terms of program operation or function. Next, they identify all potential alternatives to provide the same level of the operation or function. Unlike incremental budgeting, here budget decision makers do not start from the so-called budget base or previous year's budget amount. Instead, starting from a zero base they assess all potential programmatic alternatives to maximize efficiency and effectiveness. All programmatic alternatives are competing with all other alternatives, which implies zero-based competition. Earlier versions of ZBB were employed as far back as 1924. The U.S. Department of Agriculture adopted ZBB in 1962. Carter introduced it into the budget process of Georgia in the 1970s and further implemented it in the federal government (Kettl 2003, 91; Lewis 1988). Despite continued critiques, ZBB has recently reappeared in various levels of government.

MECHANISMS OF ZERO-BASED BUDGETING

In almost all levels of governments and nonprofit organizations, budget processes follow incremental patterns, starting from the budget base. One major limitation of incremental budgeting is that budget decision makers cannot easily respond to changing external environments or eliminate outdated and wasteful programs. In this sense, ZBB was an attempt to minimize budget waste and padding and reallocate resources where they could return maximum benefits to a whole jurisdiction that the programs cover.

DECISION UNIT AND DECISION PACKAGES

Pyhrr (1970, 1977) refined the concept of ZBB based on his managerial experience at Texas Instruments. The first step of ZBB is to identify decision units. Any meaningful elements of each organization can be identified as decision units. They might correspond to organizational units or programs that are operated by the organizational units. Even specific elements, activities, or functions of the programs can be designated as decision units. In practice, top management frequently defines decision units at organization or program levels. In that case, each line manager also has the discretion to identify additional decision units as appropriate. As an illustrative example, a specific program was chosen below as the decision unit for which ZBB mechanisms were initiated.

Once a decision unit is identified, the manager of that unit will start developing a preliminary decision package. A logically practical starting point for determining next year's resource requirements is the current year's level of organizational operations. First, the manager will need to identify all "activities" that cause the expense level for the current year. Then, he or she will look at the potential changes in next year's operations and attempt to forecast the expense level for the next year. Upper management usually provides the decision unit manager with formal assumptions about activity levels, wage and salary changes, and other elements associated with the decision unit in the next year. The decision unit manager then develops a business-as-usual package for the upcoming year, which is a compilation of programmatic activities that the decision unit intends to achieve in the next year under different assumptions of operations and cost changes. The business-as-usual package is likely to be the current level of operations measured in terms of next year's costs if there are no new activities. At this moment, readers can notice that the business-as-usual package is the major function that the decision unit must fulfill to achieve its programmatic goal.

Once the decision manager identifies the preliminary package (e.g., business-as-usual package), final sets of decision packages will be developed. There are two basic types of final-decision packages. First, mutually exclusive packages identify programmatic alternatives that perform the same function for the goal of decision units. Second, incremental packages reflect different levels of workload or expenditures on a chosen programmatic alternative. Pyhrr (1977) took a state government example in Georgia, which is depicted in Figure 8.1. The Georgia Air Quality Laboratory (Air Quality Control Program) in the state government was the decision unit in this ZBB

Figure 8.1 **An Example of ZBB Decision Packages**

The Georgia Air Quality Laboratory (Air Quality Control)

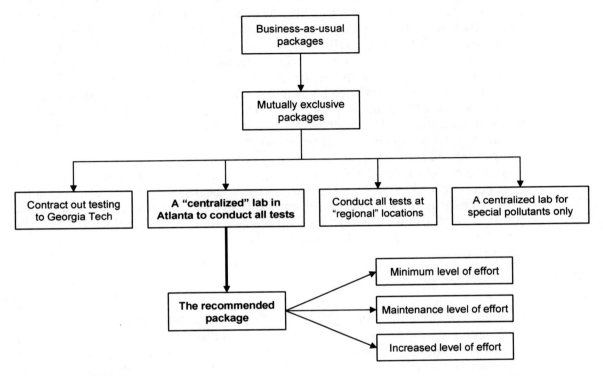

application. The goal of the Air Quality Lab (i.e., decision unit) was sampling and evaluating air quality throughout Georgia. In other words, the main function of the Air Quality Lab was monitoring air quality through sampling and evaluating. The business-as-usual package in Figure 8.1 was a compilation of all activities to deliver the function that the lab was supposed to provide on an ongoing basis.

The decision unit manager then identified four different programmatic alternatives, called mutually exclusive packages, needed to achieve the goal. Mutually exclusive packages were different ways of performing the identified function of the lab, presented in a form of the business-as-usual package (i.e., monitoring air quality through sampling and evaluating). Examples of the mutually exclusive packages included contracting out testing to Georgia Tech, conducting all tests by the central lab, conducting all tests at regional locations, and utilizing the central lab only for special pollutants. In this case, that all tests be conducted by the central lab was the recommended package. One caveat is that mutually exclusive packages may also include alternatives with different service or workload levels, although incremental packages explained below include different service or workload levels for the recommended package from all mutually exclusive packages (McKinney 2003; Pyhrr 1970, 1977).

The next step was to develop different levels of workload or effort to perform the recommended package (note that this step focuses only on choosing different service or workload levels of performing the recommended package). Typically there were three different levels of effort, called incremental packages. The first level was a minimum (reduced or base) level of effort below which the operation itself would be discontinued because there would be no viability of effectiveness at all. This level could cover only the most critical populations served or the most serious problem areas without achieving the goal pursued by the Air Quality Lab. Simply speaking, the minimum level of effort must be continued under any circumstances as long as the lab continues to exist. Without the minimum level of effort being performed, there was no reason for the lab's existence. The second level was the current (maintenance) level that was usually the status quo level of the recommended package. For instance, it measured the workload to conduct all tests currently needed by the central lab. The third level was the increased level of effort, which covered more populations in Georgia. The three decision packages would then be ranked for the decision unit of the Air Quality Lab. Since the minimum effort level was likely to cover the most critical population and areas, it tended to consist of legally obligated functions. Therefore, it was often placed at the higher end of the ranked levels: the minimum level of effort was the priority function for the lab.

RANK ORDERING AND STRUCTURAL CHALLENGES

Although rank ordering for a single decision unit was not a significant challenge, reviewing all packages from the perspective of the entire organization created too great a computational burden. This dilemma was somewhat addressed by grouping decision units together depending on three factors: the number of decision packages, line managers' ability and willingness to rank-order packages, and the need for extensive review across entire organizational units. For instance, Pyhrr (1970) showed a structure of decision unit packages with four different levels of consolidation; lowest level, lower level, upper level, and final level. The lowest level covers decision packages mostly of the lowest budgeted units (e.g., cost center). The next highest level is the lower consolidation level that consolidates decision packages grouped from the lowest consolidation level. The next level is called the upper consolidation level. The fourth and final consolidation level includes all decision packages grouped according to the hierarchically ordered four-level decision packages. If the hierarchical level were to cover all decision packages, then it might impose a ponderous task on top management. If the hierarchical level covers the decision packages only from the lowest level of the hierarchy, the top management (or upper management in general) might not have the opportunity to trade off expenditures across cost units (e.g., decision packages at the lowest level) or upper-level decision packages (e.g., the lower and upper levels in the above example). Therefore, the above-indicated three factors are very useful in deciding the nature of the hierarchical level.

In the above example, the initial ranking took place at the lowest decision unit level. Then, managers at the next-highest level reviewed the rankings with the decision unit managers, and this process would continue on to the top management. At this point, readers might notice that rank ordering of decision packages follows a somewhat bottom-up approach. In contrast, imposing cutoff lines over the rank-ordered packages pretty much follows top-down guidance. One important aspect of decision making in ZBB is how to establish cutoff lines below which decision packages will be discarded. The most practical way of establishing a cutoff line would be to identify it at the highest consolidation level. Top management can estimate the expense of business, which can be approved. If, for example, a potentially approvable budget is 80 percent of the previous year's budget, then top management is supposed to review higher-ranked decision packages (e.g., likely to be high-priority packages such as the minimum-level effort mentioned earlier) first. The decision packages below the 80 percent cutoff line will go through more stringent scrutiny because they are likely to be discretionary or low-priority decision packages. Another point worth further attention is that cutoff lines can be set at each level of the four-level hierarchy cited above. As such, managers at each level can rank-order decision packages based on the cutoff line established at his or her level, which tends to be set at a percentage of last year's budget for each level. Finally, the rank orders at various levels will be compared and adjusted from the perspective of the goal of the entire organization. Overall, ZBB was expected to reprioritize organizational programs and reallocate scarce resources where they would produce maximum benefits (McKinney 2003).

CRITIQUES OF ZERO-BASED BUDGETING

There have been numerous critiques of ZBB implementation. In practice, budget officers start from the minimum level (e.g., 90 percent of the current budget) rather than literally zero base whenever they prepare budget proposals. The maintenance level and improvement level both function to maintain or protect the budget base that ZBB is supposed to open up (Schick and Hatry 1982). Readers might also notice that the business-as-usual package in ZBB is fairly similar to the status quo level introduced in Part III rather than the zero base. The starting point of ZBB in its original mechanism is *not* the zero base.

Lauth and Rieck (1979) show evidence that ZBB in the Georgia state government was not successful due to some gamesmanship. Agency managers placed minimum-effort packages (typically legally obligated services as explained above) below the cutoff point. As a result, many low-priority programs were bundled near (or over) the legally required packages. Top managers were unable to eliminate them because it was very difficult to establish a cutoff line beyond the legally required, high-priority packages. Lauth (1978) also showed that ZBB was not successful when the general public had maintained expectation of the continuation of certain programs. Budget decision makers could not eliminate or reduce them even based on ZBB prioritization. In addition, when interest groups developed and sustained ongoing support for existing programs, budget decision makers could not successfully impose ZBB evaluation results onto those programs.

In some cases, earlier experimentation of ZBB indicated that it contributed to enhancing participatory management as indicated above. However, the desired cutoff lines for reduced spending were not realized in most state and federal cases. More importantly, ZBB implementation severely augmented the necessity of involving more people in the budget process (Draper and Pitsvada 1981). Lauth and Rieck (1979) showed a more specific example. In Georgia, there were originally about 10,000 decision packages. Since so many packages put a heavy workload on the state managers, they were reduced to about 2,000 packages. This was still a burden on state managers, especially when they had to prepare two budgets, one traditional budget and the other ZBB. More recent state examples during the 2000s indicate that the heavy workload on the part of state government managers has been one of the biggest challenges to the successful implementation of ZBB (Snell 2010).

The case of Bremerton, Washington, indicates that politicians are trying to politicize the use of ZBB. Chris Tibbs, county commissioner candidate in 2011, strongly suggested that the county introduce ZBB as a much bolder approach to counter the crisis in the county's budget. He stressed that ZBB would require each county department to prepare a new budget, each year reviewed from a zero base and without assuming that each department could get funds close to the previous year's budget. However, he clarified that his support for ZBB was tied to a programmatic priority on law and justice, road construction, and commonsense land-use decisions. It seems possible that the programs were what the candidate might have politically preferred.

Scholars have suggested some alternatives to address such political hurdles and computational burdens associated with ZBB. A more viable alternative is target budgeting (TB). With this process, unlike ZBB, subunit agencies submit skeleton cost estimates for the ensuing fiscal year to the central budget office board. Based on preliminary cost estimates, tentative government-wide budget targets are developed. Agencies are then instructed to develop more detailed budgets. TB allows lower-level organizational units more budgetary discretion (Lewis 1988). Readers can contrast this aspect with the top-down cutoff line in ZBB. Another alternative to ZBB is target-based budgeting (TBB). Under this system, organization-wide budget targets are chosen based on forecast revenue. TBB can easily adjust to recessions and is less vulnerable to political conflicts that might intensify, especially over scarce resources. With its revenue-driven target, TBB requires less work on the part of budgeters. In addition, as long as subunits stay within the target amount, they can enjoy discretion over the lump-sum budget allocations allowed to them (Koehler and Reed 2003; Rubin 1991).

Around 1980, after realizing how difficult it was to apply original forms of ZBB in the state budget process, many states actually turned to target budgeting (TB). By the early 1980s, the original form of ZBB had almost disappeared and TB was being more widely used in state budgeting. Agencies were asked to prepare their budget requests at various levels of their base budget— for instance, at 90 percent, 100 percent, and 110 percent—and then to analyze how the different budget levels would affect agency responsibilities. These actual versions of TB did not radically deviate from the original ZBB but were fairly useful in cutting budgets or reallocating resources from agency to agency. In addition, TB eliminated the tedious rank-ordering of numerous decision packages, thereby reducing the bureaucratic workload (Snell 2010, 2012).

Another alternative to ZBB is called periodic agency review budgeting. Even small scale ZBB required substantial levels of programmatic description, analysis, and budget recommendations. The analysis needed for ZBB was simply too time-consuming for agencies as well as for legislative staff and legislators. For these reasons, more recent versions of ZBB have called for four- to eight-year periodic analysis of state agency budgets. Florida was one of the first states to implement an eight-year cycle of agency budget reviews. Its eight-year agency budget review produced thorough and useful reports, but the process was still too expensive and time-consuming. Oklahoma implemented a four-year cycle of zero-base legislative review of state agency budgets. The Oklahoma Department of Education was the first agency subjected to the four-year review. The review process was valuable but so time-consuming that legislators never considered the analysis result for the agency budget. Subsequently, the Oklahoma legislature replaced the four-year agency review with performance budgeting (Snell 2010, 2012).

Despite the modified mechanisms in TB or TBB, readers might still wonder how to avoid political conflicts by setting organization-wide targets. In other words, how can we be sure that revenue-driven targets or less strict budget review can mute political competition over scarce resources? These have been the ongoing questions over rational approaches to resource allocation.

REVIVAL OF ZERO-BASED BUDGETING

ZBB has recently been reintroduced as a way of controlling budgets in the national, state, and local governments. The Federal Communications Commission's (FCC) Universal Service Fund (USF) is a program that extends telephone service to rural areas. The USF program was authorized by the Telecommunications Act of 1934 and is a typical example of an outdated program, because now even rural areas have sufficient telephone service coverage. In collaboration with Congress, the FCC attempted to establish a ZBB model, under which an organization that receives federal funds would have to present its case based on a community's need before Congress on an annual basis (Williams 2011).

Governor Paul LePage of Maine called for introducing ZBB for cost control. In particular, the Maine Department of Education and the Department of Health and Human Services distributed state funds to local school districts or health-related contractors. Governor LePage attempted to tightly review through ZBB how state monies are used by the local school districts or contractors (editorial, *Portland Press Herald* 2011). Governor John Lynch of New Hampshire instructed all state agencies to prepare their budget requests for FY 2008, FY 2009, FY 2012, and FY 2013 based on ZBB or similar approaches. The process planned to conduct a full review of agency missions, legal requirements, and relevant alternatives to existing practices for improved resource allocation. Idaho Governor C.L. Otter has recently ordered all state agencies to cut their budgets by 5 percent. ZBB was expected to help clarify the central missions of these agencies and eliminate programs that do not match current missions and priorities. At the same time, however, budget decision makers in the states cautioned that ZBB might not achieve huge cost savings (Snell 2012). The county of Bremerton, Washington, recently tried to adopt ZBB to overcome a revenue shortage by prioritizing spending categories, as noted above (Grimley 2011).

Despite the apparent revival of ZBB, it is still an open question whether ZBB can contribute to more efficient resource allocation. In recent years, seventeen states were reported to use ZBB. Fifteen state legislatures introduced bills calling for using some form of ZBB in 2009, two did so in 2010, and nine states considered similar legislation in 2011. However, none of the introduced legislations were enacted between 2009 and 2011. Although seventeen states have reported using some form of ZBB, there is no real evidence that most of them actually applied it to their budget decisions. Idaho Governor Otter launched a statewide implementation of ZBB as noted above. An Idaho budget officer indicates that even in that state, achieving the original goal of ZBB is a substantial challenge: "It is merely a tool for cost containment, used in Idaho to streamline agencies, focus them on their core missions and implement their strategic plans. It is a management tool as well as a budgetary tool" (Snell 2012, 6).

CHAPTER SUMMARY

- **Zero-Based Budgeting Systems**

Under zero-based budgeting (ZBB) systems, budget decision makers are supposed to review all programs from scratch. ZBB attempts to reallocate resources where they can return maximum benefits to the whole jurisdiction that its programs cover.

- **Steps in Zero-Based Budgeting**

  1. The first step of ZBB is to identify decision units. Organizational units or specific elements, activities, or functions of organizational programs can be decision units.
  2. The second step of ZBB is to develop a preliminary decision package. Decision unit managers first develop a business-as-usual package that delivers the current year's activity level adjusted for changes in activities and cost changes in the next year.
     a. Decision unit managers then prepare two sets of new packages detailing the chosen business-as-usual package. Mutually exclusive packages identify programmatic alternatives that perform the same function for the goal of decision units. Incremental packages reflect different levels of workload or expenditures once one of the mutually exclusive packages is chosen.
     b. Incremental packages typically include three packages: minimum-level packages, maintenance-level packages, and increased-level packages.
  3. The third step of ZBB is to rank-order all decision packages. Decision unit managers and higher-rank managers cooperate to review them below the cutoff line at the relevant consolidated level of all decision packages. This way, ZBB attempts to prioritize organizational programs and reallocate resources.

- **Actual Application of Zero-Based Budgeting**

In actual application of ZBB, the zero base was more likely to be historical bases such as 90 percent of current budgets. ZBB sometimes fell prey to some gamesmanship and interest group mobility.

- **Politics and Zero-Based Budgeting**

Politics oftentimes biased the implementation of ZBB, and scholars and practitioners have suggested some alternatives to it. Target budgeting (TB) or target-based budgeting (TBB) allows more discretion to subunit agencies. In addition, they are based on forecast revenues and, as such, might still foster intense political conflicts over scarce resources.

- **Recent Revival**

Despite many critiques of ZBB, it has been revived at various levels of governments.

9 Performance-Based Budgeting

Performance-based budgeting (PBB) is a budget system that allocates resources according to performance of programs. Recently, PBB has been targeting outcomes or results (e.g., educational capacity improvement) rather than outputs (e.g., number of school graduates). In addition, PBB has been incorporating the core features of strategic planning and program budgeting. This chapter discusses the following issues:

- What Is Performance-Based Budgeting?
- Why Is Performance-Based Budgeting Needed?
- Mechanisms of Performance-Based Budgeting
- Revival of Performance-Based Budgeting
- General Challenges to the Implementation of Performance-Based Budgeting

WHAT IS PERFORMANCE-BASED BUDGETING?

PBB starkly contrasts with line-item budgeting (LIB). Under the latter, agencies prepare their budgets based on typical objects of expenditures such as personnel and equipment. The downside of LIB is that stakeholders do not know what activities or functions the agencies achieve. Unlike LIB, PPB usually starts by defining tangible objectives of the agencies, which are supposed to realize the agencies' ultimate mission. Agencies then develop program structures that might span different subdivisions within agencies.

For instance, a state department of transportation might have two subdivisions: highway systems and transit systems. Due to declining revenue sources, many states have recently developed infrastructure bank programs to maximize resources for transportation programs. Infrastructure bank programs pool financial resources for transportation projects so state governments can loan the pooled financial resources to various entities. By loaning the resources, they can earn extra interest and thus stretch their revenue pools. They can also borrow more funds by using the pooled resources as collateral. All in all, infrastructure bank programs stretch limited financial resources for transportation projects by several times the original resource pool (Ryu 2007). Infrastructure bank programs might cut across the two subdivisions. Finally, agencies will prepare budgets for each program as well as budgets for the two organizational subdivisions. These budget formats that combine strategic goal and specific programs into budgets are broadly categorized as PBB (Melkers and Willoughby 1998). PBB intends to maximize productivity of agency performance by increasing outputs of agencies or minimizing costs for delivering agency services. This has been defined as productive efficiency. In addition, PBB intends to allocate scarce resources where they can return the largest benefits for the whole jurisdiction that agencies serve. This is defined as allocative efficiency (Robinson and Brumby 2005).

WHY IS PERFORMANCE-BASED BUDGETING NEEDED?

The Taft Commission on Economy and Efficiency of 1913 suggested that government officials tie their expenditures to results of governmental activities. In 1934, the U.S. Department of Agriculture adopted a performance budgeting system (Kettl 2003, 83–102).

Under this "old" performance budgeting system, government officials prepared budgets based on what public programs actually produced. For instance, a state-operated job training center might allocate its budget based on the number of program participants who graduated from the training center. One clear advantage of performance budgeting is that government officials are not allowed to regard the amount of their previous budgets as given. Incremental budgets closely associated with LIB tended to allow marginal increases or decreases from the previous year's budgets as discussed in Part III. Under LIB, substantial portions of input dollars, which are often called budget base, are not significantly altered. Performance budgeting intends to review at the least what those input dollars bring about on an annual basis. Budgets will then be readjusted according to what public programs actually achieve, measured in terms of program activities, performances, or outputs.

MECHANISMS OF PERFORMANCE-BASED BUDGETING

OLD PERFORMANCE-BASED BUDGETING

It is worthwhile to succinctly review the fundamental components of PBB systems. Figure 9.1 (see page 77) is a summary view of program budgets developed for the U.S. Department of Commerce (DOC) (more details will be introduced below). The DOC has twelve subdivisions. According to the traditional LIB, the DOC will prepare its budgets based on line items or objects of expenditures such as salaries and equipments for its twelve subdivisions. Line item budgets are regarded as input-oriented budget systems. Their downside is that we do not know what particular organizational entity is actually doing with taxpayers' money. To overcome the limitations of LIB, old performance-based budgeting systems relied on output measures. Up to the late 1960s, the national and state governments had employed the so-called old performance budget systems that allocated budgets based on activities or performance of organizations (e.g., number of graduates from universities). The systems were labeled as output-oriented systems. In Figure 9.1, each of the twelve DOC subdivisions will develop output measures that will be linked to budget allocations (Lee, Johnson, and Joyce 2013, 201–2; Mikesell 2011, 233–45; U.S. General Accounting Office 1997, 30–34). Thus, the old PBB could focus on the so-called productive efficiency, measured in terms of the ratio of outputs to inputs.

New Performance-Based Budgeting: Combining Outcome Measures into Program Budgeting

New PBB systems incorporated the core features of program budgeting systems, which develop hierarchically organized means-ends chains to achieve organizational missions. In addition, new PBB systems were focused on outcomes more than outputs (e.g., students' educational skill and knowledge improvement—outcome—as opposed to the number of students graduating—output). Readers can better understand key mechanisms of new PBB systems from two real-world examples.

Planning, Programming, and Budgeting System (PPBS)

During the 1960s, the federal Department of Defense (DOD) implemented Planning, Programming, and Budgeting System (PPBS). PPBS identified numerous programs called the Future Years Defense Program across different divisions in the DOD (Kettl 2003, 85–89; Lee, Johnson, Joyce 2013, 202–5). The DOD still uses PPBS under the Planning, Programming, Budgeting, and Execution System (PPBES) (Mikesell 2011, 249).

As West, Lindquist, and Mosher-Howe (2009) indicate, program budgeting such as PPBS removes activities from their home organizational divisions and evaluates them in terms of their contribution to hierarchically ordered goals and objectives. The hierarchical nature of PPBES has recently been revived in a concept called capability trees, or hierarchies. In the case of defense budgets, planners identify complete sets of capabilities needed to meet the quantitative and qualitative goals adequate for defense planning through a structured and comprehensive process. A capability hierarchy, or tree, visualizes the elemental capabilities crucial for achieving higher- and lower-level objectives. In other words, the hierarchy starts with higher-level objectives that are likely to be in general descriptions of a capability associated with higher-level defense goals. The tree then refines each level, illustrating lower-level and more precise capabilities needed to achieve the higher-level objectives described in terms of capability. The tree uses the means-ends chain typically found in PBB systems: lower-level capabilities are means to achieve higher-level capabilities but are ends to lowest-level capabilities. The tree is not necessarily identical with organizational charts (Miller, Robbins, and Keum 2011; Webb, Richter, and Bonsper 2010).

The PBB System in the U.S. Department of Commerce

Readers can better grasp the hierarchical nature of PBB through the performance evaluation scheme applied to the U.S. Department of Commerce during the Bush administration. For the U.S. Department of Commerce (DOC), annual editions of

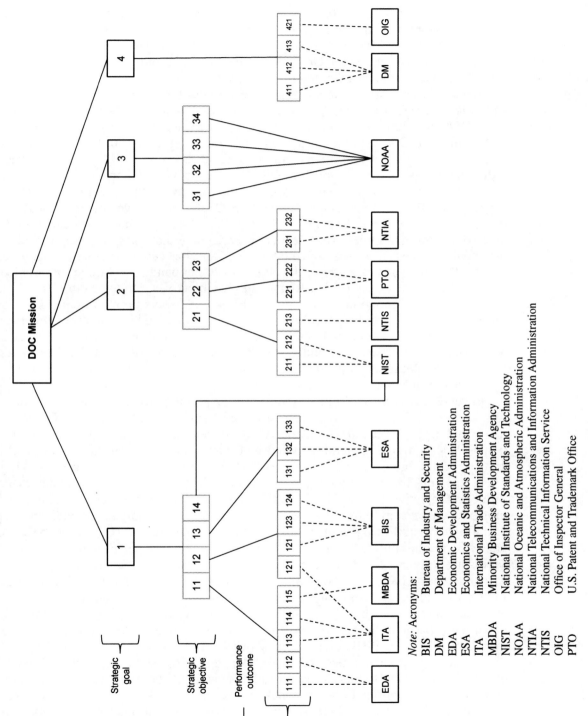

Figure 9.1 **Performance-Based Budgeting Process: The Department of Commerce**

Note: Acronyms:

BIS	Bureau of Industry and Security
DM	Department of Management
EDA	Economic Development Administration
ESA	Economics and Statistics Administration
ITA	International Trade Administration
MBDA	Minority Business Development Agency
NIST	National Institute of Standards and Technology
NOAA	National Oceanic and Atmospheric Administration
NTIA	National Telecommunications and Information Administration
NTIS	National Technical Information Service
OIG	Office of Inspector General
PTO	U.S. Patent and Trademark Office

Performance and Accountability Report (PAR) were available from ExpectMore. gov and have been available from Performance.gov as of 2011. Performance evaluation scores in the PAR series are required by the Office of Management and Budget (OMB) Circular A-11 and the Government Performance and Results Act (GPRA) of 1993 (U.S. Department of Commerce 2010, xi).

Figure 9.1 summarizes the structure of capability trees applied to DOC subdivisions. There are four strategic goals or capabilities under the highest-level capability (e.g., DOC mission). Three of them are mission-related programs—Strategic Goal 1: Maximize U.S. competitiveness and enable economic growth for American industries, workers, and consumers; Strategic Goal 2: Promote U.S. innovation and industrial competitiveness; and Strategic Goal 3: Promote environmental stewardship. The fourth strategic goal or capability is improving the overall management capacity of DOC—Management Integration Goal—to achieve organizational and management excellence. Except for Strategic Goal 4, each has its subcapabilities, labeled as Strategic Objectives. Readers need to note that the first letter of each of the capability measures is capitalized because DOC has developed its own name for it. Other departments might have developed different names for similar hierarchical capabilities. Strategic Goal 1 has four Strategic Objectives. Strategic Objective 11 is "Foster domestic economic development as well as export opportunities." Each of the Strategic Objectives has more specific capabilities, called Performance Outcomes. The Performance Outcomes include lowest-level capabilities, called Performance Measures. For instance, Economics and Statistics Administration (ESA) has eleven Performance Measures grouped into and linked to three Performance Outcomes (131, 132, and 133 in Figure 9.1).

However, as Figure 9.1 implies, there is a high potential for organizational conflict from cross-walking. Strategic Objectives 11 and 12 cover nine Performance Outcomes that span four DOC bureaus (Economic Development Administration [EDA], International Trade Administration [ITA], Minority Business Development Agency [MBDA], and Bureau of Industry and Security [BIS]), which exemplifies the cross-walking. Then, it is very likely that the four bureaus might contest for credits from achieving Strategic Objectives 11 and 12. PPBS originally develops hierarchical program structures like the capability trees in Figure 9.1 to facilitate cross-organizational analyses of multiple capabilities. But the problem is that the four bureaus (EDA, ITA, MBDA, and BIS) might contest for performance credits whenever performance evaluation scores are to be reflected into their budgets. This potential risk has been described as an attribution issue and is well evidenced in PBB experiments (Bourdeaux 2008). In fact, the federal government has been using a combination of traditional line-item budgets and functional budgets. The entire federal government budgets were based on department-based budgets and OMB function-based budgets even before the implementation of the new PBB system (Mikesell 2011, 252). OMB function-based budgets are similar to program budgets that are developed based on some forms of hierarchical capability trees. OMB function-based budgets inevitably contain a component called cross-walking mentioned above, which in this case refers to the creation of extra programs and attendant budgets spanning various organizational subdivisions (U.S. General Accounting Office 1997, 12–13). The issue of cross-walking might be one of the biggest challenges ahead for successful implementation of PBB in the future (Ellig, McTigue, and Wray 2011, 205–9; Posner and Fantone 2008, 95–97).

FOCUS ON OUTCOMES INSTEAD OF OUTPUTS

As noted above, new PBB systems focus more on outcomes than on outputs. For instance, the number of students graduated is an example of output, but it is not the ultimate goal of the education program. Real outcomes or results might be improved educational capacity of the students. The latter is frequently measured in terms of hourly wages or employment rates of the students. In sum, new PBB systems generally incorporate some functions of strategic planning, programming, and actual budgeting, which target outcomes rather than outputs and are prepared in addition to the traditional budgets based on organizational charts (Forrester and Hendrick 2003; Robinson and Brumby 2005, 5–15).

REVIVAL OF PERFORMANCE-BASED BUDGETING

PBB was less frequently used during the 1980s. During the 1990s, however, PBB systems came back. One of the most prominent examples of PBB applied to governmental budgeting is the Government Performance and Results Act (GPRA) of 1993. GPRA was the reflection of the initiative by the Clinton administration to reinvent the federal government. Similar to typical PBB systems, GPRA focused on strategic plans and required all federal agencies to write strategic plans for their activities by 2000. In addition, GPRA placed heavier emphasis on outcomes than on outputs and in this sense is an example of new performance funding systems (Ellig, McTigue, and Wray 2011; Kettl 2003, 96–97; Moynihan 2008). The PBB system applied to DOC shown in Figure 9.1 is implemented by GPRA.

The Bush administration adopted the President's Management Agenda (PMA) in 2001. It identified five areas for management improvement: strategic investment in human capital, competitive sourcing, improved financial performance, e-government, and budget and performance integration. For each of the five management dimensions, twenty-six agencies and other operating units were evaluated in terms of a traffic light grading system: green light means successful performance, yellow means mixed performance results, and red means unsatisfactory performance. The Bush administration also launched the Program Assessment Rating Tool (PART) in 2004. The OMB evaluated more than 1,000 federal programs through rounds of discussion and negotiation with federal agencies. PART scores on each program were based on weighted scores of the responses to four aspects: program purpose and design (20 percent), strategic planning (10 percent), program management (20 percent), and program results (50 percent). Each program was evaluated in the following categories: effective, moderately effective, adequate, ineffective, and results not demonstrated. PART scores for 1,017 federal programs (with 6,516 performance measures) were posted on ExpectMore.gov and are currently available from Performance.gov. The Obama administration has been using most of the performance agenda through the GPRA Modernization Act of 2010 (Joyce 2011). Many states have also adopted various versions of PBB, especially when faced with the 2008 financial crisis and attendant revenue shortages that called for more efficient use of scarce resources. Insufficient resources have driven the governments to search for cost-minimizing strategies (Clynch 2003; Easterling 2003; Hou et al. 2011; Texas Governor's Office of Budget and Planning 2003).

General Challenges to the Implementation of Performance-Based Budgeting

Empirical studies of PBB generally report that PBB systems were not successful in enhancing productive or allocative efficiency. However, some recent studies show that PBB can improve allocative efficiency of governmental programs. Indianapolis, Indiana, has launched its IndyStat, one form of PBB systems. IndyStat might have reallocated scarce resources where they can return the maximum benefits. Below the department level, there has been a substantial level of resource reallocation in Indianapolis. This is some evidence that PBB might work to improve the efficiency of governmental budget processes (Ho 2011).

Successful implementation of PBB systems in a local government might be strongly related to the scale of the problem. Local-level public agendas are not as complex as those found at the higher level of the federal tier. In addition, local government program agendas are likely to be more homogenized and less vulnerable to external political factors, quite different from higher-level federal budget processes. At the state level, for example, some external factors were more dominant in budget allocation than performance evaluation scores.

The Utah Department of Human Services had lower evaluation scores, but the governor even favored increasing its budget on the grounds that low performance is the result of changed demands (e.g., sudden increases in welfare recipients due to economic downturn). In Colorado, program-level performance measures were used and required for agency budget requests. Despite some recent success, PBB was less relevant as agency demands rose during economic crises during the first decades of the 2000s. Increased funds were still needed to fulfill the demands, even when performance was poor. In many states, PBB systems were useful only when legislators were willing to accept performance evaluation scores. Oregon has had a well-established outcome-based performance budget system. However, history and politics have played a larger role than the PBB system. In addition, many states, including California, did not have well-designed infrastructure to support PBB systems and did not have accurate accounting data to implement PBB systems (Hou et al. 2011). Chapter 8 in Part II introduced zero-based budgeting (ZBB). ZBB, which was applied to business organizations, was more adequate for service and support activities rather than manufacturing. The latter was decided by sales volume, which in turn determined the level of labor, materials, and overhead (Pyhrr 1970). Therefore, readers can easily understand that PBB systems vulnerable to external factors might not be that successful at the state level.

PBB might potentially cause numerous other problems. It tends to allow a substantial level of discretion on the part of governmental agencies. The problem is, however, that whenever there are multiple subprograms under a certain program, there is a high potential for contested credit claiming among the subprograms, as discussed above. The contested credit claiming also weakens transparency of program evaluation. In addition, if higher-level budget decision makers tighten up their control over the subprograms to enhance transparency, that control will detract from one of the strongest benefits of PBB, flexibility (Bourdeaux 2008). Lewis (1988) raised significant questions on the effectiveness of PBB. One of the key mechanisms of PPBS is cost-benefit analysis for capabilities in each level of the means-ends chain in Figure 9.1, for instance. It has been patently difficult to measure benefits from governmental programs. The grand question has always pertained to value judgments and politics. In addition, cost-benefit analysis is a microbudgeting tool, and, as such, it cannot answer the question of what projects are needed, although it can rank-order programs that compete for similar, common goals. Public programs also have multiple goals. Therefore, various stakeholders have different perspectives for public programs. Another challenge to PPBS is that goals/objectives in Figure 9.1 are oftentimes expressed in a mixture of outputs, outcomes, and impacts.

The fundamental limits of PBB were more widely evidenced at the federal level. Performance data should tell us something, but data on results or outcomes were rare. Even when obtainable, accounting systems were not capable of linking costs to outcomes. In addition, programs with quantifiable results get greater emphasis than those with results that are harder to quantify. Beginning in the 1930s, numerous attempts have been made to rationalize government budget decisions. However, budget actors with vested interests were generally opposed to the reforms. Between 2001 and 2008, some agencies reported dramatic increases in PMA scores, but there are some caveats. PMA scores might have been manipulated so they were very low at the beginning but were set higher at the conclusion. Agencies might have learned to better prepare for the PMA test. Reporting performance data should be streamlined so that congressional members and staff can utilize them. Congress was apathetic to the executive-driven performance data for budget choices. Congressional members were exposed to PART evaluations through agency budget justifications, but they were not using them significantly and instead relied more on their own knowledge. Despite OMB's assertion, Congress viewed PART scores as highly politically driven (Joyce 2011; Moynihan and Lavertu 2012).

Congress has also been more focused on bringing benefits to their district constituents than PART scores. The House Appropriations Committee deemed that PART scores were not tightly linked to their underlying authorization committee. PART did not adequately address the potential conflicts arising from the so-called cross-walking that spans different organizational subdivisions to create a common program (Frisco and Stalebrink 2008; Stalebrink and Frisco 2011).

CHAPTER SUMMARY

- **What Is Performance-Based Budgeting (PBB)?**

PBB is an endeavor to identify what activities or functions certain organizational entities attempt instead of the input dollars that they spend.

PBB typically identifies more tangible objectives of the organizations and develops programs that frequently cut across different organizational subdivisions. Budgets are then formed around the programs. PBB intends to improve productive and allocative efficiency.

- **"Old" PBB**

Old PBB focused more on output measures such as the number of graduates from universities.

- **"New" PBB**

New PBB featured two core mechanisms: program budget structures that develop hierarchically ordered sets of a means-ends chain to achieve organizational missions and outcome measures instead of output measures.

(1) The federal Department of Defense (DOD) has been employing PPBES, which identifies capability trees or hierarchies that visualize the elemental capabilities crucial for achieving higher- and lower-level objectives. The federal government has been using similar types of PBB during recent years.

(2) New PBB focuses more on outcomes (e.g., improvement in educational capacity of students) rather than outputs (e.g., head counts of students graduating from universities).

- **PPB Initiatives**

The federal government has launched PBB initiatives. The Government Performance and Results Act of 1993 was a recent example of PBB applied in governments. The Bush administration launched the President's Management Agenda in 2001, which identified five areas for management improvement. The same administration initiated the Program Assessment Rating Tool to evaluate more than 1,000 federal programs.

- **Positive Impacts**

PBB showed some positive impacts to enhance allocative efficiency in local governments, probably because the budget agendas for local governments are not complicated to the extent that the agendas defy the capacity of budget decision makers. In addition, local budget processes might not be as significantly dominated by political factors as in state or federal governments.

- **Challenges to Implementing PBB**

There are general challenges to the implementation of PBB.

(1) Cross-walking of programs tends to weaken transparency of performance evaluation due to contested credit claiming. If higher-level budget decision makers tighten up their control to enhance transparency, the control will dampen flexibility inherent in PBB systems.

(2) It is difficult to gauge benefits from governmental programs. In addition, measuring benefits does not necessarily answer the question of what projects are needed for the entire jurisdiction that PBB programs serve.

Performance-Based Budgeting

10 Challenges

The previous chapter introduced some general challenges to successful implementation of performance-based budgeting (PBB). This chapter provides more specific challenges that budget decision makers and financial managers must keep in mind when they implement PBB systems. This chapter discusses two issues:

- The Unit of Analysis and Performance-Based Budgeting
- Challenges to Successful Implementation of Performance-Based Budgeting

THE UNIT OF ANALYSIS AND PERFORMANCE-BASED BUDGETING

Scholars and practitioners have contended that PBB might not be easily applied to governmental budgets when they are too complex and heavily driven by political influence from various interest groups and partisan politics. Numerous institutional rules and procedures further prohibit budget decision makers from singularly applying PBB to resource allocation, especially when resources are scarce and competition for them is intense. This tendency is most frequently observed in the federal and state budget processes that are characterized by complex budget institutions and bipartisan political conflicts.

PBB can be applied to local government programs or single-agency programs, such as regional nonprofit or health-care organizations, which deliver more homogeneous and less complicated services. For instance, Indianapolis has adopted IndyStat, which is a type of PBB. IndyStat worked somewhat effectively in the executive budget review and program execution phases. It was operative at the subdepartment level where public administrators conducted their daily work and where strategic planning, performance goal setting, and program budgeting were logically linked. Based on performance evaluation scores, resources were more frequently moved around at the subdepartmental level (Ho 2011).

In contrast, PBB was not successfully applied to even a single agency program at the federal level. The Substance Abuse and Mental Health Services Administration (SAMHSA) implemented PBB systems. However, interunit rivalry and lack of coordination hampered PBB implementation when SAMHSA was managing multiple, complex federal and state programs. In addition, challenges of balancing diverse demands from stakeholders prohibited it from efficiently establishing its strategic planning (Ho 2007).

CHALLENGES TO SUCCESSFUL IMPLEMENTATION OF PERFORMANCE-BASED BUDGETING

Despite the disappointing evidence of the effectiveness in resource allocation, various levels of government will continue to use PBB in coming years (Joyce and Pattison 2010). As indicated in Chapter 8, some states that have used zero-based budgeting (ZBB) have opted for PBB instead of pursuing ZBB (Snell 2012). For the successful implementation of PBB, however, budget decision makers and financial managers must understand that there are numerous challenges they should carefully address.

ALLOCATIVE EFFICIENCY, COMMON DENOMINATOR, AND POLITICS

One goal of PBB is to allocate scarce resources to programs that can return maximum benefits. This concept is called allocative efficiency. However, the question is how to identify a common denominator to evaluate public programs with different value scales. Even when benefits can be accurately measured, what are the relevant theories and analytic frameworks on which to reallocate resources? Identifying the theories is a crucial challenge to improving allocative efficiency. Political obstacles are another tough challenge to allocative efficiency. When legislators or elected officials strongly support a certain program, it is very hard to readjust the program's budgets (Key 1940; Lewis 1952; Posner and Fantone 2008, 98–102; Robinson and Brumby 2005, 10–28).

Faced by the 2008 financial market crisis and state revenue shortage, the Utah state government adopted PBB systems. The Utah Department of Human Services received low performance evaluation scores, but the governor proposed increasing its budget on the grounds that low performance was the result of changed demands (e.g., sudden increases in welfare recipients due to the economic downturn). In Florida, PBB evaluation scores were useful only when legislators wanted to use them. Oregon has also been using an outcome-based performance budget system. However, Oregon's history and politics have played a heavier role than the system, as indicated in Chapter 9 (Hou et al. 2011).

George Bush's Program Assessment Rating Tool (PART) was known as an executive-driven performance evaluation tool. As such, Congress tended to perceive PART as the president's political tool to further executive budget power. Congress has been largely ignorant of or hostile to PART. If PART information was used by congressional staff members, it was because the Office of Management and Budget (OMB) consulted them in its early stage with a detailed explanation of its methodologies. In addition, federal program performance scores were of less importance to legislators' district constituents. Typical congressional committee members are more interested in parochial benefits and interests for the constituencies in their districts. Agencies' inefficient or less effective expenditures might serve the benefits of some individuals related to the congressional members. In that case, they are less likely to perform efficiency and effectiveness evaluations of agency programs. In most cases, federal programs are geared toward spreading benefits across the nation and are more likely to be monitored through such evaluation procedures as performance budgeting. However, the problem is that congressional members are less willing to devote their time to monitoring the programs with national impacts (Ellig, McTigue, and Wray 2011, 217–19; Frisco and Stalebrink 2008; Stalebrink and Frisco 2011).

PBB initiatives since the 1930s have been faced with opposition from those with vested interests (Joyce 2011). Lauth (1978) indicated that ZBB in Georgia was blocked by several challenges. When the general public showed sustained expectation of continuation of certain programs, ZBB could not downgrade the programs. The same held true when budget decision makers found strong political support for certain state programs from interest groups. In addition to the political restraint, ZBB was not successfully implemented when there were constitutional and statutory constraints. For example, the Georgia constitution stipulated that the Department of Transportation should receive at least the same amount of motor fuel tax revenue as it did in the previous year. In addition, the Georgia state government could do virtually nothing over the matching requirements of federal grant programs.

Gilmour and Lewis (2006) present another recent empirical study that PBB systems are still heavily dominated by partisan politics. The authors explored how merit or politics formed OMB recommendations for the 234 federal programs in the 2004 executive budget. The OMB claimed that there was a strong linkage between PART evaluation and budget recommendations. However, Gilmour and Lewis provided different observations. As the OMB claimed, there was a positive link between PART evaluation scores and executive budget recommendations for agency programs. However, when they controlled for partisan politics, they found interesting and provocative results. The significant relationship between PART evaluation scores and budget recommendations for agency programs was observed only for Democrat-preferred programs. Under the Republican president, Democratic programs were rewarded with budget increases when they performed well. In contrast, when they performed poorly, their budgets were reduced. However, the relationship between PART scores and budget recommendations for Republican-preferred programs was not statistically significant. Thus, Gilmour and Lewis's study evidences that PBB systems are highly vulnerable to political influence. In other words, the Republican president strictly imposed PART evaluation scores only on Democrat-preferred programs.

When external political factors heavily influence budget processes at the agency level, budgetary incrementalism rather than rational approaches to budget allocation better explains budget choices, as will be clarified in Part III. Lindblom (1959) argued that rational, synoptic approaches might be possible for small-scale problems typically found at the subagency level. Some scholars, for this reason, strongly exhort us to investigate the impact of PBB systems on resource allocations at this level (Robinson and Brumby 2005, 28–29). Moynihan (2008, 118–58) also implies that PBB systems might be more successful for subagency programs. However, a recent study shows that this might not be true, either.

West, Lindquist, and Mosher-Howe (2009) show the impact of planning, programming, budgeting, and execution systems (PPBES) in 2002 as a response to management challenges instituted by the National Oceanic and Atmospheric Administration (NOAA) housed within the U.S. Department of Commerce. PPBES had mixed effects. It clarified a definition of agency goals and facilitated communications across organizational divisions. However, it required substantial amounts of time and effort and was inimical to NOAA's scientific mission. Moreover, it did not have any significant impact on actual resource allocation. Very similar to earlier experimentation in the 1960s, new and complex routines competed with established norms and were not supported by adequate resources. Overall, NOAA could not overcome internal organizational politics when it implemented PPBES.

PRODUCTIVE EFFICIENCY

Though improving allocative efficiency causes one of the biggest challenges to PBB, productive efficiency causes a somewhat less significant obstacle. Productive efficiency measures the ratio of outputs (e.g., program graduates from a job training program) to inputs (e.g., budgets allocated to the program) (Kelly and Rivenbark 2011, 115–32; Robinson and Brumby 2005, 5). This has been the core measurement target for the old performance budget systems introduced in the previous chapter. Compared with allocative efficiency, productive efficiency was observed to be somewhat improved by PBB systems.

Reddick (2003) surveyed the impacts of the rational approaches on eight state functional expenditures. He found some spending restraint in selective state functions, and that state aggregate expenditures were also somewhat contained. Although Reddick's findings still serve as evidence of improved productive efficiency, he suggests that there might be some other rivalrous explanations for budget constraints. For instance, states under fiscal stringency might take PBB systems more seriously, and that attitude might explain tighter fiscal control or improved productive efficiency.

Similarly, Robinson and Brumby (2005, 33–34) introduce the so-called Prospective Payment System (PPS) for Medicare payments to hospitals, initiated by the federal government in 1984. The key idea behind the PPS program was to allow preset price schedules for hospitals for certain medical payments. If hospitals performed poorly, then the preset cost reimbursement would be an obvious penalty for the hospitals. This was closely related to productive efficiency in the hospitals. Overall, the PPS program somewhat improved productive efficiency of the hospitals participating in it. As in Reddick's (2003) study, however, numerous problems were also reported on improved productive efficiency. The main limit was the fact that the PPS program focused only on output or cost control and was negligent of the "quality" improvement. Services to patients were reduced in general. Hospitals did not invest in technology that would improve service quality but cost too much. They did not maintain research with longer-term potential for service improvement. The hospitals were also engaged in creaming: overservicing of low-cost patients. Robinson and Brumby (2005, 39–40) indicate that some hospitals maintained high quality as well as high quantity. However, they attributed the high quality to generally strict regulatory requirements and strong professional ethics for quality service in the health industry field, not the PPS program.

In addition, as closely related to the measurement issue below, many public organizations are involved in output maximization simply because it is easier to measure outputs than outcomes or quality of services. For instance, Barzelay and Thompson (2006) introduce an illustrative case of responsibility budgeting implemented by the Air Force Material Command (AFMC). Responsibility budgeting is a different name for the PPBES systems mentioned above. A newly committed manager of the AFMC intentionally focused on cost control at the very beginning of implementing responsibility budgeting. Overall, the AFMC has been successful in controlling program costs. This is a rare example that shows an improvement in productive efficiency. However, readers should also note that the key rationale of the responsibility budgeting is to improve "allocative" efficiency as well. Thus, simply improving productive efficiency does not mean that PBB systems are successful.

Attribution

Gilmour presents an insightful question on the attribution issue or linking performance to outcomes (2006, 26–28; Kelly and Rivenbark 2011, 100–2). In 2006, ExxonMobil made a record-high annual profit of $36 billion. Did ExxonMobil manage its operation so efficiently and effectively? The high profit can probably be attributed more to high international oil prices and a sudden increase in oil demand caused by Hurricane Katrina. In PBB systems, it is very difficult to link certain outputs to performance management of public organizations. This is especially the case for new PBB systems that focus more heavily on outcomes. Outcomes are typically one or two steps removed from outputs, and it is very likely that there might be other reasons for improved outcomes.

The Migration and Refugee Assistance Protection program has as its outcome goal percent reduction in long-standing global refugee population. Whether or not the Bureau of Population, Refugees, and Migration (PRM) can achieve this ambitious goal, is there any logical link between the achievement of the goal and PRM's performance management? There might be so many other factors that contribute to the goal (Gilmour 2006, 26–28). In addition, public programs usually have multiple goals and outcomes. Many federal programs have fairly abstract outcome targets. Of course, there are many departments that implement part of such functions (U.S. General Accounting Office 1997, 17). Therefore, we cannot be sure which public programs brought about the improved outcomes (Kasdin 2010).

It also takes years to realize the intended outcomes of public programs. For example, the EPA's Superfund program is supposed to clean up groundwater pollution. However, it takes at least several years to achieve improved water quality. How can we accurately measure the impact of performance management in a given year? In addition, some programs were fundamentally limited in their legal authority. EPA is supposed to provide cleaner air and water. However, it does not have any legal authority over local zoning or land-use decisions. How can we evaluate EPA for program outcomes that it cannot control (Gilmour 2006, 28; Hou et al. 2011; White 2012)?

A closely related issue is the trade-off between flexibility and transparency of budget choices. One rationale for PBB systems is that they can allow more discretion to agency budget administrators. This is obviously a strong merit compared with the traditional line item budget system. However, one problem is the difficulty linking certain outcomes measured at the agency level to subagency programs. Without an adequate link between aggregated outcome measures and disaggregated subagency programs, PPB systems are inherently flawed (Bourdeaux 2008; see also White 2012). The Obama administration, in extending the GPRA performance initiatives, emphasized the utilization of program evaluation to control various types of attribution problems (Joyce 2011). Researchers need to pay attention to how enhanced program evaluation can help control the attribution issue in coming years.

MEASUREMENT ISSUE

The fact that some public programs were successfully improving productive efficiency is partly because of the possibility of measuring outputs more easily (Moynihan and Lavertu 2012; Robinson and Brumby 2005, 16). Some programs have an either/or feature. For instance, the outcome goal of the Secure Transportation Asset Program (STAP) is preventing thefts of nuclear bombs or fuel. However, there have never been stories of such thefts within U.S. territory. The STAP instead chose output measures such as annual average overtime hours of its federal agent. The Bureau of Statistics has as its outcome goal better-informed business decisions, but this measure is too abstract to be used as a single agency program. Too many external factors affect this abstract goal. The bureau instead chose percentage of scheduled data releases (Gilmour 2006, 22; Joyce 2011; Kasdin 2010). This problem of measurement is aggravated when powerful stakeholders, especially legislatures or Congress, have different views of performance measurement. Of course, the result is that legislators do not pay much attention to performance evaluation results when they view performance scores differently (U.S. General Accounting Office 1997, 7–12; see also Heinrich 2012).

TRANSACTION COST

Just because a performance management system can be implemented does not mean that it should be. If the cost of monitoring or oversight due to the performance measures is greater than the outcomes, it does not make much sense to implement such a system (Kasdin 2010). At the beginning stage of ZBB in Georgia in the early 1970s, managers were supposed to review over 10,000 decision packages "in addition to" their traditional line item budget formats as introduced in Chapter 8 (Lauth and Rieck 1979). One of the main reasons why PPBS programs were not quite successful was the extraordinary burden put on budget decision makers (Lee, Johnson, and Joyce

2013, 202–5). In fact, this is one of the main reasons budgetary incrementalism has been suggested as "both" descriptive theory and normatively better decision strategy. It can relieve budget decision makers of the heavy computational burden. Whenever there is disagreement over performance measurement for public programs, executive agencies have been engaged in multiple rounds of time-consuming negotiation with legislatures or Congress (Joyce 2008, 56–57; U.S. General Accounting Office 1997, 12–16). In sum, the cost incurred by implementing PBB systems oftentimes outweighs the benefits achieved from those systems (Kelly and Rivenbark 2011, 128; White 2012).

THE QUESTION OF UTILIZATION

Along with the above limitations is another fundamental question: Are PBB scores effectively reflected in budget choices? Robinson and Brumby (2005, 18–22) provide a comprehensive summary of previous research on this topic. Most of the results were based on surveys of state and city budget officers, and they are bifurcated. A study conducted on behalf of the Government Accounting Standards Board reveals that only a small number of state budget officers perceived PBB systems to be effective in changing state budget appropriations (Robinson and Brumby 2005, 19). In contrast, Jordan and Hackbart (1999) and Poister and Streib (1999) report that state and city budget officers perceived that PBB systems moderately or substantially modified budget allocations. With respect to budget officers' perception of "use" of PBB systems (rather than the general effectiveness in changing budget allocations), the above studies reported somewhat more positive results. They reported overall budget officers' positive perceptions of the "use" of PBB systems in internal resource allocations within agencies.

There were some caveats about the somewhat positive findings, however. One clear pattern was that when survey results were positive, the cases mostly pertained to the states with well-developed performance measures and explicit introduction of performance budget procedures (Robinson and Brumby 2005, 21). In addition, the key point of PBB is to link performance evaluation results to funding decisions (Heinrich 2012). Unlike the bifurcated findings, results on the impact of PBB systems on "actual funding decisions or resource allocations" are clearly negative. Most studies report that performance evaluation results were not actually reflected in the final budget choices (Robinson and Brumby 2005, 20–22). As introduced in Chapter 2 in Part I, the Texas legislative budgeting system has heavily utilized performance measures in agency budget preparation. Agencies differed in terms of whether they applied performance evaluation results in their budget requests. Some prepared detailed budget requests utilizing such results, but some others did not because they were concerned that the detailed information might invite budget cuts for the programs with detailed performance data. Governors and legislators also tended to ignore the priorities shown in the priority allocation tables (Texas Governor's Office of Budget and Planning 2003). A recent study also revealed that PART evaluation scores were not reflected in funding changes (Heinrich 2012). GPRA initiatives improved allocative efficiency of some federal agencies such as the Small Business Administration. However, a study on the cost-effectiveness of job training programs reported that there was no expected resource reallocation. The U.S. Department of Labor had implemented job training programs such as Youth Transition, Welfare to Work, and Job Corps. The study shows no correlation between job placements per one million dollars for the three programs and actual appropriations dollars. In this case, there was an even inverse relationship between them (Ellig, McTigue, and Wray 2011, 178–91).

CHAPTER SUMMARY

- **Performance-Based Budgeting and Efficiency**

When governmental budgets are too complex and driven by political influence, budget decision makers cannot easily apply PBB to budget processes. PBB systems applied to small jurisdictions such as local government budgets sometimes improved efficiency. In contrast, PBB systems applied to even a single agency at the federal level were not successfully implemented.

- **Allocative Efficiency**

Allocative efficiency means that resources are allocated to the programs that return maximum benefits. However, there are various challenges to allocative efficiency.

(1) Measuring benefits from public programs is difficult, especially because of the lack of common denominators among them. Even when they can be measured, there are no adequate theories or frameworks on which to reallocate resources.

(2) When politicians, beneficiary groups, or political parties support certain programs, they tend to receive increased budgets even when their performance evaluation scores are low.

(3) Empirical studies indicate that even subagency programs are exposed to internal organizational politics.

- **Productive Efficiency**

Productive efficiency means the maximization of outputs per given inputs. It has been the main target of old PBB systems.

(1) Some states reported cost reduction from PBB implementation. However, states under fiscal stringency might have taken PBB more seriously.

(2) The Prospective Payment System (PPS) for Medicare payments reported some cost control during the 1980s. However, it was achieved at the expense of quality improvement. When some hospitals maintained high quality as well, it was attributable to generally stricter regulatory requirements and strong professional ethics.

(3) Even when some governmental agencies improved productive efficiency, the impact of PBB on allocative efficiency is unidentifiable.

- **Performance-Based Budgeting Challenges**

It is difficult to link performance evaluation scores to certain programs. This is particularly the case for new PBB systems focusing more on outcomes than on outputs because outcomes are one or two steps removed from outputs. One merit of PBB is to give more discretion to budget decision makers. However, without an adequate link between aggregated outcome measures at the higher organizational level (i.e., agency-level) and disaggregated subagency programs, PBB systems are inherently flawed.

When some programs report improved productive efficiency, it is more because they might have chosen more easily measurable outputs.

Regardless of benefits from PBB, costs incurred from implementing it are non-negligible.

Most critically, PBB evaluation scores were not effectively reflected in budget choices. PBB results were sometimes utilized in internal resource allocations within agencies. Overall, however, PBB results were not meaningfully incorporated into jurisdiction-wide funding decisions.

Cost-Benefit Analysis
Measurements and Time Values

11

Cost-benefit analysis (CBA) is an economic tool to measure costs and benefits for public programs. When public programs generate more benefits than costs, decision makers tend to support those programs. CBA is usually conducted over investment projects with useful lives of several years or longer. This chapter briefly discusses three key CBA issues: measuring costs and especially benefits, time values of costs and benefits, and challenges to CBA.

- Why Is Cost-Benefit Analysis Emphasized Again?
- What Does Efficiency Mean in Cost-Benefit Analysis?
- Measurement of Costs and Benefits
- Time Values of Costs and Benefits
- Challenges to Successful Implementation of Cost-Benefit Analysis

WHY IS COST-BENEFIT ANALYSIS EMPHASIZED AGAIN?

Economists have long been using cost-benefit analysis (CBA) in evaluating various public programs. As discussed later in this chapter, however, policy scholars and practitioners have criticized CBA techniques as much as their supporters have embraced them. In response to the critiques, economists assert that CBA has not been dominating the real world of program evaluation as much as their critiques have alleged. Therefore, they assert that we pay more attention to potential strengths from, rather than critiques of, CBA (Vining and Weimer 1992). As indicated in Chapter 9 in Part II on performance-based budgeting (PBB), rational approaches to resource allocation have been revived during the recent decades. Despite the general critiques over rational approaches including CBA, these approaches have been employed at various levels of government in the United States and abroad, thanks primarily to the call for more efficient service delivery. CBA conducted from a perspective of welfare economics is based on numerous principles and assumptions and analytical techniques. Readers who are interested in more details are referred to advanced CBA books (Bardach 2012; Boardman et al. 2006, 2011; Dunn 2012, 210–18; Gramlich 1990, 1–133; Stokey and Zeckhauser 1978, 134–58; Weimer and Vining 2005, 380–451, 2011, 383–423; Wheelan 2011, 405–43).

What Does Efficiency Mean in CBA?

Readers need to understand what efficiency in standard CBA denotes in the first place. This section illustrates how efficiency is defined and measured, when the efficiency is lost or reduced, and whether policy interventions can prevent or augment such efficiency loss. Readers who are not familiar with economics can selectively read this section to grasp the overall rationale suggested in standard economics-oriented CBA.

Definition of Efficiency or Social Surplus

In conducting CBA, measuring costs and benefits is heavily linked to the concept of efficiency. Public administration scholars and practitioners tend to define "efficiency" as the ratio of outputs to inputs as discussed in Chapters 9 and 10 in Part II. This ratio is known as productive efficiency. In contrast, economists generally define efficiency in terms of the changes in welfare or utility from public projects. Since CBA has mostly originated from economic analyses, measuring benefits and costs in terms of welfare changes is first illustrated through simple diagrams of demand and supply schedules. Figure 11.1 shows the concept of efficiency in typical economics-oriented CBA conducted by economists. Suppose D denotes a demand curve, or marginal benefit schedule, for a certain private economic commodity and MPC denotes a marginal producer cost that is a supply schedule of the producer of the commodity. The market equilibrium is held at point h where the quantity of the commodity is Q and its price is b: where the demand curve, D, intersects with the marginal producer cost, MPC. In that case, demanders for this commodity enjoy consumer surplus equal to the area bhi because they pay only the area $bhQO$, while their total benefit equals the area $ihQO$. Likewise, the producer of the commodity enjoys a producer surplus equal to the area bhj because the total production cost equals the area $jhQO$ but the total profit equals the area $bhQO$. The sum of consumer and producer surplus is called social surplus (Weimer and Vining 2011, 92–94). When the social surplus is maximized, efficiency is also maximized. This condition also applies to public goods (Hyman 2011, 160–63).

Efficiency Loss: The Case of Negative Externality

What if the producer causes air pollution due to its manufacturing activities? (Readers may skip to the last sentence of this paragraph for the answer to this question.) This means that the producer incurs a certain amount of cost due to air pollution affecting nearby residents. This is an example of negative externality. To have an accurate depiction of efficient market equilibrium from the perspective of the entire society, the cost imposed on the residents, in addition to the production cost incurred by the producer, should be accounted for. Marginal social cost (MSC) combines MPC and

Figure 11.1 **Negative Externality and Overproduction**

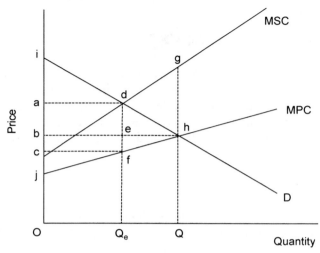

the extra costs caused by air pollution and imposed on the residents. Now, an adequate level of production should be Q_e, rather than Q. Therefore, the society is producing more than the efficient level of quantity Q_e. If the society produced an efficient level of the commodity by accounting for the negative externality (i.e., producing an adequate level of the commodity at Q_e), then consumers might have enjoyed a consumer surplus equal to the area *adi*. At the quantity of Q, however, their consumer surplus increases by the area *adhb*. The producer might have enjoyed a producer surplus equal to the area *adfj* at the efficient quantity of Q_e because the producer does not pay for the external costs. At the overproduced quantity level, its producer surplus is the area *bhj*. In sum, its final producer surplus decreases by the area *adeb* but increases by the area *ehf*. The external costs for the nearby residents increase by the area *dghf*. If all these costs and benefits (e.g., consumer and producer surpluses, and external costs) are combined, the final social surplus will decrease by the area *dgh* (Gramlich 1990, 18–20; Weimer and Vining 2011, 92–94).

REMEDYING EFFICIENCY LOSS: GOVERNMENTAL INTERVENTION TO PREVENT NEGATIVE EXTERNALITY

Further assume that the government decided to prevent overproduction and negative externality by imposing a tax on the producer, with the tax level equal to the distance *df*. The government will receive tax revenues equal to the area *adfc*. After adjusting all costs and benefits, the final change in social surplus will be the area *dgh* which was exactly the loss in social surplus due to the negative externality when there is no governmental intervention. (See Boardman et al. 2011, 91–92, to see how the efficiency loss turns into an efficiency gain.) This logic is also applied as a rationale for intergovernmental grant systems to address interjurisdictional externalities as explained in Figure 21.1 in Chapter 21 in Part V (e.g., spatial externalities). Thus, according to a standard CBA analysis, the governmental taxation program to address the negative externality turns the loss in social surplus (i.e., sum of consumer and producer surpluses) into a social surplus gain.

GOVERNMENTAL INTERVENTION CAUSES EFFICIENCY LOSS WITH NO NEGATIVE EXTERNALITY

If the tax was imposed on the producer when there was no negative externality (i.e., efficient market), what happens? In that case, there will be a loss of social surplus equal to the area *dhf*. The loss is called deadweight loss or excess burden. (See Hyman 2011, 450–54, for more details.) For the above case of taxation that addresses the negative externality, public administrators or budget officers are more likely to compute the area *adfc* as "government tax revenues," rather than recording the area *dgh* as the gain in social surplus. Likewise, for the second case of taxation over the market with no negative externality, budget officers are likely to record the governmental tax revenues without accounting for the excess burden (the area *dhf*).

This disparity is a significant difference between economists and public administrators or budget officers regarding cost-benefit analysis. Similarly, if a job training program increased the working hours of program participants, economics-based CBA tends to report a different (probably smaller) impact than CBA conducted by public administrators (Boardman et al. 2011, 297–301). Readers should be aware that there are two versions of CBA in the field of budget and finance: one preferred by economists and the other pursued by public administrators. This disparity also exemplifies one of the key challenges facing the rational approaches to resource allocation discussed in previous chapters in Part II: How can we accurately measure costs and especially benefits for public programs that do not have price tags? At the same time, as clarified above, rational approaches have gradually been applied to evaluation of public programs despite the challenges. For instance, the U.S. Office of Management and Budget (OMB) Circular A-94 provides guidelines and discount rates for cost-benefit analysis of federal programs. The circular specifies that twenty-five cents per dollar of revenues should be recorded as excess burden from taxation.

MEASUREMENT OF COSTS AND BENEFITS

It is often very difficult to accurately measure the social value of public goods. Sometimes their observed prices do not even exist. Therefore, researchers rely on an approach called shadow pricing to measure benefits and costs of public goods; they attempt to measure them in the shadows (Boardman et al. 2011, 80). There are roughly three ways of shadow pricing to measure costs and benefits. Readers also need to be cautious of challenges to measurement of costs and benefits.

MEASUREMENT OF COSTS AND BENEFITS FROM OBSERVED BEHAVIOR

First, analysts have attempted to measure costs and benefits from observed behaviors. For instance, many public programs such as health, education, job training, employment, and welfare programs implement demonstration or pilot projects on a small-scale basis. Demonstration projects might provide analysts with relevant costs and benefit data (Boardman et al. 2006, 279–313, 2011, 288–319). Alternatively, analysts can directly collect relevant data from actual public programs. For instance, analysts can obtain the quantity of waste disposal service and the price for units of the services, along with other factors that affect the demand for the services. Then, they can run regression models and derive demand curves for the service. Economics-based CBA will trace the changes in social surplus as explained in Figure 11.1 (Boardman et al. 2011, 320–40).

Measurement of Costs and Benefits From Indirect Market Behavior

If analysts cannot obtain relevant data directly from demonstration or actual programs, they collect data from indirect market behaviors (Weimer and Vining 2011, 396–99). Since there are no price tags for human life, analysts use average earnings of individuals for their entire lifetime to impute such value. They use the sum of present values of future earning streams as a proxy measure for human life. Although there are various other techniques to measure the value of human life, this method is used in some U.S. courts (Boardman et al. 2011, 344–49). Another technique, called hedonic pricing, applies regression analyses to gauge the price of public goods, which is virtually unobtainable directly from the market. For instance, what is the price for a better scenic view from a house? Analysts can collect data sets on various factors affecting a housing price, including the indicator for houses with a better view. When they conduct regression analyses with the housing price as a dependent variable and all other factors as independent variables, the coefficient value of the indicator for the houses with a better view in regression models might be an indirect measure of the price for a better scenic view (Boardman et al. 2011, 353–57). Similarly, how can analysts measure the price for recreational sites? The zonal travel-cost method traces the relationship between average total cost per person to travel from people's homes to the recreational sites and the average number of visits per person. Based on the data collected, analysts can develop demand schedules for the recreational sites (Boardman et al. 2011, 358–65). Analysts can then measure the changes in social surplus based on the demand schedules derived "indirectly" from the market.

Contingent Valuation and Shadow Pricing From Secondary Empirical Findings

When none of the above methods are available, analysts typically rely on contingent valuation. Contingent valuation surveys demanders, through typical surveys or more advanced surveys such as dichotomous choice technique, for public services about their willingness-to-pay (WTP) for the services on a hypothetical ground because they are not actually paying for them (Boardman et al. 2011, 372–405). Recent studies measured benefits and costs of public goods based on contingent valuation. Donahue, Robbins, and Simonsen (2008), based on contingent valuation, determined citizens' WTP for new terrorism-related technologies and services. Robbins, Simonsen, and

Feldman (2008) conducted a Web-based survey by teaming up with the town of West Hartford, Connecticut. They found there is little or no relationship between the taxes paid by local residents and their use of a particular service, that is, there is no match between residents' WTP (i.e., residents' willingness-to-pay for the service) and their actual tax payment. Similarly, Chen and Thurmaier (2008) conducted contingent valuation surveys with more than 400 firms to measure WTP for e-transactions with state governments.

Analysts can also impute WTP for costs incurred from public services using results from published empirical studies when even surveys are not feasible. As indicated above, OMB Circular A-94 specified twenty-five cents per dollar as excess burden from governmental taxation, which was based on empirical findings (Boardman et al. 2011, 406–42). Greenberg and Cebulla (2008) conducted a meta-analysis of numerous empirical reports on the effectiveness of welfare-related job-training programs. Based on the shadow-pricing technique, they found that most of the programs were not effective and some specific programs performed better than others.

RISK OF DOUBLE COUNTING

As shown so far, measuring costs and benefits of public programs might be one of the biggest challenges to CBA. There is another challenge that makes the application of CBA more difficult: the risk of double counting (i.e., counting the same cost or benefit twice). A real-life example illustrates the challenge. In 1981, under strong pressure from the U.S. government, the Japanese government agreed to voluntarily limit the number of automobiles sold in the United States. This was called a voluntary export restraint agreement (VERA). Boardman et al. (2006, 118–20) succinctly summarized CBA analyses conducted by Tarr and Morkre (1984) and Gomez-Ibanez, Leone, and O'Connell (1983). They analyzed how a ceiling on the number of Japanese cars exported to the United States (e.g., a quota limit on Japanese imported autos) affects social surpluses (i.e., sum of consumer and producer surpluses) in both the Japanese and U.S. auto markets. The quota limit on Japanese imported autos would increase the demand for U.S.-manufactured autos. One notable finding was that the changes in social surplus in the secondary market (U.S. auto market) were already reflected in the long-run social surplus change in the primary market (Japanese auto market). Therefore, if analysts added up the changes in social surplus in the secondary market, there was a risk of double counting.

Chapters 23 and 24 in Part VI introduce the Keynesian multiplier effect. For instance, the construction of a new manufacturing plant in a local jurisdiction will increase the personal income of the workers living in the jurisdiction. If they go to local restaurants more often with their increased income, the local restaurant business will reap additional profits. Adding the profits, however, is likely to cause double counting as well. The increased profits have already been reflected in the increase in personal income. The increase in personal income is called the direct effect, and the increased profits of the local restaurant business are called the indirect effect from the manufacturing plant construction. In general, excluding indirect effect is a safer way to avoid the risk of double counting unless analysts are fully assured that indirect effect is completely separate from the direct effect (Boardman et al. 2011, 115–32, 297–303).

TIME VALUES OF COSTS AND BENEFITS

The second crucial issue in CBA is the time values of costs and benefits (Gramlich 1990, 92–114; Weimer and Vining 2011, 399–406). This is not as complicated as identifying and measuring costs and benefits, but there are some issues regarding what would be the most desirable discount rate to compute present values of future streams of costs and benefits. A discount rate for public projects is usually called a social discount rate.

Table 11.1 illustrates how net benefits vary depending on different discount rates (i). Assume that the upfront cost for this capital project is $1 million. The project incurs annual maintenance costs as shown under the column Cost. The costs increase for later years of the project life. Similarly, benefits from the project increase for the later years. In this case, however, the project will return much larger benefits for the later years, as shown under the column Benefit. The third column shows the net benefit stream for the entire project year. Since dollars in future years are probably less valuable than the same dollars in current years, future dollar values need to be discounted into current-year dollar values. The column Net Present Benefit (i = 10 percent) converted future net benefit streams to current-year (i.e., year 0) values at the discount rate of 10 percent. The final column converted future net benefit streams to current-year values at the discount rate of 2 percent. If 10 percent is used as the discount rate, the project is not worthwhile because it results in a loss of $97,409. If 2 percent is adopted as the discount rate, then the project will return a net present benefit of $261,270. So the question is, which result is a more accurate estimation of net benefits from the project? The answer is: We do not know. Economists have made numerous suggestions on how to select an adequate discount rate. There are three possible approaches (Boardman et al. 2011, 238–73).

MARGINAL RATE OF TIME PREFERENCE

The first approach is an individual's marginal rate of time preference (MRTP). Individual persons are likely to prefer dollars in their pockets right now rather than the same amount in dollars to be obtained after many years. Therefore, MRTP approximates the time preference placed over current dollars. In particular, time preference is typically associated with the choice between individuals' current consumption vs. future consumption (i.e., current savings). The flip side of this logic implies that if people want to borrow money from others, they need to compensate for what lenders currently forgo for future consumptions. Considering that individuals generally prefer current consumption to savings for future consumption, borrowers need to pay interest to borrow from the savings at MRTP. In real-life situations, an after-tax return on savings is an ideal proxy for MRTP. Economists further contend that it is more appropriate to discount costs and benefits at a risk-free rate. Thus, the return on holding government bonds, which hovers around 1.5 percent, is practically used as a proxy for MRTP (Boardman et al. 2011, 252–53).

Table 11.1

Discount Rate and Net Benefit (in dollars)

Year	Benefit	Cost	Net benefit	Net present benefit (i = 10%)	Net present benefit (i = 2%)
0		1,000,000	−1,000,000	−1,000,000	−1,000,000
1	100,000	10,000	90,000	81,818	88,235
2	100,000	10,000	90,000	74,380	86,505
3	100,000	20,000	80,000	60,105	75,386
4	300,000	20,000	280,000	191,244	258,677
5	400,000	30,000	370,000	229,741	335,120
6	500,000	30,000	470,000	265,303	417,347
Total				**−97,409**	**261,270**

MARGINAL RATE OF RETURN ON PRIVATE INVESTMENT

The second approach to discount rates is the marginal rate of return on private investment (MRRPI). While individuals might consume private resources, producers can use the same resources to produce economic commodities. If the producers borrow the private resources to expand their investment for their production, they need to reap sufficient profits to make up for the borrowing costs. In that case, the return on producers' private investment will be a good measure for borrowing private resources. In terms of CBA, this aspect gives some clues to what discount rate is adequate for governmental programs. When governments launch public projects, they tend to use private resources that might have been used for private projects. If the public projects use up the private resources that might otherwise have been used for the private projects, governments should be able to legitimate that the return on the public investment exceeds or at least is equal to that on private investments. This implies that the return on private producers' investment or MRRPI will be a good proxy measure for governments' borrowing costs. The real, before-tax rate of return on corporate bonds is a good proxy for MRRPI. The before-tax rate is used because firms can deduct from taxation interest payments made out to holders of corporate bonds. In addition, returns on corporate equities such as stocks have been very volatile, and thus more stable rates of returns on corporate bonds are preferred. The rates have been around 4.5 percent (Boardman et al. 2011, 244–47, 249–52).

WEIGHTED AVERAGE APPROACH

The third approach is the weighted average between MRTP and MRRPI. Debt-financed public projects are likely to displace private investment as the increased demand for loanable funds drives up interest rates and thus crowds out private investment. In this case, using MRRPI would be more relevant as a social discount rate. Tax-financed public projects are more likely to reduce individual consumers' disposable incomes. Considering that individuals tend to spend, rather than save, most disposable income, MRTP would be a better measure for a social discount rate for tax-financed projects, because taxes are levied on disposable income. If analysts can trace the sources and proportional shares of funds for public projects, the weighted average of MRTP and MRRPI would be a better choice for a social discount rate. Some economists suggest using a long-term "actual" government borrowing rate in addition to MRTP and MRRPI. In that case, the weighting would include the third, government borrowing rate as well (Boardman et al. 2011, 254–55).

DISCOUNT RATES IN THE REAL WORLD

Discount rates in real-life cases sometimes differ from the rates suggested by analysts. The OMB had been using 10 percent for a social discount rate but has recently preferred 7 percent. In contrast, the Government Accountability Office (GAO) and the Congressional Budget Office (CBO) have been using a lower rate around 2 percent (Boardman et al. 2006, 263–65). As shown in Table 11.1, if 10 percent is used, then the net present value in Year 6 is $265,303 (= $470,000/(1 + .10)^6$. If 2 percent is used, it will be $417,347. As discussed in Part I on executive budgeting systems, central budget offices in the executive branch, such as the OMB, generally exert tight control over agency budget proposals. This tendency is described as a guardian's perspective (Boardman et al. 2011, 16–18). Guardians tend to discount future benefits more heavily, as shown when 10 percent is used as the social discount rate. In contrast, spenders are more likely to support public investment projects that produce larger benefits, typically in later years like the example shown in Table 11.1. Spenders tend to support 2 percent as the social discount rate and are more likely to support investment projects with positive net present benefits (Boardman et al. 2011, 18–20).

CHALLENGES TO SUCCESSFUL IMPLEMENTATION OF CBA

Discussions of measurement and time values naturally lead to the fundamental critique of CBA: It might be based on arbitrary assumptions. In addition, analysts should be familiar with complicated methodologies. As Wildavsky (1969) indicated earlier, most agencies have only a few qualified personnel to conduct policy analysis. Greenberg and Cebulla (2008), as noted above, provided a highly executable measurement approach to costs and benefits. Even when the measurement is possible, however, Kelman (1981; see also Rhoads 1999, 131) asserts that measuring the value of what should not be put to a value scale, such as human dignity and life, will start devaluing such significant values.

The second challenge to CBA is its negligence of equity or fairness (Suranovic 1997). Maximization of welfare raises a question of whose welfare is maximized. Recently, economists have developed distributionally weighted CBA. For instance, analysts can assign the value of 1 for the benefits of wealthy individuals but assign the value of 2 or higher to relatively poor individuals (Boardman et al. 2011, 495–503). However, developing the weights will obviously add to the already heavy computational burden for public administrators. Finally, rationality has almost always been dominated by political, institutional, and legal procedures and limitations in human capacity (see Williams [1972] for an earlier discussion of this issue). Chapters in Parts II and III illustrate numerous cases evidencing these challenges.

CHAPTER SUMMARY

- **Why Is Cost-Benefit Analysis Emphasized Again?**

Cost-benefit analysis (CBA) has recently been revived at various levels of government in the United States and abroad.

- **Efficiency in Economics-Oriented Cost-Benefit Analysis**

Efficiency in economics-oriented CBA tends to mean welfare or utility changes.

(1) The efficiency concept is typically measured in terms of consumer and producer surpluses (e.g., social surplus).

(2) Negative externalities generally reduce the amount of social surplus. CBA accounts for negative externalities in order to accurately measure the change in efficiency for any economic activities or governmental policies.

(3) Tax is often imposed to remedy negative externalities and thereby increase or retrieve social surplus. If a tax is imposed when there are no negative externalities, the tax incurs deadweight loss or excess burden.

(4) CBA conducted by economists tends to differ from that public administrators pursue. Public administrators are likely to measure *budgetary* costs or benefits.

- **Shadow Pricing**

Due to the difficulty in measuring the social value of public goods, researchers measure their benefits and costs in the shadow.

(1) Analysts can sometimes obtain relevant data from actual or demonstration public programs. When analysts cannot obtain data directly from demonstration or public programs, they can impute values for them through various statistical techniques.

(2) When the above methods are not available, analysts can rely on contingent valuations such as typical surveys or dichotomous choice technique surveys. When analysts cannot even utilize surveys, they conduct meta-analyses of numerous empirical studies.

- **Double Counting Costs and Benefits**

There is often a risk of double counting costs and benefits with public programs. In general, analysts need to avoid double counting.

- **Selecting a Discount Rate**

Most public programs generate benefits and incur costs for their entire useful lives. In that case, analysts should select an adequate discount rate to convert them to present (or current year) values. There are three possible approaches to selecting a discount rate.

(1) Individuals tend to prefer current consumption to future consumption. They have to pay interest on their borrowing as compensation for what lenders forgo with their preferred current consumption (e.g., MRTP).

(2) Private producers of economic commodities borrow funds for their investment expansion. They need to earn at least as much as they pay in borrowing costs (e.g., MRRPI).

(3) When analysts have data on the sources of funds for public projects, a weighted average of MRTP and MRRPI will be a good proxy measure for a social discount rate.

Central budget offices in executive branches tend to use higher discount rates and are likely to underestimate future benefits. Supporters of public projects are likely to use lower rates to overestimate them.

• Computational Burden

One challenge of CBA is that it adds to the computational burden of analysts.

12 Activity-Based Costing

In the field of financial management for public and private organizations, cost accounting is very important in accurately gauging the amount of resources used for delivering services, producing products, and serving clients. Miscalculation of costs for final products, services, and clients will result in misjudgment of overall financial management. An activity-based costing (ABC) system has been widely employed as an advanced tool to measure more accurate costs for products, services, and clients, primarily in the private sector and secondarily by public sector organizations. With the advent of performance-based budgeting (PBB) systems, ABC systems were repeatedly emphasized for the successful implementation of PBB systems. This chapter discusses the following issues:

- Direct and Indirect Costs
- Five-Stage Costing Systems
- Traditional Stage II Costing Systems
- Why Are the Traditional Stage II Costing Systems Distorted?
- Steps of Activity-Based Costing Systems
- Illustrative Examples of Activity-Based Costing Systems
- Challenges to Activity-Based Costing Systems

DIRECT AND INDIRECT COSTS

To understand what ABC systems are and why they are needed, we first need to understand two concepts related to cost controlling. A simple illustrative case will expedite that understanding and the two cost concepts. Assume that a local government has just one department, a fire department. The fire department has only two functions or subdivisions: firefighting and fire safety inspection. Direct labor hours for the employees in the two subdivisions and direct materials used by them are called "direct" costs for the two subdivisions. In contrast, some other resources used to support the operation of the subdivisions are called "indirect" costs on their part. If we want to know the accurate cost of fire safety inspection, then fire safety inspection is defined as "cost objects." Any final services, products, or clients can also be defined as cost objects as appropriate. Finding financial data on direct costs for all functions, including fire safety inspection, is called "cost tracing." Finding financial data on indirect costs incurred from fire safety inspection and allocating the indirect costs to fire safety inspection is called "cost allocation" (Horngren, Datar, and Rajan 2012, 99–100).

FIVE-STAGE COSTING SYSTEMS

Five-stage costing systems are used for cost tracing and allocation. Stage I costing systems are not adequate as financial reporting systems and are frequently found in starting businesses. Stage II systems are driven toward financial reporting and are used as standard costing mechanisms. They minimally satisfy financial reporting requirements and collect cost data by cost objects or responsibility centers. However, they are still limited in that they report highly distorted product costs and do not have customer-focused cost data. In addition, they provide feedback to managers, but it is done too late and is too aggregate. Stage III systems are more customized and managerially relevant. ABC systems are typical of Stage III systems. Stage IV systems pursue integrated cost management and financial reporting. They move activity-based management systems and operational and strategic performance measurement systems toward integrated financial reporting systems (Kaplan and Cooper 1997, 11–27). Cokins (2006, 83) adds the fifth-stage cost management system. Stage V goes beyond simply applying accurate cost information to cost allocation. In this stage, managerial accounting shifts to managerial economics. Since most resources cannot be quickly readjusted in the short-term, the focus moves from cost control to cost planning. Financial managers are more concerned about what level and type of resources are needed for future demands and plans. Therefore, forecasting and predictive analyses become much more important in Stage V.

TRADITIONAL STAGE II COSTING SYSTEMS

Brown, Myring, and Gard (1999) provide a succinct and clear financial data set for the above-mentioned fire department, as shown in Table 12.1. This table illustrates how overhead or indirect costs incurred by the operation of the entire department are allocated to fire safety inspection. Overhead or indirect costs identified by the entire fire department include those incurred by administration and maintenance as well as depreciation of fire trucks, equipment, and the station itself. The departmental record also shows that direct labor costs for employees in the two subdivisions are $30 per hour and there are 1,500 total direct labor hours for the fiscal year. In addition, the total overhead costs are estimated at $300,000 for the period.

What is the total cost incurred by a two-hour fire inspection at a local business in this case? First, direct labor costs for labor hours of employees in the fire inspection subdivision are $30 per hour. Thus, the direct costs for two-hour fire inspection are $60 as shown in Table 12.1 (see Traditional column in Table 12.1). Under traditional

Table 12.1

Cost of Fire Inspection: A Traditional vs. an ABC Cost-Accounting System

	Traditional	ABC
Direct labor (fire inspection service)	$60 (= 2 hours × $30 / hour)	$60 (= 2 hours × $30 / hour)
Overhead/indirect cost allocated based on direct labor hours (the entire fire department)	$400 $\left(=\dfrac{\$300{,}000\ overhead\ cost}{1{,}500\ hours} \times 2\ hours\ of\ labor\right)$	
Administrative overhead cost		$200 $\left(=\dfrac{\$10{,}000}{50\ inspections}\right)$
Inspection overhead cost		$100 $\left(=\dfrac{\$5{,}000}{100\ hours} \times 2\ hours\ per\ inspection\right)$
Total cost	$460	$360

Source: Adapted from Brown, Myring, and Gard (1999, Tables 1 and 2).

Stage II costing systems, overhead or indirect costs incurred from the operation of the entire fire department are likely to be allocated to the cost object (fire inspection, in this case) on the basis of labor hours of the entire department. This is because the traditional Stage II costing systems do not maintain adequate financial data that link the indirect costs to fire inspection on a cause-effect basis. The overhead or indirect costs per direct labor hour are $200 (= $300,000 / 1,500). Therefore, the indirect costs to be *allocated* to the two-hour inspection are $400. Finally, the total costs incurred from two hours of inspection are $460.

WHY ARE THE TRADITIONAL STAGE II COSTING SYSTEMS DISTORTED?

The problem with this Stage II traditional cost-accounting system is that the total labor hours for the fire safety inspection subdivision include some functions such as maintenance on fire trucks and other equipment that are not directly linked to fire inspection. Under the traditional Stage II cost systems, therefore, organizational overhead costs are allocated to cost objects based on arbitrary bases such as direct labor hours or head counts of employees (Kaplan and Cooper 1997, 83–85). As clarified later in this chapter, this traditional cost allocation leads to distorted cost measurement for cost objects.

The potential risk of distorted cost measurement has been heightened recently. Indirect or overhead costs have become a greater portion of the total cost of business operations. Overhead costs were traditionally around 5–15 percent of total production costs. By 1985, overhead costs had risen to around 35 percent of the total, and in 1991, overhead ranged around 55 percent of total production costs. In addition, as business processes of private business corporations have been relying substantially more on technology and less on labor, cost allocation based on labor hours has resulted in misallocation of indirect costs to cost objects.

Organizations have also been faced with increased global and domestic competition, privatization, and the need for increased effectiveness. As a result, they have been driven to take a closer look at ways to more accurately allocate indirect costs. The traditional costing system failed to adequately allocate the overhead costs to final products or services because a single allocation base did not accurately reflect the cause-effect relationship between indirect costs and final products and services. In addition, as businesses produce more diverse products, cost allocation based on a single allocation basis leads to distorted cost measurement. Public sector organizations have experienced similar situations (Brown, Myring, and Gard 1999; Horngren, Datar, and Rajan 2012, 149). No doubt, misjudgment of total costs will lead to misjudgment in managerial decisions.

STEPS OF ACTIVITY-BASED COSTING SYSTEMS

Four typical steps in ABC systems make up one of the main Stage III costing approaches.

STEP 1

The first step is for the ABC project team to develop an activity dictionary that lists all relevant activities that drive up the costs for a cost object, the fire safety inspection subdivision in the above case. Since ABC systems were first developed in the mid- to late 1980s, numerous formats have been created, such as the one developed by the International Benchmarking Clearinghouse. Some organizations rely on a bottom-up approach so that front-line employees take the lead in defining the activity dictionary. However, doing so incurs higher costs of implementing ABC (Horngren, Datar, and Rajan 2012, 147; Kaplan and Cooper 1997, 85–86).

STEP 2

The second stage is to determine costs/expenses for each item in the activity dictionary. Under traditional Stage II costing systems, the financial manager will collect the organization's financial expense data by spending codes such as salaries and fringe costs, occupancy costs, equipment and technology costs, indirect material costs, and maintenance costs. These indirect costs will then be allocated to production cost centers or objects (e.g., the fire safety inspection subdivision in the above case) based on somewhat arbitrary bases under the Stage II costing systems (e.g., labor hours in the above case).

In contrast, ABC systems collect more detailed data on items in the activity dictionary. Activities may include processing customer orders, purchasing materials, designing products and processes, scheduling production orders, setting up machines, inspecting items, maintaining product information, and administering overall business processes (Horngren, Datar, and Rajan 2012, 147; Kaplan and Cooper 1997, 87). The project team can conduct surveys with individual employees other than front-line employees who are working in the production line or cost object center to estimate the percentage of time they spend in any of the support activities. For nonpersonnel resources, the ABC project team can directly measure the resources or estimate the percentage they are used for each activity. Finally, the indirect costs will be allocated to each of the activities based on the collected data set (Kaplan and Cooper 1997, 86–89).

There is a hierarchical structure in a typical ABC activity schedule. Unit-level activities are those performed for every unit of product or service produced and, as such, are directly proportional to production and service volumes. An example is machine operation costs (e.g., energy cost, machine depreciation and repair). Traditional cost systems, based on labor hours, machine hours, units produced, or sales dollars, rely on unit-level cost drivers to allocate indirect costs to cost objects as shown in Table 12.1. One of the main differences between traditional Stage II costing systems and the Stage III ABC systems is the use of nonunit cost drivers such as batch, product-sustaining, and customer-sustaining activities. Batch-level activities are performed for each batch or group of work performed, such as setting up a machine for operation in a cost object center, purchasing materials, or processing a customer order for typical business corporations. ABC systems can assign the costs incurred from batch-level activities to the products, customers, and services that triggered the activities.

Product-sustaining activities enable production of individual products (or services) to occur. Customer-sustaining activities enable a company to sell its products to individual customers. These two activities include designing/updating product specifications, special testing for individual products and services, and technical support for individual customers. Sometimes, customer-sustaining expenses cannot be adequately linked to final products or services if the expenses are incurred by providing different levels of customer support. Increased volume of products does not necessarily mean increased levels of "specialized" customer support, for example.

Some other categories cannot be directly traced to individual products and customers. They are brand or product-line sustaining activities (e.g., product development and advertising), order-related activities specific to a particular order, facility-sustaining activities (e.g., plant manager and administrative staff), and channel-sustaining activities (e.g., trade shows, advertising, catalogs) (Horngren, Datar, and Rajan 2012, 149; Kaplan and Cooper 1997, 89–91).

STEP 3

The third step is to identify specific products, services, and customers of organizations as cost objects. As noted above, any of the three items in organizations can be defined as a cost object.

STEP 4

The final and fourth step is to link activity costs to organizations' products, services, and customers (e.g., cost objects). The ABC project team can develop a quantitative measure of activities, called the activity cost driver, and then allocate the costs incurred from activity cost drivers to cost objects. The ABC project team may bundle all activities triggered by the same event into the same activity cost driver. There are roughly three different types of activity cost drivers.

Transaction drivers only count how often certain activities are performed. Examples include numbers of setups, receipts, and products supported. When outputs require the same demands of certain activities (e.g., scheduling a production run or processing a purchase order) and thus the same quantity of resources, the transaction driver is useful. Its limitation is, however, that if the quantity of resources varies across activities, more accurate cost drivers are needed.

Duration drivers reflect the amount of time needed to perform certain activities. Simple products may need 10–15 minutes for setup, while complex, high-precision products may require several hours. Costs incurred from duration drivers can be measured on the basis of setup hours, inspection hours, and direct labor hours. For materials movement, distance moved can be used as a duration driver.

Intensity drivers charge separately for the resources used for each activity. A particularly complex product may need special setup and quality control workers. In these cases, activity costs might be higher. The ABC project team can also use complexity indexes by weighting the various drivers (Horngren, Datar, and Rajan 2012, 150–54; Kaplan and Cooper 1997, 94–99).

ILLUSTRATIVE EXAMPLES OF ACTIVITY-BASED COSTING SYSTEMS

Although the ABC systems are somewhat complicated, we can apply them to the above simpler case of fire safety inspection in Table 12.1. In contrast to the traditional Stage II costing systems, an ABC system identifies more detailed support activities that are strongly related to fire safety inspection on a solid cause-effect basis.

Assume that through a closer investigation, an ABC system identifies three types of overhead or indirect costs incurred by firefighting, inspection system administration, and inspection. Obviously, the latter two categories (i.e., costs incurred by the two activity cost drivers for cost objects) are more directly linked to fire inspection. The inspection system administration costs include such items as administrator's salary and office costs (e.g., facility-sustaining expenses). Inspection overhead costs consist of maintenance and depreciation on an office and on inspection equipment (e.g., unit-level expenses). Since there was a "one-time" two hour inspection, the administrative indirect cost to be allocated to the cost object, the fire safety inspection subdivision, will be $200 (= total administrative indirect costs of $10,000/50 annual inspections). The total inspection overhead costs of $5,000 are allocated based on inspection hours. The department expects to spend 100 hours for fire inspection for the period. Since there were two hours of fire safety inspection, the inspection indirect cost to be allocated to the fire safety inspection subdivision will be $100. The fourth column in Table 12.1 shows that the final cost for fire inspection is $360, a more accurate total for two hours of fire inspection.

From a management perspective, an ABC-based cost estimation is more relevant. For instance, if a nearby local fire department offered to deliver the same service for $400, the above fire department might be tempted to accept the offer if it relies on the traditional cost-accounting system. However, if it uses an ABC system, it is clear that it should not accept the offer because its own total cost for two hours of fire inspection is just $360. An ABC system in this case is very useful in making the so-called make-or-buy decision (Brown, Myring, and Gard 1999).

Chapters 9 and 10 introduced numerous cases of performance-based budgeting (PBB) in the federal government. In 2003, the OMB mandated agencies to integrate GPRA-mandated annual agency performance plans into congressional budget justifications (i.e., agency budget requests) beginning with FY 2005. The main purpose of the change was to link costs with performance information on goals and outcomes. Some performance goals cut across multiple programs that were also funded by various appropriations accounts. The OMB attempted to restructure agency appropriations accounts so that agencies would have greater discretion to reallocate resources across different appropriations accounts. George Bush's President's Management Agenda also attempted to integrate budget and performance as one of its five management priorities (Ellig, McTigue, and Wray 2011, 204–5).

As a part of the PBB initiatives, some federal agencies implemented ABC systems for their budget and performance integration. In the case of NASA, various items of indirect costs had not been allocated to specific projects or programs (i.e., cost objects). General and administrative (G&A) costs were not allocated to relevant projects (or programs). G&A costs were about 5.4 percent of NASA budgets. Costs of individual centers such as the Kennedy Space Center, which amounted to about 9.1 percent of the total, were not allocated to specific projects either. NASA had attempted to allocate these indirect costs to each project or program on a more solid cause–effect link in ABC systems. As a result, NASA managers were able to more tightly monitor costs incurred for each project. Unfortunately, the successful efforts of NASA had not continued after 2005. Another agency that implemented ABC was the Small Business Administration (SBA), which implemented ABC systems as early as 1999. In 2002, the SBA found that 81 percent of its operating costs were labor (personnel) costs. It conducted an agency-wide survey to allocate SBA-wide labor costs to each SBA program by tracking SBA employees' time spent on specific program activities (Ellig, McTigue, and Wray 2011, 205–9). Cokins (2006, 275–308) introduces multiple success stories with federal agencies that implemented ABC systems.

CHALLENGES TO ACTIVITY-BASED COSTING SYSTEMS

Despite the accuracy of ABC systems, there are limitations when implementing them. Resistance to change (i.e., using a new costing system) is the biggest challenge. When organizational members are forced to change, they are likely to maintain a defensive posture. The cost of change incurred from higher compensation and time needed for its implementation is sometimes very high. Organizational members are also concerned that implementation of ABC systems will cause a sudden shift in the organizational balance of power (Brown, Myring, and Gard 1999). There is a trade-off between the accuracy of costing systems and implementation costs. Cost of errors declines as the accuracy of costing systems increases. In contrast, cost of measurement (or implementation) increases as the accuracy increases. Therefore, Stage III ABC systems might be obtained where the total costs are lowest at the point the two cost curves intersect (Kaplan and Cooper 1997, 102–4). However, finding a middle ground to accommodate all these issues is still a significant challenge for successful implementation of ABC systems (Finkler 2010, 150–55; Finkler et al. 2013, 143–48).

In particular, Mullins and Zorn (1999) suggest a different view on the so-called make-or-buy decisions based on ABC systems. Standard ABC systems tend to allocate unavoidable costs, such as fixed costs, to cost objects. As long as an organization continues its operation, fixed costs are unavoidable, and they need to be excluded from allocation cost pools. In terms of make-or-buy decisions, marginal costs of service production are more relevant than average costs, which include fixed costs that are unavoidable (i.e., sunk), while marginal costs compute resources needed for additional units of services or products. Therefore, ABC systems that rely heavily on average production costs are not highly relevant for managerial decision-making. In addition, ABC systems, when applied to make-or-buy decisions, are likely to ignore other costs. Transaction costs are incurred by searching for reliable suppliers and enforcing contracts. Coordination costs are incurred from monitoring contract performance and coordinating activities between in-house and outside suppliers. Additional costs are incurred by maintaining competition among potential suppliers. Mullins and Zorn (1999) also indicate that ABC systems cannot easily overcome most challenges for performance-based budgeting discussed in Chapter 10 in Part II.

CHAPTER SUMMARY

- **Direct and Indirect Costs**

Finding out direct costs for cost objects is called cost tracing. Finding out indirect costs for cost objects is called cost allocation.

- **Five-Stage Costing Systems**

There are five-stage costing systems for cost tracing and allocation.

(1) Stage I costing systems generally do not provide meaningful financial data.

(2) Stage II costing systems have been most frequently used for cost allocation. However, they are limited, especially because indirect costs are not allocated to cost objects on a solid cause-effect basis. Instead, they have been based on a somewhat arbitrary allocation basis such as labor hours. Overhead costs for private and public organizations have been rapidly increasing, and substantial portions of support functions rely on technology and less on labor. Therefore, the Stage II costing systems cannot accurately allocate indirect costs to cost objects.

(3) ABC systems are a typical example of Stage III costing systems.

(4) Stage IV costing systems integrate cost management and financial reporting.

(5) Stage V costing systems shift from cost control to cost planning. Forecasting future demands becomes more important in this stage and managerial economics replaces managerial accounting.

- **Steps of Activity-Based Costing Systems**

ABC systems have four typical steps.

(1) The ABC project team develops an activity dictionary that lists all potential activities driving up costs for cost objects.

(2) The ABC project team collects more detailed cost data on all activities in the activity dictionary. The cost data will cover: unit-level activities, batch-level activities, product-sustaining activities, customer-sustaining activities, product-line sustaining activities, facility-sustaining activities, and channel-sustaining activities.

(3) The ABC project team identifies specific cost objects.

(4) The ABC project team identifies activity cost drivers to link to cost objects. There are three types of activity cost drivers: transaction drivers, duration drivers, and intensity drivers.

- **Challenges to Activity-Based Costing Systems**

There are several challenges to ABC systems.

(1) Organizational members are likely to sustain their defensive posture against new techniques, especially when they are concerned about sudden power shifts caused by ABC systems.

(2) Implementation costs for ABC systems are high.

(3) When indirect costs include fixed costs, even the cost allocation based on ABC systems are misleading, because fixed costs are sunk. Financial managers need caution in employing the ABC systems for make-or-buy decisions.

PART III

INFORMATION CAPACITY AND BUDGET CHOICE

13 Bounded Rationality and Budgetary Incrementalism

Budget decision makers usually do not have the capacity or resources to process all information inputs they obtain from their surrounding budget environments. Even when they have good information-processing capacity, numerous rules and institutional procedures prohibit them from adopting potentially better budget alternatives. The overall condition in which budget decision makers are limited in their information processing is called bounded rationality. Since they cannot process all information inputs or budget alternatives, they tend to focus only on those that are marginally different from ones in previous years. This is called incrementalism. This chapter discusses the following issues:

- Limited Capacity of Budget Decision Makers
- An Example: Limited Capacity and Limited Search for Alternatives
- Incrementalism
- Budgetary Incrementalism
- Critiques of Incrementalism
- Prospects of Incrementalism

LIMITED CAPACITY OF BUDGET DECISION MAKERS

Decision makers do not have the cognitive and analytical capabilities needed to process all pieces of information flowing from decision environments. Decision makers tend to have pre-established levels of decision aspiration. Once certain alternatives are minimally satisfactory with respect to the aspiration levels, decision makers are likely to select them as their final choice. Decision makers do not conduct comprehensive reviews of all alternatives. This aspect of the decision-making process is known as bounded rationality. In practice, decision makers have attempted to enhance rationality in decision making by adopting techniques such as performance budgeting or organizational restructuring. There is dominant evidence from empirical observations that such efforts were not highly successful in enhancing rationality. The cognitive capacities of decision makers are fundamentally limited, especially for public programs that are restricted by political, legal, and institutional constraints (Fry and Raadschelders 2008, 221–22).

Readers can better understand the bounded rationality in the case of the governmental budget process. Budget decision makers are bombarded by masses of information. They obtain political and policy cues from elected politicians. Interest groups usually convey strong signals to budget decision makers regarding their favorite programs. Budget decision makers also get informational cues on the resources available for coming fiscal years. Since they cannot process all these inputs, they tend to ignore some of those from budget environments. Instead, they are likely to start from the status quo or current budget levels. Yearly budget changes, therefore, typically follow stable, predictable growth patterns, which is more specifically described as budgetary incrementalism.

AN EXAMPLE: LIMITED CAPACITY AND LIMITED SEARCH FOR ALTERNATIVES

In the wake of the 2008 financial market crisis, numerous policy suggestions were proposed to revive the U.S. economy. Supporters of the Keynesian approaches contended that rapid governmental intervention through massive deficit spending would effectively stimulate the national economy, creating financial credits needed for investment and consumption flow again. In addition, Keynesians have recently recommended that the Federal Reserve Bank pump more cheap credits into the financial market as introduced in Chapters 23 and 24 in Part VI. In contrast, supporters of supply-side economics assert that tax cuts are the most effective way of increasing private savings, which in turn can be loaned to business investors and expedite the circulation of financial credits.

Other approaches call for reviving the classical approach to macroeconomics. They contend that the private market system has a self-clearing power, so leaving the market to the law of supply and demand is the best policy alternative. Furthermore, they oppose the Keynesians' proposal, saying that the increased circulation of dollars gives the wrong signal to business investors, who are likely to expand their production capacities only because they have access to cheap credit. Another group of scholars and practitioners argue that increasing cheap credit created various bubbles in the U.S. economy—the housing bubble, the stock market bubble, the discretionary spending bubble, and ultimately the governmental debt bubble. When all the bubbles popped up, the 2008 crisis followed. These varied approaches recommend minimizing governmental intervention into the private market system. More details will be introduced in Part VI of this book.

Looking at the policy alternatives that the federal government actually adopts, one can see that either Keynesian suggestions or supply-siders' proposals have been dominating the national fiscal and monetary policy debates. From 2009 to 2011, the federal government pumped huge amounts of stimulus funds into the private market system through bailouts, rounds of quantitative easing, and tax-cut extension. Democrats generally support Keynesian methods, and Republicans support supply-side economics. In practice, policy alternatives seldom deviate from the two macroeconomic approaches that have been implemented for several decades, even when new ones have gained stronger support from scholars and practitioners.

INCREMENTALISM

Lindblom (1959, 1979) systematically observed the pattern of marginal policy changes known as incrementalism. Limited capacity to process information efficiently and lack of time and resources prevent decision makers from adopting comprehensive, synoptic solutions to complex social problems. Budget decision makers are further constrained by prescribed political and institutional procedures. Consequently, the decision makers tend to pay selective attention and analysis to a few policy alternatives that marginally deviate from the status quo. The incrementalist approach has obvious advantages over the comprehensive approaches. Synoptic and rational decision making can easily result in ill-designed, accidental incompleteness. In contrast, incrementalism leads to deliberate, designed incompleteness. Therefore, one normatively superior merit of incrementalism is that it targets identified ills to avoid rather than abstract and unattainable goals to pursue.

Furthermore, partisan mutual adjustment can enhance the analysis of budgets or policies. For instance, interest groups or beneficiaries of governmental programs try to influence through partisan analysis (as opposed to centralized analysis by governmental agencies) to bring budget-relevant information to budget decision makers. Interest groups or lobbyists actively provide budget-relevant information to state legislatures or agency bureaucrats. In addition to their advocacy roles, they function as important information sources because they know what budget alternatives might be best for their group interests. The alternatives might be locally optimal but offer a lot of budget-relevant information to budget decision makers (Esterling 2004; Ryu et al. 2007; Swain and Hartley 2001; Wildavsky 2007, 3–19). This partisan analysis is augmented by partisan mutual adjustment among various stakeholders (Lindblom 1979). Overall, a limited search for alternatives and mutual adjustment among diverse stakeholders results in incremental and predictable policy changes.

BUDGETARY INCREMENTALISM

Davis, Dempster, and Wildavsky (1966, 1974) applied incrementalism to explain and predict the patterns of federal budgets. Governmental budgeting is extraordinarily complex, defying the computational capacity of budget decision makers. For this reason, they almost never review budget alternatives in their entirety. Instead, they review marginal deviations from the current budget level, described as the *budget base*. If budget actors agree on the expected base of their ongoing expenditure levels, the agreement functions as a powerful means of securing budgetary stability.

The stabilized budgetary process is frequently simplified to interaction among agencies, chief executive officers and central budget offices, and legislative appropriations committees. Agency bureaucrats tend to advocate their own programs. Agency budget officers especially have learned that requesting abnormally high increases invites scrutiny from central budget offices and appropriations committees. They have also learned that requesting budgets without any allowances might result in cuts. Therefore, agency budget decision makers intentionally request budgets that are neither too high nor too low. Scholars have observed that agency budget requests typically increase by about 5–10 percent, seldom larger than 30 percent. Central budget offices tend to closely review and cut the requests. Appropriations committees and their staff are likely to conform to what chief executive officers and central budget offices recommend for agency budgets (Wildavsky and Caiden 2004, 44–57).

CRITIQUES OF INCREMENTALISM

As much as budgetary incrementalism has dominated the study of budget processes in the United States, it has also been exposed to numerous critiques from three directions: the unit of analyzing budget choices, the concept of budget base, and overall conceptual confusion.

MORE FREQUENT BUDGET FLUCTUATIONS BELOW THE AGENCY LEVEL

Earlier studies showed that there were more fluctuations in budgets below the agency level that had been the study target for incrementalism (agency programs are highly complex and characterized by intense partisan politics). For instance, the aggregated budgets for twenty-three programs administered by the Atomic Energy Commission (AEC) throughout the 1960s showed stable growth patterns, as incrementalism suggested. Below the agency level, however, there were much more frequent budget fluctuations for the twenty-three programs, and the stable budget patterns were no longer observed (Natchez and Bupp 1973). Similar findings were observed in local governments. Local government budget documents in the 1970s revealed that the institutionalization of local budget processes was explained by the concept of budgetary base and incrementalism. However, these processes were more rational at the lower organizational level. At that level, local governments employed even cost-benefit analysis or computer-assisted simulations (Cornia and Usher 1981). More recent observations present a similar story. The aggregated local government expenditures per capita by a state from fiscal year 1994 to fiscal year 2004 followed fairly stabilized change patterns as in incrementalism. However, when the aggregated expenditures were disaggregated by major functional categories, budget fluctuations were observed more frequently than in incrementalism (Kelly and Rivenbark 2008).

An analysis using U.S. government appropriations data from 1955 to 2002 reported similar findings. Budget choices fluctuated more at the subaccount and subfunction levels than did those at the agency level. Changes in party control were strongly reflected in budget decisions at the disaggregated level. In contrast, more prescribed political and institutional conditions, such as divided governments, which Lindblom (1979) identified as a cause for bounded rationality, clearly explained aggregate-level budget choices at the agency level. Of course, budgets at the more aggregate level were stickier and featured budgetary incrementalism (Anderson and Harbridge 2010). One reason for the above observations might involve the scale of problems to address: At the subfunction level, budget-related information might not be extremely complex, and so budget decision makers are able to process them into budget choices, but at the agency level, this scenario might not hold true (Lindblom 1979). In addition, agency-level budget allocations are characterized by interdependence or contentious zero-sum trade-offs among subagency programs. In contrast, bureaucratic competition tends to be dynamic over the budget allocations at the program level below agencies, with a more volatile decision process. Two contrasting views are not necessarily mutually exclusive, though. The crucial point, therefore, is the unit of analysis (Gist 1982).

Much in line with the critiques, Boyne, Ashworth, and Powell (2000) show that incrementalism is not a strong tool to analyze even local budgets. Using fiscal data of 403 English local governments during the 1980s and the 1990s, they tested whether budget decision makers' tendency to protect budget base could explain local budget changes. They also tested whether external, prescribed procedures constrain budget choices—whether central government's imposition of expenditure limits restricts local governments' discretion and thus leads to stable budget change patterns. Their empirical results do not support these assumptions. The authors report more diverse observations on local budget choices. Stanford (1992) reports another very interesting observation against incrementalism. She analyzed more than 12,000 questions asked by legislators during agency budget hearings before the appropriations committees of the Florida House and the Senate during the 1980s. As Schick (1966) posits, budget functions have three orientations: control, management, and planning. Stanford adds a fourth orientation, funding. Unlike the assumptions inherent in incrementalism (readers should note that incrementalism focuses heavily on control), her findings are very provocative. Legislators paid substantial attention to the four orientations over agency budget requests and gubernatorial budget recommendations. They showed particularly higher interest in management-related issues. In addition, they made a detailed analysis of services or programs that directly affect their legislative districts by bringing in jobs, education, highways, training, and transfer payments. Both the English and Florida cases illustrate that budget decision makers pay more attention to budget-related information inputs even at the *agency* level.

Revisiting the Concept of Budget Base

Earlier studies also criticized incrementalism from various other fronts. Wanat (1974) developed "random" numbers with boundaries for incremental budget changes ranging between 10 and 160 percent. His repeated simulations obtained results almost indistinguishable from those of Davis, Dempster, and Wildavsky (1966, 1974). He also analyzed congressional hearings on the budgets of the Department of Labor around 1970. There were three components in the agency budget requests: the base, the agency's mandatory needs, and the agency's programmatic increases. As incrementalism predicted, the budget base was almost untouched. However, Congress also passed most of the mandatory needs that were new costs to keep the agency operating budget at the same level as in the current year: new costs are likely to be cost increases caused by inflation. In contrast, Congress cut primarily the agency's programmatic increases. According to Wanat, mandatory needs were more reflective of such external factors as inflation or increased population, but most of them were kept intact. This contrasts with incrementalism in that even the agency's mandatory needs, as well as the base, were unchanged. Furthermore, top-down budget constraints were exerting more influence on agency budget requests. This aspect also contrasts with the incrementalist view that budget choices are fundamentally a reflection of bottom-up forces arising from main budget actors.

Kamlet and Mowery (1980) presented similar observations. They analyzed U.S. budget data from 1952 to 1975 and revealed three different concepts of the budget base: the current estimate, the cost of ongoing activity levels (close to the sum of the base and the mandatory needs in Wanat), and the mandatory budget levels (close to the sum of the base and the programmatic increases in Wanat). Unlike in incrementalism, Kamlet and Mowery identified that adequate concepts of the budget base might differ, depending on the nature of agency programs. There was substantial discrepancy between the Office of Budget and Management (OMB) and agencies over the definition of budget base. For any given year of the Eisenhower administration, disagreement over the base was greater than that over increments. Thus, Kamlet and Mowery's analysis indicates that agreement among budget actors on the budget base is not necessarily guaranteed.

Wildavsky and Caiden (2004, 83–102) also evidenced heightened conflict over the budget base for the decades since the early 1970s. They have claimed for numerous reasons that the agreed base has disappeared. Party systems have been more polarized, and these polarized parties were even more fragmented by different preferences about deficit control. Keynesian doctrines were also challenged by monetarism and supply-side economics. Most of all, Wildavsky and Caiden attribute the disappearance of the base to the focus on budget targets or totals prescribed in the Congressional Budget and Impoundment Control Act of 1974. With the advent of top-down budget control such as budget resolution and reconciliation procedures (see Chapter 25 in Part VI for more details), budget conflicts intensified among various budget actors. This has jeopardized the budget stability asserted for incrementalism because the intensified conflicts tended to accelerate tighter reviews of even budget bases.

MORE COMPREHENSIVE CRITIQUES OF INCREMENTALISM

LeLoup (1978) makes another comprehensive critique of incrementalism. Incrementalism did not account for many restrictions on long-term budget changes such as revenue estimates, taxation decisions, deficit size, and expenditure ceilings. Uncontrollable spending authorized by permanent laws dramatically increased throughout the 1960s and 1970s. These facts imply that the study of budgetary decisions needs a longer time frame, not a single-year perspective as shown in incrementalism (see also Meyers [1996] for more diverse strategies that budget actors apply).

Davis, Dempster, and Wildavsky (1966, 1974) and Ryu et al. (2007, 2008) indicate that budget environmental factors did not exert significant influence on budget choices. LeLoup (1978), however, contends that there was a more subtle dimension. When the dependent variable was changed into the percentage change in appropriations rather than final appropriations amounts, new sets of environmental factors explained budget choices. Presidential support was related to budget changes, while changes in previous appropriations showed virtually no impact on percentage changes in agency budget requests or appropriations. In other cases, congressional political coalitions, the level of congressional support for the president, and congressional conflict did influence budget results. In addition, agency size and experience of agency administrators were correlated with greater appropriations.

As noted above, uncontrollable budget categories have dramatically increased, and congressional budget procedures have changed since 1974. LeLoup (1978) stresses that authorization committees in charge of uncontrollable budget categories should be investigated as one main budget actor. In addition, top-down budget processes need to be more elaborate studies, similar to that of Kamlet and Mowery (1980). LeLoup also shows that budgetary decisions varied in three broad categories, such as priority decisions (mostly on budget totals), program decisions (e.g., program authorizations, agency appropriations, entitlement programs), and operational decisions (mostly related to agency-level operations). Decisions at all three levels might be affected by such external budget factors as economic, social, and political fluctuations, but who the key budget actors might be depends on which of the three levels is chosen as the study target.

Berry (1990) also made a comprehensive critique of incrementalism. He decomposed incrementalism's fundamental logical assumptions into six concepts found in earlier studies and six budget-specific concepts. He then identified from those twelve concepts three general ones in incrementalism: regularity of relationships, simple decision rules, and lack of effect of external variables. Berry contends that the extent to which other concepts are related to regularity of relationships utterly depends on how other concepts are defined. The simple decision rules are so general that all other concepts are somehow related to them. The third general concept of incrementalism, lack of external variables' effect, does not have a strong connection to other concepts, and the scope of being external should be more specifically delineated first. Nine other specific concepts are also very loosely interrelated. Only three variables—smallness of change, sequential consideration of alternatives, and negotiation among participants with narrow roles—are related to each other. However, the relationships are not strong enough, either.

Dezhbakhsh, Tohamy, and Aranson (2003) make a more recent critique of incrementalism by using data similar to what Davis, Dempster, and Wildavsky (1966, 1974) used. Since the cutoff point to define budgetary increments is arbitrary, they standardized budget changes across agencies and years. Their analysis first clarified that marginal budget changes were reported more frequently for medium-sized agencies. They also strictly limited themselves to budget increments that showed at least three consecutive years of small changes. Then, they tested what budget environmental factors affected incremental versus nonincremental budget changes. Overall, rapid political changes often caused nonincremental budget changes. A high revenue growth reduced nonincremental budget changes because it might be easier for politicians to build a high increase into the base spending as implied in incrementalism. Budget deficits would make it harder for legislators to keep promises to continue similar levels of governmental spending and thus caused nonincremental budget changes. In sum, budget environmental factors affected budget outcomes more strongly than envisioned in earlier studies of incrementalism.

PROSPECTS OF INCREMENTALISM

These critiques of incrementalism warrant continued future empirical research. One recent real-life story supports incrementalism, however. In 2011, South Carolina Governor Nikki Haley explicitly tried to augment central budget control with expected revenue shortage. State agency heads developed some budgetary strategies. For instance, the State Law Enforcement Division has added training of local enforcement agencies to enforce state alcohol laws. The state Forestry Commission has called for legislation that would allow some existing taxes that flowed to the state's general fund so the commission can retain some of the taxes. The Department of Natural Resources has attempted to increase the price of hunting and fishing licenses. All these are examples of budget gimmicks or strategies to maximize or retain the current level of agency budgets even under tighter budget control. These budgetary activities exemplify causes of budgetary incrementalism or budget padding. In addition, some politicians supported the movements of resources to these agencies in that they are responsible for providing the general public with stable services. This support obviously helped the agencies sustain their budget padding. In addition, Governor Haley explicitly tried to stabilize the fluctuations in the agency budget cycle, which obviously gave momentum for agencies to retain their current budget levels. In sum, agencies were freer to pad their budgets (Beam 2011).

Budget shortfalls that have recently plagued various levels of government might drive budget decision makers to exert tighter budget controls. Various versions of performance-based budgeting as introduced in Part II have swept the federal, state, and local governments, pressing them for more efficient and effective use of scarce resources. Therefore, one might expect more budget fluctuations from recent budget choices at various levels of government. However, as implied by the above case, incremental budget change patterns might also sustain their momentum in U.S. budget processes.

Schick (2009) and Caiden (2010) also emphasize why budget reforms might face significant challenges and why incrementalism can stand the test of budget reality. Budget reforms devoid of underlying understanding and cultural changes cannot be successful. Performance budgeting has been widely adopted throughout countries, but the evaluation results have rarely been used and incorporated into budget allocation decisions. Performance budgeting is an old, recurring idea with a disappointing future. Another example is accrual budgeting. Although it might be more accurate, many governments still deem a cash basis of accounting a more convenient way of recording. In addition, though rationalists deride incrementalism as irrational, it is still alive and well. When Organization for Economic Cooperation and Development (OECD) countries try to make room for targeted enhancements, they tend to snip existing programs at their margins. In addition, governmental programs are very sticky temporally. Governmental budgets are "the means of continuing the past into the future," and "it is time to call a halt to the reformist war against incrementalism" (Schick 2009, 208, 356).

Chapter Summary

- **Limited Capacity of Budget Decision Makers**

Budget decision makers do not have the capacity or resources to process all information inputs from budget environments. This is typically known as bounded rationality, and its result is that governmental budget processes tend to follow incremental change patterns.

- **Partisan Analysis in Incrementalism**

Interest groups or beneficiaries of governmental programs often know the best benefits from the programs. Their analysis is known as partisan analysis. Partisan analysis is augmented through partisan mutual adjustment that, in turn, results in incremental changes.

- **Budgetary Incrementalism**

Budgetary incrementalism reveals a systematic interaction among main budget actors. Agency budget officers tend to avoid requesting budgets that are too high or too low. Chief executive officers or central budget offices are likely to exert tighter review over agency budget requests, and legislative appropriation committees conform to executive budget recommendations.

- **Critiques of Incrementalism**

There have been numerous critiques of incrementalism.

(1) Programs and budgets below the agency level, which have been the target of budgetary incrementalism, have experienced more frequent fluctuations. More recent empirical studies have shown that budget decision makers pay more attention to budget-related information inputs even at the agency level.

(2) Budget base has more diversified dimensions than incrementalism simply defined. In addition, there have been disagreements over how to define the budget base. Recent changes in partisan politics and enhanced top-down budget controls intensified budget conflicts among main budget actors, which has expedited tighter reviews of budget bases.

(3) When analysts used different measures of agency budgets, many environmental factors significantly affected budget choices, contrary to incrementalism's expectations. Who the key budget actors might be depends on which level of budgets (i.e., priority decisions, program decisions, or operational decisions) is chosen as the study target.

(4) Many concepts in incrementalism are not meaningfully interrelated.

- **Prospects of Incrementalism**

Despite the critiques, a recent state budget example implies that incrementalism might persist in state budget processes.

14 Stable Interactions Among Budget Actors

There are three main budget actors in U.S. budget processes: executive agencies, chief executive officers or central budget offices, and legislatures. Numerous empirical observations of the budget processes revealed a highly stable and predictable interaction among the three main budget actors. This chapter discusses the following issues:

- Three Main Budget Actors and Their Interactions in U.S. Budget Processes
- Earlier Findings on the Interactions Among the Main Budget Actors
- A Summary View of the Interactions Among the Main Budget Actors
- Prospects of the Interactions Among the Main Budget Actors

THREE MAIN BUDGET ACTORS AND THEIR INTERACTIONS IN U.S. BUDGET PROCESSES

Budget changes typically show stabilized, predictable change paths. Three main budget actors drive budget choices, especially at the national and state levels: agencies in the executive branches, chief executive officers or their central budget offices, and legislatures. Studies have consistently shown a stable interaction among the main budget actors. Agency budgeters in the executive branches have superior knowledge of the true costs of their agency programs as well as programmatic details. Based on their superior knowledge and years of experience, agency budget officers are likely to pad their budget requests. But they know that if they request too much, higher-level budget decision makers might conduct a detailed scrutiny of their requests. If their requests are too small, their budgets might get cut. Therefore, their requested budgets are a bit high but not too high, based on their institutional memory and political experience. Chief executive officers or central budget offices tend to exert tight reviews over agency budget requests based on forecast revenues for upcoming fiscal years. Legislatures generally do not have access to detailed information on agency programs or the information-processing capacity that their executive counterparts have. Legislatures mostly conform to what chief executive officers recommend for agency budgets. This highly predictable relationship among the main budget actors has been supported for the past several decades, although the relative power has been shifting somewhat among them.

EARLIER FINDINGS ON THE INTERACTIONS AMONG THE MAIN BUDGET ACTORS

Several major empirical studies have investigated the interactions among agencies, chief executive officers and central budget offices, and legislatures. Some of the studies are fairly old but provide succinct and relevant observations of the interactions among these main budget actors. As introduced in Chapter 13, empirical analyses conducted by Davis et al. (1966, 1974) are among the most influential studies to reveal the stable interactions among the main budget actors in the federal budget process (see also Green and Thompson 2001; Wildavsky and Caiden 2004). Other earlier studies also have shown the stable interactions in state and local budget processes.

CRECINE'S STUDY OF MUNICIPAL BUDGET DECISIONS IN THE 1960S

Davis et al. (1966, 1974) identified three models to explain how federal agencies mostly based their budget requests on the previous year's congressional appropriations. They also established three models to explain how Congress responded to the current year's agency budget requests in terms of congressional appropriations. The key point of the six federal agency budget models is characterized by a simple linear relationship between agency budget requests and congressional appropriations. Crecine (1967, 1969) also found linear relationships between current and previous budget amounts in local budget processes, very consistent with the incrementalism approach discussed in Chapter 13. He analyzed agency budgets for three local governments—Pittsburgh, Detroit, and Cleveland—throughout the 1950s and the 1960s. Crecine attributed the incremental budget changes across years to highly stable and predictable budget aspirations and behaviors among local budget actors.

In what he described as governing or budgeting by precedent, Crecine detailed how three main budget actors in local governments—department heads, mayors, and local councils—formed local budgets. When department heads prepared budget requests, the budget forms they dealt with heavily affected their budget aspirations. For instance, budget forms automatically compared next year's budget requests with this year's appropriations. Therefore, the most salient tendency of department heads was to ensure their departments had funds to continue the operation of ongoing programs. More importantly, department heads realized through their experience and institutional learning that their budget requests were likely to be cut by the mayor's office or council. Thus, they tended to ask for more than they expected to get. This budget padding was based on one common observation of mutual expectations and roles. Department heads' calculations played an important role in figuring out acceptable amounts for their budgets, but the calculations were about what would be acceptable to the mayor's office, thus securing reasonable shares of increases in total budgets for their departments.

In contrast to the expansionist attitude of department heads, the mayors' basic role was that of economizers, especially because they were responsible for balancing local budgets. Mayors' strategies to balance local budgets targeted increasing or decreasing tax rates, but their formal targets usually focused on spending control: How to cut lower-priority expenditures or allow supplemental requests under anticipated deficits or surplus. Under anticipated surplus, mayors typically attempted to increase general salaries or allow supplemental requests. Under anticipated deficits, there were also highly predictable patterns of mayoral budget actions. The mayors first made sure that preliminary budget recommendations were within budget limits. Then, they tried to eliminate the increases recommended over nonsalary budget items. If all these measures failed, they imposed across-the-board budget cuts. While mayors were reviewing departmental budget requests, the strictness of their review differed depending on how honest and realistic the requests were.

In contrast to the aspirations and behaviors of department heads and mayors, those of councils were rather simple and straightforward. The primary limit of the councils was cognitive and informational constraints. They had no professional staff assistance in line with the state cases on budget stability introduced below. Given the fundamental limitations, councils generally used mayors' budget recommendations as the reference point for their budget choices. In sum, the entire process of local budget decisions featured a systematic, bureaucratic, administrative decision-making process and highly predictable interactions among the three budget actors. The primary reason for the highly stable interactions could be explained by an implicit assumption that since this year's problems were similar to last year's, this year's solutions would be nearly identical to last year's solutions.

Crecine (1967, 1969) also investigated the influence of external budget environmental factors on local budget choices. He identified several categories of random errors in his linear models to explain yearly budget changes. Changes in external budget environments, such as changes in intergovernmental transactions or catastrophic emergencies, often caused sudden budget changes. Altered internal organizational environments, such as new administration or changes in departmental functions, also caused sudden and huge budget changes. Such factors as changes in state and federal subsidies and regulations or budget accounts also explained big lurches in annual local budget choices. However, the impact of budget environmental factors was minimal, such that the stable interactions among the three main budget actors explained significant portions of local budget processes. At this moment, readers should be aware of a strong caveat about local budget choices. As detailed in Chapter 17, external budget factors such as the median voter's tax price and income exert a much stronger influence on local budget choices, especially when jurisdictional boundaries are very narrow (three cities in Crecine's studies are examples of big localities) and voters can shop around multiple local jurisdictions. It is very likely that budget problems might not defy the capacity of budget decision makers and voters. Therefore, budget environmental factors (in this case, voters' preferences) might more strongly affect local budget choices. But what Crecine's studies imply is consistent with expectations on budget interactions based on the assumptions of bounded rationality introduced in Chapter 13.

SHARKANSKY'S 1968 STUDY

Sharkansky (1968) empirically observed the interactions using state agency budget data mostly from the mid-1960s. Throughout the 1960s, total state and local government expenditures, often categorized by functional areas such as highway, education, public welfare, etc., were the main focus of budget studies. In contrast, Sharkansky focused on what mechanisms and patterns explain how state agency budgets, instead of state total expenditures, were formed. This approach is meaningful in understanding and testing incrementalism because it attempted to explain budget processes and outcomes at the agency level, where the complexity of budget-related information defies the capacity of budget decision makers, and where prescribed political, institutional rules further augment the budget decision makers' bounded rationality as discussed in the previous chapter.

Budget Behaviors of the Main Budget Actors

Sharkansky (1968) found governors and legislators to be more or less fiscally conservative. Therefore, they are likely to cut agency requests that in most cases attempted to expand. At the same time, however, the expansionist attitude of agencies might be a prerequisite for budget increases for the agencies in the long run. Thus, the agencies requesting more tended to get more. In the long run, governors would recommend larger budgets and legislatures would approve increased resources for those agencies that tried to secure more resources. In the state budget processes, gubernatorial support was the most critical factor for agencies' short-term and long-term budget increases. In contrast, state legislators had been limited in terms of resources, skills, and information-processing capacity and were likely to get budget cues from gubernatorial recommendations. Legislative appropriations were likely to conform to gubernatorial budget recommendations for the agencies.

Sharkansky's (1968) empirical findings mostly supported these expectations. The agencies requested on average 24 percent more than their current outlays. Governors overall trimmed 14 percent from the agency requests. Legislatures granted about 13 percent below the request but about 13 percent higher than the agencies' current outlays. In the short run, legislatures cut the budgets of the agencies that attempted to pad their budgets. In the long run, however, the more acquisitive agencies received larger budgets.

Budget Base, Budget Environmental Factors, and Stable Interactions

Sharkansky (1968) further investigated whether the main budget actors, especially governors and legislatures, carefully reviewed the budget base, which in most cases was the previous year's budget. He also investigated whether budget environmental factors affected the stable interactions among the main budget actors.

Total dollar amounts of agency budget requests did not significantly explain governors' budget recommendations or legislative appropriations. As shown in the previous chapter, budget decision makers were less likely to review the budget base. Budget reviewers were more likely to focus on the budget increment that was marginally different from the current budgets, rather than on the sheer size of agency budget requests, substantial portions of which were the budget base. Sharkansky's (1968) finding resonated well with the incrementalist insight. Main budget actors paid primary attention to the marginal budget changes. In other words, they mostly did not touch the budget base and focused instead on the portion of about 5–10 percent annual budget changes. This significantly led to stable interactions because of the marginal or minimal budget changes and adjustments among the main budget actors.

Similar to Davis et al. (1974), Sharkansky (1968) showed that some environmental factors influenced budget outcomes at the agency level but for the most part did not significantly affect agency budget outcomes. In the states where governors retained stronger veto power and state expenditures were higher, governors tended to tightly control agency budget requests. In contrast, a low debt rate, high personal income, relatively intense party competition, and high voter turnout led governors to accept agency budget expansion. When legislatures curbed agency budget requests, there were high state expenditures and a low number of elected executive officials. Overall, however, budget environmental factors did not significantly change the stable interactions among the main budget actors.

THOMPSON'S 1987 STUDY

Thompson (1987) replicated Sharkansky's (1968) analysis using the fiscal year 1978–1980 data. There had been substantial changes in the interactions among the main budget actors since the mid-1960s. Governorships had been strengthened through the governors' increased tenure potential. Gubernatorial budget and appointment powers had also expanded. Administrative executive organizations were streamlined, state employee merit coverage expanded, state agencies became more professionalized in grantsmanship and accounting, and federal-state interactions substantially increased. Legislatures had also been professionalized through increased committee staff assistance and reduced membership turnover. The legislative professionalism might have enabled legislators to develop more durable relationships with their constituencies and placed them in a better position to compete with governors.

The changing institutional settings might have influenced budget outcomes at the state agency level. According to Thompson (1987), however, agencies still requested about 38 percent more than their current outlays, governors reduced the requests by about 12 percent, and legislatures appropriated what governors recommended. One difference from Sharkansky's (1968) findings was that state agencies were more acquisitive and legislatures tended to cut original agency requests less. One possible reason for the increased acquisitiveness was that many states with progressive income tax systems might have raised more revenues. Thus, governors and legislators were more lenient. In addition, agencies played more crucial roles in securing legislative appropriations than did governor's recommendations. This observation was another minor departure from Sharkansky's (1968) findings. However, the stabilized interactions among the main budget actors remained almost unchanged. Executive agencies tended to request more budgets, governors or central budget offices were likely to curb budget increases, and legislatures tended to conform to governors' budget recommendations for the agencies.

CLARKE'S 1997 STUDY

Clarke (1997) conducted a similar study. He originally investigated how the methods of selecting state agency heads affected a governor's budget recommendations for state agencies using fiscal data from 1985 to 1995. This is what Thompson (1987) briefly investigated. Elected agency heads from the governor's political party received greater gubernatorial support for both short-term and long-term budget increases. But all in all, this study reported almost similar stable relationships among the main budget actors in line with Sharkansky and Thompson. State legislatures took their budget cues from governors. In most cases, legislative appropriations were closer to gubernatorial budget recommendations than agency budget requests, which is closer to Sharkansky's findings.

OTHER RECENT STUDIES

Ryu et al. (2007, 2008) investigated the interaction among the main budget actors based on self-reported survey responses from more than 1,000 agency heads in the fifty states for 1998. They found a similar stable interrelationship among the main budget actors. Governors tended to control agency budget requests. Legislative appropriations closely conformed to what governors recommended for agencies. One difference from the earlier studies was that agencies were not as acquisitive as was observed earlier. They were much more moderate in their budget requests. As high as 82 percent of agencies requested budget increases by 0–10 percent from previous legislative appropriations. In addition, governmental budget growth was also attributed to legislative assertiveness. Finally, they tested numerous environmental factors to verify whether the stable interactions among the main budget actors still held true. Their models controlled for legislative professionalism, governor's item veto power, tax and expenditure limits, balanced budget requirements, state economic conditions, centralized gubernatorial and legislative budget reviews, interest group mobility, etc. as environmental factors. Ryu et al.'s (2007, 2008) findings confirmed that the stable relationship remained almost unchanged as well.

The above studies, except for Thompson (1987), revealed that governors were the most pivotal actors in the stable relationships among the main budget actors. Many scholars have recently observed that governors have been losing their dominant budget power, however. Based on 2000–2001 surveys, Goodman (2007) found that state legislatures' enhanced capacity regarding budget information and agenda substantially increased legislative budget power. Dometrius and Wright (2010), based on surveys spanning from 1978 to 1998, reported that legislatures have gained more budget power, which can be attributable to some political changes. They also found that the strongest governor dropped in influence from 1978 through 1988 but regained control from 1994 through 1998. In contrast, the strongest legislatures have maintained their power across most of the time periods.

A SUMMARY VIEW OF THE INTERACTIONS AMONG THE MAIN BUDGET ACTORS

Rosenthal (1998, 50–80) provides a more comprehensive overview of the interactions among the main budget actors, especially between governors and legislatures, and gives clues to the subtly different views on the interactions in more recent findings. During the 1960s and the 1970s, the model for legislative reforms for states was Congress and the California legislature. Recommendations for legislative reforms were made in five areas: space, sessions, structure, staff, and salaries. Physical space for state legislators expanded. The length and frequency of legislative sessions expanded. Structure was also streamlined. Throughout the 1970s and the 1980s, legislative staffs have grown substantially and have become highly professionalized. Salaries for members of state legislatures have also steadily increased. The professionalization of the legislature itself contributed to the professionalization of individual legislators in the legislature. Democrats are believed to be more active in participating in governmental affairs than their Republican counterparts. In many cases, the outside jobs of Republican legislators have been too attractive to give up. In contrast, Democrats usually have less attractive outside jobs and sacrifices are easier to make. They are more ready to enter politics and to be professional legislators. Data show that the membership turnover rate in the lower houses had been declining substantially from the 1950s to the 1990s. Possible reasons for the high institutionalization might be the high proportion of legislators who were committed to political careers and the professional skills and capacity they accumulated. In this regard, professionalization of state legislatures also contributed to their institutionalization.

Legislative professionalism led to legislative independence. Kentucky was a good example. Its legislature made the first serious review of gubernatorial budget recommendations. It also pushed through a constitutional amendment that moved legislative elections away from the gubernatorial election year so as to reduce the governor's influence on the choice of legislative leaders. As discussed in Chapters 1 and 2 in Part I, on executive and legislative budgeting systems, central budget offices in the executive branch typically review agency requests. However, in thirty-seven states throughout the 1990s the legislatures also reviewed the agency requests before the executive budgets were prepared. One executive staff functional responsibility was the authority to predict revenues. However, legislative staffs in three-fifths of the states prepared their own revenue estimates during the time period. In some states, consensus-estimating conferences between the governors and the legislatures developed state revenue forecasts. This allowed both sides to start from the same assumption for budget preparation. Even under executive budgeting systems, governors could not completely dominate legislatures (Rosenthal 1998, 302–8; 2004, 195–99).

After a period of institutionalization, however, state legislatures now have entered a period of deinstitutionalization. The turnover rate in state legislatures has been rising recently. From 1987 to 1997, the rate for the upper chambers changed by 72 percent on average, while that for the lower chambers changed by 84 percent. In addition, state legislatures are under strong constitutional and statutory restrictions in legislative terms. Furthermore, outside controls over the length of legislative sessions and the salaries of legislators have been enhanced (Rosenthal 1998, 72–80). Since the late 1990s, governors have been exerting much stronger budget power over their legislative counterparts. Numerous illustrative cases have shown how legislatures did not succeed in remedying an extreme imbalance of budgetary power (Rosenthal 2004, 201–5). Rosenthal's observations echo well what Dometrius and Wright (2010) reported (especially that stronger governors regained budget powers during the second half of the 1990s), as introduced above. However, readers should be cautious of one caveat. Abney and Lauth (1998) contended that gubernatorial executive budget power has been declining for almost the same period investigated in the above studies. One of the reasons for the decline is the increased informational advantages of state legislatures. Despite the potential controversy over the relative budget power between governors and legislatures, Rosenthal's comprehensive summary of the stable relationships between governors and legislatures indicates that the interactions among the main budget actors are fairly stable and predictable even when they are changing. Future research is warranted to investigate, by using more recent empirical budget data, whether governors or legislatures are gaining stronger budget control.

PROSPECTS OF THE INTERACTIONS AMONG THE MAIN BUDGET ACTORS

Since the 2008 financial market crisis, the national and state governments have been going through fiscal stringency. Faced with scarce resources, tensions among claimants over governmental budgets might intensify. In addition, as the above studies showed, revenue shortages generally accelerate centralized budget control and coordination in governmental budget processes. Therefore, one can expect that the stable interactions among the main budget actors might become less predictable under fiscal stress. However, Schick (1983) suggests some insightful clues on how fiscal stringency might affect the interactions among various budget participants. When revenues are sufficient, budget controllers tend to be more generous to various demands for increased budgets. In contrast, scarce resources invite tighter budget reviews as noted above. But one caveat is that the process of budget adjustment to revenue shortage was gradual and predictable even when budgets had been steadily "decreasing," rather than increasing. Schick aptly labels this phenomenon "decrementalism." The notion of decrementalism predicts that the interactions among the main budget actors might still follow predictable change paths.

In addition, virtually all states have employed some form of performance-based budgeting. Stronger and more professionalized legislatures and government-wide implementation of performance-based budgeting might cause turbulence in budget processes due to potentially tighter budget review and competition among various programs. These are significant research questions to fill the current gap in the budgeting literature. Currently, almost all fifty states posted their executive budget documents on the websites of their central budget offices or departments that perform budget coordination. Somewhere between ten and twenty states provide budget data on agency budget requests, governor's budget recommendations, legislative appropriations, and actual outlays. Although researchers still need to standardize budget formats across the states, these formats are important sources for budget data to replicate the earlier studies and test whether and how the fiscal stringency and performance-based budgeting systems affect the stable interactions among the main budget actors.

CHAPTER SUMMARY

•   **Historical Findings on the Interactions Among the Main Budget Actors**
Scholars have observed stable interaction among agency budget requests, governors' budget recommendations, and legislative appropriations. The relative power in the interaction has recently shifted slightly.

(1) Crecine's studies conducted in the 1960s revealed highly predictable and stable interactions among department heads, mayors, and councils in three large cities. Department heads realized through their institutional learning that it would be in their best interest to ask for slightly more than they expected to get. In contrast, mayors were responsible for balancing local budgets and their role was that of economizer. Crecine found that mayors relied on highly predictable and systematic heuristics when reviewing departmental budget requests. City councils tended to use mayors' budget recommendations as their reference points for budget choices. Overall results were very stable interactions among the three budget actors.

(2) Sharkansky's 1968 study showed that agencies generally requested increased budgets, while governors and central budget offices tended to cut agency budget requests. Governors' support for agency budget requests was most critical for agencies' short-term and long-term budget increases. Legislators tended to conform to governors' budget recommendations. In addition, more acquisitive agencies managed to receive larger budgets in the long run. Budget environmental factors did not significantly change the stable interaction among the three main budget actors.

(3) Thompson's 1987 study reported the stable interaction among the three main budget actors, similar to Sharkansky's findings. Thompson's findings had minor departures from Sharkansky's. State agencies were less acquisitive and legislatures were more lenient toward agency budget requests. In addition, agencies were most critical for securing legislative appropriations.

(4) Clarke's 1997 study, using more recent fiscal data, found that state legislative appropriations were closer to governors' budget recommendations. The study is closer to Sharkansky's findings.

(5) More recent empirical studies reported subtle changes in the stable interaction among the main budget actors. Agencies were less acquisitive in requesting agency budgets. Legislatures have been gaining more budget power. All in all, however, they generally confirmed the stable interaction among the main budget actors.

•   **Prospects of the Interactions Among the Main Budget Actors**
Since the second half of the 1990s, state legislatures have been less powerful and governors have been gaining more budget power again. During the 2000s, many states experienced fiscal stringency. Most of them have also employed performance-based budgeting systems. Future research is warranted to test whether and how the fiscal stringency and performance-based budgeting systems affect the stable interaction among the main budget actors.

Disproportionate Information Processing

Scholars have frequently observed that sudden, dramatic budget changes occur. For instance, 50–100 percent of budget changes are obviously dramatic, compared with 5–10 percent incremental budget changes. In the literature of public budgeting, the dramatic budget changes are known as budget punctuations. Scholars have intensively investigated why they take place and have found that the causes of punctuations are virtually the same as those for incremental budget changes. This chapter will first explain budget punctuations as opposed to small, marginal changes and then show how budget punctuations are related to incremental budget changes. Disproportionate information-processing theory is further explained as a comprehensive theory linking small and huge budget changes. This chapter investigates the following issues:

- Controversies on the Magnitude of Budget Changes
- New Perspectives on Dramatic Budget Changes: Budget Punctuations
- Why Do Budget Punctuations Occur? Institutional Approach
- Why Do Budget Punctuations Occur? Information Processing Approach
- Disproportionate Information-Processing as a Comprehensive Theory
- Reillumination of Earlier Cases of Budget Punctuations

CONTROVERSIES ON THE MAGNITUDE OF BUDGET CHANGES

INCREMENTALISM: BUDGET MODERATION

According to incrementalism, the consensus on agency budgets is that agencies will continue operations at the going level of expenditures, or budget base. In addition, the concept of fair share denotes not only the budget base, but also the expectation that the agencies will get some portion of that base. The concept of fair share further implies that agencies will exert some level of moderation in budget requests under a sort of zero-sum game because there is likely to be a convergence of expectations on roughly how much they will receive in comparison to other agencies. This budget-moderation behavior is the main reason that budget change patterns are highly predictable and incremental as discussed in the previous chapters (Wildavsky and Caiden 2004, 46–47).

CRITIQUES OF INCREMENTALISM: AGENCY BUDGET ACQUISITIVENESS

Some studies, however, indicated that budget moderation was not the modal observation in budget changes. Earlier empirical observations reported that agency budget requests were much larger than incremental changes, which were seldom larger than 30 percent (LeLoup and Moreland 1978). In the previous chapter, this phenomenon was called agency budget acquisitiveness.

UNSOLVED QUESTION OF THE CUTOFF POINT FOR BUDGET MODERATION

One question that is unsolved in the budgeting literature is what the cutoff point would be for budget moderation of marginal, incremental changes. Earlier, Bailey and O'Connor (1975) strictly defined the range of incremental changes as less than 10 percent. They defined budget changes larger than 10 percent but less than 30 percent as intermediate changes, and budget changes over 30 percent as nonincremental changes. Under the stricter definition, about half of budget changes reported in incrementalist studies fell outside the concept of incremental changes. The definition of the cutoff point for incremental changes has been highly controversial (Baumgartner and Jones 1993, 2009; Jordan 2003; Robinson et al. 2007; Ryu 2009, 2011a).

NEW PERSPECTIVES ON DRAMATIC BUDGET CHANGES: BUDGET PUNCTUATIONS

Despite the ambiguity of the cutoff point for incremental changes, however, scholars have recently observed more frequent cases of sudden, dramatic changes in budget outcomes (e.g., 50–100 percent budget changes). The cases of agency budget acquisitiveness defined above might be the target of this investigation, but much more importantly, scholars also attempted to explain why dramatic budget changes much larger than even the acquisitive changes (e.g., slightly larger than 30 percent, for instance) happen in the first place. These sudden changes were known as *budget punctuations*.

OBSERVATIONS OF BUDGET PUNCTUATIONS: U.S. BUDGET CHANGES

Baumgartner and Jones (1993) showed that most U.S. policies did not follow incremental change patterns. There were huge, sudden, and dramatic changes in U.S. policy processes. Scholars have recently suggested a creative way of defining the controversial cutoff point for budget lurches. They developed a hypothetical normal curve line using actual budget change distributions (Jones and Baumgartner 2005a, 2005b; Robinson et al. 2007). The observations of budget changes outside the normal range for a given budget data set were aptly defined as dramatic budget changes or budget punctuations. Ryu (2011a) reported, based on this method of defining budget lurches, that budget punctuations explained substantial portions of U.S. budget authority and state government subfunctional expenditures.

Another way of identifying budget punctuations is more straightforward than the normal curve-based approach. Scholars have observed long-term trend lines of budget outcomes; sometimes these trend lines exhibit sudden upward or downward shifts and the new trend lines are sustained for a long period of time. These sudden upward or downward shifts are deemed budget punctuations (Kettl 2007, 128–38). Using U.S. budget authority data from FY 1947 to FY 1995, Jones, Baumgartner, and True (1998) found that U.S. budget changes were characterized by periods of stability interspersed with unpredictable budget punctuations. They categorized U.S. budget changes into three different epochs divided by two large-scale punctuations. The first epoch was post–World War II adjustment lasting until FY 1956. The second was the period of robust growth up to FY 1974 when the Congressional Budget and Impoundment Control Act was enacted. The third epoch was the period of restrained growth since FY 1976. These were not explained by the stable, predictable budget changes depicted in incrementalism. Instead, the three epochs were characterized by sudden upward or downward shifts of long-run stable trend lines.

OBSERVATIONS OF BUDGET PUNCTUATIONS: STATE AND LOCAL BUDGET CHANGES

When Breunig and Koski (2006) used annual state expenditures in ten state functions from 1982 to 2002, they found that substantial portions of state budget changes were explained by budget punctuations not envisioned in incrementalism. Jordan (2003) analyzed six functional expenditures of thirty-eight large cities from 1966 to 1992. There were more frequent observations of budget punctuations in local government expenditures. Robinson et al. (2007) explored expenditure data of over 1,000 K–12 public school districts in Texas from 1989 to 2001. They also reported that some budget changes were outside the normal range, explained by budget punctuations. Using longer decades of state budget and policy data ranging from the early twentieth century to the late 2000s, many scholars have reported much more frequent observations of dramatic changes in state budgets and policies (Boushey 2010, 2012; Breunig 2011; Breunig and Koski 2009, 2012; Breunig, Koski, and Mortensen 2010; Robinson 2004; Ryu 2011a, 2011b)

WHY DO BUDGET PUNCTUATIONS OCCUR? INSTITUTIONAL APPROACH

Faced with numerous observations of budget punctuations that incrementalism did not predict, scholars have attempted to learn why such budget punctuations occur in the first place. Jones, Sulkin, and Larsen (2003) present a very sophisticated analysis of policy choices under institutional settings to identify such potential causes for budget punctuations. They specifically raised two questions: What are the characteristics of output changes from human decision-making institutions? And are any of these output changes associated with heightened institutional frictions or conflicts?

COSTS INCURRED FROM HUMAN DECISION-MAKING INSTITUTIONS

In terms of the magnitude of institutional conflicts, the authors ranked a diverse set of institutions in the following order: markets, elections, and policy/budget processes. Institutional conflicts incur institutional costs, two examples of which are decision and transaction costs. Decision costs are incurred by reaching an agreement, and transaction costs are incurred by complying with the contractual agreement. Markets are characterized by low transaction and decision costs, combined with freely available information (e.g., information in modern stock and bond markets). Elections are generally associated with relatively low transaction and decision costs, although less information is available for House elections than for presidential elections. Complex interactions among policy and budget actors explain policy and budget processes. As such, high decision and transaction costs feature them. The decision and transaction costs explain the bounded rationality of decision makers in previous chapters.

INSTITUTIONAL COSTS AND CHARACTERISTICS OF DIFFERENT DECISION OUTPUTS

Jones, Sulkin, and Larsen (2003) offer a very insightful framework to predict what types of output changes are associated with markets, elections, and policy/budget changes. First, they discuss what would happen in a hypothetically fully efficient decision-making setting such as a competitive market economy. Decision makers under the cost-free institutional settings can process all information flowing from their decision environments. Therefore, output or decision results are likely to be a function of all the information they receive from their decision environments. More detailed discussions of this procedure are beyond the scope of this book, but one interesting observation is that the statistical distributions of the output changes in market systems tend to be normally distributed. For instance, empirical analysis of the Dow-Jones Industrial Average indicated that the average was closer to normal distributions. Here again, discussion of distributions of output changes associated with elections and policy/budget processes is beyond this book's scope. One thing is clear, however. Output changes from elections featured leptokurtic distributions with high peaks around the mean values of election-to-election swings (i.e., minimal changes across years) and more sudden, dramatic election-to-election changes. Output changes from policy and budget processes were characterized by Paretian distributions with much steeper peaks around mean values of policy and budget changes (i.e., incremental budget changes) and extremely large policy and budget changes. In sum, high institutional costs are likely to lead to sudden, dramatic budget changes—that is, budget punctuations. The following section shows a simple example.

AN EXAMPLE: INSTITUTIONAL COSTS AND BUDGET PUNCTUATIONS

Let us take an illustrative example based on Jones and Baumgartner (2005a). Suppose a state department of transportation is planning to construct a new road leading to a big manufacturing plant within its jurisdiction. Of course, the company and related industries that might benefit from the products of the company would lobby strongly for quick implementation of the road construction plan. Others, such as Sierra Club members, might oppose its implementation. This might incur some institutional costs because decision costs might increase to reach an agreement. In addition, the state department might face the numerous institutional rules detailed in Part I. When overall institutional costs are high, the department might not make the effort to implement the plan. If there is strong mobilization of the groups supporting the plan, however, and its initiative is more powerful than opposing forces the department can ride on the bandwagon effect. In that case, institutional costs will suddenly decrease. What happens? Of course, the department can suddenly mobilize to implement the plan. If it is successful, there will be a sudden budget allocation for the project and attendant budget punctuation (see also Boushey 2010 for an excellent analysis of punctuations in state policy adoption for the past 100 years).

WHY DO BUDGET PUNCTUATIONS OCCUR? INFORMATION PROCESSING APPROACH

Disproportionate information-processing theory presents a very comprehensive explanation of why there are budget punctuations, improving upon *both* incrementalism and budget punctuations (known as punctuated equilibrium theory). Surprisingly, the reason for budget punctuations is almost the same as that for incremental budget changes. This is a highly significant advance in the budgeting literature.

DISPROPORTIONATE INFORMATION-PROCESSING OR INDICATOR LOCK

In budget processes, budget decision makers tend to lock onto one specific indicator that functions as a heuristic for future decision making. Due to bounded rationality, decision makers leave some aspects of environments unmonitored, unattended to. Errors in their decisions due to the ignored factors will accumulate, and episodic adjustments will eventually follow. Budget decision makers suddenly realize that previously disregarded facets of the environment are relevant for budget choices. They cannot ignore them anymore and must suddenly incorporate them into budget processes. Choice is attention-driven because budget decision makers suddenly reflect the ignored facets of the budget environment in budget choices. This occurs because they pay selective attention to the facets at a certain point in the budget process. Incrementalism failed to recognize the full implications of this mechanism of budget dynamics. This mechanism is called *disproportionate* information processing because budget decision makers now pay disproportionately heavier attention to the previously ignored factors. When budget decision makers do so, there are likely to be episodic but dramatic budget adjustments (Jones 2003; Jones and Baumgartner 2005a; 2005b, 115–32).

AN EXAMPLE: DISPROPORTIONATE INFORMATION PROCESSING AND BUDGET PUNCTUATIONS

A simple illustration explains the dynamic process more easily. Assume that state agency budgeters obtain information on inputs from their program beneficiaries, shifting partisan configurations, forecasts of revenues available for their agencies, changing gubernatorial policy priorities, changing workloads, rising input costs, changing target populations, and so on. Due to bounded rationality or limited information-processing capacity, budgeters lock onto one specific indicator with which they are familiar, in what is known as disproportionate information processing or indicator lock. In the above case, the state budgeters might have continuously disregarded the inputs from their program beneficiaries. At some point during state budget processes, they can no longer ignore the inputs and suddenly pay disproportionately heavier attention to the inputs from the beneficiary groups. Therefore, sudden, dramatic budget changes are likely to take place because they might allocate higher budgets for the beneficiary groups. Disproportionate information-processing theory further contends that institutional costs incurred by institutional conflicts further augment the disproportionate information processing (i.e., the institutional approach introduced above) and thus increase the likelihood of budget punctuations. At this point, readers should note that budget punctuations also mean that budget environmental factors are reflected in budget outcomes *but* in a delayed manner.

DISPROPORTIONATE INFORMATION-PROCESSING AS A COMPREHENSIVE THEORY

According to incrementalism, budget decision makers pay virtually no attention to environmental factors. Disproportionate information-processing theory suggests that they do pay attention to the environmental factors but in a selective and delayed manner. The greatest contribution of disproportionate information-processing theory is combining both incrementalism and punctuated equilibrium theory (i.e., budget punctuations). In the above case, assume that the weight for the inputs from beneficiary groups is 0.9, while the weight for all other four factors (assume just four factors) is 0.025 for each. If budget decision makers pay 90 percent of their attention (e.g., weight of 0.9) to the inputs from the groups, they are highly likely to reflect a substantial portion of the signal from the groups into budget choices. This will result in sudden budget punctuations. In the same case, all other four factors are virtually ignored, and the mean value of budget changes associated with the four variables will be close to zero due to the insignificant weights. These cases will translate into more frequent observations of mean budget changes close to zero changes because about 80 percent of all observations (four of five factors) weighted by 0.025 that is close to zero. In other words, 0.025 times each of the four factors will be mathematically close to zero and about 80 percent of budget environmental factors will be associated with almost zero changes. Therefore, modal observations of budget changes will be found around mean values close to zero budget changes. There will be high peaks around mean budget changes in budget change distributions. At the same time, about

20 percent of cases (e.g., inputs from beneficiary groups) will be weighted by a factor of 0.9, which is closer to one. This means that the original values of the budget inputs from the beneficiary groups will be reflected in the budget change distributions. The values will show up as big changes rather than the modal observations of zero budget changes. Disproportionate information-processing theory thus explains the incremental budget changes as well. Therefore, the greatest contribution of disproportionate information-processing theory is that it clarifies that bounded rationality causes *both* incremental budget changes and budget punctuations (for more details, see Ryu 2011a, 11–31).

REILLUMINATION OF EARLIER CASES OF BUDGET PUNCTUATIONS

Of course, there are challenges to disproportionate information-processing theory. For instance, Berkman and Reenock (2004) present empirical findings somewhat contrary to disproportionate information processing, especially policy punctuations, but in line with incrementalism. They analyzed state agency consolidation data from 1950 to 1992, containing both incremental and comprehensive organizational changes. In no way, however, did incrementalism give way to punctuated, dramatic changes. Their study is provocative in that empirical findings were based on decades of state government data. Therefore, researchers need to more carefully investigate whether and how policy or budget punctuations take place. However, numerous earlier studies show how institutional settings can cause budget punctuations in a much more detailed manner. They also reveal how budget decision makers pay selective attention to external budget environmental factors and budget punctuations could take place in line with disproportionate information-processing theory.

HOW DO BUDGET OFFICERS PROCESS EXTERNAL POLITICAL FACTORS?

Natchez and Bupp's (1973) study (see Chapter 13 in Part III) on Atomic Energy Commission programs revealed that the nuclear weapons program enjoyed higher priority around 1970, attributable to the great thermonuclear debate that took place more than ten years earlier. Jones, Sulkin, and Larsen (2003) indicate that small amendments to the Social Security Act in 1939 resulted in dramatic program benefit expansion ten years later in the early 1950s. These are typical examples of budget punctuations where external budget factors were suddenly reflected in budget outcomes years after the factors were first introduced.

HOW DO BUDGET OFFICERS PROCESS COURT RULINGS?

Straussman (1986) shows how rights-based budgeting (see Chapter 6 in Part I for details on rights-based budgeting) could affect state and local budgets. He also developed a framework that describes how agency bureaucrats reacted to budget-related information flowing from budget environments, in this case court-mandated standards. For instance, courts mandated state agencies to redress harsh conditions of state and local prisons pursuant to the Eighth Amendment prohibiting cruel and unusual punishment. There were several scenarios of agency reactions to court litigations, but some of them strongly lent support to disproportionate information processing. As noted in Chapter 6, there are more recent cases of rights-based budgeting, so these somewhat dated but very relevant scenarios warrant our renewed attention.

Scenario 1

If agencies agreed with the policy intent in court decisions, they were more likely to implement them because courts' objectives of compliance and agencies' objectives of budget expansion were compatible. Judges typically facilitated negotiations between the involved parties, which often resulted in some variation of plaintiffs' demands. Prison conditions in Rhode Island in the late 1970s support this assumption. A district court decision in 1977 to address the violation of the Eighth Amendment by the state's security facility was implemented without significant resistance. Legislative resistance was also minimal because some federal monies were used to defray parts of increased budget costs of compliance.

Unfortunately, however, court decisions were not implemented to the satisfaction of the courts because some contingencies different from the above scenario might take place. The passage of time allowed both budget offices and legislatures to assess the consequences of noncompliance. In addition, factors not directly related to the litigations might develop, such as an intergovernmental dispute. In this case, both compliance and budgetary expansion were more problematical. The *Holt v. Sarver* (1969) decision in Arkansas illustrates this scenario. In the long run, state agencies were not able to persuade legislatures to appropriate required funds. It took several years for the state agencies to implement the court policy intent. In no way was this intent "incrementally" implemented. It took at least several years before the state agencies seriously accounted for the court ruling in their budget decisions.

Scenario 2

A second scenario involved court litigations as a threat to agencies. Agencies were concerned about nonbudgetary issues that as courts encroached on executive budgetary discretion, executive agencies might not be able to expand their budgets. Ohio's prison case, *Chapman v. Rhodes* (1977), exemplifies this scenario. The director of the Department of Rehabilitation and Correction in Ohio was opposed to the policy intent in the court decision. He believed that judges were not the allies of the administrators and the court decision exacerbated the difficulty of his negotiations with the state legislature. The result, of course, was a significantly delayed implementation of the court's decisions.

Scenario 3

A third situation developed fairly quickly (one to three years) after the beginning of litigations where defendant executive agencies were opposed to the *policy* of the court rulings. Agencies were overtly delaying the implementation of the rulings, in relation to the severity of policy objections and the extent of judicial involvement. The degree of resistance was also dependent on alternative programmatic options available to agencies. In court cases involving school desegregation, delays became routine responses to court rulings. While agencies might sit on the fence to see what would happen in the first scenario, in this case agencies explicitly objected to the policy content of court decisions.

Scenario 4

When agencies were opposed to the policy and three or more years had passed since the onset of litigations, a fourth situation took place. If the policy shift and attendant resource reallocation from the court decisions were much larger than expected, the legislature or executive was likely to resist the implementation. Overcrowding conditions in local jails was a typical example of this scenario.

These cases illustrate that administrators are likely to give selective attention to budget-related information from budget environments and that their reactions to the information are highly delayed, as suggested by disproportionate information-processing theory. Without doubt, when they implement court orders several years later, there will be sudden budget punctuations. Compiling and analyzing more recent court cases illustrating budget punctuations would be a significant future research agenda. Readers can also collect more recent cases showing how external budget factors are incorporated into budget outcomes in a delayed manner and investigate the reason.

CHAPTER SUMMARY

- **Controversies on the Magnitude of Budget Changes**

Agreement on budget bases for agencies and their fair share results in agencies' budget moderation. Budget moderation leads to highly stable budget change patterns. However, some early studies revealed that agency budget requests were much larger than incremental changes (changes less than 30 percent).

Scholars have reported that dramatic budget changes (much larger than those envisioned in incrementalism and even by its critics) take place in various governmental budget changes.

- **Approaches to Explaining Dramatic Budget Punctuations**

There are two main approaches to explaining dramatic budget punctuations: an institutional approach and disproportionate information-processing theory.

(1) An institutional approach to explaining budget punctuations first indicates that the magnitude of institutional costs such as decision and transaction costs differs across different institutional settings. Markets and elections are characterized by relatively lower institutional costs. In contrast, policy and budget processes are marked by high institutional conflicts and costs. In institutional settings with higher institutional costs, there were more frequent observations of dramatic budget punctuations.

(2) Disproportionate information-processing theory is the most comprehensive theory, combining both incrementalism and punctuated equilibrium theory. Due to

bounded rationality, budget decision makers tend to ignore certain facets of budget-related information flowing from budget environments. At a certain point in temporal budget processes, they can no longer ignore the previously disregarded facets and must suddenly incorporate them into budget choices. This sudden, selective attention to the facets results in budget punctuations.

• Reillumination of Earlier Cases of Budget Punctuations

Many early studies have shown in a much more detailed manner whether and how policy or budget punctuations take place. One promising research agenda on dispro-portionate information processing and attendant budget punctuations is the so-called rights-based budgeting. Straussman's (1986) various scenarios on how state agencies process state court rulings into their agency budgets are worth our new attention.

16 Budget-Maximizing Bureaucrats

Agency bureaucrats are likely to maximize their bureau budgets based on their superior information about bureau budget and program details. In most cases, their legislative supervisors (or sponsors) do not have such detailed information. When agency bureaucrats have accurate data on the amount of resources their legislative supervisors would allow for their bureau programs and how much cost is incurred from delivering the programs, they will attempt to obtain the maximum resources possible. Previous chapters showed how agency bureaucrats attempted to increase their bureau budgets, but their attempts were primarily based on political deliberation and experience. Instead, budget-maximizing bureaucrats in this chapter attempt to maximize their bureau budgets based on their superior information capacity. This chapter specifically discusses these issues:

- Budget Moderation, Budget Expansion, and Budget Maximization
- Niskanen's Model of Budget-Maximizing Bureaucrats
- Critiques of the Niskanen Model

BUDGET MODERATION, BUDGET EXPANSION, AND BUDGET MAXIMIZATION

According to budgetary incrementalism, budget actors are self-moderating when they request budgets for their organizations, although they are likely to request resources that are slightly more than what they might actually need. Typical budget change patterns are 5–10 percent, seldom larger than 30 percent. Highly stabilized budget change patterns are substantially attributable to bounded rationality, as discussed in previous chapters. Budget decision makers are limited in their capacity to process all budget-related information, so they do not consider much of the information in making budget choices. Instead, they tend to form mutual consensus on fair shares for all budget actors, which are likely to be close to their current budget levels or budget bases. The concept of fair shares does minimize the computational burden of budget actors and potential political conflicts that might resurface if they attempt to scrutinize all budget alternatives. In addition, budget actors learn from their political experience that requesting slightly increased budgets is the most beneficial strategy for their organizational budgets. The stable budget change patterns are augmented by political and legal institutions, leading to marginal budget changes.

As also discussed in previous chapters, some budget actors, such as executive agencies, learned that when they request more money, they are likely to receive more in the "long run." Numerous studies showed that executive agencies are highly acquisitive and tend to pad their budget requests based on their political maneuvering.

All these approaches are in one way or another related to the concept of budget-maximizing bureaucrats. In the literature of public budgeting, however, the term "budget-maximizing bureaucrats" refers to the bureaucrats who retain monopolistic power over accurate information on bureau programs and budgets. In addition, they are maximizing (as opposed to optimizing) their bureau budgets even based on their "rational" computation. Their motive of maximizing, thus, is quite rational rather than political or boundedly rational.

Niskanen's Model of Budget-Maximizing Bureaucrats

Niskanen (1971) contended in *Bureaucracy and Representative Government* that much of governmental budget growth is attributable to government bureaucrats' budget-maximizing behavior. A bureau manager's utility typically increases in proportion to the bureau's budget, and the manager is likely to maximize that budget. The bureau has a tremendous strategic advantage over elected legislative sponsors due mainly to its monopolistic power over the information on bureau programs and budgets. In addition, it is assumed that the bureaucratic agents are aware of legislative sponsors' willingness to pay for any output level. The result is an oversupply of bureau programs and social inefficiency.

Niskanen's model is based on several assumptions (Miller and Moe 1983; Niskanen 1971; 1991, 16–17; 1994; 2003). First, the bureau is a monopolistic supplier of bureau programs. Legislative sponsors, too, are monopoly demanders for the programs (i.e., monopsonists), such that most bureaucrats face the monopoly demander rather than ultimate consumers of their bureau services. Second, the bureau and legislative committees are in a hierarchical relationship. The committees subject to the full legislature can make final budgetary decisions. The bureau has primary advantages over the cost information on service production, but legislative sponsors' budget powers are further weakened by two factors. First, prior budget decisions reveal more information on sponsors' demand function, and agency bureaucrats can take advantage of that information for their budget maximization. Second, the sponsors tend to monitor service production only when it serves the specific interests of their constituents, which leaves substantial portions of bureau budgets less carefully examined.

Figure 16.1 presents a diagrammatic explanation of the key assumptions in Niskanen's model of budget-maximizing bureaucrats. The thicker portion of the inverted U-shape curve is the legislative sponsors' budget-total evaluation curve, which traces the relationship between output levels of bureau services and legislative willingness to approve budgets for the service levels. Therefore, Niskanen's model investigates

Figure 16.1 **Budget Maximizing by Government Bureaucrats**

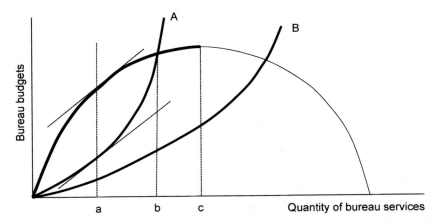

legislative monopoly buyers' demand schedules in terms of a *total* social benefit curve. Total benefits from bureau services grow at a decreasing rate up to a peak point. The slope of the total benefits curve will get less steep as the quantity of bureau services increases. It becomes zero at point "*c*," where marginal benefits from bureau services are zero.

In contrast, bureaucratic providers' cost curves increase as the quantity of bureau services rises at an increasing rate. In Figure 16.1, curve A shows a relationship between the quantity of bureau services and the bureau's production costs. According to the rule of efficiency-maximizing resource allocation, societal utility is maximized when the marginal cost of a certain good equals the marginal benefit from that good. Similarly, when marginal benefits from bureau programs are equal to the marginal costs of producing the programs, social efficiency is maximized. At point "*a*" in Figure 16.1, the marginal cost of producing bureau programs and the marginal benefit from the total benefit evaluation curve are equal; that is, the slopes of the two curves are identical. At point "*a*," social *net* benefit, measured as the distance between the evaluation curve and the total cost curve, is maximized, as readers can visualize. Niskanen's fundamental question was whether bureaucrats are willing to deliver the socially optimal quantity of bureau services and live with the budget level associated with the total benefit evaluation curve (see also Cullis and Jones 2009, 389–90).

According to Niskanen, the answer is clearly no. Bureaucrats are least likely to reveal their true production cost curve to legislative sponsors. For example, under the cost curve A in Figure 16.1, bureaucrats might pursue the output level of bureau services at point "*b*" and seek bureau budgets higher than the budgets associated with the socially optimal output level (e.g., point "*a*"). Under this condition, they cannot opt for the highest budget level associated with point "*c*" because, in that case, bureau budgets approved by legislative sponsors would not be sufficient to cover the cost of service production. This condition is denoted "cost-constrained" bureau budgets. If a cost curve looks like curve B instead, then bureaucrats can pursue the maximum bureau budgets associated with point "*c*" because production costs are now below the total budget evaluation curve. This condition is described as a "demand-constrained" bureau budget. In both scenarios, bureaucrats try to maximize their bureau budgets. The result is always an oversupply of bureau services and inflated bureau budgets, with efficiency loss. According to Niskanen, this mechanism explains why government budgets expand. The basic motive of bureau managers is based on rational deliberation of utility, yet rational computation does not necessarily result in efficiency maximization but entails budget maximization.

CRITIQUES OF THE NISKANEN MODEL

There are two lines of critique to the Niskanen model.

THEORETICAL CHALLENGES

Despite its elaborate mechanism, Niskanen's model has been exposed to numerous earlier critiques (Lynn 1991, 59–83), which Kiewiet (1991, 151–62) succinctly summarizes. Government bureaus deliver essentially the same services with a higher price tag than with private firms. However, the inefficiency might be the result of legislative sponsors who enjoy the poorly managed bureaucracies. The inefficient service delivery can ironically provide opportunities for their constituents. The bureaucratic inefficiency or waste might not be singularly attributable to bureaucrats.

In addition, the bureaucratic inefficiency or oversupply is less likely when citizens are free to register their preferences for bureau services by voting with their feet in a Tiebout-like world (refer to Chapter 17 in Part IV for definitions of these concepts). The quasi-market pressure from footloose consumer-voters would minimize oversupply and maximize social efficiency. Many studies have indicated that bureaucratic (e.g., governmental) competition at the local level was negatively correlated with local government expenditures. An earlier empirical study also supports Kiewiet's critique. Competition, as reflected in multiple providers and by a wider range of choice for the tax burden of local government, restrains the size of government and thereby enhances the ability of voters and politicians to control the budget maximization of local bureaucrats (Schneider 1989).

Another line of critique is directed at the assumption that bureaucrats retain a monopolistic power over the information of service delivery. If bureaucrats have such a price-discriminating monopoly power, the Niskanen model maintains some explanatory power. Under a bilateral monopoly power (e.g., information power shared between bureaucrats and legislative sponsors), the oversupply of bureau programs is less likely (Casas-Pardo and Puchades-Navarro 2001). In a similar vein, Miller and Moe (1983) revealed that when legislative committees were more representative of the full legislature and were concealing their true preference for bureau programs, bureaucrats were much less likely to maximize bureau budgets.

EMPIRICAL OBSERVATIONS

Another group of critiques has considered whether bureaucrats actually do maximize their bureau budgets. Many scholars have contended that bureaucrats are not single-minded in maximizing their bureau budgets in the first place (Avant 1993; Blais and Dion 1991; Wood 1993). More recent empirical observations strongly support these scholarly propositions that state agency bureaucrats do not always pursue budget expansion (Sigelman 1986). For instance, Bowling, Cho, and Wright (2004) used four decades of survey data with state agency administrators, spanning 1964 to 1998, to show that agency administrators' preferences for budget expansion substantially varied over the survey period. Most notably, lots of agency administrators did not pursue budget expansion in their agency budgets or in their state's overall budgets. In fact, frequently agency bureaucrats have even been minimizing or disciplining.

Ryu et al. (2007, 2008) reported that almost 80 percent of state agency heads pursued budget increases of less than 10 percent. Dolan (2002) reported similar findings based on multiple surveys conducted in 1996 and 1997 with respect to Senior Executive Service (SES) members in the federal government. She investigated whether federal employees actually tried to maximize their bureau budgets. Senior Executive Service members might either mirror the attitude of the general public in terms of bureau budgets or inflate their bureau budgets as predicted in Niskanen's model. However, Dolan found that the federal administrators were more likely to discipline their budget aspirations and preferred less spending than even the general public in almost all spending categories. Most surprisingly, they preferred smaller budgets even for their bureau programs.

CHAPTER SUMMARY

- **Niskanen's Model of Budget-Maximizing Bureaucrats**

Niskanen's theory of budget-maximizing bureaucrats is based on the assumption that agency bureaucrats tend to maximize their bureau budgets based on their rational computation. This approach is in stark contrast to incrementalism in which agency bureaucrats pad their agency budgets based on their political experience.

(1) Niskanen's model assumes that executive bureaus are monopolistic suppliers of governmental programs and legislative sponsors are monopoly demanders for the programs.

(2) If legislative sponsors reveal more information with their demand for the programs, agency bureaucrats can take advantage of the information for maximizing their bureau budgets.

(3) A socially efficient level of bureau budgets will be obtained when legislative sponsors' marginal benefit from bureau programs equals agency bureaucrats' marginal cost of delivering the programs. However, agency bureaucrats tend to take advantage of their superior information power over bureau programs and budgets. As a result, bureau budgets are likely to be larger than the budgets associated with the socially efficient level of service delivery.

- **Critiques of the Niskanen Model**

There have been numerous theoretical critiques of Niskanen's model.

(1) Budget maximization is also attributable to legislative sponsors' prefer-

ence for poorly managed bureaucracies because they offer opportunities for their constituents.

(2) When consumer-voters are more footloose and shop around governments for the best services, the ability of the voters and politicians can control budget-maximization of local bureaucrats.

(3) When bureaucrats and legislative sponsors share information power, the oversupply of bureau programs is less likely. In addition, when legislative sponsors concealed their true demand for bureau programs, bureaucrats were less likely to maximize their bureau budgets.

•   Empirical Findings
Numerous empirical findings on federal and state budget data indicate that agency bureaucrats are not maximizing their bureau budgets as much as Niskanen predicted.

PART IV

PUBLIC CHOICE AND TAXATION

17 Public Goods and Public Choice

Public finance scholars have developed a field called public choice. The theory of public choice analyzes how the amount of public goods is selected, especially in local jurisdictions. Its main framework is demand-and-supply schedules for public goods based on microeconomics. The theory also accounts for political, legal, and institutional conditions that might affect the fiscal choice over public goods. Therefore, the public choice theory is often called the theory of political economy. This chapter investigates the following issues:

- Political Economy of Fiscal Choice: *The Calculus of Consent*
- Efficient Provision of Public Goods
- Political Institutions and Fiscal Choice
- Service Diversity and Fiscal Choice

POLITICAL ECONOMY OF FISCAL CHOICE: *THE CALCULUS OF CONSENT*

Buchanan and Tullock in their seminal 1962 book, *The Calculus of Consent*, developed an interesting framework to analyze the mechanism of fiscal choice. The book's fundamental assumption is that individuals are primary decision-making units and their motive of decision-making is utility maximization. In addition, they are well informed and make rational choices. However, some groups apart from their individual members are also highly swayed by many other considerations. In their political behavior, they are not perfectly informed or rational.

More specifically, Buchanan and Tullock (1962) suggested two models to explain the mechanism of fiscal choice. According to a logical model, individual constitutional choice is closer to rational choice models. Individuals follow utility-maximizing rules of behavior and are fully informed and rational. According to an operational model, observations of the real world often refute the logical model. Buchanan and Tullock contended that the logical, economic model could not explain all aspects of the complicated political process; it could explain only certain elements of modern political activities (1962, 298–300).

Buchanan and Tullock elaborated their view of the nature of fiscal choice from the perspective of two conflicting costs. The costs of collective action are the sum of political externalities plus the transaction costs of collective choices. Any political process except for unanimity might incur external costs. If the majority of citizens in a certain jurisdiction voted for a tax increase to finance increased public services, external costs might be incurred. Some individuals who opposed the measure might be dissatisfied with the collective decision, but they must bear the political externalities and external costs as a result of collective choices. The probability that individuals must bear the external costs declines as the percentage of the community population required for collective choices increases. As the percentage rises, the individuals are less likely to belong to the losing coalition of voters. Under the extreme case of unanimity, no individual would be forced to bear the external costs. If the external costs are the only cost incurred from reaching collective choices, a unanimity rule would be the optimal voting mechanism.

Unfortunately, political transaction costs are incurred from inducing unanimous agreement on unattractive policy alternatives. These are called decision-making costs. They tend to increase because of the time needed to reach unanimous agreement. In addition, some individuals might withhold their consent until they receive some side payments from those individuals who strongly demand a certain alternative. This type of individual strategic action also increases decision costs. Of course, rational individuals will choose the decision rule that minimizes both external and decision costs. One caveat is that cost functions associated with each decision rule vary depending on the nature of decision issues and personal preferences (Buchanan and Tullock 1962, 63–116; Cullis and Jones 2009, 109; Forrester 2001; Forte 2012; Holcombe 2005; Hyman 2011, 197–99).

Wagner (2012a) introduces the key point in *The Calculus* from a slightly different angle. The mechanism operating in marketplaces cannot singularly translate into collective decision processes due mainly to the nonscalability of collective actions within democratic settings. In a small town with a small number of representatives, the relationship between the population and the representatives might be scalable. For instance, each representative might know his or her constituents. However, a town with larger population might need more representatives. In that case, the relationship between representatives and their represented populations might be scalable but the relationship between the representatives might not be. This aspect differs from the market mechanism. *The Calculus* sought an economic logic inherent in the complex structure of the American constitutional structure, which was polycentric, not monocentric. An important corollary is that polycentric politics cannot be reasonably reduced to some median preference. In a sense, the public choice perspective in *The Calculus* is a comprehensive view of public decision making from the perspective of individuals acting simultaneously both in marketplaces and in political organizations (Congleton 2012; Cullis and Jones 2009, 97–123; Forte 2012).

Some scholars harshly criticize one of the most important assumptions in *The Calculus*. Block (2010) is skeptical of the possibility of making an analogy between the market's dollar vote and the political ballot box vote in the first place. The price analogy in the marketplace, he contends, cannot be directly applied to political processes, and there is no self-interested reason why individuals might get involved in the public sector just to minimize costs. Despite the critiques, Forte (2012) supports *The Calculus* in that the logic of collective decision making in Buchanan and Tullock (1962) can be aptly applied to more complex institutional settings such as bicameral legislatures under interest groups' game-theoretical interactions. This nature of the collective-decision process places their theory in the center of public-sector economics. Decision costs incurred by bargaining suggest that the theory of public-sector economics must account for transaction costs. The external costs along with the transaction costs place the theory of public choice as a solid contracting game.

EFFICIENT PROVISION OF PUBLIC GOODS

As implied in Buchanan and Tullock's (1962) framework of collective decision making, public choice approaches have at least attempted to develop rational choice models to explain the mechanism of public goods. This section first explains what public goods are, and second what rationality means when providing public goods (e.g., the Lindhal equilibrium).

PUBLIC GOODS

Fisher (2007, 44) and Hyman (2011, 162) succinctly explain the nature of public goods, and details of their explanations are worth introduction in this chapter. Suppose there are three individuals in a local jurisdiction, A, B, and C. Note that public choice theorists often call them consumer-voters in that they can shop around local jurisdictions for the best package of services and taxation as discussed below. Further assume that their income schedules are $Income_C < Income_B < Income_A$. Figure 17.1 shows the demand schedules of the three consumer-voters for a public good: for instance, MB_A denotes marginal benefit that individual A enjoys from the public good. Since state and local government services are likely to be normal goods (i.e., as individuals' incomes grow, their demands for normal goods grow as well), individual A's demand for the public good will be highest, and individual C's demand will be lowest. Three marginal benefit curves therefore visualize the three different levels of demand for the public good. Even when all three individuals' incomes are the same, the demand schedules will hold true as long as A's demand is highest and C's demand is lowest (Fisher 2007, 44; Hyman 2011, 164–65).

Pure public goods are characterized by nonexcludability from and nonrivalry of consumption. Nonexcludability means that no individual can be excluded from enjoying the public good. Nonrivalry of consumption (or joint consumption) means that individual A enjoys benefits from the public good while individual B and individual C can still jointly consume the public good. A good example is public radio and television programs. They are mostly financed from voluntary contributions of listeners and viewers. Even when an individual does not pay for the service, he or she cannot be excluded from it. In addition, multiple individuals can jointly and simultaneously benefit from public radio and television programs (Cully and Jones 2009, 64–68; Hyman 2011, 169; Weimer and Vining 2011, 72–91).

Figure 17.1 **Fiscal Choice for Public Goods**

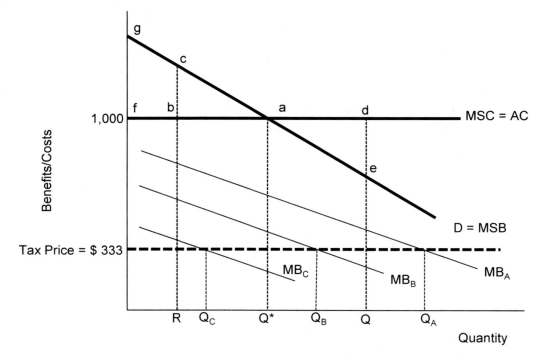

Especially due to the nonrivalry of consumption for public goods, social marginal benefit of a public good is the sum of individual marginal benefits from consuming one more unit of the public good. This means that marginal benefit curves for the three individuals should be vertically summed up to derive the social marginal benefit curve or the social demand curve for the public good (Fisher 2007, 40–43; Hyman 2011, 160–63; Weimer and Vining 2011, 73–76). In Figure 17.1, the social demand curve, D, is the same as the marginal social benefit curve for the public good, MSB. The marginal social benefit curve, as noted above, is the vertical summation of the three individual marginal benefit curves. This means that the three individuals separately enjoy a given amount of the public goods. For ease of analysis, further assume that the marginal social cost (MSC) of providing the public goods is fixed at $1,000. This also means that the average cost (AC) of providing the public goods is $1,000. By construction, a social equilibrium is held at Q^* amount of the public goods with the marginal cost of production at $1,000. The equilibrium, where marginal social benefits equal marginal social costs, is the most efficient condition for producing Q^* amount of the public good (Samuelson 1954, 1955; Thompson 2007, 1074–75).

However, a common problem associated with public goods is that they will be underprovided if delivery of public goods is decided solely by the private market system due mainly to the free-rider problem (Cullis and Jones 2009, 71–8; Hyman 2011, 168–70; Samuelson 1954, 1955). In Figure 17.1, individual B and individual C are highly likely to conceal their true preference for the public goods because they learned that individual A would demand the public goods anyway. Then, they might think they should wait until individual A provides the public goods at his or her expense. In Figure 17.1, MB_A (i.e., individual A's demand schedule) does not intersect with the marginal social cost curve by construction, but readers can simply think of a case where it intersects with the cost curve. If it does intersect with the cost curve, readers can find that the quantity of the public goods is much smaller than the socially efficient quantity Q^*. This situation will also result in built-in deadweight loss (Rosen and Gayer 2010, 61–64; Samuelson 1955; Thompson 2007, 1074–75). Readers are referred to Weimer and Vining (2011, 81–85) for more details of the deadweight loss. Samuelson (1954, 1955) also asserted that no decentralized pricing system can guarantee the optimum condition of collective consumption (Fisher 2007, 41–43).

EFFICIENT PROVISION OF PUBLIC GOODS: LINDHAL EQUILIBRIUM

Despite the efficiency loss in the provision of public goods, public finance scholars have investigated whether there might be any conditions that should prevent the free-rider problem and its attendant deadweight loss. What if the community where the three individuals in Figure 17.1 live is small enough for all three individuals to know each individual's preference and income level very well? In that case, the three individuals can police potential free-riding attempts. Then, the three individuals could pay certain portions of the total $1,000 cost incurred from providing the public goods. For instance, once the local community can identify each individual's benefit share, then each individual can pay a tax proportional to his or her share of benefits from the public goods. In Figure 17.1, assume that individual A's benefit share is $450, individual B's is $350, and individual C's is $200 when the jurisdiction delivers Q^* amount of the public good. Then each individual will pay a tax equal to his or her benefit share. This condition is called the Lindhal equilibrium (Cullis and Jones 2009, 78–80; Fisher 2007, 43–45; Gramlich 1990, 40–41; Hyman 2011, 164–65). Under the Lindhal equilibrium, the social surplus will be equal to the area *afg* in Figure 17.1.

MODELS OF DEMAND FOR PUBLIC GOODS

Public finance scholars have developed formal models to explain what factors affect the demand curve in Figure 17.1. Three studies stand out: Barr and Davis's 1966 study on "an elementary political and economic theory of the expenditures of local governments"; Borcherding and Deacon's 1972 study on "the demand for the services of nonfederal governments"; and Bergstrom and Goodman's 1973 study on "private demands for public goods."

Inman (1979) succinctly summarized the models into Equation 17.1 (see the next paragraph for major factors of demand for public goods):

$$I + \tau z = \Sigma_i \tau c_i (1 - m_i) G_i + Y \qquad (17.1)$$

where I is an individual's before-tax income, τ is the individual's net share of per capita taxes, z is lump-sum aid per capita, Σ is a sum operator, c is the unit cost of producing a public good, $(1 - m_i)$ denotes how much the individual's tax burden is reduced by matching share of matching grants (readers are referred to Chapter 21 in part V for more details), G_i is a public good i, and Y is after-tax income of the resident. τ is further defined as (b/B) π where b/B is the ratio of the individual's tax base to the average tax base in the local jurisdiction where the individual lives, and π is the individual's net burden per dollar of local taxes after deductions and credits.

Equation 17.1 is fairly complex, but readers need to focus on two factors that influence the level of public expenditures: income and tax burden of an individual living in a local jurisdiction. The measures of tax burden in the above equation, τc $(1 - m_i)$, are generally defined as the tax price of the individual. In particular, the ratio of the individual's tax base to the average tax base in the local jurisdiction, (b/B) in τ, and $(1 - m_i)$ have been the most frequently employed tax price measures in the literature of public finance (Duncombe and Yinger 1998, 2009; Fisher 2007, 77–81).

In general, an inverse relationship exists between tax price and the quantity of public goods. In contrast, as an individual's income rises his or her demand for public goods also increases. This implies that most public goods are normal goods. Empirical findings indicate that the price elasticity of demand for public goods ranges between –.25 and –50. This means that if the tax price for public goods declines by 1 percent, the demand for the public goods will increase by about 0.25 to 0.50 percent. The income elasticity of demand for public goods ranges between 0.60 and 0.80. This means that if an individual's income rises by 1 percent, his or her demand for public goods will increase by about 0.60–0.80 percent (Barr and Davis 1966; Bergstrom and Goodman 1973; Borcherding and Deacon 1972; Duncombe and Yinger 1998, 2009; Fernandez and Rogerson 2001; Fisher 2007, 82–84; Gramlich and Rubinfeld 1982; Merrifield 2000; Poterba 1997; Turnbull and Mitias 1999). Readers are referred to Chapter 21 in Part V on how $(1 - m_i)$ affects the demand for public goods. In short, when the local tax price is reduced by matching share m_i, the demand tends to grow.

POLITICAL INSTITUTIONS AND FISCAL CHOICE

In real-world cases, however, the Lindhal equilibrium raises one lingering question. Individual residents are most likely to live in a geographically large and dispersed community. When the community is too large for the residents to know all the details of other residents' preferences and income levels, it is unlikely that each individual will be inclined to reveal his or her true preference for the public good (Hyman 2011, 168–70). In addition, it cannot be guaranteed that each individual in the above case will sincerely vote if the community adopts voting as a way of revealing individual preferences for the public goods. If an individual knows how much others demand the public good, he or she will behave strategically, one example of which is the free-riding problem discussed above. Second, it takes a very long time to identify mutually agreeable Lindhal prices (Cullis and Jones 2009, 80; Rosen and Gayer 2010, 110).

Since the transaction cost of identifying each individual's marginal benefit (i.e., Lindhal price) might be too high, the community in Figure 17.1 is more likely to impose an equal share of contributions to deliver the public good. This method of equal payment schedules is what governments frequently adopt as a way of financing public goods. In the above case, if the local jurisdiction decided to levy an equal amount of tax price on all three individuals (e.g., $333 = $1,000/3), the three individuals' desired quantities of the public good will be Q_C, Q_B, and Q_A, respectively. Under this condition, if the governmental jurisdiction decides to provide the same quantity level to each individual, each with a different preference for the quantity of the public goods, some compromise has to be made by voting (Fisher 2007, 55–57). At this moment, readers might notice that the rational choice models deviate somewhat from marketplaces (efficient solution) toward political institutions (less efficient solution) as Buchanan and Tullock's *The Calculus of Consent* has posited. Then, the question pops up: Whose preferences for the public goods dominate under political institutions?

MAJORITY VOTING AND THE MEDIAN VOTER

The most common voting mechanism is majority voting, such as a local property tax-rate referendum or the election of officials. Fisher (2007, 57–60) provides a succinct and clear example of typical results of majority voting. In Figure 17.1, if the local jurisdiction chooses between Q_A and Q_B, Individual A will vote for Q_A but Individual B will vote for Q_B. Individual C will support Q_B because it is closer to his or her preferred quantity. Thus, Q_B will get the majority vote. If the jurisdiction chooses between Q_B and Q_C, Q_B will still get the majority vote using similar logic. One caveat here is that Q_B gets the majority vote not because it is the most preferred but because it is the only choice that can receive majority support.

One problem with majority voting is that winners might be different depending on the order in which alternatives are suggested or there might not be a clear-cut winner. This condition is highly likely, especially when voters do not show single-peaked preferences. If, for instance, an individual's utility from consuming a certain good decreases until it becomes extremely low and then it increases again, obviously there are two "peaks" in his or her utility or preference. In real-life majority voting, however, inconsistent or intransitive results might not take place. A typical downward-sloping marginal benefit curve (or demand curve) as shown in Figure 17.1 implies single-peaked preference (Cullis and Jones 2009, 105–6). Therefore, if all policy alternatives are represented along a single continuum, if all policy alternatives are voted on, and if voters vote based on their true preferences, then the final choice selected by majority vote will be the median of the alternatives.

In Figure 17.1, Q_B will be the median outcome that will be chosen from the majority voting. The case is somewhat unrealistic in that just one person is associated with each potential spending level. In a real-world situation, more voters might support each alternative. As long as the distribution of the frequency associated with the voters for each alternative is close to normal (i.e., bell-shaped curves), the median alternative is still likely to get the most votes by majority voting. The median voter theorem primarily explains voting procedures under participatory democracy. However, the theorem generally applies to a representative democracy as well. In particular, if elections are held often, then public officials tend to be pushed toward the median choice to stay in power (Cully and Jones 2009, 105–10; Fisher 2007, 60–62; Hyman 2011, 187–95; Kearns and Bartle 2001).

In his earlier study, Holcombe (1980) showed that the actual level of public expenditure tended to be close to the median voter's preferred level. Holcombe used referendum data on millage (property tax rate) increases in Michigan school districts in 1973 because property tax rates would translate into local expenditures. He calculated the median voter's preferred millage using the actual percentage of "yes" votes under the assumption that the millage data were normally distributed. He then compared the estimated median voter's preferred millage rate with actual millage rates chosen by the electorate and found no statistically significant difference between the two values: The median-preferred property tax rate was almost the same as actual property tax rates. In line with Holcombe's earlier finding, numerous surveys have consistently confirmed that voters prefer median levels of public expenditures (Fisher 2007, 62–64). Trimidas and Winer (2005) assert that the median voter theorem has been fading away somewhat in the public choice literature. Comparing several competing models to explain governmental budget growth, however, Maux (2009) concluded that the median voter's income and tax share prevail in the decision of the public good and tax package (see also Holcombe 1989).

BUDGET-MAXIMIZING BUREAUCRATS

Since Niskanen (1971) developed his model of budget-maximizing bureaucrats introduced in Chapter 16 in Part III, many similar models have been suggested. Romer and Rosenthal (1979a, 1979b, 1982) developed a monopoly model to analyze local government spending. They contend that providers of public goods, rather than consumer-voters or median voters, are more likely to dominate local budgets, similar to Niskanen's model. They further suggest that to better understand decision-making about public expenditures, researchers need to further analyze the process of political resource allocation. Specifically, Romer and Rosenthal's dominant bureaucrat model assumes that the actual expenditure level of public goods will usually be larger than the median voter's preferred level of demand for public expenditure (Romer and Rosenthal 1979a, 1982). Because there is no complete competition between suppliers of public goods and the information asymmetry between bureaucrats, and legislators and consumer-voters may prevail in reality, the median voter's preference cannot accurately depict the decision of the actual expenditure level for public goods even in local jurisdictions. Budget-maximizing bureaucrats with their better information of the true cost of service delivery threaten consumer-voters with the "reversion rate," or statutorily specified minimum service level, of public programs that may be triggered if consumer-voters do not vote for the proposal suggested by bureaucrats. This supply-side approach to local government expenditures assumes that the consequence of the threat is always the selection of a public-expenditure level that is higher than that preferred by the median voter (Romer and Rosenthal 1979a, 1982).

Romer and Rosenthal's original theory (1979a) is extremely complicated, so its synopsis is briefly introduced here. In Figure 17.1, the equilibrium for the locally delivered public goods was held at point "*a*." The equilibrium is assumed as the median-preferred spending level. If the reversion rate is larger than the median-preferred spending level, then the reversion rate will be chosen as the final expenditure level by a simple majority. In contrast, when the reversion rate is less than the median-preferred level, the final expenditure level varies but is larger than the latter. In Figure 17.1, the reversion level of public expenditures or quantity of public goods is denoted as R. When the bureaucratic budget-setter proposes a budget level that is larger than the median-preferred spending by the amount by which the median-preferred spending level exceeds the reversion rate, there will be no difference in consumer voter's surplus (i.e., the sum of consumer surplus is zero). In Figure 17.1, this condition denotes that the distance between points a and d is equal to the distance between points a and b. With the reversion budget, R, the loss in consumer surplus will be the triangular area abc. With the budget-setter's budget, Q, consumer surplus loss will be the triangular area ade, which will be equal to the area abc by construction. Hence, consumer voters will be indifferent to either the reversion rate or the setter's budget, because they will suffer from the same amount of consumer loss.

In contrast, if the budget-setter proposes a budget that is at least one dollar smaller than the proposed budget level Q, then the consumer-voter's surplus will be slightly larger than that when the reversion rate will be selected. In Figure 17.1, if the setter's budget is less than Q even by a dollar, the forgone consumer loss will be smaller than the triangular area ade, which is equal to the loss under the reversion budget. Therefore, consumer-voters will vote for the budget proposal smaller than the proposed budget level but larger than the median-preferred budget level (Fisher 2007, 66–69; Holcombe 1980; Romer and Rosenthal 1979a; Trimidas and Winer 2005). Thus, the reversion point drives consumer-voters to choose a budget level larger than that preferred by the median voter. This, they argue, is a strong, albeit partial, support for the monopolistic bureaucratic budget-setter model. The budget setter's behavior is also known as Leviathan bureaucratic monopolies (Cullis and Jones 2009, 439–40).

Despite some empirical support for the monopoly model (Romer and Rosenthal 1979a, 1982), there are some critiques of the model. Munley's 1984 study shows that when the reversion rate is not sufficiently low for bureaucrats to exploit voters, the actual level of spending is almost the same as the median voter's preferred level. Kiewiet (1991) issues some similar cautions for the monopoly model. While a negative correlation exists between the reversion rate and school district spending, there is no linear relationship between the reversion rate and the magnitude of spending. In other words, once the threat of closing schools is accounted for, low reversion points do not lead to an equivalent budget increase. Bureaucratic budget-setters might try to maximize budgets by exploiting the reversion rate. However, Kiewiet asserts that voters merely respond to whether school will be closed or not, rather than whether administrators might exploit the level of the reversion points. Overall, the monopoly model is not as strongly supported as the median voter theorem has been.

EFFECTS OF BUDGET INSTITUTIONS

Other scholars have contended that political, legal, and institutional procedures and conditions affect the decision about the level of public expenditures. Although the median voter theorem has been frequently employed to observe fiscal choice in local jurisdictions, it has been criticized for its negligence in accounting for other variables such as "political and institutional factors" in deciding public expenditures (Duncombe 1996; Fisher 2007, 81–82; Merrifield 1991, 2000; Mueller and Stratmann 2003; Noonan 2007; Rowley 1984; Trimidas and Winer 2005). In particular, such institutional factors as constitutional or statutory limitations on public spending, balanced budget requirements, and line-item veto power granted to the executive sometimes play significant roles in deciding the level of public expenditures (Abrams and Dougan 1986; Holtz-Eakin 1988; Merrifield 1991, 2000; Poterba 1994, 1995a, 1995b, 1996). Political environments surrounding decision-makers about public expenditures, such as political ideology, interest group activities, and legislative structures, play significant roles as well (Abrams and Dougan 1986; Alt and Lowry 1994; Becker 1983; Holtz-Eakin 1988; Merrifield 1991, 2000; Mueller and Murrell 1986; Poterba 1994, 1995b).

Based on the comprehensive review of literature and criticisms of the median voter theorem, Merrifield (1991, 2000) developed an alternative model that put more emphasis on political and institutional environments while controlling for major explanatory factors in the median voter model. As he shows, the political system is usually defined as a "conversion mechanism that transforms the preference of the median voter into the public policy" (Merrifield 2000, 26). Once researchers focused on the collective decision-making institutions, mean values (as a composite measure reflecting collective decision making) of explanatory factors for governmental spending, rather than the characteristics of the median voter, were viewed as more adequate variables for public expenditures. The approach using the mean values of the explanatory factors was called the ad hoc approach, which prevailed in the 1960s (Inman 1979, 272). Once again, readers might notice that the rational choice models based on the median voter are drifting somewhat toward political institutions (less efficient solution) as Buchanan and Tullock's *The Calculus of Consent* (1962) posited.

Turnbull and Mitias (1999) tested the extent to which the median voter model better explained governmental spending than did the mean value model with respect to government levels. The authors used county data from 437 county governments in five Midwestern states for the years 1970 and 1980, as well as samples from the forty-eight contiguous states for the same years. City-level data were drawn from another study done by the authors. In sum, they found that the median voter model had a stronger explanatory power for the lowest tier of government (e.g. cities). In contrast, they reported, "the ad hoc model dominates the median model for counties and states" (1999, 119). It is obvious that state and county governments have more-complicated institutional procedures than do city governments. Thus, it is no wonder that the ad hoc model explains fiscal choice of state and county governments better.

SERVICE DIVERSITY AND FISCAL CHOICE

As discussed in Figure 17.1, Q^* is the most efficient amount of public goods. With Q^* amount of the public goods, consumer surplus will be maximized at an amount equal to the area *agf*. Since it is virtually impossible to obtain this Lindahl equilibrium in real-world cases, most local jurisdictions rely on majority voting as indicated above. Typical results of majority voting are the amount of public goods, which the

median voter prefers. In Figure 17.1, the median voter's preferred am(
goods is Q_B. The problem is that Q_B is larger than the socially efficien
Therefore, majority voting does not necessarily render socially effici
of public goods.

In his trailblazing paper, however, Charles Tiebout (1956) suggested that the inefficiency associated with public goods could be resolved if consumer voters could move around subnational jurisdictions. Tiebout asserted that they can freely move around the jurisdictions and form groups that have similar preferences for public goods. If they do so, they can influence fiscal choices by participating in local political processes (e.g., voice) or by voting with their feet (exit). The result is that locally provided public goods can entail efficiency without majority voting (Cullis and Jones 2009, 372–73; Fisher 2007, 100). If Tiebout's assumptions are correct, public choice mechanisms will mirror private market choices.

TIEBOUT THEOREM AND ITS VALIDITY

According to Tiebout, individuals can shop around local governments in search of the best mix of taxes and benefits, a condition analogous to the private market system. Individuals can choose what they want and need not compromise through voting. There are several assumptions for the Tiebout choice, but its key assumptions suggest that individual consumer-voters have perfect information about the best mix of taxes and governmental benefits. In addition, consumer-voters are footloose, willing to find the government that provides their desired mix of taxes and benefits. If these assumptions are satisfied, any community will have residents with the same preferences for service benefits, and an individual's marginal benefit will be the same for all residents in each community. It is also likely that each individual's share of service costs would be equal to his or her marginal benefit. Unlike majority voting without mobility, all consumer voters (residents in each community) would be perfectly satisfied with the level of public service, and provision of the good would be efficient (Anderson 2012, 664–71; Cullis and Jones 2009, 373–74; Fisher 2007, 101–2; Hyman 2011, 715–17; Tiebout 1956). In Figure 17.1, this Tiebout equilibrium means that all three individuals will have exactly the same demand curves, and there will be no deadweight loss. In this regard, the Tiebout equilibrium is a special case of the Lindhal equilibrium.

However, there have been numerous controversies over the validity of the Tiebout model. For instance, people do not enjoy full mobility. They do not have perfect information on tax and service packages rendered by locals. Sometimes, family ties, career opportunities, geographic climate, and other factors influence people's relocation decisions. In addition, locals might not have such complete control over local services. Despite the controversies over the Tiebout model, Brunori (2007, 20–21) summarizes various studies on the model, which were conducted during the 1990s and the 2000s. Tax rates and public service quality are important factors in determining metropolitan-area choices for individuals and firms. Variations in metropolitan household income were associated with the creation of more-diversified schools and special district governments. Counties and cities match their policy actions with those of their competitor governments. Students learn more at a lower cost in more-competitive public economies. Even in the absence of mobility, Tiebout's theory gains support. "Citizens can also become involved in the electoral process and support politicians who will provide the mix of services and taxes they desire. Local policymakers, in turn, are likely to listen to local constituencies, which have both electoral power and the ability to migrate" (Brunori 2007, 22). Most of all, the underlying Tiebout assumptions have stood the test of time. Citizens gravitate toward localities with tax and service packages they prefer and can afford. Localities also try to attract individuals and firms by being cognizant of their desires (Brunori 2007, 20–21).

THREATS TO THE STABILITY OF THE TIEBOUT MODEL AND FISCAL ZONING

Even when all of its assumptions suffice, the Tiebout model might still fail to provide an efficient amount of local public services. If local services are chosen by factors other than benefit charges or head taxes, the Tiebout equilibrium might not hold. For instance, the amount of tax prices depends also on the value of houses individuals choose to consume.

As Fisher (2007, 105–8) illustrates, assume that a community with small houses imposes a higher property tax rate than a community with large houses (note that this is one possible scenario: readers can think of numerous others). Further assume that the two communities spend similar budgets for their local public goods. Then, an individual living in the former might be tempted to move into the latter because if a purchaser acquires a relatively small house in the community with large houses he or she can enjoy the same level of public goods at a much "lower" tax burden. The community with large houses obviously becomes less homogeneous, and this is a threat to the stability of the Tiebout model.

In sum, the potential efficiency of the Tiebout world can be blocked if individuals can purchase cheaper-than-average houses and thus pay less than the average cost of local public services. One mechanism to prevent such a condition is introduced in various forms of land-use restrictions or fiscal zoning laws. Simply put, a community may prohibit building houses cheaper than its average housing value. Alternatively, many communities impose rules on minimum lot size, minimum setback from streets, and required construction methods and materials. Under the strictest imposition of fiscal zoning, local taxes (typically property taxes) become a benefit tax or user charge. This is in line with the so-called benefit view of property tax (Fisher 2007, 109–11). However, developers or local residents could easily get exceptions to the zoning regulations and use the land in a way that is not consistent with the local community's zoning plan (Anderson 2012, 667). In addition, even when fiscal zoning is possible, there is still one problem. Since the demands for housing and public services tend to rise with income, the regulations might cause inter-jurisdictional equity issues: Wealthy individuals are more likely to get more public services (Fisher 2007, 111).

FISCAL CAPITALIZATION

In fact, there is another mechanism that more effectively maintains the stability of the Tiebout model. If, in the above case, tax advantages of the small-house consumer in the big-house community are offset by higher prices for small houses in the big-house community, in the long run, big and small houses may coexist in the big-house community. This process is called tax or fiscal capitalization (Fisher 2007, 111–14; Hamilton 1976).

If we can assume that service benefits B are reflected in the rental price of houses and the discount rate is r, then the value of the houses V will be $V = \frac{B}{r}$ (readers are referred to Stokey and Zeckhauser [1978, 54–57] and Boardman et al. [2011, 159–62], for mathematical derivation of the equation). If local residents pay property tax T annually, then the value of the houses will be $V = \frac{B}{r} - \frac{T}{r}$ (Anderson 2012, 568–71). This simply means that benefits from locally delivered public goods and costs incurred by property tax payment will eventually be reflected in the values of small houses in the above big-house community. Since the two communities were assumed to provide similar levels of public goods, the values of the small houses owned by the individual who moved from the small-house community into the big-house community will be the same (just think about $V = \frac{B}{r}$). However, the individual will clearly pay less property tax, and thus the value of his or her house V will be increasing. Therefore, the instability of the Tiebout model will somehow be adjusted, although not perfectly, and the big-house community might be more homogenized again. In conclusion, the Tiebout model is a fairly robust framework to observe local fiscal choice.

CHAPTER SUMMARY

- **Buchanan and Tullock's *The Calculus of Consent***

Buchanan and Tullock's *The Calculus of Consent* presents the key aspect of collective decision making or political economy.

Individuals can jointly consume public goods, so social marginal benefit curves for public goods are the sum of individual marginal benefits. When the private market system alone decides delivery of public goods, free-rider problems are likely to develop.

- **Lindhal Equilibrium**

When governmental jurisdictions are geographically small, their residents can police free-riding problems and can pay their shares of service delivery costs. This is called the Lindhal equilibrium, which maximizes social surplus.

- **Median Voter Theorem**

In general, tax prices and incomes of consumer-voters significantly affect the level of public goods. A 1 percent decrease in tax price increases the demand for public goods by about 0.25–.50 percent. A 1 percent increase in income raises the demand by 0.60–0.80 percent.

It incurs transaction costs too high to obtain the Lindahl equilibrium. Therefore, governmental jurisdictions often rely on voting to decide the level of service delivery. The median voter theorem suggests that the median voter's income and tax share prevails in deciding the service level.

• Monopolistic Budget-Setter Model

Unlike the median voter theorem, the monopolistic budget-setter model predicts that governmental budgets will always be larger than those preferred by the median voter. This is because budget-setters threaten consumer-voters by way of reversion budgets that will be triggered if the voters fail to choose adequate service levels.

• Ad Hoc or Mean Value Models

Ad hoc or mean value models indicate that mean values, as more composite measures for collective decision making, better explain state and county government expenditures. The mean values are proxy measures for political, institutional settings. As such, the mean value models emphasize that institutional conditions are more influential in deciding service levels than are median voters.

• Tiebout's Assumptions

The service level preferred by the median voter is not necessarily an efficient service level. Tiebout asserted that when consumer-voters can freely shop around different jurisdictions for the best package of tax and services social surplus will be maximized even without majority voting.

(1) There have been numerous critiques of Tiebout's assumptions. However, many empirical findings consistently show that Tiebout's model retains a substantial level of explanatory power over local expenditures.

(2) When consumer-voters purchase cheaper-than-average houses in Tiebout communities, they can enjoy public goods at a lower tax burden. The communities will become less homogeneous, which threatens the stability of the Tiebout model. In the long run, however, the lower tax burden will be reflected in increased housing values. Therefore, the stability of the Tiebout model can still obtain.

Taxation

Revenue Collection and Efficiency

Governments exercise their sovereign authority to raise tax revenues for their delivery of services. Since tax payments are involuntary and coercive, scholars and practitioners have suggested numerous principles to render taxation acceptable to taxpayers. There are various criteria to evaluate whether taxation is good or bad. However, there are three major criteria for tax evaluation: adequacy of revenue collection, efficiency, and equity. These principles for sound taxation do not always dominate tax decisions. Partisan political preferences and interest group mobilization frequently nullify the principles of sound taxation. This chapter focuses on the following issues:

- Adequacy of Revenue Collection
- Efficiency

ADEQUACY OF REVENUE COLLECTION

We all know that the best tax is no tax. Unfortunately, governments need resources to deliver public goods and services that the public want. In this sense, taxation is unavoidable. If taxation is unavoidable, the number one rule for sound taxation is the potential of revenue collection. Without tax revenues being collected, all other criteria are meaningless. If no revenues are collected, why do we have to think about other issues at all? Thus, any taxes should be able to raise an adequate amount of revenues (Cullis and Jones 2009, 307–9; Lewis and Hildreth 2013, 206–10).

TAX RATE AND REVENUE COLLECTION

A simple arithmetical computation might suggest that if governments want to raise tax revenues, they can simply raise tax rates. As shown in Figure 18.1, as an effective tax rate increases, tax revenues will grow in proportion to the increasing tax rate. The relationship is depicted as a linear relationship between effective tax rate and tax revenues.

Figure 18.1 **Tax Rate and Tax Revenues: Laffer Curve**

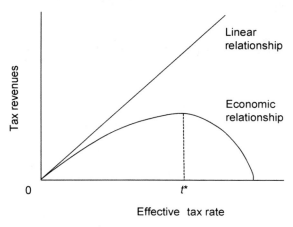

The linear relationship, however, ignores how individual and business taxpayers will respond to an increasing tax burden. A more realistic relationship is depicted as the inverse U-shaped curve in Figure 18.1. In real-life cases, workers might not work more or might leave the taxing jurisdictions if most of their earned income is to be taxed. This means that when governments impose extremely high tax rates, they might lose some of the tax base on which they levy taxes. Similarly, if local jurisdictions impose extremely high property tax rates on commercial and industrial properties, many business firms might leave the jurisdictions in search of a lower tax burden. As introduced in the previous chapter, this phenomenon is known as voting with feet. As jurisdictions lose their tax bases due to higher tax rates, their tax revenues will also decline. Thus, a more probable scenario between an effective tax rate and tax revenues will look like the inverse U-shaped curve in Figure 18.1. As the effective tax rate increases, tax revenues might grow as well. Beyond a certain point, however, tax revenues will decrease due to declining tax bases. The inverse U-shaped curve is known as the Laffer curve (Barro 1989, 200; Cullis and Jones 2009, 335–36; Mikesell 2011, 344–50). Therefore, a practical issue for taxing jurisdictions is how to find the effective tax rate to maximize their tax revenues. In Figure 18.1, the rate is t^*. In reality, however, there are numerous challenges to attempts to maximize tax revenues.

REVENUE LOSS: TAX EXPENDITURES

The first challenge is that tax laws have allowed numerous exceptions to taxation. These exceptions are called tax expenditures or tax breaks (Lewis and Hildreth 2013, 216–17). For instance, the federal income tax excludes certain income categories from taxable income (Hyman 2011, 582–83). Employer contributions for medical insurance premiums and medical care are excluded from taxable income. Mortgage interest on owner-occupied homes is exempted. Charitable contributions are deducted from the taxable income. State and local property taxes on owner-occupied homes are deducted. In many cases, these exemptions and deductions are allowed to taxpayers for policy purposes. The federal government might exempt charity contributions to encourage public donations to charitable organizations. The exemption of mortgage interest on owner-occupied homes encourages home ownership. Other types of federal tax exemptions are meant to assist the poor more. The child tax credit reduces the final tax liability of taxpayers with dependent children. The Earned Income Tax Credit (EITC) provides tax credits to low-income earners. The credits allow reduction of tax liability by the credit amounts, so they have much stronger tax-reducing impacts (Mikesell 2011, 396–405, 585–89). Although many tax breaks achieve some policy purposes, they are among the major challenges to maximizing tax revenues. As of 2011, tax exemptions of federal individual and corporate income taxes are estimated at $1 trillion (Palmer and Penner 2012).

One of the main revenue sources for state governments is sales tax. Many sales tax exemptions are allowed for administrative reasons or to ease regressivity (as will be detailed in the next chapter, regressivity means that poor individuals' tax burden is greater than that of wealthy people). For instance, many states exempt food, prescription drugs, education, and clothing from the tax. A sales tax imposes a disproportionately heavier tax burden on low-income earners. The exemption of necessities would therefore reduce the sales tax burden. As of 2005, thirty-two states had some form of exemption for food for home consumption, forty-five states had a prescription drug exemption, and twelve states exempted nonprescription medicine. The exemption of necessities from sales tax reduces regressivity, but at a cost. The percent of sales subject to the sales tax fell from 51 percent in 1990 to 43.3 percent in 2003. Food for home consumption that is exempt from sales tax amounts to about 20 percent of the sales tax base alone. Due to widespread exemptions, sales tax rates have steadily increased because taxing jurisdictions cannot help but make up for the revenue loss caused by the exemptions. The median sales tax rate was 2.7 percent in 1978, but had increased to 5.1 percent by 1993. The median sales tax rate in 2011 was 6 percent. The exemptions add up to sales tax revenue loss, but there is another problem. Since there are so many different exemptions, neither individuals nor politicians know for sure which items are exempt and which are not. Business vendors sometimes collect taxes on items that are exempted from the sales tax. The complexity for businesses gets further complicated when a plethora of different exemptions exist across states. Examples include: Eleven states tax transportation charges, nine states tax interest and finance charges, and forty-one tax some form of telecommunications services. Different sales tax rates further complicate the problem (Brunori 2011, 63, 67–68; Ulbrich 2011, 231–33).

After the property tax, local-option sales taxes (LOST) are the most important revenues for local governments. In 2006, 7,488 localities (about 9 percent of all local governments) imposed LOST. In 1977, LOST raised about 7 percent of total local tax revenue. In 2005, LOST raised about 11 percent of that total and about 7 percent of total own-source revenue. Since California established Proposition 13, which restricted property revenue growth, LOST has been more frequently used as an alternative revenue source for many local governments. Urban communities in particular relied on LOST to export tax burdens to nonresidents. In terms of its share of total local revenue, LOST accounted for about 3 percent of total local revenue. This pattern has remained almost unchanged for nearly fifty years. Local governments also exempt necessities such as food, medicine, and utilities from LOST. The exemption of necessity items will reduce the tax burden for lower-income earners because such items constitute a relatively larger portion of their income. However, the exemption significantly shrinks local tax bases (Brunori 2007, 69–70).

Property tax is the main revenue source for local governments. However, there are numerous exemptions for charitable organizations and economic development, and thus the property tax base has shrunk. Economic development exemptions in particular have caused a loss of a substantial amount of property tax revenues, as have charitable exemptions allowed for nonprofit organizations. Although some states have solicited payments in lieu of taxes (PILOTs) from exempted organizations, PILOTs amounts are far less than the forgone revenues. Farmland has been enjoying tax relief meant to preserve the viability of family owned farms. Environmentalists have backed this relief as a move to slow urban and suburban sprawl. Farm tax relief is frequently given in the form of preferential assessments that value farmland at current-use value rather than its market value. Of course, the former is much less than the latter in metropolitan areas. In Kansas in 2006, current-use farm relief was 600 percent less than market value. Many studies indicated that the relief failed to preserve family farms or prevent urban sprawl, however. Thus, government property exemptions also aggravate the problem of shrinking tax bases and forgone revenues (Brunori 2007, 61–63).

Similar to the federal income tax and state sales tax, some property tax exemptions target a reduction of the tax burden on low-income earners, although it is somewhat unclear whether property tax is regressive or not. A New Jersey study shows that the poorest 20 percent of homeowners pay property taxes that are, relatively speaking, four times higher than those paid by the wealthiest 1 percent of homeowners. Another study showed that the property tax burden for younger households is heavier. Some studies indicated, however, that the burden is proportional. Thus, property tax is slightly regressive (this equity issue is discussed in more detail in the next chapter). But there are some measures to relieve the regressivity of property tax. Washington, DC, along with twenty-eight states, offers homestead exemptions for owner-occupied housing. Some states allow property tax credits to eligible households. Another form of exemptions, called circuit breakers, sets an income threshold that property tax liability cannot exceed, ranging from 1 to 9 percent of income. Since states grant the reliefs, local fiscal burdens do not amplify. In addition, they reduce the regressivity of state tax systems. The elderly and disabled are oftentimes allowed deferrals until they sell their homes or die. Localities will collect property taxes and interests accrued over delayed payment amounts, but these legally provided exemptions also shrink property tax revenues (Anderson 2012, 575–80; Brunori 2007, 63–65).

The above-mentioned LOST further aggravates property tax revenue loss. Once LOST is in place, local taxing jurisdictions are likely to encourage the building of retail shopping centers to obtain additional LOST revenues. To attract retail development, localities ironically allow more property tax breaks to the retailers, thus further weakening the property tax base. Although LOST was used as an alternative to the property tax, the former eventually aggravates the revenue potential of the latter. In addition, once retailers locate in a jurisdiction, they become the most ardent opponents to LOST, contending that it weakens their competitiveness (Brunori 2007, 74–75).

REVENUE LOSS: OTHER CAUSES

Numerous other conditions further weaken governmental tax bases.

In this age of electronic commerce, the issue related to remote sales became more salient (Hyman 2011, 662–63). In the 1992 *Quill Corp. v. North Dakota* decision, the U.S. Supreme Court ruled that unless a vendor has a physical presence in a state, the state cannot compel the vendor to collect sales and use taxes. Usually, vendors that depend on remote sales do not have physical outlets and thus are not obligated to collect and remit sales and use taxes to the states in which they sell their products. This is known as the nexus clause. Because vendors are liable for uncollected sales and use taxes when they are responsible for them (i.e., have a physical presence) and the state defrays part of the administrative expenses, compliance with adding the taxes to sales is very high. However, states have become concerned about the loss of tax revenues from remote sales, especially because they have been rapidly increasing. In addition, remote sales that are exempt from sales and use taxes pose a threat to horizontal equities between traditional in-store purchases and transactions made via remote sales. States must find ways to impose a use tax on remote sales. One such effort was the Streamlined Sales and Tax Project (SSTP) of 1999. This was a project to ease the administrative complexity of collecting use taxes borne by businesses. Its secondary objective was to secure the passage of a federal law that enables Congress to trigger its authority, based on the Commerce Clause, to require remote vendors to collect use taxes for states and localities. The Streamlined Sales and Use Tax Act was introduced in 2003 in Congress. Many states had tried to align their state sales tax laws with the main provisions in the act. As of 2011, forty-four states and the District of Columbia were involved in the SSTP (Anderson 2012, 532–37; Brunori 2011, 69–70, 77–78; Cornia, Sjoquist, and Walters 2004; Sonnier and Lassar 2012).

Despite continued efforts to close the loopholes in electronic commerce and tax revenue collection, many scholars suspect that states can successfully generate sufficient revenues from electronic commerce (Cornia, Sjoquist, and Walters 2004; Lee, Johnson, and Joyce 2013, 167–68). At the same time, however, many states have been attempting to address the challenges of collecting sales and use taxes by remote sellers. Recent state legislation includes provisions to address the challenge through one or more of the following options: click-through nexus, notice requirements, and affiliate nexus.

According to the click-through nexus provision, some remote sales would be subject to sales or use taxes even without the physical presence of remote sellers in states where the products are sold. For instance, if a certain person in a state is paid a referral fee by the remote sellers to find consumers of the products, then the remote sellers need to collect sales or use taxes in the states where they sell their products. The second option, notice requirements, also closes loopholes in remote sales tax administration. In 2010, Colorado was the first state to require remote sellers to provide notice to consumers of their products that their purchase might be subject to sales or use taxes. They were also required to provide their customer list to the taxing authority of the states where they sold their products. Many states have adopted the third option, affiliate nexus statutes. A typical statute determines whether there is a physical presence within certain states for remote sellers by investigating whether the remote sellers have affiliates in the state. Indiana has recently introduced House Bill 1119, which declares a physical presence if the remote sellers sell products similar to their affiliates' products in the state, the affiliates are significantly involved in advertising and promoting sales of the remote sellers' products, or the affiliates use trademarks similar to those used by the remote sellers in Indiana (Hall and Garn 2012; Sonnier 2010). While there are numerous challenges to closing the loopholes in remote sales tax administration, many states have attempted to fix the loopholes through new administrative alternatives as well.

In February 2013, a bill, the Marketplace Fairness Act of 2013 (H.R. 684), was introduced in the U.S. House. The bill was referred to and passed the U.S. Senate as S. 743 in May 2013. The act authorizes each member state under the Streamlined Sales and Use Tax Agreement to collect sales taxes on remote sales when the remote sellers sell their products in the state. In short, the bill kills the nexus clause mentioned above and enables states to levy sales taxes on remote sales without significant legal challenges (Norquist 2013). However, it is not certain yet whether the bill will be finally legislated into a law and state governments can successfully collect sales taxes on remote sales.

Local governments have also been damaged by increasing remote sales. Technological advances have increased remote transactions. Even small and medium-sized businesses can sell goods and services throughout the United States through the Internet. Localities have lost billions of dollar revenues from sales taxes. Electronic commerce has made businesses less dependent on plants and equipment and made them more mobile. Increased mobility makes it more difficult for localities to impose business taxes. Remote workers pose a further challenge to personal income and wage taxes. Employers and employees might be tempted to avoid these taxes. Modern businesses do not own heavy equipment, land, or plants. They rely on computers and technology, so localities lose property tax revenues as well (Brunori 2007, 115–16).

There are other factors that weaken tax bases. Americans are aging. As a result, personal income tax revenues might decline due to increased tax preferences for older people. Another important effect is that between 1970 and 1990, fringe benefits such as health insurance, pretax contributions to pension plans, and flexible spending accounts substantially grew from 8.0 percent to 11.7 percent of total compensation (Brunori 2007, 118–19; 2011, 91). The economy has recently shifted from manufacturing to services and intangible properties, which weakens revenues from sales and property taxes (Brunori 2007, 8–9, 74).

Deregulation of electricity, gas, telecommunications, and financial services presents three issues. First, the industries were monopolists, and localities levied taxes at rates almost twice those for other industries. Now, the revenues are in jeopardy because the utility industries demand lower tax burdens. In addition, falling utility prices have resulted in decreases in the value of utility-owned land, which has, in turn, led to the decrease in property tax revenues. Second, even when localities own the utility industries, competition from private companies due to deregulation tends to decrease the revenue yield (e.g., Tallahassee, Florida, finances 40 percent of its total budget from a city-owned electricity company, which is threatened by private competition). Third, localities have collected rights-of-way and franchise fees from the regulated industries. Deregulation will affect such revenues as well (Brunori 2007, 117–18).

As of 2005, sixteen states had constitutional or statutory laws requiring a supermajority (e.g., two-thirds, three-quarters, or three-fifths) vote for a tax increase in each chamber. The supermajority requirements have been criticized as undemocratic because of the exceptional advantage over the minority (in effect, the minority subverts the will of the majority). More critically, the requirements impede sound state tax policies. They require a simple majority to increase state spending. Granting exemptions requires a simple majority. With the supermajority requirements for tax increases, the mismatch between the two requirements leads to tax policy deadlock. The simple majority requirement for tax exemptions necessarily results in a narrower tax base. With the narrower tax base, governments have no choice other than increasing tax rates. However, due to the supermajority requirement for a tax rate increase, they cannot easily raise tax rates (Brunori 2011, 55–57).

EFFICIENCY

The second important principle for sound tax policies is that any taxation not distort the private market economy. However, taxation itself almost always causes distortion to the market economy, as shown in this section (Bosworth and Burtless 1992).

NEUTRALITY OF TAXATION

Figure 11.1 in Chapter 11 (see page 94) on cost-benefit analysis indicates that any kind of taxation generally causes efficiency loss, deadweight loss, or excess burden. In this sense, no taxation is neutral with respect to economic activities on which taxation is imposed. The deadweight loss was estimated at about twenty-five cents per one dollar tax revenue. For tax administrators and scholars, the biggest question has been how to minimize the efficiency loss from taxation, with the Ramsey rule and the Corlett and Hague rule being the most promising attempt (Cullis and Jones 2009, 459–62; Fisher 2007, 388–90; Lewis and Hildreth 2013, 205–6; Poterba 2011).

To clarify this economic analysis of efficiency loss, some more specific examples show how taxation distorts the behaviors of individuals and businesses. As discussed earlier, just as individuals might not work more if tax rates on their earned incomes increase, businesses might relocate to other jurisdictions with lower property tax rates. Individuals who are living in the border counties between two states might shop across the state line in search of lower state and local sales tax rates (Bosworth and Burtless 1992; Fisher 2007, 390–93; Hyman 2011, 468–88; Mikesell 2011, 360–62).

Sales and use taxes are not imposed on business purchases for resale, ingredients for manufactured products, and sales of machinery. However, as of 2009, over $100 billion in sales tax was imposed on business purchases. Theoretically, when business-input purchases are taxed, the ultimate business-product price will carry the tax.

Thus, consumers will then be taxed on the tax itself, an effect known as pyramiding or cascading. Businesses also tend to prefer vertical integration, and to avoid sales tax, businesses will decide to produce needed services or products on their own rather than purchasing them (Brunori 2011, 73–75; Ulbrich 2011, 230–31). Some states rely on local-option income and business income taxes. However, these are not strongly supported because local governments are worried that they might impel businesses to migrate out of their localities (Brunori 2007, 8–10). These examples show how taxation influences the behaviors of individuals and businesses, evidence that taxation is not neutral with respect to economic activities.

NON-NEUTRALITY OF TAXATION: FISCAL POLICY

In Chapter 24 in Part VI, we will discuss details of supply-side economics. This type of economics suggests that a tax cut will stimulate the market economy through increased savings and attendant expanded business investments and that, in contrast, a tax hike will dampen economic growth. The federal income tax has been used as a major tool of the national fiscal policy, which clearly indicates that the federal income tax is not neutral with respect to the national economy. It either stimulates or dampens economic growth. Ironically, the federal income tax quality of non-neutrality has been applied as a tool of the national fiscal policy (Cullis and Jones 2009, 346–48; Lewis and Hildreth 2013, 203–4). In a similar vein, taxation has been used as a strong incentive for economic development at the state and local levels.

NON-NEUTRALITY OF TAXATION: TARGETED TAX INCENTIVES

State tax policy has been more frequently used as an instrument to foster economic development, but interstate competition through targeted tax incentives has had undesirable effects. It shrinks state tax bases. It has also pitted states against each other in the endless and wasteful quest for economic development and job creation. To some degree, the Commerce Clause of the U.S. Constitution prohibits states from imposing greater tax burdens on out-of-state products than on in-state products and transactions. However, the clause does not prohibit states from offering nondiscriminatory incentives to companies that invest in them. In 2004, a federal appellate court ruled unconstitutional Ohio's investment tax credit under the Commerce Clause. In *Cuno v. Daimler Chrysler*, a federal court declared a tax incentive program unlawful. A bipartisan group of lawmakers ultimately enacted the Economic Development Act of 2005, allowing states to eventually continue such tax incentive programs (Brunori 2011, 27–39).

The political payoff—jobs created from tax incentives—is immensely attractive to politicians. Since patronage-based recruitment, one of the major benefits politicians could render to constituent groups, has been greatly curtailed, politicians have been trying to create jobs by providing incentives to companies. In this way, they could create multiple jobs, not just a small number under the patronage system. Jobs allow earnings for individuals and their families. Politicians understand this aspect well. All needed arrangements for tax incentives, such as negotiations and approval of tax incentives, can be achieved in a matter of months. Politicians can move quickly to achieve some measurable results. They do not want to be perceived as having lagged behind the competition with other states by doing nothing (Brunori 2011, 27–39).

Types of Targeted Tax Incentives

Typical examples of targeted tax incentives include "property tax abatements, sales and use tax exemptions, job and investment credits, and accelerated depreciations deductions" (Brunori 2011, 32). The incentives are allowed to a limited number of corporations even when they are provided in general statutes. For instance, the Virginia Code, sec. 58.1-439, specifies that an income tax credit of $1,000 for each new job created after the first 100 jobs will be allowed to qualifying entities (Brunori 2011, 32). Numerous corporations were expected to enjoy targeted incentives related to corporate income taxes as well as sales and property tax incentives, but the problem is that only a small number of corporations have received the incentives. The Mercedes-Benz law in Alabama is the most notorious example. Companies investing at least $50 million and employing at least fifty people can issue tax-exempt bonds. Corporate income tax credits for servicing the debt are further allowed. In some cases, corporations request tax incentives even after they have decided to locate in certain states. In addition, once states allow incentives to a few corporations, it gets harder to deny them to others (Brunori 2011, 100–1).

Local governments also rely on tax policies to attract businesses, jobs, and individuals. They maintain their tax burdens at levels competitive with their neighboring jurisdictions. Sometimes, they develop enterprise zones with tax breaks for businesses. They also provide targeted tax incentives because other location-decision factors such as transportation and labor costs are almost equal across metropolitan areas. Although targeted incentives are inefficient, inequitable, and mostly unnecessary, politicians prefer this option because the benefits from claiming credits for creating jobs outweigh all other factors (Brunori 2007, 35–36; Hanson 2009).

Revenue Impacts of Targeted Tax Incentives

The above section on the adequacy of revenue collection revealed that preferential tax breaks decrease tax bases. Targeted tax incentives are most strongly related to declining tax bases. This section is also related to the section on the adequacy of revenue collection. The case of state corporate income tax exemplifies how targeted tax incentives significantly damage state tax bases. These days, most corporations conduct multistate business. As a result, a uniform rule in determining how corporations are taxed is greatly needed. If all states can impose the same rule, they can also reduce administrative costs.

Following the weighted three-factor apportionment formula in the 1957 Uniform Division of Income for Tax Purposes Act, corporate incomes are apportioned based on the relative amount of sales, property, and payroll that corporations have in a certain jurisdiction (Anderson 2012, 494–97). However, many states have adopted different apportionment formulas for economic competition, and as of 2010, only twelve states

Table 18.1

Illustration of Double-Weighted Sales-Factor Apportionment

Tax component	State A	State B	All states
Payroll	$3,000	$800	$8,000
Property	$6,000	$1,500	$12,000
Sales	$700	$7,000	$25,000
Profit			$13,500
Payroll factor	0.375	0.10	
Property factor	0.50	0.125	
Sales factor	0.028	0.28	
Three-factor formula	0.301	0.168	
	= (0.375 + 0.5 + 0.028)/3	= (0.1 + 0.125 + 0.28)/3	
Taxable profit	**$4,063.50**	**$2,272.50**	
Double-weighted sales formula	0.233	0.196	
	= (0.375 + 0.5 + 0.028 + 0.028)/4	= (0.1 + 0.125 + 0.28 + 0.28)/4	
Taxable profit	**$3,142.10**	**$2,649.40**	

follow the traditional one. Eighteen states have adopted some variant of a double-weighted sales factor, which usually lowers tax liability for business corporations that have more operations within a state (in terms of payroll and property), but sell most of their products out of state. However, studies show that a double- or single-sales factor ultimately results in state revenue loss (Brunori 2011, 101–3). Fisher (2007, 444–49) illustrates the revenue loss that is depicted in Table 18.1.

A certain multistate business corporation has total amounts of payroll ($8,000), property ($12,000), and sales ($25,000) from "all" states. Assume that their profit ratio is 30 percent. Thus, their total profit is $13,500. The question here is what portion of the business corporation's profit can be apportioned to state A and how much to state B. The first panel in Table 18.1 shows the amounts of payroll, property, and sales the corporation has in each of the two states. The second panel shows the relative portions of payroll, property, and sales in each state compared with payroll, property, and sales in all states (e.g., the payroll factor for state A is 0.375 = 3,000/8,000). When the three-factor formula is used, the taxable profit apportioned to state A is $4,063.50. When a double-weighted sales formula is used (i.e., sales factor is added one more time and the sum of all factors is divided by 4), it is $3,142.10. The corporation might be more tempted to increase its production in state A, but from a revenue perspective, state A will lose its corporate income tax revenue by a significant amount.

Economic Impacts of Targeted Tax Incentives

Numerous studies have investigated whether tax incentives affect state and local economic growth, job creation, or business location decisions. Most of the studies have focused on the economic impacts of targeted tax incentives (Bartik 1989; Dalenberg and Partridge 1995; Garlino and Mills 1987; Hanson 2009; Hicks and LaFaive 2011; Papke 1991; Plaut and Pluta 1983; Wasylenko 1997). Buss (2001) offers a comprehensive review of the tax literature.

In the late 1950s and early 1960s, tax research first employed simple comparative studies and then more sophisticated econometric analyses. Scholars continued this stream of research until the mid-1980s. They generally reported no meaningful relationship between taxes and economic growth or business location decisions. The flipside of the findings is that tax incentives might not have any significant impact on economic growth or business location decision either.

Throughout the 1970s and 1980s, economic turbulence precipitated development of federal and state economic development programs. These programs reignited interest in tax incentives, and scholars have used somewhat new approaches to analyze their impact. One significant feature of the new approaches is that they began to separate tax incentives from other nontax factors such as public services, infrastructures, and amenities. The nontax factors included various ones encouraging or discouraging business activities. However, they specifically attempted to separate the impacts of tax incentives from the levels of public services or infrastructures.

Helms (1985) made a notable contribution to this stream of studies (Buss 2011). States and localities with higher overall tax rates for business firms might also have higher levels of public services or infrastructures rendered by higher state and local revenues. Better public services and infrastructures are likely to stimulate regional economies or boost business location decisions. Since state and local taxes are closely linked to the quality of public services and infrastructures, the previous studies that included only tax variables in their models might be somewhat biased. High taxes might drive businesses out of taxing jurisdictions but at the same time, increased tax revenues might render better public infrastructures that will attract businesses and boost the jurisdictions' economy. When the new studies controlled for public services or infrastructures, state and local taxes on business firms showed much more negative impacts on regional economic growth and business-location decisions. Again, the flip side of these findings is that tax incentives might have a stronger impact on business activities.

In line with the new approaches to tax studies, business climate studies have emerged since the mid-1970s. The purpose is to investigate how more comprehensive measures for business activities, defined as the overall business climate, affect economic growth and business location decisions. Business firms prefer jurisdictions with lower taxes, lower wages, right-to-work laws, minimal business regulation, lower utility costs, and higher subsidies for capital. Business climate studies analyzed the economic impacts of the more composite indices for favorable business operations. However, they weighted state and local taxes heavily in computing state business-climate rankings. In this regard, business climate studies are closer to the new approaches discussed above. Overall findings from business climate studies have indicated that taxes matter significantly (Buss 2001).

More recent studies report findings very similar to those from the new approaches and the business climate approaches. Hanson and Rohlin (2011) investigated new business establishments entering a local area in 1994, 1996, and 2000, induced by the federal Empowerment Zone (EZ) program. The EZ wage tax credit was shown to attract about 2.2 new establishments per 1,000 existing business establishments in EZ areas, particularly from the retail and service sectors. Chad and Skidmore (2010) analyzed the relationship between ethanol production capacity and subsidies/tax credits for the ethanol production industry during 1980–2007. They found that some tax incentives for ethanol production had a significant impact on a state's production capacity.

In general, taxes or tax incentives have either negative or positive impacts on state and local economic growth, job creation, or business location decisions. Therefore, state and local taxes are not neutral with respect to regional economies. However, targeted tax incentives employed by states and localities have been widely used as a tool to stimulate regional economies.

CHAPTER SUMMARY

- **Adequacy of Revenue Collection**

Any taxes should first raise revenues. Without revenues being raised, it is meaningless to evaluate tax schedules. The first criterion for taxation is the adequacy of revenue collection.

(1) Raising tax rates does not necessarily guarantee maximum tax revenues.

(2) As jurisdictions increase their tax rates, tax revenues will begin to decline because individuals might stop working or businesses might migrate out of the jurisdictions in search of a lower tax burden. This relationship is best depicted in the Laffer curve.

- **Tax Expenditures**

One challenge to tax-revenue maximization is tax expenditures.

(1) The federal income tax allows numerous exemptions, deductions, and credits. States and local jurisdictions exempt food, prescription drugs, education, and clothing from sales taxation.

(2) Local governments exempt charitable organizations and economic development from property taxes. They also reduce or defer property tax payment for owner-occupied housing or the elderly and disabled.

(3) These tax exemptions have been allowed in order to stimulate certain economic activities or improve the equity of taxation. However, if taxing jurisdictions lose revenues from tax exemptions, they cannot help but increase tax rates for other existing taxes.

- **Other Challenges to Tax Revenue Maximization**

There are other challenges to tax revenue maximization.

(1) Increasing remote sales by Internet and other electronic means significantly reduce sales tax revenues for states and localities.

(2) As Americans are aging, taxing jurisdictions allow more tax preferences to older people, leading to tax revenue loss.

(3) Due to deregulation of electricity, gas, telecommunications, and financial services, local governments especially have lost taxes that were much higher for the regulated industries.

(4) Many states require a simple majority for increasing state spending or granting tax exemptions. In contrast, they usually require a supermajority for increasing tax revenues. The disparity accelerates state revenue shortages.

- **Taxes and Private Market Activities**

No taxes should interfere with private market activities.

(1) In actuality, any taxation will generate excess burden or deadweight loss. In addition, it will modify the behavior of individuals and businesses.

(2) Ironically, the non-neutrality of federal and state taxes has been applied as a fiscal policy tool or an economic policy to boost economic growth, job creation, and business location decisions.

Taxation

19 Equity and Politics of Taxation

The previous chapter introduced three major principles for sound tax policies. Taxes should first be able to raise adequate amounts of revenues. In addition, they should not distort economic activities in the private market system. The third important rule for taxes is that the tax burden on taxpayers should be fair and equitable. As noted in Chapter 18, the politics of taxation often bypasses these principles. This chapter focuses on the following issues:

- Equity
- Politics of Taxation

EQUITY

In Chapter 17, "Public Goods and Public Choice," we learned various approaches to the economic analysis of how the level of public goods and services is chosen. One approach to public choice is known as the Lindhal equilibrium. When individuals pay taxes proportional to the relative share of benefits they enjoy from the public goods and services financed by tax revenues, the economic efficiency will be maximized. Since each taxpayer pays taxes equal to his or her benefits, tax schedules based on the Lindhal pricing are regarded as fair and equitable. In the parlance of tax analysis, this is called the benefits-received principle (Cullis and Jones 2009, 65; Lewis and Hildreth 2013, 212–14; U.S. Government Accountability Office 2005, 26–27; Wagner 2012b). In practice, however, equity in taxation usually refers to the ability-to-pay principle. This assumes that those who can afford to bear a higher tax burden should pay more taxes than those with less ability. The ability to pay is measured in terms of overall wealth, income, or consumption. One caveat is that a taxpayer's ability to pay taxes might vary depending on which measure is chosen to define that ability. For instance, the ability measured by overall wealth will be different from that measured by income (Lewis and Hildreth 2013, 214–16; U.S. Government Accountability Office 2005, 27; Wagner 2012b). Once one selects an adequate measure of the ability to pay taxes, the key question is how to evaluate vertical equity and horizontal equity.

Table 19.1

Proportional, Progressive, and Regressive Tax Schedules

Taxpayer	Income ($)	Proportional tax liability ($) and rate (%)	Progressive tax liability ($) and rate (%)	Regressive tax liability ($) and rate (%)
A	10,000	1,000 (10%)	1,000 (10%)	1,000 (10%)
B	50,000	5,000 (10%)	10,000 (20%)	2,500 (5%)
C	200,000	20,000 (10%)	60,000 (30%)	4,000 (2%)

VERTICAL EQUITY

Definition

Vertical equity means different treatment of taxpayers with different abilities to pay taxes. Table 19.1 succinctly illustrates the concept of vertical equity or inequity. There are three taxpayers, A, B, and C. The second column in Table 19.1 shows each taxpayer's income level, illustrating a case of proportional tax liability and rate. If taxpayer A pays $1,000 in taxes, then that tax rate is 10 percent. Individual B pays $5,000 in tax and that tax rate is also 10 percent. Finally, individual C also pays 10 percent of his or her income as tax. In this case, the tax rate for the three individuals is 10 percent. This is called a proportional tax schedule.

In contrast, the third column shows that tax rate increasing as taxpayers' incomes rise. Individual A still pays $1,000 in taxes, and the tax rate is 10 percent. Individual B now pays $10,000 at a tax rate of 20 percent. Finally, individual C pays $60,000 in tax and his or her tax rate is 30 percent. Thus, the relative tax burden increases as a taxpayer's income increases. This is called a progressive tax system. While tax payments according to the proportional tax schedules are neutral with respect to the taxpayer's income levels, those pursuant to the progressive tax schedules are obviously larger for those with higher capacities to pay taxes. For instance, individual C's income is much higher than that of individual A, and as such, individual C pays a relatively larger share of his or her income. The federal income tax and most of state income taxes impose higher, graduated tax rates on those higher-income earners. Progressive tax schedules are vertically equitable because those with higher capacities pay more taxes.

The last column shows a case of regressive tax liability and rate. Individual B now pays $2,500 in taxes and the tax rate drops to 5 percent. Individual C now pays $4,000 in taxes with a tax-rate drop to 2 percent. As a taxpayer's income level rises, the relative tax burden decreases. This tax schedule is called a regressive tax system. The system is vertically inequitable because lower-income earners pay disproportionately more taxes (Gravelle 1992; Mikesell 2011, 352–55; Mirlees et al. 2012; U.S. Government Accountability Office 2005, 27–28).

If the tax rates in Table 19.1 are specified in tax laws, they are called statutory tax rates. However, statutory tax rates are not necessarily the same as effective tax rates, which are more frequently used as a measurement of vertical equity. As shown in the previous chapter, there are numerous cases of tax exemptions for either business firms or individuals. If taxing jurisdictions give tax breaks to individuals B and C under the proportional tax systems (the third column in Table 19.1), their tax rates will be lower than 10 percent. Then, the statutory tax rate is not the same as the effective tax rates for the two individuals. Sometimes, effective tax rates from consumption-based taxes such as sales taxes are different from statutory tax rates. If a low-income earner (individual A) and a high-income earner (individual C) each purchased $2,000 worth of food, each of them would pay $200 when the sales tax rate is 10 percent. The statutory sales tax rate is obviously the same for the two individuals. However, the effective tax rate for the low-income earner is 2 percent (= 200/10,000), whereas that for the high-income earner is 0.1 percent (= 200/200,000). So, most sales taxes are regressive. To ease the regressivity, many states allow exemptions of sales taxes on necessities such as food for home consumption or medicine. The exemptions will reduce the sales tax burden of low-income earners.

Empirical Observations on Vertical Equity

Scholars have analyzed the distributional impacts of the Economic Growth and Tax Relief Reconciliation Act of 2001 (EGTRRA), also known as the George Bush tax cut. The federal income tax rate schedule, as noted above, is a progressive tax system. The Bush tax cut further reduced statutory tax rates for all four income tax brackets and created a new 10 percent bracket applied to the first $12,000 of taxable income for joint returns. Statutory tax-rate schedules after the tax cut are progressive. When all tax expenditures for entire income tax brackets were accounted for, effective tax-rate schedules were still progressive. However, there was one notable pattern in the effective tax rates for all income tax brackets. Effective marginal tax rates for the $25,000 income bracket decreased. This is some evidence for vertical equity. However, effective marginal tax rates for the income tax brackets beyond $400,000 also significantly decreased. On average, effective marginal tax rates decreased from 26 percent to 24 percent, but the benefits from the Bush tax cut were heavily concentrated in lower- and higher-income brackets. Therefore, the Bush tax cut dampened the progressivity or vertical equity a little bit (Gale and Potter 2002; Kiefer et al. 2002).

Due to the economic downturn since the 2008 financial market crisis, the U.S. government extended the Bush tax cut until the end of 2012. Many scholars and practitioners have been concerned that ending the tax cut, as well as other tax cut provisions and emergency governmental spending, might further dampen the U.S. economy, as aptly demonstrated by the fiscal cliff (U.S. Congressional Budget Office 2012a, 2012b). Both political parties once again made a dramatic compromise to avoid the fiscal cliff that ending tax cuts and emergency spending might cause. Among the compromise measures, a change in federal income tax warrants our attention. The federal income tax rate for individuals earning more than $400,000 and couples earning more than \$450,000 was raised from 35 percent to 39.6 percent. Federal income tax rates for other income brackets remained the same as those under the Bush tax laws: 99.3 percent of taxpayers would experience no change in their income tax payment. Wealthy people have to pay additional taxes on their dividends and capital gains. They have to pay two new surcharges on investment income and regular income. By some measures, the new tax code might be the most progressive in decades (Lowrey 2013).

Poorer people tend to pay relatively larger portions of their income for state sales tax, which causes regressivity. Numerous studies support this assertion. A 1993 Minnesota study showed that the bottom 10 percent in the income spectrum paid 5.2 percent of their income in sales tax, but the upper 10 percent paid only 1.3 percent. According to a 1990 Connecticut study, those earning below \$5,000 paid 8.15 percent of their income in sales tax but those earning between \$100,000 and \$200,000 paid 2.18 percent of their income. Although necessities are exempt from sales tax, thus relieving the regressivity for the poor, wealthier people also benefit from those exemptions. If tax rates for nonexempted items are raised, then the poor will get further hurt. In addition, most of them already receive food stamps, and therefore food tax exemptions do not relieve the regressivity very much. Some states attempted to reduce the regressivity by introducing back-to-school sales-tax holidays. Some states provide income tax credits or refunds over sales tax purchases. All in all, however, sales tax is still regarded as regressive.

In addition, when sales and use taxes were implemented, services were just a small segment of the national economy. Since 1979, however, services have grown from 47.4 percent to 57.5 percent of personal consumption. Many services are untaxed. But the real issue is that wealthier people are likely to spend more on legal, accounting, and medical services that are exempt from sales tax. This obviously increases the regressivity of state sales tax systems (Brunori 2011, 70–72).

State income taxes are the most progressive, compared to other state taxes, especially sales and excise taxes. Even Pennsylvania, with a flat 3.07 percent income tax rate and no deductions/exemptions, exempts persons with an income at or below the poverty line. Thirty-four states rely on a graduated rate schedule. Seven states (Colorado, Illinois, Indiana, Massachusetts, Michigan, Pennsylvania, and Utah) use a single flat rate, with some tax breaks. During the 1990s, narrowing the income tax base and a lot of tax breaks benefited the wealthy more than the poor, thus lessening the tax progressivity. By 2005, most state income tax schedules had become just mildly progressive. Still, the state income tax is the most progressive among state taxes (Brunori 2011, 87–89).

As briefly discussed in the previous chapter, local property taxes are viewed as mildly progressive with various tax relief measures. Together with state and local sales taxes, local-option sales tax (LOST) increases the regressivity. A North Carolina study indicates that increased LOST burdens the least-wealthy 20 percent of income earners six times more than the wealthiest 1 percent (Brunori 2007, 75–76). In 2005, Local-Option Income and Wage Taxes (LOIWT) composed about

1.5 percent of total local revenues and about 4 percent of total local tax revenues. In 2002, local personal income taxes composed about 24 percent of the latter for cities with populations over 300,000. LOIWT takes the form of a wage (payroll) tax or a general income tax (a piggyback tax because localities piggyback on state administration like sale tax implementation). The former usually is not applied to unearned income such as dividends, interest, and capital gains. Since the piggyback taxes are mostly tied to state income taxes, they are mildly progressive and thus somewhat increase the overall progressivity of local taxes. In contrast, local wage taxes are more regressive because lower-income earners earn most of their income from wages. They also do not allow a lot of exemptions or deductions for the poor employees (Brunori 2007, 83–88).

HORIZONTAL EQUITY

Definition

Horizontal equity means that taxpayers with equal capacities should shoulder equal tax burdens. Again, simple examples will illustrate the concept of horizontal equity. Until very recently, the federal income tax contained provisions of the so-called marriage penalties. Assume that there are two individuals, A and B. Each earns $40,000 annually. Further assume that the income tax rate is 10 percent for the first $20,000 but increases to 50 percent beyond that. Under two separate single income tax returns, each individual will pay $12,000 in income tax (0.1 × $20,000] + 0.5 × $20,000]). The combined total income tax payment is $24,000. Between 1948 and 1969, even when these two individuals were married and filed a joint tax return, the federal government allowed a rule called income splitting for an administrative purpose. If the income splitting were not allowed, the married couple would have a total income of $80,000 and their income tax liability would be $32,000 (0.1 × $20,000] + 0.5 × $60,000]). However, when their total income was split (i.e., two annual incomes of $40,000), their income tax liability would still be $12,000 apiece. The 1969 federal income tax law change disallowed income splitting, and married couples have thus had to pay more taxes under joint income tax returns. This is one example of marriage penalties in the federal income tax schedule. Couples have to pay more taxes only because they are married, although their ability to pay taxes measured by income is the same. This is an example of horizontal inequity (McIntyre and McIntyre 1999).

Another example of marriage penalties in the federal income tax schedule is the standard deduction. Previously, the amount of standard deduction for married couples was less than twice that of single tax filers. For the filing year 1998, the amount of standard deduction for single filers was $4,250. Therefore, if two individuals were not married, the total amount of standard deduction would have been $8,500. However, the amount of standard deduction for married couples was $7,100. This is another clear example of horizontal inequity because married couples have to pay more taxes only because they are married. The Earned Income Tax Credit (EITC) exemplifies similar disadvantages for married couples (Gravelle 1992; McIntyre and McIntyre 1999).

Empirical Observations on Horizontal Equity

The Bush tax cut addressed most of the provisions related to marriage penalties. About 11 million couples were expected to enjoy lower marriage penalties, and about 5 million couples were free from marriage penalties. Thus, the Bush tax cut somewhat improved horizontal equity (Kiefer et al. 2002).

As noted in the previous chapter, in the age of electronic commerce, the tax issues related to remote sales became more salient. In the 1992 *Quill Corp. v. North Dakota* decision, the U.S. Supreme Court ruled that unless a vendor has a physical presence in a state, the state cannot compel the vendor to collect sales and use taxes. Often, vendors, depending on remote sales, do not have physical outlets in the states where they sell their products and thus are not obligated to collect and remit sales and use taxes to the state. Since vendors are liable for uncollected sales and use taxes when they are responsible (i.e., have a physical presence) and the state defrays parts of their administrative expenses, compliance with the tax was fairly high. However, states have been concerned about the loss of tax revenues from remote sales, especially because remote sales have been rapidly increasing. In cases where remote sales are exempt from sales and use taxes, the exemption poses a threat to horizontal inequities between traditional in-store purchases and transactions made via remote sales (Brunori 2011, 69–71). As shown in the previous chapter, many states have recently developed new measures to improve the horizontal equity over remote sales tax by more clearly identifying the link between remote sellers and their physical outlets.

While current state sales and use tax systems threaten horizontal equity, the state corporate income tax was created to reduce horizontal inequity. Property taxes do not account for varying degrees of property inputs to produce business products. Capital-intensive (manufacturing) companies are taxed more heavily than labor-intensive companies (e.g., knowledge-based companies such as high-tech). The inequality is augmented by the difficulties in assessing property taxes for intangible properties. As a result, two companies similar in total asset size might have to pay different amounts of property taxes. In some sense, the inclusion of the state corporate income tax was meant to relieve the horizontal inequity between capital-intensive and labor-intensive companies by taxing corporate profits that might implicitly reflect the advantages from intangible assets (Brunori 2011, 97–99).

Local wage taxes discussed above also cause a horizontal equity issue. Residents who earn most of their income from dividends, interest, and capital gains are not taxed, while those whose wages are the sole source of their income do pay taxes (Brunori 2007, 87–88).

POLITICS OF TAXATION

Although tax administrators and scholars are familiar with the principles of sound tax policies, political motives frequently nullify those principles (Fisher 2009, 23–42; Lewis and Hildreth 2013, 187–90).

Electoral politics shape state tax policy in two ways. First, politicians seeking office typically raise broad issues such as tax relief for education or repealing sales tax on food. The second way to shape state tax policy is by reinforcing the antitax American culture that has prevailed since the Ford administration. Democratic and Republican presidents have based their electoral campaigns on tax cuts (for either low- and middle-income earners or high-income earners). At the state level, gubernatorial and legislative candidates have pledged to cut taxes. Few have successfully increased them. Even when they needed to increase public services, they cautiously avoided debates on how to finance them. Ample evidence shows that voters likely judge incumbent governors on their tax policies. When incumbent candidates have not significantly increased taxes or voters are not seriously concerned with tax fairness, taxes are minor issues. However, in most gubernatorial races, tax policies are critical issues for both incumbents and challengers.

Unlike electoral politics, legislative politics involve a more limited number of individuals who try to affect state legislators on specific policy or tax outcomes. Studies consistently show that business groups are the most influential in lobbying before legislatures than are any other interest groups, although other lobbyists working for small businesses, labor unions, local government associations, civic associations, and environmental groups still try to influence state legislatures. Legislators sometimes lend their support to other lawmakers who try to bring tax breaks to particular industries in their districts in exchange for political assistance on issues important to the legislators through logrolling (Brunori 2011, 42–50; 2007, 27–29; Rubin 2010, 49, 57–67). Electoral and legislative politics mostly threaten the adequacy of revenue collection and the equity of taxation.

When political leaders cannot avoid taxing, they try to obscure the taxpayers' burdens. Excise taxes and corporate income taxes seem to be less burdensome to taxpayers, although they tend to be passed on to consumers. Since the sales tax is levied on incremental amounts of purchases, consumers usually are unaware of their overall sales tax burden. State lawmakers often try to reduce income taxes that are progressive but most visible. Instead, they prefer to retain the less visible but more regressive consumption taxes. Most state legislators have some idea of the regressivity of state sales taxes, but the general public does not have accurate information on the unfairness of the levy. Poorer people, who are most damaged by sales taxes, are least likely to vote on election days, and politicians tend to increase sales tax rates if they cannot avoid taxing. As noted earlier, legal, accounting, and medical services are not subject to sales taxes in most states. One of the main reasons for the lack of a sales tax on those services is strong resistance from political power groups such as lawyers, accountants, and doctors (Brunori 2011, 52–54, 62–63, 72–73, 89–90). Rubin (2010, 50–57) also illustrates numerous cases of how politics detracts from revenue collection and equity of taxation through various kinds of breaks on the federal income tax. Sound tax principles are frequently confused with mundane political matters, such as pressures from interest groups that would benefit from specific tax breaks. The recent debates over how to control the runaway federal deficits are another good example illustrating how vulnerable tax policies are to political pressures (Palmer and Penner 2012).

CHAPTER SUMMARY

- **Principle of Taxation**

The benefits-received principle of taxation means that those who benefit from public services should pay taxes proportional to their benefit share.

The ability-to-pay principle of taxation means that those who can afford to bear a higher tax burden should pay more. The two concepts in the ability to pay are vertical equity and horizontal equity.

- **Vertical Equity**

Vertical equity means different treatment of taxpayers with different capacities to pay taxes. Based on vertical equity, tax schedules can be proportional, progressive, or regressive. The most accurate measure of vertical equity is effective tax rates.

(1) The federal income tax is progressive. After the 2001 Bush tax cut, effective marginal tax rates for low-income and high-income brackets decreased the most significantly, which slightly dampens the vertical equity of the federal income tax schedules. The 2013 income tax code as a way around the fiscal cliff created the most progressive federal income tax schedule in decades. State income taxes are also mildly progressive.

(2) State sales taxes are mostly regressive. Many states exempt some necessity items from sales taxes to ease the regressivity of sales taxes.

(3) Local optional sales and income taxes are mostly regressive.

- **Horizontal Equity**

Horizontal equity means that taxpayers with equal capacities should shoulder equal tax burdens.

(1) Married couples previously had larger tax liabilities due to many provisions in the federal income tax law. The Bush tax cut substantially addressed marriage penalties.

(2) Increased electronically remote sales placed higher sales tax burdens on traditional in-store transactions. This is an example of horizontal inequity.

(3) State corporate income taxes were introduced to address horizontal inequity between capital-intensive companies and labor-intensive companies.

- **Politics of Taxation**

The principles of sound tax policies are frequently bypassed by the politics of taxation.

(1) Politicians have attempted to cut taxes for their constituency groups through electoral and legislative politics. The politics of taxation often reduces tax bases and raises issues of equity.

(2) When politicians cannot avoid taxation, they try to obscure tax burdens. Politicians try to reduce income taxes because their burdens are most visible. In addition, low-income earners, who are disproportionately affected by a sales tax, are least active in voting, so politicians tend to increase sales tax rates if they cannot avoid taxing.

Measures of Fiscal Capacity and Stress

One important dimension in the fiscal decision-making process is how to gauge the fiscal capacity of certain jurisdictions. Budget decision makers have to estimate how much they can raise the revenue based on their jurisdictions' economic capacities. They also need to make decisions on how much they can spend based on those estimated tax revenues. The measures of fiscal capacity or tax revenues have frequently been used as a basis of allocating intergovernmental grants as introduced in Part V. This chapter discusses the following concepts:

- Measures of Fiscal Capacity and Stress
- Revised Measures of Fiscal Capacity and Stress
- Other Critiques of the Representative Tax System
- Why Are Measures of Fiscal Capacity and Stress Needed?

MEASURES OF FISCAL CAPACITY AND STRESS

REPRESENTATIVE TAX SYSTEM AND TAX EFFORT INDEX

A conventional way of measuring the fiscal stress of a given jurisdiction is to gauge the amount of taxes collected relative to its fiscal capacity. Developed by American economists such as Selman Mushkin and Alice Rivlin in association with the U.S. Advisory Commission on Intergovernmental Relations (ACIR), the Representative Tax System (RTS) has been widely used for the purpose of measuring the fiscal capacities of various governmental jurisdictions, including two federal governments, Canada and the United States (Hawkins 1990, 3). RTS selects about twenty-seven principal taxes levied by state and local governments for which comparable data across states can be obtained. Regardless of whether they actually collect revenues, RTS estimates the output of all possible tax bases of states and the nationwide standard tax base (Hawkins 1990; Tannenwald 1998, 1999). Tannenwald (2002) used slightly different categories for FY1997. The RTS for FY1997 covered twenty state and local tax sources, such as general sales and gross receipts, selective excise taxes, licenses, personal income, corporate income, property taxes, estate and gift taxes, severance taxes, and others. Benoy and Hendrick (2013, 11–41) succinctly explain the difference between actual revenues and fiscal capacity such as revenue capacity, revenue base, and economic base.

The actual nationwide collection from each tax is divided by the nationwide standard tax base for each tax to get a nationally determined representative tax rate. This rate is applied to the RTS base of each state to determine the fiscal capacity of each state with respect to a certain tax. In a formulaic form, the representative tax rate for each base equals:

$$r = \frac{\sum_{i=1}^{50} T_i}{\sum_{i=1}^{50} B_i}$$

where r = the representative tax rate, T = tax actually collected from the specific tax in the state, and B = the imaginary base for that tax in the state. Based on the representative tax rate, one can compute a certain state's fiscal capacity. Mikesell (2007) explains: "For example, state sales tax capacity for an individual state would equal sales receipts in the retail trade reported in the quinquennial U.S. Bureau of Census economic census reports (with a few adjustments) multiplied by the national average tax rate, which itself has been calculated by dividing national sales tax collections by national retail trade receipts (as in the above formula)" (534). The sum of the computations for all categories of tax will measure the fiscal capacity for each state for all potential tax bases as reported above. The RTS approach thus extends beyond a single tax category and can also allow heavier weight to some fiscal options and account for tax exporting such as tourism, energy extraction, and financial services.

A state's tax effort index is estimated by dividing its actual tax collections by this fiscal capacity to collect revenues from the tax (Hawkins 1990; Tannenwald 1998, 1999). A state's tax effort indicates "the extent to which a state is utilizing the tax bases available to it, relative to the national average" (Hawkins 1990, 15). This process is repeated to obtain the overall tax effort index including all tax categories.

REPRESENTATIVE EXPENDITURES SYSTEM AND FISCAL NEED INDEX

The tax effort index based on RTS, however, does not take into consideration different levels of demand for public programs across states. For example, if a certain state's overall demand for public programs is higher than that of another state with a similar fiscal capacity, then the former state's fiscal capacity may be relatively lower than the latter's. To address this limitation of the fiscal capacity measure, the Representative Expenditures System (RES) approach has been developed.

The first step in RES is to identify seven workload measures for representative expenditures of state and local governments: elementary and secondary education, higher education, public welfare, health and hospitals, highways, police and corrections, and all other direct general expenditures (Rafuse 1990). Each state's workload measure for each function as a share of the national total workload is calculated and is multiplied by the nationwide spending for the category to determine "how much the state would have spent if it had spent an average amount per workload measure unit" (Tannenwald 1998, 67; 1999, 14). The estimated spending is then adjusted for relative costs of inputs for that function. For each state, the per capita spending levels on each function are totaled to get a state's per capita spending on a standard expenditure package that is an overall fiscal need index for each state (Rafuse 1990; Tannenwald, 1998, 1999). For instance, Massachusetts accounted for about 1.81 percent of the national workload measure for highways for FY1997. In FY1997, all states spent $82.06 billion on highways. With a workload share of 1.81 percent, Massachusetts might have spent about $1.49 billion (= 0.0181 × $82.06 billion). Per capita state spending was $243. When the latter was divided by the national average, Massachusetts' average was 81 percent. This process was repeated for all expenditure categories to obtain fiscal need indices (Tannenwald 2002, 25).

COMBINED TAX AND EXPENDITURES SYSTEM AND FISCAL COMFORT INDEX

The fiscal comfort index is computed by dividing the fiscal capacity index based on RTS by the fiscal need index. The fiscal comfort index shows the relative fiscal capacity compared with fiscal needs in each state.

REVISED MEASURES OF FISCAL CAPACITY AND STRESS

Tannenwald (2002) indicates that the above methodology is vulnerable to potential measurement errors. He suggested a revised methodology to estimate fiscal capacity indices.

ADJUSTING FOR PROPERTY VALUES

A state's property tax capacity was divided into four different bases: residential, commercial and industrial, farm, and utility. However, estimating the value of residential property has been especially challenging. To estimate fiscal capacity for certain years (e.g., FY1997), the latest data that could be obtained was from the 1990 Census of Housing. Since the latest data available was outdated, state-specific residential property values should be estimated using annual statistics of house prices, new residential construction value, per-square-foot prices for rental properties, etc. Concerned about the risk inherent in the estimation method, Tannenwald (2002) pursued an alternative method.

In 1997, many states estimated fair-market values of properties located within their jurisdictions. In some cases, the states provided both market values of taxed properties and those of properties exempted from taxation (e.g., homestead exemption, economic development incentives, and properties owned by nonprofit organizations). These states provided the means to estimate the value of potentially taxable properties because the sum of market values of taxed and tax-exempt properties might be more accurate than those values estimated based on the latest data available from the

1990 Census of Housing, for instance. In some other states, only the values of taxed properties were provided. In theory, market values of taxed properties should be less than the total of potentially taxable properties. However, the market values of taxed properties exceeded the total of potentially taxable properties in some states, and as such, the market values of taxed properties might be biased. In such unexpected cases, whichever was a larger value was used as a superior measure to estimate property values.

ADJUSTING FOR REMOTE SALES

Tannenwald (2002) also accounted for the increasing share of remote sales of goods and services through Internet or mail order. Based on this method, the relative size of sales tax capacity (e.g., between in-state and out-of-state sales) could be more accurately translated into sales tax capacity. As introduced in Chapter 18 in Part IV, some states have developed new approaches to taxing goods and services through Internet or mail order. Measures of fiscal capacity need to account for these new developments in remote sales taxes.

REVISED FISCAL MEASURES

Based on his modified methodology, Tannenwald (2002) presented indices of fiscal capacity for fiscal years 1997, 1996, 1994, 1991, and 1987 for all fifty states and Washington, DC. The indices ranged from the lowest of 65 (Mississippi for FY1987) to the highest of 178 (Alaska for FY1991) with the national average of 100. For the five years examined, the national ranking has remained almost similar to that developed under the old measurement schedules. For instance, Mississippi was ranked 51st for the five years. Alaska was ranked first for the five years except for 1994 and 1996, when it was ranked second and third, respectively. Another pattern was that Pacific Coast states and upper Atlantic Coast states showed much higher indices of fiscal capacity.

Fiscal need indices report findings very similar to those on fiscal capacity. The national ranking has remained very stable across 1997, 1996, 1994, and 1987. Washington, DC, has been ranked first in terms of fiscal need for public expenditures except FY1987. New Hampshire has been ranked 51st in terms of fiscal need for the four years except FY1994. Indices of fiscal need show another interesting finding. The Pacific Coast states, with relatively higher fiscal capacity indices, still reported higher fiscal need indices. In contrast, the upper Atlantic Coast states, similarly with relatively higher capacity indices, reported consistently lower fiscal need indices for FY1996 and FY1997.

Fiscal comfort indices combined the two measures, fiscal capacity and fiscal need indices, into one measure. As such, they are supposed to show how much in fiscal resources states have in response to fiscal needs for public expenditures. Pacific Coast states still reported the highest values of fiscal comfort. This means that these states faced strong needs for public expenditures but at the same time they had more than enough fiscal capacity to cover the needs for the selected fiscal years.

OTHER CRITIQUES OF THE REPRESENTATIVE TAX SYSTEM

Despite the improved methodology, some scholars have raised further potential limitations in the fiscal capacity measures, especially the RTS (Mikesell 2007).

METHODOLOGICAL LIMITATIONS IN THE RTS

A problem with the RTS is that the computation is based on national surveys conducted every five years, as noted above. As a result, interpolation for missing years is unavoidable, which reduces the independence of between-year estimations. Another closely related problem is that the measures cannot be applied to panel data analysis. If one state increased the sales tax rate for a certain year, for instance, the state's tax collection would increase and, as a result, the RTS tax rate would increase. If the increased RTS tax rate were applied to potential tax bases of all states, then the overall fiscal capacity of all states would increase. A corollary is that fiscal capacity for other states would also increase due to the increased RTS rate. Thus, one cannot be sure whether the increase in fiscal capacity is attributable to tax base increases or to RTS rate increases.

A third problem is that the RTS measure mixes capacity and fiscal choices. A state with residents who spend a larger share of their income on retail sales might show greater fiscal capacity than a state with those spending a smaller share on retail sales. This is misleading, because total resources for the first state might not necessarily be larger than those in the second state. A closely related example is that fiscal capacity gauged by resident income cannot accurately capture sales to nonresidents via tax burden export. Fourth, selected tax bases for the RTS measure might differ from what state legislatures actually selected as legal tax bases. The RTS measure prescribes that the sale of all goods and services at the retail level be included as a tax basis other than selective excises such as motor fuel. Not all states necessarily tax all potential bases, although many tax experts contend that the exclusion is a policy mistake.

Fifth, the RTS measure neglects the fact that heavy use of one tax basis precludes heavy use of another. Neglecting that fact might result in double counting of tax bases (Mikesell 2007). What Mikesell implies is that one needs to exert caution when employing one specific type of fiscal capacity such as that from sales tax. As explained earlier, fiscal capacity measures that include all potential tax bases might mitigate this possible risk of double counting. Of course, readers still need to be cautious of the difference between potential and actual tax bases.

ALTERNATIVES TO THE RTS

Alternative capacity approaches use macroeconomic indicators without the need for accounting for state revenue structures. Although the indicators are important for analyzing fiscal federalism, many available state economic indicators are not without limitations. State personal income includes only household income excluding business income. In addition, personal income does not account for the unequal capacity to export the tax burden. It tends to understate the capacity of energy-producing states, tourism states, and states with financial service sectors. The Ladd-Yinger (1989) concept of revenue-raising capacity for cities adjusts for the varying capacity to export tax burden from property, general sales, and earnings taxes. Its weakness, however, is that all burden exports and burden imports do not accurately cancel each other out. Gross state product adds business income, but even the latter still omits income from outside sources (Mikesell 2007).

A more reasonable alternative measure is called total taxable resources (TTR). TTR measures the sum of the income flows within a certain state and those that its residents received and the state can potentially tax. As Mikesell (2007) puts it, "The measure equals gross state product less flows that are not available for the state to tax (federal indirect business taxes, social insurance contributions, and federal civilian enterprise surpluses) plus income flows not included in gross state product (dividends and interest earned from out-of-state, certain transfers from the federal government, net realized capital gains, and earnings of residents who live out of state)" (537). This measure was developed by the U.S. Department of the Treasury and was used as a redistributive factor for federal substance abuse and mental health grant programs. It is a more realistic measure of state fiscal capacity. In addition, TTR can be used for pooled cross-section/time series analysis on an annual basis because the data needed for constructing TTR are annually available. Unlike RTS, TTR is not linked to arbitrary definitions on tax structure and policies. However, there is still a potential limit in TTR: it does not accurately account for tax exporting (Mikesell 2007).

Using TTR indices from 1981 to 2003, Mikesell (2007) also presents useful findings on fiscal capacity. Average real state fiscal capacity per capita has increased from 1981 to 2003. Fiscal capacity varies dramatically across states, unlike what Tannenwald (2002) reported, as introduced above. However, Mikesell also indicates, in line with Tannenwald, that many states' fiscal capacity indices have remained consistently low, while others have been consistently high. Both state tax effort and state-local tax effort have grown for the period. Despite the dramatic variation in the two tax-effort measures, however, there is less overall fluctuation now than in the early 1980s. In addition, Mikesell found no statistically significant correlation between fiscal capacity and tax effort.

Mead (2013, 77–124) indicates that RTS and RES have been criticized for their limits. The nationally focused measures overall employ federal economic data rather than information derived from individual governmental financial reports. Thus, the financial approach to fiscal stress and capacity was developed to replace fiscal approaches such as RTS and RES. In particular, the Government Accounting Standard Board's (GASB) Statement No. 34 announced in 1999 suggested that state and local governments use more comprehensive financial reports based on both an accrual basis and a modified accrual basis of accounting. The financial reports could thus enable financial managers to develop financial-condition indices more specific to state and local financial stress and capacity (see also Benoy and Hendrick 2013, 18–34; Maher and Deller 2013, 409–14). Hendrick (2011) applied this stream of measuring fiscal capacity and need to local government fiscal analysis. She identified much more detailed categories of revenues, assets, and other resources for local governments. They were thoroughly compared with expenditures and liabilities as well as net financial conditions. When analyzing fiscal conditions of selected governments, Hendrick's approach seems the most promising. It is also obvious, however, that applying her approach to multiple jurisdictions might be a daunting task. Thus, there is a tradeoff between a much more detailed approach based on financial reports and the more representative measures of fiscal condition introduced earlier.

WHY ARE MEASURES OF FISCAL CAPACITY AND STRESS NEEDED?

The measures of fiscal capacity and stress are patently complicated and so might overwhelm policymakers by the complexity and attendant time needed for computation. However, these stress measures can be usefully applied to various areas of public finance, especially intergovernmental grants. In particular, Brunori (2007) introduced various court-induced litigations regarding state educational funding to local governments, as Chapter 6 in Part I detailed. One issue was how to develop accurate indices to measure the fiscal capacity of local governments. Oftentimes, lawsuits were filed based on fiscal capacity measures that were deemed less objective. Refined fiscal capacity and stress measures could be applied to the controversial cases.

CHAPTER SUMMARY

- **Representative Tax System and Tax Effort Index**

The Representative Tax System (RTS) has been used as a tool to measure fiscal capacities of various governmental jurisdictions. Jurisdictions' actual tax collections divided by the fiscal capacity computed based on the RTS approach is called the tax effort index.

- **The Fiscal Need Index**

The tax effort index does not account for different levels of demand for public programs across jurisdictions. The Representative Expenditures System (RES) measures jurisdictions' representative workload. The RES then develops standardized expenditure measures of the jurisdictions. These measures are called the fiscal need index.

- **The Fiscal Comfort Index**

The fiscal comfort index is computed by dividing the fiscal capacity index based on RTS by the fiscal need index.

- **Revised Measures of Fiscal Capacity and Stress**

There are numerous suggestions for revising the above fiscal capacity measures.

(1) Since property values are dependent on periodic surveys, some states use market value data of properties, which are available at the time of computing fiscal capacity measures.

(2) Remote sales are likely to be excluded from the sales tax base, so some adjustments have been made to account for the lost sales tax base from remote sales.

(3) Fiscal capacity and stress measures developed from revised methodologies are similar to those developed under the old approaches.

• Critiques of the Representative Tax System

Scholars have also criticized many methodological limits in the RTS.

(1) Due to periodic survey-based estimations of the RTS, some data must be interpolated. This causes high dependence between yearly data sets. An increase in certain jurisdictions' tax rate causes an increase in overall fiscal capacity indices, which has nothing to do with actual improvements in fiscal capacity. The RTS measures do not distinguish between fiscal capacity and fiscal choices. It does not cover all tax bases, and it double counts some tax bases.

(2) A more reasonable alternative measure is called total taxable resources (TTR). TTR measures the sum of the income flows within a certain state and those that its residents received and the state can potentially tax.

(3) Practitioners called for using financial-condition indices that are developed based on GASB Statement No. 34 to more specifically measure fiscal stress and capacity of state and local governments.

PART V

INTERGOVERNMENTAL FISCAL RELATIONS

Intergovernmental Grants

21 Rationales and Types

There are various rationales for intergovernmental (IGR) grants. Wallace Oates (1999, 1126) lists three major functions of IGR grants: "the internalization of spillover benefits to other jurisdictions, fiscal equalization across jurisdictions, and an improved overall tax system." There are three typical types of IGR grants: matching, categorical, and general grants. This chapter introduces the following issues:

- Rationale I: Internalization of Spillover Benefits or Costs
- Rationale II: Fiscal Equalization
- Rationale III: Improved Tax System
- Critiques of the Traditional Theory of Fiscal Federalism
- Types of IGR Grants
- Status of IGR Grants

RATIONALE I: INTERNALIZATION OF SPILLOVER BENEFITS OR COSTS

First, IGR grants typically are distributed to lower-level governments from higher-level ones to account for spillover benefits or costs of delivering public services by the lower-level governments. The main reason for IGR grants in this case is to internalize spillover benefits or costs. To better understand this concept, one needs to examine two principles in identifying the range and level of governmental jurisdictions.

THE PRINCIPLE OF SUBSIDIARITY

The first criterion of assigning governmental services is the principle of subsidiarity. This principle recommends that the lowest level of government primarily deliver governmental services. Because subnational governments can closely monitor the preferences and demands of taxpayers, they can provide the services their residents want much more effectively than central governments can. The principle of subsidiarity leads to devolution, a trend that is a reflection of political evolution toward more democratic and participatory governments with heightened responsiveness and accountability. The participatory governments can ensure a closer correspondence between the quantity and quality of governmental goods and services and the preferences of their residents (Mikesell 2011, 599).

When diverse public services are provided by a single government, consumer-voters with different preferences and demands for services will be less happy and less satisfied. The greater the number of different service demands, the more governments are needed. More governments means smaller ones, and services need to be provided at the most decentralized level of the federal system (Fisher 2007, 120), which can better satisfy diverse demands from consumer-voters. As we have discussed in Chapter 17 in Part IV, Tiebout's (1956) voting with feet allows consumer-voters to choose localities with the best mix of taxes and services (Hyman 2011, 713–17, 726–28), although Oates (2008) calls for some caution, because Tiebout's voting is not exactly the same as fiscal federalism.

THE PRINCIPLE OF CORRESPONDENCE

A second and closely related criterion for identifying the level of governmental jurisdictions is the range of spillover benefits or costs of delivering public services. If governmental jurisdictions serve a set of individual residents who consume their goods and services, this condition satisfies the correspondence principle in defining geographic boundaries of jurisdictions (Mikesell 2011, 598; Oates 1972, 34). Based on this principle, the governmental jurisdictions can prevent problems that occur when beneficiaries of goods and services do not pay for them. The principle is very useful in analyzing intergovernmental systems. A pure private service does not have any spillover effects. When private individuals make decisions on the provision of a purely private service, there is no distortion. In contrast, public goods and services generate external benefits. For instance, police and fire protection services benefit the residents beyond the community that delivers the services. Therefore, higher-level governments need to deliver the services whose benefits spill beyond local jurisdictions. Mismatch between the spillover range and the provision range might result in misallocations of resources (Mikesell 2011, 598–99).

From the perspective of the entire society, a spillover of costs results in overproduction of certain services due to an underestimation of the true social costs. A benefit spillover leads to underestimation of benefits and thereby underproduction of services (thus a mismatch between the spillover range and the provision range). There are other examples of the mismatch. Nonresident landlords partly bear the expense of property taxes, which is an example of local tax-cost spillover. When nonresidents drive on well-paved city streets, there is a benefit spillover. When a student is educated at the cost of a city and migrates to other areas, there is a spillover of educational service benefits. An economic solution to spatial externalities is to internalize the externality by considering true costs and benefits. A simple alternative is to create bigger governmental jurisdictions. As a result, more centralized governments or IGR grants from these governments are justified (Fisher 2007, 120–21; Ulbrich 2011, 282–83).

Figure 21.1   **Internalization of Externalities Across Jurisdictions**

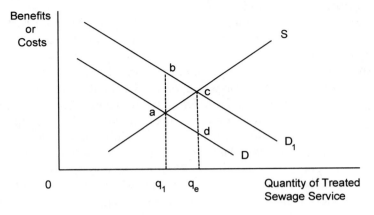

AN ILLUSTRATIVE EXAMPLE OF CORRESPONDENCE

Mikesell (2011, 600) gives an excellent example of the correspondence and internalization of spatial externalities, which is slightly modified here for clarity. City A's sewage treatment plant used to dump partially treated waste into a river that flows past city B, but now it completely treats waste. City B draws water from the river for its water utility. More complete treatment of waste by city A is obviously a benefit for the residents of city B. Higher-level governments can provide a corrective subsidy to city B so the residents in city B can demand more water. Alternatively, they can provide the same subsidy to city A to reimburse city A's waste treatment costs incurred by providing cleaner water for the residents of city B (Anderson 2012, 620–25; Boadway and Wildasin 1984, 518–21; Hyman 2011, 112–13; 1986, 63–34; Mankiw 2012, 199–201). Figure 21.1 shows how higher-level governments can internalize the spillover benefits.

As shown in Figure 21.1, the quantity of completely treated sewage service delivered by city A is on the horizontal axis. The vertical axis denotes benefits from enjoying the local service or costs incurred from delivering the service. D and S denote demand curves and supply curves for the service. When city A's sewage treatment facility dumps completely treated waste into the river, the activity obviously creates some positive externalities on the part of the residents in city B. The original equilibrium for the sewage treatment service is held at the quantity of q_1. However, when the amount of positive externalities is "internalized," the social benefit, or demand curve, for the service should now be D_1, rather than D. This implies that the adequate level of producing the treatment service is q_e. In this case, the original level of treatment service is an underproduction compared to the socially efficient (i.e., internalizing the positive externalities) level of service production.

Under the original condition, the deadweight loss (i.e., efficiency loss) to the entire society will be the triangular area, *abc* (Weimer and Vining 2011, 94–97; see also Chapter 11 in Part II on cost-benefit analysis for the case of negative externalities). One way to address the positive externalities is to provide a corrective subsidy to city B to stimulate the demand for cleaner water. The amount of the subsidy at the new equilibrium of treated sewage service will be *cd* (Hyman 2011, 112–13). Another way to address the positive externalities is to give a corrective subsidy to the producer of services, in the above case City A's sewage treatment plant. In this case, a higher-level government might offer grant funds to city A so that it can increase its waste treatment service from q_1 to q_e. In this case, the higher-level government has chosen to subsidize city A for wastewater treatment. Diagrammatic analysis of the subsidy to city A will be slightly different from that in Figure 21.1. The computational formula for the subsidy amount also differs from that for the subsidy distributed to city B (Boadman and Wildasin 1984, 517–18; Cullis and Jones 2009, 382–83). These corrective subsidies are called intergovernmental subsidies, known as grants-in-aid to internalize the positive externalities (Weimer and Vining 2011, 224–27). When City A increases treated waste service, social surplus will increase as well, which will correct the spatial externalities. The internalization of spatial externalities is one of the most frequently listed rationales for IGR grants (Fisher 2007, 201–2).

TRADEOFF BETWEEN CORRESPONDENCE AND SUBSIDIARITY

There is almost always a tradeoff between the two principles: having governments large enough to avoid cost or benefit spillovers (i.e., the principle of correspondence) but small enough to provide uniform desired amounts of public services to local residents (i.e., the principle of subsidiarity). The optimal size of governments maximizes social welfare. Social welfare might increase by choosing geographically adequate jurisdictions when there are spillover costs or benefits as shown in Figure 21.1. However, there is then a possibility that in the now larger jurisdictions or wider service coverage rendered by IGR grants with no externalities, some residents might prefer different amounts of public services. Therefore, the welfare gain from suppressed spatial externalities should be compared with the welfare loss due to increasing dissatisfaction caused by less desired and less diverse sets of public services. Of course, in principle, the optimal size of governments can be obtained when marginal benefits of public services can be compared with marginal costs of delivering the services (Fisher 2007, 125–27). However, this is a daunting task for budget decision makers.

RATIONALE II: FISCAL EQUALIZATION

As noted above, Oates (1999) suggested fiscal equalization across jurisdictions as the second rationale for IGR grants. The property tax provides a relevant illustration. If two communities with different levels of property tax bases are to provide the same level of public services, then the community with the lower tax base will be faced with a higher property tax rate or higher tax effort (see Chapter 20 in Part IV for details of tax effort). If higher-level governments intervene in this type of fiscal disparity, they can raise revenues through their tax systems and redistribute them to communities with lower tax bases. Fiscal disparity is the most pronounced between urban cities and their suburbs. It may also be large between urban and rural areas. Some federal grant formulas do include equalizing elements (Boadman and Wildasin 1984, 521–29;

Cullis and Jones 2009, 383–84; Mikesell 2011, 600–3). If IGR grants with formulas favor states and localities in greater fiscal need (e.g., in terms of poverty rates, per capita income, etc.), they can address fiscal disparity across the states and localities (Fisher 2007, 203; Ulbrich 2011, 281–82).

RATIONALE III: IMPROVED TAX SYSTEM

Oates (1999) also listed an improved overall tax system as another rationale for IGR grants. Mikesell (2011, 603–7) offers clear examples. In general, lower-level governments can mutually benefit from relief in tax-base use and assistance with tax administration and compliance. For instance, if an individual is in the 35 percent federal income tax bracket and her state income tax increases by $100, then the real tax burden increases only by $65 because the state income tax is deducted from the federal income tax. There are other examples of such benefits. Payments under a qualifying state tax act as an 80 percent credit to the federal death tax. These are examples of implicit fiscal assistance to lower-level governments from higher-level ones.

Governments have continued cooperative tax administration. With coordinated tax bases, several states key their income tax filings to federal adjusted gross income. Tax supplements and central administration are other types of intergovernmental fiscal coordination. These are also examples of fiscal assistance to lower-level governments by way of reduced administrative cost for those governments.

CRITIQUES OF THE TRADITIONAL THEORY OF FISCAL FEDERALISM

The traditional theory of fiscal federalism introduced above, which is primarily based on the principles of correspondence and subsidiarity, is often dubbed first-generation fiscal federalism (FGFF) (Oates 2008; Weingast 2009).[1] Oates (2008) indicates that there have been some criticisms of FGFF, but they do not necessarily nullify the fundamental framework of FGFF. First, critics assert that public agents do not always seek to maximize the well-being of jurisdictional constituents out of benevolence but have their own incentives. Oates indicates, however, that local jurisdictions can achieve approximately efficient outcomes even without assuming benevolence. The second criticism is that central provision of public goods might result in the same level of public outputs. Central governments might not fashion local outputs in accordance with local tastes. There are numerous political and legal needs to maintain equity across jurisdictions, as shown in environmental federalism. However, there might be some cases where central governments, as well as local jurisdictions, can still bring different levels of public programs across different jurisdictions as in the case of pork-barrel politics. Despite the minor critiques and attendant modifications over FGFF, Oates indicates that fiscal decentralism can still contribute to welfare maximization. When there are spillover effects, central governments can introduce corrective IGR grants that can internalize such external benefits. For other cases, central governments can rely on IGR grants for fiscal equalization.

More critical critiques of FGFF come from a different perspective. Second-generation fiscal federalism (SGFF) builds on FGFF but assumes that subnational officials have different goals induced by political and fiscal institutions. These goals often diverge significantly from the maximization of citizen welfare assumed in FGFF. SGFF "emphasizes how fiscal institutions create incentives for subnational political officials that affect their policy choice and hence their jurisdiction's performance" (Weingast 2009, 283). Similarly, Oates (2008) summarizes two strands of critiques of FGFF, which are the rationales for SGFF. Strand One indicates that local jurisdictions might fall into moral hazard in anticipating that, in the case of fiscal crisis, central governments will come to their rescue as evidenced during the recent financial crisis. Under the framework of Strand Two, local public agents pay more attention to legislative structure and electoral processes to have a better understanding of different fiscal outcomes under centralized and decentralized polities. In sum, Strand Two applies formal models of fiscal and political institutions to the analysis of fiscal decentralization. Oates further discusses why IGR grants result in unexpected fiscal impacts from the fiscal decentralization theory and in some cases should be cautiously distributed. At this point, readers might have noticed that the transition from FGFF to SGFF echoes the logic developed in the public choice theory introduced in Chapter 17 in Part IV: Market-based rational choice models incorporate political institutions.

TYPES OF IGR GRANTS

IGR grants are characterized by four main factors: use for a specific service or general purpose (categorical vs. general grants), automatic allocation based on formula or application required for a specific project (formula-based or project grants), matching requirement by recipient governments (matching vs. nonmatching grants), and limits on grant size. Most federal and state grants are categorical. There are either formula or project grants. Grants can also be lump-sum (nonmatching) or matching grants. Amounts of lump-sum grants generally do not change as recipient governments change taxes or expenditures. The recipient governments cannot alter the amounts of lump-sum grants. Matching grants may be either closed-ended (i.e., grant amount limited) or open-ended (i.e., no limit on grant amount) (Cullis and Jones 2009, 378–82; Fisher 2007, 203–5). In practice, three types of IGR grants warrant readers' attention: matching, categorical, and general grants.

MATCHING GRANTS

Specific matching aid matches each dollar of recipient tax or expenditure with R grant dollars, or the matching rate. If $R = 0.5$, each local dollar generates 50 cents per each recipient government's dollar spent on specific services. The share financed by the grant, M, is $0.33 = (0.5/(0.5 + 1))$: $M = R (1 + R)$. The matching grant reduces the cost of delivering the aided service by the recipient government. The local tax price (P) of an additional dollar incurred for service delivery (the local marginal cost) is $P = 1 - M = 1 - [R / (1 + R)] = 1 / (1 + R)$. Therefore, if $R = .25$, the local tax price is \$.80: Local residents will pay \$.80 for each dollar of expenditure for the aided service (Chernick 1998; Fisher 2007, 203–5).

CATEGORICAL GRANTS

Categorical grants can be either open-ended (no limit on the grant amount) or closed-ended (the grant amount is limited by a fixed upper boundary) (Cullis and Jones 2009, 378–82; Fisher 2007, 203–5). There are three difficulties associated with categorical grants in particular. First, they are very complicated administratively. For instance, federal grant systems contain elaborate control mechanisms, and different programs usually have different planning, reporting, and accounting requirements. Second, some communities do not participate in the programs, while others aggressively seek such funds. In addition, recipient governments might use the funds to meet other programs' matching requirements. Third, categorical grants can distort local program priorities (Mikesell 2011, 612–15).

GENERAL GRANTS

In contrast, general grants do not have restrictions. They typically provide general fiscal assistance and are almost always distributed by formula. If the formula includes factors that recipient governments cannot control, such as population or per capita income, the grant is called a pure lump-sum grant. If the formula includes some factors within the control of recipient governments, such as tax collections or tax efforts, recipient governments can alter the amount of the grant by adjusting their tax collections or tax efforts. Some federal and state revenue sharing grants use this method, and the grants are then de facto matching grants. The best-known general-purpose grant was the U.S. General Revenue Sharing Program that started in 1972. The funds were first allocated to states based on a formula including population, per capita income, and tax effort. One-third of them were distributed to states, and the remaining went to local governments in each state, again based on formulas. States were removed from the program in 1984, and the program for localities expired in 1987. Recently, numerous categorical grants have been combined into a few block grants. In practice, they are closer to general-purpose grants (Fisher 2007, 205–6; Hyman 2011, 725; Mikesell 2011, 615–16; Ulbrich 2011, 284–86).

STATUS OF IGR GRANTS

In 1971–1972, about 28.4 percent of state revenues came from grants from other governments. In 2001–2002, the share of state revenues from these grants was about 30.3 percent. It remained almost unchanged at 30.1 percent in 2005–2006. The share of local revenues from grants was about 37.7 percent in 1971–1972, 38.2 percent in 2001–2002, and 38.2 percent in 2005–2006. Federal grants as a percentage of state-local revenues were around 15 percent until 1970, but hovered around 21 percent during the late 1970s. They declined until 2005, when the percentage was about 21.1 percent. One of the main reasons for the recently increasing share of state-local revenues from federal aid is the increase in such entitlement programs as Medicaid and other public assistance programs (Mikesell 2011, 607–11). From 1960 to 2007, federal grants to states and localities for health and income security grew the most in terms of dollar amounts. In 2007, about 64 percent of all federal grants to states and localities were accounted for by Medicaid and other public aid payments to individual recipients. The grants in the areas of education, training, employment, social services, and transportation also grew substantially during the same period (Hyman 2011, 725–27).

Most of federal grants-in-aid made directly to localities have been allocated for education, housing and community redevelopment, waste treatment facilities, and airport construction. These service categories have been more likely to have spillover effects beyond local regions (Hyman 2011, 726). Another important type of IGR grant is state aid to local school districts. Chapter 6 in Part I on rights-based budgeting introduced the state aids, separate from the above IGR grants.

CHAPTER SUMMARY

• **Principles of Subsidiarity and Correspondence**
Two principles identifying governmental jurisdictions are relevant for understanding why we need IGR grants.

(1) The principle of subsidiarity means that the lowest levels of government should deliver governmental services because they know the demands from consumer-voters the best.

(2) The principle of correspondence is satisfied when governmental jurisdictions precisely serve a set of individual residents who consume their goods and services. Spatial externalities take place when there is a mismatch between the benefit/cost spillover range and the service provision range. IGR grants are supposed to internalize the spatial externalities.

There is almost always a tradeoff between the two principles. Spatial externalities can be minimized through creation of larger jurisdictions or wider service coverage rendered by IGR grants. In that case, however, some residents prefer different amounts of public goods.

Second-generation fiscal federalism modifies the traditional theory of fiscal federalism. Subnational public officials might pursue their own interests rather than maximizing the welfare of their jurisdictions. In addition, political and fiscal institutions can also affect subnational governments' fiscal decisions.

• **Fiscal Equalization**
Another rationale for IGR grants is fiscal equalization. There is a large disparity in fiscal capacity between urban and rural areas as well as cities and their suburbs. If IGR grant formulas favor jurisdictions in greater fiscal need, they can improve fiscal disparity across the jurisdictions.

• **Improved Tax System**
When higher-level governments allow relief in tax-base use, lower-level governments benefit from implicit IGR fiscal assistance. Cooperative tax administration also provides for fiscal assistance to lower-level governments.

- **Types of Intergovernmental Grants**

Three types of IGR grants warrant further attention: matching, categorical, and general grants.

(1) Matching grants reduce tax burdens on the residents in recipient governments.

(2) Some IGR grants limit the purposes on which they are spent. These are categorical grants. Despite the limit, they are often used for other programmatic purposes or programs' matching requirements.

(3) General grants usually do not carry the limits attached to categorical grants. They are almost always distributed by formula.

- **Status of Intergovernmental Grants**

Federal grants as a percentage of state-local revenues had increased during the 1970s, but decreased until about 2005 when they started increasing slightly. The relative increase in federal grants during recent years is substantially attributable to the increase in entitlement programs such as Medicaid and other welfare programs.

NOTE

1. Weingast succinctly summarizes five conditions for an ideal type of fiscal federalism, called market-preserving federalism. First, a hierarchy of governments with delineated authority lines exists for each level of government. Second, subnational governments retain authority over local regulation of the economy and provision of public goods and services. Third, product and factor mobility across jurisdictional boundaries enables effective competition, hence the common market condition. Fourth, a corollary of the third condition is a hard budget constraint. Subnational governments should bear the full financial consequences of their fiscal choices such that they cannot spend more than their capacity or bail out failing enterprises. The federal government may not rescue subnational governments through transfers. Fifth, an allocation of political authority is institutionalized in federal systems. The central government cannot singularly impose its will upon subnational governments. The absence of one or more of the five conditions leads to inefficiency or pathology in fiscal federalism. FGFF, based on the principles of correspondence and subsidiarity, is a condition of fiscal federalism close to the ideal type.

22 Intergovernmental Grants
Fiscal Impacts

The previous chapter introduced the rationales and types of intergovernmental (IGR) grants. This chapter shows that fiscal impacts of IGR grants vary significantly depending on the rationales and types of the grants. This chapter covers the following issues:

- Fiscal Impacts of Intergovernmental Grants
- Price Effect of Intergovernmental Grants
- Income Effect of Intergovernmental Grants
- Side Effects of Intergovernmental Grants
- Empirical Findings on Fiscal Impacts of Intergovernmental Grants
- Money Sticks Where It Hits
- Recent Findings on Fiscal Impacts of Intergovernmental Grants

FISCAL IMPACTS OF INTERGOVERNMENTAL GRANTS

When the price of a certain product drops, consumers are affected by two factors. The product with a lower price is less expensive than other goods, which is an incentive for consumers to demand the now less expensive commodity. This effect is called the substitution, or price, effect. Consumers demand the commodity more, if it is a normal good, when its price decreases. Second, when consumers' incomes grow, their purchasing power increases. As a result, they are likely to demand the commodity more. This is called an income effect (Mankiw 2012, 448–53).

Analysis of income and price effects can be applied to the analysis of fiscal impacts of IGR grants. When IGR grants only increase the wealth of recipient governments, one might observe income effects. The residents in the recipient governments might increase their demand for the public service that IGR grants support. In contrast, if IGR grants reduce the price of services delivered by the recipient governments, the grants generate primarily price effects. The following sections show the price and income effects of IGR grants. Other side effects of IGR grants are also introduced.

PRICE EFFECT OF INTERGOVERNMENTAL GRANTS

Fisher (2007, 207–9) presents an excellent example of IGR grants' price effect. Assume that the price elasticity of demand for a public service by a local government is –0.5: When the tax price for the service decreases by 1 percent, the demand for it in terms of local expenditure for the service increases by 0.5 percent (see Chapter 17 in Part IV for details on elasticity). Assume that initial expenditures on the service, financed from taxes by the local government, are $1,000 per capita. Assume further that the matching rate by its state government is $.50: The state government gives the local government $.50 per every dollar spent by the local government. This means that the tax price for a decisive voter in the local government decreases. More specifically, the tax price drops to $.67: The tax price is equal to 1/ (1 + .50) (see Chapter 21 for more details). Therefore, the tax price decreases by 33 percent and the original local spending increases to $1,165, by 16.5 percent (a 16.5% *increase* = 33% × –.5) because the decisive voter will now demand the aided service more due to its cheaper price. This is called the price effect of IGR grants (Baicker 2001; Chernick 1998, 2000; Ribar and Wilhelm 1999).

The price effect of IGR grants also has a significant aspect regarding revenue financing by the recipient government. Because one-third of the fiscal burden, or tax price, of the decisive voter is financed from the state IGR grant, the local government does not have to finance the full amount of $1,165. In other words, one-third of the new total spending, $388.33 (= $1,165 × .33) is financed from a matching grant. The local government now does not need the full $1,000 for its local expenditures on the service because of the IGR grant.

INCOME EFFECT OF INTERGOVERNMENTAL GRANTS

In the above case, assume instead that the same amount of $388.33 is distributed in the form of a lump-sum grant, and per capita income in the locality is $5,000. Further assume that the income elasticity of demand for the local service is 0.5: When per capita income increases by 1 percent, the demand for the service increases by 0.5 percent. With the aid of the lump-sum grant, per capita income rises by 7.76 percent (e.g., $388.33 of $5,000). As a result, local spending on the service will increase by 3.88 percent (= 7.76% × .5) to $1,038.80 (= $1,000 × .0388) (see Chapter 17 in Part IV for details) (Baicker 2001; Chernick 1998, 2000; Ribar and Wilhelm 1999).

The fiscal impact induced by the lump-sum grant is much smaller than is the $1,165 that is induced by the equal amount of the matching grant in the above case. In general, matching grants have more stimulative fiscal impacts on recipient governments' expenditures on aided services than do pure lump-sum grants (Fisher 2007, 207–9; see also Anderson 2012, 627–35; Rosen and Gayer 2010, 528–32; Ulbrich 2011, 292). Matching grants are generally used to compensate for positive externalities across lower-level governments, and efficiency gain will be measured in terms of increased social marginal benefits, as indicated in the previous chapter (Hyman 2011, 734–35).

SIDE EFFECTS OF INTERGOVERNMENTAL GRANTS

GRANT FUNGIBILITY

There is another interesting theoretical observation in the above scenarios. An open-ended matching grant of $388.33 was matched to $776.67 in the new spending total of $1,165 in the case of matching grants (see the above discussion of the price effect). It is obvious that the new "local" spending decreased from the original $1,000 to $776.67. This implies that $223.33 might have been used for other service categories or tax relief. This observation tends to hold true whenever the demand for local goods is fairly price-inelastic.[1] As discussed in Chapter 17 in Part IV, most empirical studies reported that the demand for state and local public goods is inelastic and the above scenario is likely to hold true (Fisher 2007, 209–10). This observation is oftentimes called grant fungibility, and many scholars have assumed that grant fungibility might be more frequently found for general grants without any use restrictions.

However, even when the use of IGR grants is specified, there is still a chance of grant fungibility. For instance, specific lump-sum grants with use restrictions might not be significantly different from those without restrictions. The use restriction matters only when intended expenditures by recipient governments are less than what the grant will purchase for them. If they are already spending more than what the grant might buy for them, local funds equal to the grant amount (or part of the grant amount) might be shifted to other service categories. This is a typical case of grant fungibility. In other words, if recipient governments are spending more than the specific lump-sum grants with use restrictions, there is no guarantee that they will use the full amount of the grants for aided services. They might not increase local spending by the full amount of the grant (Anderson 2011, 728–89; Fisher 2007, 210–12; Ulbrich 2011, 289–92).

To prevent grant fungibility, some grants add provisions for maintaining local efforts. The provisions require that grants be used for aided services and that local funds not be reduced. However, if local expenditures increase annually, the lump-sum grant with the maintenance-effort provision is not as effective as it might look. For instance, recipient governments might use the grant for aided services but shift the annual increase in local expenditures for the aided services to other services (Fisher 2007, 210–12).

REVENUE DISTORTION FROM THE REVENUE SHARING PROGRAM

Finally, the Revenue Sharing Program discussed in the previous chapter sometimes has the same fiscal impact as matching grants when the program uses a formula based on, for instance, tax effort (see Chapter 20 in Part IV on measures of fiscal capacity and stress for details on tax effort). When a jurisdiction increases tax effort, it increases its tax revenues. The Revenue Sharing Program distributes larger grants to the jurisdiction with the higher tax effort. The increased grant amount will further reduce the local tax price for the aided service. At this moment, other jurisdictions will competitively increase their tax efforts to increase their grant dollars. However, when all localities raise their tax efforts, though no one's revenue-sharing grant changes, local tax rates have been hiked (Fisher 2007, 212–13).

EMPIRICAL FINDINGS ON FISCAL IMPACTS OF INTERGOVERNMENTAL GRANTS

Empirical findings mostly support the theoretical expectations on the fiscal impacts of different IGR grants on recipient governments' spending on aided services. Despite some variation in empirical findings, there are fairly common conclusions about the impact of grants on recipient governments' spending.

PRICE EFFECT: STIMULATIVE EFFECTS OF MATCHING GRANTS

First, open-ended, categorical matching grants tend to increase local expenditures more than do equal-size specific lump-sum grants. Since price elasticities of demand for most public goods are less than 1, local expenditures do not increase more than the grant amounts (i.e., grant fungibility). Some funds might have been diverted to other expenditure categories or tax relief as discussed above. Although they were not the most common type of federal grants, open-ended, categorical matching grants have been used for two federal grants: Aid to Families with Dependent Children (AFDC) until 1996 and Medicaid. Despite potential grant fungibility, however, open-ended, categorical matching grants have reported a stronger fiscal impact on recipient governments' spending than lump-sum grants (Fisher 2007, 216; Ulbrich 2011, 286).

Chernick (1998, 2000) and Ribar and Wilhelm (1999) provide a comprehensive review of empirical findings conducted on the price elasticities of open-ended matching grants such as AFDC and Medicaid from the 1960s to the 1990s. Chernick reports that the price elasticities have ranged from about –.96 to .58. Ribar and Wilhelm report that the price elasticities of open-ended matching grants have ranged from about –1.24 to .58. Baicker (2001) raises some caveats over the previous empirical findings. Since the amounts of the open-ended categorical matching grants were often inversely related to recipient governments' income levels, there is a possibility that statistical models in the previous studies might have suffered from two-way causality between recipient governments' income levels and grant amounts. Baicker corrected for this potential two-way causality for AFCD grant data and found that the price elasticity was fairly stable between –.4 and –.3.

Second, closed-ended categorical matching grants are often more stimulative than open-ended, categorical matching grants are, unlike theoretical expectations. There are a couple of potential reasons for the anomaly. Closed-ended categorical matching grants were heavily used for services that state and local governments usually do not provide or may include maintenance efforts as introduced above. In either case, the possibility of grant fungibility is very low. In addition, price elasticities of demand for the aided services were more likely to be higher than those of the services receiving open-ended categorical grants, which might also explain the higher-than-expected impacts (Fisher 2007, 217).

One good example of grants that suffice for the condition is federal highway grants to states. These are closed-ended matching grants, with a federal share of spending ranging from $.75 to $.80 (Gamkhar 2002, 33; Knight 2002). As the relatively higher share of federal funds implies, state and local governments do not provide highway, especially interstate, services. In addition, previous studies revealed that the price elasticities of demand for public works like highways range from –0.40 to –0.90, which are more elastic than those for other public services such as education, police, and fire protection (Fisher 2007, 82).

Empirical evidence strongly supports these assertions.[2] Stotsky (1991) reported that up to the point requiring state governments' matching funds, one dollar of federal highway grant boosted state highway spending by as much as $2.9, although beyond the matching point the fiscal impact from the grant dropped to only $.05. Congleton and Bennett (1995) indicated that one dollar of federal highway grant increased state highway spending by $1.75 to $1.92. Goel and Nelson (2003) reported that the fiscal impact of the grant on state highway outlays was about $1.26. Ryu (2006) showed that the grant increased state highway expenditures by about $.98. This finding is quite close to the increase of about $.87 that Gamkhar (2000) found. Ryu (2006, 2007) also reported some interesting findings from a new type of federal highway grant. The National Highway System Designation Act of 1995 and the Transportation Equity Act for the Twenty-First Century of 1998 allowed state governments to leverage federal grant monies. They were allowed to loan the federal funds to various public and private infrastructure projects and borrow more funds by using the federal funds as collateral. His studies showed that federal highway grants used for leveraging fund programs, called State Infrastructure Bank programs, increased state highway spending by $5.24 to $7.6. The mechanism allowing fund leveraging might further explain those exceptionally higher fiscal impacts.

INCOME EFFECT

Lump-sum grants mostly increase recipient governments' expenditures less than equal-size matching grants do. Empirical findings show that the fiscal impacts of the grants fall between $.25 and $.50. The range of the fiscal impacts (i.e., income effect) from lump-sum grants is significantly lower than that (i.e., price effect) for the closed-ended, categorical matching grants introduced above. This also has some significant implications for grant fungibility, especially for lump-sum grants. Given the fiscal impacts of $.25 to $.50, lump-sum grants of $1 provide somewhere between $.50 and $.75 for expenditures for other services or tax relief. A substantial portion of lump-sum grants might have been used for different services of the recipient governments (Fisher 2007, 217–18; Hyman 2011, 728–29; Ulbrich 2011, 288–92).

Chernick (1998, 2000) and Ribar and Wilhelm (1999) also provide comprehensive reviews of empirical findings conducted from the 1960s to the 1990s on the income elasticities of such open-ended matching grants as AFDC and Medicaid. Chernick reports that the income elasticities have ranged from about –0.39 to 2.32. Ribar and Wilhelm report that the income elasticities of open-ended matching grants have ranged from about –0.64 to 2.09. Baicker (2001), when controlling for the two-way causality between recipient governments' income levels and grant amounts mentioned above, found that the income elasticity of AFDC grants was again fairly stable around 0.50.

FLYPAPER EFFECT

Finally, empirical findings also showed that fiscal impacts of lump-sum grants are higher than increases in residents' incomes. A one-dollar increase in the latter typically increased local expenditures by about $.05 to $.10 (Cullis and Jones 2009, 388). In contrast, a one-dollar increase in lump-sum grants increased local expenditures by about $.25 to $.50 as noted above. This phenomenon has been known as the flypaper effect (Fisher 2007, 218; Hines and Thaler 1995; Hyman 2011, 732–33; Rosen and Gayer 2010, 532–33; Ulbrich 2011, 293–94). The following section has more discussions on this highly controversial issue.

MONEY STICKS WHERE IT HITS

As mentioned above, the flypaper effect is much more complicated and controversial than it looks. According to the median voter theory introduced in Chapter 17 in Part IV, local expenditures might be heavily swayed by the most decisive voter, a median voter. The median voter's personal wealth might increase either by an increase in personal income or by grants. Thus, the fiscal impacts of lump-sum grants are supposed to be the same as those from increases in personal income (Fisher 2007, 218–19).

Empirical studies, however, reported that the fiscal impacts from lump-sum grants are much higher than those from personal income, also reported above: Money will stick in recipient governments that it hits. There have been numerous scholarly suggestions about why that might be the case. One possible explanation is the theory of fiscal illusion: Local residents perceive that lump-sum grants reduce the marginal, as opposed to average, cost of service deliveries by the recipient governments. If local governments spend $100 per capita for a certain service and receive a $30 per capita grant, the governments pay only 70 percent of the cost incurred for service deliveries. Residents might equate the reduction in the cost with a decrease in their tax price. This will lead to a similar effect from matching grants by reducing tax prices through decreasing marginal costs of service deliveries (Courant, Gramlich, and Rubinfeld 1979; Oates 1979).

King (1984) applied Niskanen's model of budget-maximizing bureaucrats, introduced in Chapter 16, to explaining the flypaper effect (Cullis and Jones 2009, 389–90). As explained in Chapter 16, bureaucrats tend to request budgets larger than socially efficient ones. When marginal benefits equal marginal costs of delivering public goods and services, social efficiency will be maximized but bureaucrats tend to pursue budgets until average benefits equal average costs (recall point "b" in Figure 16.1; see page 145). If the bureaucrats in local jurisdictions, receiving lump-sum grants, believe that the grants reduce average costs of delivering public goods and services, they are likely to request larger budgets. In Figure 16.1, for instance, total cost curve A will now cut through the section of the total benefit curve, which is associated with point *b* and point *c*. In short, lump-sum grants will raise the local budgets more than increases in residents' incomes do. Some empirical observations support King's expectation. When bureaucrats in grant-receiving local governments retained stronger budget-manipulation power, stronger flypaper effect was reported (Bae and Feiock 2004; Schneider and Ji 1987).

The flypaper effect also can result from the political process. Budget-maximizing bureaucrats can control the information about the grants and induce voters to approve taxes for desired services and at the same time spend the grant funds. In this case, the grant funds will significantly increase the spending for the services (Filimon, Romer, and Rosenthal 1982).

Other, competing theories contend that the flypaper effect results from analytical errors. When choosing the recipients for lump-sum grants, granting governments usually tend to distribute their grant funds to recipient governments that are likely to spend the largest amount of local funds. This process actually turns lump-sum grants into matching grants with much higher stimulative fiscal impacts. Analysts misunderstand the former as the latter. For instance, Chernick (1979) specified the donor-recipient contract as an auction. Recipient governments bid for the right to provide aided services through potential grants by offering to share the costs of provision. Donor governments select recipient governments until their grant budgets are exhausted to the extent that the marginal contributions of recipient governments are equal to the marginal benefits from the provision of the services provided by the recipient governments. Recipient governments with the highest bidding price will provide more services and receive more aid. The process of the auction game partially explains the flypaper effect.

Another possibility implies that as income levels of jurisdictions increase, the cost of service deliveries by the jurisdictions might decline. For instance, especially high-income communities might have private educational services other than governmental education services. This will reduce the burden of the governments. As income levels rise, demands for public education go up. At the same time, the cost of service deliveries will be reduced because education services are partially delivered by *private* educational services. This will partially reduce the cost of service delivery by the governments, and, therefore, supply curves for the service will make a parallel shift that increases the educational service quantity and expenditures. This leads to slightly higher expenditures for the aided service (Fisher 2007, 220–21; Hamilton 1983).

Continued future research into the confusing flypaper effect is warranted. However, Inman (2008) contends that politics might explain the flypaper effect the best. He cited Chernick (1979), introduced above, as a study supporting the logic of politics. In addition, he cited Knight (2002) as another study supporting the logic. Knight specifies a model of political contracting for grant allocations. Those legislators whose districts value the aided service most highly, and, thus, are willing to spend more on the aided services, are likely to make the winning offers for grants. The result is a positive correlation between grants awarded and the spending by the recipient districts. This also will explain the flypaper effect. Knight further reported one of the most provocative findings on fiscal impacts of IGR grants. When the political process is adequately controlled for, one dollar of federal highway grant astonishingly "reduced" state highway outlays by as much as $.87 to $1.12.

In contrast to the above, a recent study by Grizzle (2011), using a panel data for all fifty states from 1997 to 2006, reported the impacts of nonmatching, lump-sum grants on state expenditures, which are significantly smaller than those associated with the flypaper effect. When she used logarithmic model specifications instead of linear specifications between lump-sum grants and recipient governments' expenditures, she found a significantly weaker flypaper effect.

RECENT FINDINGS ON FISCAL IMPACTS OF INTERGOVERNMENTAL GRANTS

While the above-introduced issues are an ongoing research agenda, one recent study suggested a very interesting and promising theory about the impacts of IGR grants on the budget processes of recipient governments. The federal government has long distributed the so-called seed grants to state drug courts. These have mostly been used as start-up funds for no more than three to five years. Douglas and Hartley (2011) indicate that short-term seed grants will eventually lead to considerable funding uncertainty and program elimination when the seed IGR funds expire. The temporary nature of seed grants will, therefore, detract from the budget capacity of recipient governments. Douglas and Hartley aptly defined the fiscal aspect of seed grants as "fly ball effect." A continued future research effort is warranted for this topic.

CHAPTER SUMMARY

- **Fiscal Impacts of Intergovernmental Grants**

IGR grants generate price effects and income effects in recipient governments.

(1) Matching grants reduce tax prices for consumer-voters in recipient governments. The decrease in tax prices increases the consumer-voters' demand for aided public goods. This effect is called the price effect of IGR grants.

(2) Lump-sum grants increase the incomes of consumer-voters. An increase in their incomes increases their demand for aided public goods. This effect is called the income effect of IGR grants. The income effect tends to be smaller than the price effect.

- **Side Effects of Intergovernmental Grants**

IGR grants often cause unexpected side effects. While recipient governments use grant funds for aided programs and services, they might free up the funds used for the services for other programs. This effect is called grant fungibility and is reported even with grants with use restrictions. When IGR grants are distributed based on tax efforts, there is a chance that only recipient governments' tax rates will increase.

- **Empirical Findings of Fiscal Impacts of Intergovernmental Grants**

Empirical findings on fiscal impacts of IGR grants mostly support theoretical expectations.

(1) Open-ended, categorical matching IGR grants stimulate recipient governments'

spending on aided services more than do equal-size lump-sum grants. Slightly different from expectations, closed-ended categorical grants are often more stimulative than open-ended, categorical grants. For instance, federal highway grants are closed-ended matching grants with the federal matching share of about $.80. Their fiscal impacts range approximately between one and two dollars.

(2) Lump-sum grants stimulated recipient governments' spending by about $0.25 to $.50. This implies that substantial portions of the grants might have been used for programs other than aided programs, evidencing strong grant fungibility.

• **Flypaper Effect**

Theoretically, an increase in personal income or that from IGR grants should result in same fiscal impacts on recipient governments' spending. However, increases in lump-sum grants increase recipient governments' spending more than an equal amount of increases in personal income. This phenomenon is called the flypaper effect. There have been numerous scholarly suggestions for why the effect takes place: Fiscal illusion of residents in recipient governments, political processes, analytical errors, or reduced service delivery costs.

• **Fly Ball Effect**

Some IGR funds used as seed funds for recipient governments' programs ultimately detract from the budget capacity of recipient governments. This phenomenon is called the fly ball effect.

NOTES

1. In this case, if the price elasticity is 1.5, then the local expenditure will increase by about $500 ($1,000 × 0.33 × 1.5). When the total expenditure is $1,500, the full local spending will be about the same as the original expenditure of $1,000. Therefore, if the price elasticity is less than 1.5, one might observe grant fungibility.

2. It is difficult to directly compare elasticity measures with dollar values. However, the dollar values reported here are generally much higher than fiscal impacts from other types of grants.

PART VI

MACROBUDGETING

23

Macroeconomic Theories
Classical, Keynesian, and New Approaches

Classical and Keynesian approaches to macroeconomic activities have dominated scholarly and practitioners' debates over the factors affecting the national economy and policy suggestions to stimulate it. Recently, however, a variety of new theories have been developed to explain the anomalies that the two major theories could not successfully explain. The diagnoses of and prescriptions for the ailing national economy made by the new approaches substantially deviate from the major viewpoints. The new theories have made fairly accurate predictions about the national economy, especially the Great Recession of 2008. This chapter briefly summarizes the main features of the diverse approaches to macroeconomic analysis of the national economy, focusing on the issues below. Readers might wonder whether understanding something of macroeconomic equations is really needed for public budgeting processes. Surprisingly, budget decision makers have been more deeply involved in the debates that necessitate a certain level of understanding the equations. With careful attention to this chapter, readers can grasp why scholars and practitioners suggested such theories and equations without significant challenges. In sum, they will find that there are clear patterns in macroeconomic theories that repeat themselves.

- Classical Approaches to Macroeconomic Activities
- Keynesian Approaches to Macroeconomic Activities
- New Approaches to Macroeconomic Activities

CLASSICAL APPROACHES TO MACROECONOMIC ACTIVITIES

Although Keynesian views have been dominating the field of macroeconomic theories, readers need first to understand the Classical approach to macroeconomic analysis. It covers three main components: the labor market, linking both saving and investment to interest rates, and a theory of price level.

217

LABOR DEMAND AND SUPPLY

Classical views of employment in the labor market are explained in terms of demand for and supply of labor. Business firms, which instigate the demand for labor, tend to require less labor when its marginal productivity declines as more units of their goods are produced. Thus, the demand curve for labor slopes downward to the right like typical demand curves for economic commodities. Consumer workers, as the suppliers of labor, tend to work more (i.e., increase their labor supply) only when extra work gives them more utility or satisfaction in terms of real wage. The classical supply curve of labor therefore slopes upward to the right, again similar to supply schedules for typical economic commodities. A closely related and important point in Classical views of the labor market is that the labor market equilibrium will be held at a full-employment level, and labor is the most critical input for national output. Classical approaches assume capital stock and technology as a given (Mankiw 2013, 47–100; Peterson and Estenson 1996, 79–83). Despite some fluctuations, shares of capital stock and labor in the national income account during recent years have been 35 percent and 65 percent, respectively (Gale and Potter 2002).

SAY'S LAW AND THE ROLE OF INTEREST RATE

Contemporary economists tend to reject Say's Law, but their general theoretical assumptions have remained the same as what Say identified in 1800 (Sherman and Meeropol 2013, 28). According to Say's Law, every supply creates its own demand. Production creates sufficient income (e.g., consumer workers earn personal wages) to buy back what is produced. This aspect of Classical theory is vulnerable to one theoretical loophole. If consumer workers decide to save some of their personal income for future consumption, the demand for what is produced tends to be less than their money income generated by overall production activities. Classical approaches fill in the gap by applying the classical theory of interest. When consumer workers save parts of their personal income for future consumption, money supply through increased savings in the economy will grow. This will decrease interest rates due to the increased money supply. In addition, the amount of overall savings in the economy will be a signal for future demand for goods and services. Business firms can borrow from the savings at a lower interest rate and expand their investments for the future demand. Therefore, savings through interest-rate changes will translate into more or less business investments (Mankiw 2013, 47–100; Peterson and Estenson 1996, 84–86; Sherman and Meeropol 2013, 28–32). A corollary of this observation is that saved current consumptions (e.g., savings) will be loaned to business investors. The supply of and demand for goods and services will automatically reach a market equilibrium. Under this condition, governmental intervention into the private market system is unnecessary. Loanable funds theory expands the Classical theory of interest by analyzing financial markets (e.g., bond markets). Monies additionally come from business firms, governments, and foreigners. Governmental borrowing, perceived business profit opportunities from investment projects, and the expected inflation rate also can influence demands for loanable funds. However, the loanable funds theory relies on a framework similar to that of the Classical theory of interest (Krugman and Wells 2013, 281–89; Mankiw 2013, 70–71; Peterson and Estenson 1996, 151–58).

CLASSICAL VIEW OF THE PRICE LEVEL

Another important part of the Classical viewpoint is its theory of the price level. Classical approaches to money are based on the quantity theory of money and treat money only as a medium of exchange. Details of the quantity theory are beyond the scope of this chapter, but its key ideas are worth our attention here. In sum, there is a perfect inverse relationship between the overall price level and national output. The perfect inverse relationship also implies that increased money supply raises only the overall price level and has no impact on the level of national output (Peterson and Estenson 1996, 86–87).

Post-Keynesian scholars offer a simpler interpretation of this rather abstruse assumption. If the overall price level goes up in the labor market, the "real" wage will decrease. This will result in excess demand for labor (i.e., readers can simply think of typical demand and supply curves: When price drops from the equilibrium price, demand is higher than supply). With the excess demand for labor, now the "nominal" wage of labor tends to be bid up until the real wage level goes back to its original level at its previous equilibrium in the labor market. The only thing that changed is the overall price level, but the labor quantity remains the same. Thus, when money circulation increases, the level of real output will not change *in the short run*. Only the overall price level will go up (Mankiw 2013, 101–32; Peterson and Estenson 1996, 89–98; Sherman and Meeropol 2013, 73–79). This starkly contrasts with the Keynesian view discussed below.

KEYNESIAN APPROACHES TO MACROECONOMIC ACTIVITIES

Classical approaches could not explain why mass unemployment and idle production facilities resulted from the Great Depression. Keynesian theory, unlike Classical, starts with the "capacity" of the whole national economy, rather than the labor market.

GENERAL CONCEPTS IN KEYNESIAN APPROACHES

The level of national output will rely on the extent to which capacity is utilized. Then the key question to Keynesian theory is what determines the extent to which the overall productive capacity is being utilized. The answer includes two parts. First, whenever business firms anticipate that their products will be in demand (and sold), they will produce them. Second, it is necessary to investigate what drives the demand for the business products to identify the extent to which the overall productive capacity is being utilized (Peterson and Estenson 1996, 102–3). Unlike Say's Law in Classical theory, Keynes contended that demand creates its own supply. Therefore, policies need to focus more on the aggregate demand, such as household and government consumption, because the latter will decide whether to produce more (Eyler 2010, 157–59; Sherman and Meeropol 2013, 75).

SPECIFIC CONCEPTS IN KEYNESIAN APPROACHES

Accordingly, Keynesian economics links national output to the *expected* proceeds from the sale of business products (note that Keynesian theory used employment rather than national output because data on the latter were not available in the 1930s). When business firms expect that sales of their products will increase, they will increase their production. In short, there will be a linear, positive relationship between the expected proceeds (i.e., prices) and the national output even in the short run unlike the Classical theory as noted above (Krugman and Wells 2013, 526–29). In a similar vein, Keynesian demand schedules trace the relationship between the amounts that major spending units in the national economy prepare to spend (i.e., expected expenditures) and their real income levels (Peterson and Estenson 1996, 103–12). The aggregate demand schedules can be more easily understood under given budget constraints of major spending units in the national economy (Eyler 2010, 157–59; Krugman and Wells 2013, 341–76; Mankiw 2013, 303–54).

Consumption vs. Saving

Individuals either consume or save their income. Once their consumption (C) exceeds their saving (S), a borrowing need develops. The building block of the Keynesian aggregate demand schedule is that individuals are likely to spend a certain portion of their income: marginal propensity to consume is positive (Eyler 2010, 159–60; Krugman and Wells 2013, 315–21; Mankiw 2013, 466–67; Peterson and Estenson 1996, 114–16).

Investment vs. Savings

As another economic entity, business firms make physical, real investment in capital (I) to produce their products. Somewhat similar to Classical approaches, business dividends are part of individual incomes. Individuals make a choice between consumption and saving, and if business firms borrow funds from individuals, they must pay interest. The goods market is in equilibrium at aggregate expenditures (AE) = $C + I$. Individual households have a budget constraint: Income (Y) = $C + S$. The equilibrium of the national economy will be held when $S = I$. When there are more savings, interest rates fall and investment rises, and vice versa. Thus, interest rate is a crucial factor in deciding the level of individual consumption and savings (Eyler 2010, 160–62; Krugman and Wells 2013, 321–30).

Government Spending vs. Savings

If government is added, then governmental budget constraint is *government spending (G) – taxation (T) = borrowing (B)*. When G exceeds T, government borrows from individual consumers' savings. Now individual consumers' budget constraint is $Y = C + S + T$, and the new goods market equilibrium is $AE = C + I + G$. The new equilibrium will be $S + T = I + G$. Savings and taxes are leakages from the national economy because they drain the economy's capacity to consume domestically produced goods and services. Business investment and governmental spending are injections into the economy because they stimulate consumption of goods and services (Eyler 2010, 162–65; Krugman and Wells 2013, 377–409).

Net Exports and Savings

When the foreign sector is added, the new equilibrium is $S + T + import (IM) = I + G + export (EX)$. When IM exceeds EX, domestic disposable income will decline and the need to borrow will increase. In contrast, when EX exceeds IM, the demand for domestically produced goods and services will increase (Eyler 2010, 165–66; Krugman and Wells 2013, 127–58; Mankiw 2013, 133–75). Overall, Keynesian aggregate demand schedules (i.e., $C + I + G + EX$) are the key aspect in determining the extent to which the entire production capacity is utilized.[1] One notable change in macroeconomic theories, especially since the 2008 financial market crisis, is that the standard macroeconomic theories incorporate the fact that financial institutions (e.g., financial intermediaries such as banks) affect the aggregate demand schedule (readers more interested in this topic are referred to Burton and Brown 2009; Krugman and Wells 2013, 275–307; Mankiw 2013, 63–65; Olsson 2012, 101–14).

LIQUIDITY PREFERENCE

Another very important Keynesian departure from Classical views is the liquidity preference theory of interest. Keynesians perceive individuals as assigning extra values to monies as the most liquid, or readily available, asset. Thus, monies are not just a medium of exchange but also have their own asset value. Again, details of the theory are beyond the scope of this chapter, but there are two significant implications from the liquidity preference theory. First, the forces affecting monetary equilibrium are quite different from those inducing equilibrium in employment and income (i.e., $AE = Y$ above). Second, money is not neutral. Classical approaches predict that an increased money supply will increase only the overall price level without changing the national output level. In contrast, Keynesian approaches contend that money exerts a powerful influence on both national output and employment through interest rate changes (Krugman and Wells 2012, 453–67; Mankiw 2013, 317–19; Peterson and Estenson 1996, 160–62, 181–87).

NEW APPROACHES TO MACROECONOMIC ACTIVITIES

In 2008, the U.S. economy experienced one of the most devastating economic debacles since the Great Depression. Many scholars have suggested new frameworks or have revived Classical theories (e.g., Austrian approaches introduced below) to explain the 2008 financial market collapse. Others presented elaborate models to explain or predict the economic crisis long before Austrian approaches were revived. Although they are not mainstream macroeconomic theories, one thing is certainly worth our attention: they have predicted and explained the 2008 crisis fairly well.

AUSTRIAN APPROACHES TO MACROECONOMIC ACTIVITIES

Too Many Cheap Credits in Circulation

Woods (2009, 2011) asserts that the main culprit in the 2008 financial market crisis was the federal government, especially the Federal Reserve Bank (Fed). The Fed had injected too many cheap credits into the private, especially the financial, market system. Between 2000 and 2007, the Fed increased the money supply more than at any other time in the entire U.S. history (Woods 2009, 11–32).

How Did Too Many Cheap Credits Create the Boom-Bust Cycle?

Based on revived Austrian approaches to the macroeconomy, Woods succinctly explains the recent patterns of business cycles. He emphasizes that busts in typical boom-bust cycles are found more frequently in the so-called higher-order activities such as capital-goods industries like raw materials, construction, and capital equipment than in lower-order activities such as retail stores and services. Why does this happen? According to the Classical ideas introduced above, when individuals save more, the money supply increases and interest rates drop. The mechanism will automatically entail an interperiod equilibrium between current consumption and future consumption (i.e., savings and attendant investment for future consumption). This is how interest rates coordinate production across time (Woods 2009, 63–67; 2011, 45–47).

When the Fed artificially lowers interest rates by pumping in cheap credits, the rates do not reflect the true state of consumer preferences over present versus future consumption. This will mislead investors. Business firms might interpret the money supply and lower interest rates as signals for their long-term investment. In fact, however, consumers have not yet decided to save for future consumption. In addition, they will also consume more now due to the low rate of return on their savings. In the future, the business firms will learn that the amount of real savings is smaller than expected, and they will realize there is not enough demand for their products. Labor, materials, and replacement parts for their production will fall short of their demands. Business costs will rise accordingly, and firms will have to borrow more funds. This will further increase interest rates. Mismatched projects will be abandoned, and the whole economy will suffer great losses (Woods 2009, 68–70; 2011, 42–51).

Some scholars contend that such boom-bust cycles were reported even before the Fed was established. Woods rebuts this contention. The bank panic of 1819 was partially caused by the Second Bank of the United States in 1816. The Bank overissued paper money at such a level that paper money circulation was much higher than the corresponding value of specie holdings in banks' vaults. The Panic of 1857 resulted from a five-year boom also induced by a similar kind of substantial credit expansion (Woods 2009, 88–93; 2011, 76–80). Similar to Classical theory, Austrian viewpoints indicate that an increased money supply leads to an increase in the overall price level or inflation. One departure of the Austrian from the Classical approach, however, is that the injection of cheap credits by the Fed was the main cause of misallocated resources and the ultimate failure of the national economy.

America's Bubble Economy and the Financial Debacle

Economic Bubbles

Another stream of scholars put forth intuitive insights into various bubbles in the U.S. economy. From 2001 to 2006, personal income grew by 2 percent, but housing prices went up 80 percent. Housing price index data show that housing prices exploded after 2001. The housing crunch was not confined to a subprime mortgage problem. As long as the house equity value continued growing, individuals with poor credit scores could purchase homes. From 1928 to 1982, the Dow increased by 300 percent. In the next twenty years, it increased 1,200 percent, while company earnings increased only four times. This is called a stock market bubble. In addition, from 1960 to 1990 the proportion of financial assets as a percentage of GDP increased from about 500 percent, but it has hovered around 900 percent since 2000. The popping of the housing bubble resulted in large losses in the massive mortgage-backed securities market. This roiled the entire credit market because investors were struck with fear. The loss of market confidence ultimately resulted in the bursting of stock bubbles (Wiedermer, Wiedermer, and Spitzer 2011, 28–60; Wiedermer, Wiedermer, Spitzer, and Janszen 2006).

With the help of cheap credits, individuals could borrow a lot. According to a 2009 study, more than 50 percent of U.S. households did not have enough savings to pay their monthly expenses for more than two months. The problem is that when people with low savings are laid off, even nondiscretionary spending will decrease. Those who still have their jobs will cut back on their discretionary spending, due to the fear that they might also be laid off. Economic activities will contract due to reduced aggregate demand. More jobs will be lost. Consumers will lose interest in purchasing more items. Banks will be less willing to lend to unqualified borrowers. This will further drive down consumption, the economy will contract, and jobs will decline. Most importantly, when the bubbles pop, dollar values will fall, and even with the printing of more money, they will keep falling. Since foreign investors will withdraw their investments in dollar-denominated assets, the government debt bubble will also pop (Wiedermer, Wiedermer, and Spitzer 2011, 28–60; Wiedermer et al. 2006).

Why Do Economic Bubbles Grow?

Quite in line with Austrian approaches, the above assertions contend that the main reason for the bubbles and associated inflation is an increased money supply. Since 2008, the money supply has tripled, which implies another doomsday scenario in the near future. According to monetary policy, the money supply will lead to lower interest rates. However, Wiedermer, Wiedermer, and Spitzer (2011, 64–87) assert that money supply is the main cause of inflation. Under inflation, lenders would lend you dollars after accounting for the decreasing purchasing power of dollars, but they will require higher interest rates to compensate for inflation rate plus a profit on the loan. As it gets harder to borrow dollars, demand for assets—homes, stocks, savings, and all dollar-denominated assets—will decline further. With declining demand, asset prices will fall (also caused by supply going up due to fewer buyers). For instance, if the mortgage rate increases to 7.5 percent, home values will drop by 32 percent. Businesses cannot borrow when interest rates are too high, which will decrease business investment and employment. In sum, the increased money supply causes numerous malfunctions in the economy, contrary to the Keynesian point of view. Swain and Reed introduces a similar viewpoint as "the alarmist representation of macroeconomics" (2010, 213).

THE FINANCIAL INSTABILITY HYPOTHESIS

The above approaches share in common the belief that money is not neutral to the national economy. In actuality, Hyman Minsky (1982, 1986, 1993) decades ago developed a theory called the financial instability hypothesis. It emphasized the non-neutrality of money and a much more important role of financial institutions in the economy.

Minsky's View of Economic Agents

According to Minsky (1982, 1986, 1993), capitalism is essentially a financial system, and financial institutional processes have their own life cycles. The Keynesian approaches assert that money is not neutral to the national economy. Money has its own value as an asset. This is in stark contrast to the Classical view that money is only a medium of economic exchange. Keynesians also list households, nonfinancial firms (e.g., businesses), and governments as the three major domestic economic agents. In Minsky's view, money plays an even stronger role in the economy, that an economy consists of households, nonfinancial firms, governments, and, most importantly, financial institutions.

To Minsky, the key mechanism to understanding an economy, especially a capitalist economy, is the logic of financial institutional arrangements that can never be separated from the real-sector economy. In particular, the most important element of the logic of finance is the survival constraint imposed upon economic agents, who try to maintain cash inflows from cash commitments higher than cash outflows incurred from cash commitments (e.g., investments). For instance, economic agents attempt to earn more in the future from their current investments. In this sense, the balance sheets of economic agents are the most crucial tool to understand financial institutional arrangements. A simple accounting equation on balance sheets looks like: Assets = Liabilities + Net Assets. Balance sheets show how yesterdays, todays, and tomorrows are linked. For example, today's borrowing (e.g., cash commitments incurred from investment = Liability) leads to future cash outflows (e.g., expense under Net Assets). Economic agents might attempt to maintain their future cash inflows (e.g., revenue under Net Assets) from the investment at a higher level than their borrowing. Minsky contended that the system of a balance sheet, linking yesterdays, todays, and tomorrows, is not a well-behaved, linear process. There is almost always either fragility or robustness in financial institutional arrangements. Furthermore, this fragility or robustness decides whether the economy will be fragile or robust (Galbraith 1987–1988; Mehrling 1999; Minsky 1982, 1986, 1993).

What makes Minsky's view of economic agents' activities unique is that the financial institutional arrangements generally tend to move from robust to fragile finance. Basically, economic agents' expectations of future cash flows from current cash commitments are highly likely to be misleading. Economic agents believe that future cash flows will exceed the cash commitments needed to finance investments. In reality, however, some expected future cash flows do not materialize. Under robust finance, supported investments and a kind of attendant upward instability will eventually succumb to fragile instability. The conditions under robust finance will give way to weak investments and slow economic growth under fragile finance. This overall framework is called Minsky's financial instability hypothesis (Mehrling 1999). The next section presents a more succinct explanation of the financial instability hypothesis, with an example to explain the 2008 financial market collapse.

The Minsky Moment

When the U.S. economy was going through the 2008 crisis, many observers said that the Minsky moment had ultimately arrived. Minsky's view of evolutionary instability rests on two distinctive cycles: the basic Minsky cycle and the super-Minsky cycle.

The basic Minsky cycle begins with hedge finance in which economic agents make current and future payment commitments (e.g., interest and principal payments) of as much as they can earn from their current and future earnings. The cycle then progresses to speculative finance whereby revenues can cover interest payments only. Economic agents need to make multiple rounds of refinancing and arrange new borrowing to pay existing debt to reflect market uncertainty that is typically found under floating debt instruments. Finally, speculative finance moves on to Ponzi finance when cash inflows from indebted investments are much too short for even interest payments from the debts. Economic agents (e.g., borrowers in this case) will have to rely on other sources of capital gains to meet their obligations for interest and principal (Minsky 1986, 1993; Palley 2010).

McCulley (2009) nicely applied Minsky's financial instability hypothesis to the subprime mortgage crisis in 2007 and 2008. For instance, hedge borrowers relied on a traditional mortgage loan and made both interest and principal payments. Speculative borrowers tend to have interest-only loans. They will pay back interest only and make principal payments through refinancing. Finally, Ponzi borrowers tend to have negative amortization loans. Their payments do not cover interest, and their principals are likely to grow in actuality. Lenders loaned to Ponzi borrowers only because they expected housing values to continue growing (e.g., other sources of capital earnings noted above). This process of the basic Minsky cycle exists in every business cycle, but the super-Minsky cycle ultimately breaks what Minsky called thwarting institutions important for ensuring the stability of capitalist economies: "business institutions, decision-making conventions, and the structures of market governance" (Palley 2010, 31). Therefore, it is the super-Minsky cycle that causes a full-blown financial crisis (Palley 2010).

At this moment, then, readers might wonder why the super-Minsky cycle takes place in the first place. There are two fundamental reasons: regulatory relaxation and increased risk-taking. First, regulatory institutions were captured by the entities they were supposed to regulate. Regulators, as human beings, forgot the lessons of the past. Various financial innovations bypassed regulatory nets. Second, the financial innovations led borrowers to take on more debt by purchasing new financial products. Like regulators, financial market participants also suffered from memory loss (Palley 2010).

STRUCTURAL KEYNESIAN INTERPRETATIONS OF ECONOMIC CRISIS

Although Minsky is popularized for his prediction of the 2008 financial market collapse, structural Keynesian economists call for cautions about Minsky's financial instability hypothesis. For the period 1945–1975, the U.S. economy was explained by the so-called virtuous Keynesian cycle. The U.S. economic policy was pursuing full employment and the mindset of wages-grow-with-productivity. Productivity improvement would lead to wage increases for consumer-workers. The wage increases for consumers would boost aggregate demand as indicated in the section on Keynesian approaches in this chapter. The increased aggregate demand would be likely to achieve full employment that, in turn, would motivate producers to increase their business investments. With the enhanced investments, their productivity would further rise and consumer-workers' wages would also grow.

Palley (2010, 2012), as a structural Keynesian economist, contends that a neoliberal growth model replaced the virtuous Keynesian model and severed the link between wages and productivity growth. After 1980, debt and asset price inflation, rather than wages, became the engine of U.S. demand growth. The U.S. economic policy based on the neoliberal growth model weakened the position of consumer-workers and instead strengthened the position of business corporations, especially financial companies. Some statistical data support this assertion. Between 1979 and 2007, the income of the top 1 percent of households increased by 275 percent. The income for middle-class households increased by 40 percent and for those in the bottom quintile increased by only 18 percent (Gosling and Eisner 2013, 171). Globalization put consumer-workers in unprotected international competition. Attacks on the legitimacy of government resulted in privatization and tax cuts that in turn warped income equality. The support for labor market flexibility further weakened legal protection for consumer-workers such as the minimum wage and unemployment benefits. The adoption of inflation targeting instead of full employment accelerated financial interests' control of the Fed and its monetary policy. The Fed might not have had a strong incentive to prevent asset price inflation on its way up under inflation targeting. In contrast, the Fed tends to be pressured to block asset-price declines on the way down. The attitude of the Fed under inflation targeting provides investors with a clear message to take advantage of the Fed's asymmetrical policy intervention. The Fed conveys a signal of too-big-to-fail mentality and raises the moral hazard of financial institutions (Palley 2002).

According to structural Keynesian economists, one of the great contributions of

Minsky's financial instability hypothesis is that it clarified how the financial system could keep expanding the supply of credit through financial innovation and deregulation. It also showed how the neoliberal model could prolong the outburst of the market collapse that it might have caused without expanded credit supplies. Under stagnant wages and income inequality, increased debt sustained consumer-workers' consumption. Under a financial boom, both consumer-workers and firms were provided collateral that enabled debt-financed spending. In contrast, structural Keynesian economists assert that more "structural" factors, rather than financial instability, cause an economic crisis (Palley 2010).

CHAPTER SUMMARY

- **Classical Approaches to Macroeconomic Activities**

Classical approaches to macroeconomic activities analyze the labor market, link both saving and investment to interest rates, and develop a theory of price level.

(1) The labor market will automatically maintain equilibrium at a full-employment level. Thus, governmental intervention in the private market system is unnecessary.

(2) When consumer-workers save their income for future consumption, business firms can borrow from the savings at a lower interest and expand their investments for production. Savings will translate into business investments through interest rate changes.

(3) When the money supply increases, the only thing that changes is the overall price level, with no change in real output.

- **Keynesian Approaches to Macroeconomic Activities**

Keynesians focus more on the capacity of the national economy than on the labor market.

(1) When business firms anticipate that they can sell their products, they will produce more. The expected demand for business products is an important factor in gauging the capacity of the economy. Therefore, Keynesians pay more attention to the aggregate demand level.

(2) Aggregate demand consists of: aggregate consumption, business investments in physical capital, governmental spending, and export.

(3) Liquidity preference theory suggests that individuals place extra value on monies as the most liquid asset. Unlike Classical economists, Keynesians assert that money exerts significant impacts on both national output and employment.

- **New Approaches to Macroeconomic Activities**

New approaches to macroeconomic approaches contend that too many cheap credits were the main culprit for the recent financial debacle.

(1) Austrian approaches suggest that increased artificial cheap credits circulated by the Fed give a wrong signal to business firms, so they produce products that consumers will not demand in the future. Since real resources might have been used for other activities, business firms will need to borrow more in the future, and the economy will suffer more.

(2) In a similar vein, some scholars have asserted that an increased money supply will cause inflation. With ongoing inflation, lenders will demand higher interest rates to compensate for the decreasing purchasing power of dollars. If it becomes harder to borrow, asset prices will fall. As a result, the national economy will suffer another crisis.

(3) Minsky's financial instability hypothesis emphasizes the importance of financial institutional arrangements that can never be separated from the real-sector economy. There are three fundamental financial arrangements: hedge finance, speculative finance, and Ponzi finance. The financial system tends to move from robust to fragile financial conditions. Financial innovations and deregulations accelerate the development of the fragile financial condition.

(4) Structural Keynesian economists indicate that the lack of the virtuous Keynesian cycle, committed to full employment and the mindset of wages-grow-with-productivity, is the main reason for economic crises.

NOTE

1. More complete models of Keynesian approaches were derived through the so-called IS-LM curves. In addition, macroeconomic textbooks introduce combined Classical-Keynesian demand and supply curves. These discussions are beyond the scope of this book. To read more, see Peterson and Estenson (1996), Krugman and Wells (2006, 2009, 2013), Mankiw (2013, 303–54), and Eyler (2010).

24

Macroeconomic Policies

Fiscal Policy, Monetary Policy, and New Policy Suggestions

As introduced in the previous chapter, Classical approaches to macroeconomic activities suggest that the private market system has the power to regain market equilibrium and that this system should be left alone. In contrast, Keynesians contend that the national economy will not reach equilibrium or utilize its full capacity if all economic activities are left to the private market system. Keynesians assert that governments should intervene more strongly in the market, especially through increased money injection to boost the aggregate demand in the national economy. Keynesian approaches have dominated the debate over national macroeconomic policies, although new approaches have recently emerged and gained attention. This chapter focuses on the following issues:

- Tendency Toward Governmental Intervention
- Governmental Intervention: Fiscal Policy and Monetary Policy
- Minimizing Governmental Intervention
- Other Policy Suggestions
- The Hidden Dimension in Macroeconomic Policies: Politics

TENDENCY TOWARD GOVERNMENTAL INTERVENTION

Since the 2008 financial market crisis, the federal government has been injecting billions of dollars into the U.S. economy. It has also extended the Bush tax cuts (Tanglao and Wolf 2010). In November 2010, the Federal Reserve Bank announced that it would initiate another round of money injection into the fragile economy. The Fed planned to buy $600 billion in long-term Treasury securities or mortgage-backed securities until June 2011 to stimulate the U.S. economy. The bond purchase, known as quantitative easing (QE), was expected to boost consumer spending and private investment, and ultimately spur the national economy. By June 2010, the Fed had purchased about $2.1 trillion worth of the securities through two rounds of QE. The Fed announced its intention to purchase up to $85 billion worth of the securities each month from September to December 2012 through QE3 to keep short-term interest rates low until mid-2015 (Censky 2010; Plumer 2012; Sherman and Meeropol 2013, 318–19). In addition, President Obama signed into law the Dodd-Frank Wall Street Reform and Consumer Protection Act of 2010 (P.L. 111–203). The main target of the act was to enhance government oversight over a variety of financial institutions. In particular, the regulation focused on how to regulate shadow banking systems dealing with financial derivatives ("Times Topics" 2010).

GOVERNMENTAL INTERVENTION: FISCAL POLICY AND MONETARY POLICY

Macroeconomic policies have been heavily gravitating toward governmental intervention as the recent macroeconomic policy measures evidence. Keynesian economic theory suggests that increased governmental expenditures are the most effective tool to boost the aggregate demand—especially through increased consumer spending—and the national economy. In addition, governmental taxes are closely related to aggregate demand, as introduced in the previous chapter. Governmental tax cuts are also regarded as an incentive to stimulate business production. As such, they have been viewed as a tool to enhance the aggregate supply, as discussed below. Broadly speaking, governmental expenditures and taxes are the main vehicles for the national fiscal policy. As also shown in the previous chapter, Keynesian approaches viewed the money supply as another tool to stimulate the national economy. This is generally viewed as the federal monetary policy. The Fed purchases or sells U.S. Treasury securities or corporate bonds (since 2008) based on decisions made by the Federal Open Market Committee (FOMC). The Fed manipulates the money supply and, eventually, the Federal Funds Rate (FFR) at which depository financial institutions can charge one another for overnight loans (Burton and Brown 2009, 46–65; Gosling 2009, 86–87; Krugman 2009, 176; Krugman and Wells 2013, 377–409, 447–71; Mankiw 2013, 72–74, 81–100, 308–33, 449–59; Sherman and Meeropol 2013, 291–306). Recent scholarly debates have centered on whether these fiscal and monetary policies can save the deteriorating national economy.

ENHANCED GOVERNMENTAL INTERVENTION THROUGH REGULATION AND MONEY INJECTION

Krugman (2009), as a leading Keynesian scholar, contended that the 2008 financial market crash was the result of the malfunctioning market system. He calls for much more enhanced regulation over the so-called shadow banking systems and stronger governmental interventions through fiscal and monetary policies. According to Krugman (2009, 31–138), the economic crises in Latin America and Asia throughout the 1990s were primarily attributable to the lack of timely or strong enough governmental intervention. Krugman also asserts that the same holds true for the U.S. economy. He asserts that there was a more risky institutional setting in the financial market than the economic bubbles, especially the housing bubble. The problem originated in the shadow banking system. In the first place, some financial systems were not regulated at all. The Financial Stability Board (FSB), working for G-20 countries, has defined shadow banking as credit intermediation entities and activities outside the regular banking system. The FSB estimated the size of global shadow-banking activities at roughly 25 to 30 percent of the total global financial system (Evans 2011).

One example of the shadow banking system is an auction-rate security that Lehman Brothers invented in 1984. Individuals loan their money to the borrowing institution, and the institution frequently holds an auction. When new investors (i.e., potential buyers of the loans) bid for the loans with lower interest rates, the new investors can replace current investors. The institution could raise funds through the auction process, rather than through deposits. The process had some advantages. It was not subject to bank regulation, and borrowers could earn higher interest payments. But the downside was that it was not protected by the Fed. The crucial problem in the 2008 financial market crash was not the housing bust. The real problem was that lack of consumer confidence in the U.S. economy suddenly froze the circulation of funds in the shadow banking system. This was similar to the bank runs that depository banks experienced during the early part of the twentieth century. Thus, Krugman (2009) recommends a much more enhanced oversight over the financial transactions in the shadow banking system (Krugman 2009, 139–90; Roubini and Mihm 2010). Evans (2011) makes similar suggestions. One option is to move the trading transactions in the shadow banking system into a centralized clearinghouse, where oversight authorities can more easily monitor and regulate the transactions. Another step is to tighten oversight over the riskiest participants in shadow banking. For instance, the Securities and Exchange Commission could monitor risky money-market funds.

Krugman (2009) also contends that since 2008 the United States has been on the way to recovery. However, the effort is far too weak. First, the government bailout funds are too small compared to the entire financial market. Second, the bailout funds might not reach the shadow banking system, which is the main problem. Third, we cannot be sure whether other depository banks can loan out the funds that they can augment from the increased credit circulation courtesy of the Fed. Krugman suggests that the credit injection be much bigger and broader (2009, 185–90). Through the enactment of the American Recovery and Reinvestment Act of 2009, the federal government has developed Build America Bonds to stimulate infrastructure and development spending at the local level, which are a recent example of governmental intervention. Local governments are allowed to issue taxable debt, as opposed to the traditional tax-exempt municipal bonds, and to receive either a direct subsidy of as much as 35 percent of the debt issuance or return the subsidy to bondholders in tax credits (Martell and Kravchuk 2012). Overall, since February 2009, the Act has distributed about $777.8 billion in tax benefits, contracts, grants/loans, and entitlement funds (U.S. Government 2012).

SUPPLY-SIDE ECONOMICS

During the Reagan era, a widespread new classical movement, called supply-side economics, was popularized. In short, supply-side economics was based on Classical theory of macroeconomics introduced in the previous chapter. According to Classical approaches, the labor supply curve is sloping upward to the right. For instance, higher wages induce workers to supply more labor (i.e., work more). A corollary is that consumer-workers might work more if their after-tax income would be higher. In addition, Classical approaches assume that market interest rates will function as a tool based on which consumer-workers make a decision between current consumption and further consumption (i.e., savings). They will increase savings because their after-tax income (i.e., interest earnings) will be higher as well. If savings increase, money supply will increase, as discussed in the previous chapter. The increased money supply will reduce the going market interest rate. Thus, business investors can borrow more funds at lower interest rates and increase their business investments. Therefore, if there are tax cuts on workers, savers, or anyone involved in any kind of productive activities, the quantity of labor, savings, investment, and, ultimately, national output will increase (Krugman and Wells 2013, 538; Mankiw 2013, 312; Peterson and Estenson 1996, 646). As also noted in the previous chapter and above, tax cuts are closely linked to the aggregate demand through the national income account equations. In general, tax cuts or increases are deemed as one measure of governmental fiscal policy. Recently, supply-side macroeconomic recommendations have picked up again (Gosling and Eisner 2013, 52–53; Meltzer 2011; Sherman and Meeropol 2013, 333–34).

REVIVAL OF SUPPLY-SIDE ECONOMICS

Arthur Laffer (2011a), who popularized supply-side economics around 1980, has reemphasized its importance: immediately eliminate the Alternative Minimum Tax and make Bush tax cuts permanent. More than that, the United States should adopt a flat-rate tax with the lowest possible tax rate on the broadest possible tax base. This would decrease the incentives for tax avoidance and evasion. In addition, it would boost the incentives to produce, invest, and save, and this would in turn bring about more stable revenue streams. A value-neutral flat tax rate needs to be at around 13 percent on business net sales and personal unadjusted gross income (Laffer and Moore 2010, 283–84).

Laffer (2011a) also specifically focuses on the fact that the overall U.S. unemployment rate is 9.1 percent, but black unemployment has jumped to 16.7 percent since the 2008 Great Recession. Black teenage unemployment rate is bordering on 50 percent. Laffer makes one suggestion based on supply-side economics: developing enterprise zones for the areas with exceptionally high concentrations of poverty and unemployment. Among many detailed provisions, enterprise zones are needed to give tax benefits to inner-city residents and employers by eliminating payroll taxes. Politicians, especially Republican presidential candidates, were more sanguine about embracing supply-side suggestions; 2012 presidential candidate Herman Cain suggested elimination of the current federal income tax, corporate income tax, and payroll tax. These taxes would be replaced by a 9 percent national sales tax, a 9 percent business flat tax, and a 9 percent individual flat tax (Laffer 2011b). Rick Perry, Republican presidential candidate, made a similar tax cut proposal. He suggested a "Cut, Balance, and Grow" plan with a 20 percent flat-rate income tax and capping national spending at 18 percent of GDP (Perry 2011). Some contend that the proposals might eliminate many of the deductions and exemptions in the current federal tax code, which might dampen investment for the weak economy. In addition, a flat tax or a national sales tax would place heavier tax burdens on middle- and lower-income people (McKinnon 2011).

CRITIQUES OF THE FISCAL POLICY

There are also critiques of governmental fiscal policy measures, especially Keynesian approaches. Meltzer (2011) lists four reasons why Keynesians are wrong. First, big increases in governmental spending and future deficits drive individuals to be concerned about future tax increases (see also, Cullis and Jones 2009, 322–25, for Ricardian equivalence). Concern over a future tax increase is one of the main reasons for reduced confidence. Second, most governmental spending programs redistribute income from workers to unemployed people. However, once resources are shifted away from productive investment to redistribution, overall productivity declines. Third, Keynesian models ignored the costs incurred from regulations. Fourth, U.S. fiscal and monetary policies have been primarily focused on short-term impacts. The bonds that financed fiscal stimulus packages remain in the future and must be serviced. The multiplier effect will be offset by the medium- and long-term fiscal burden. Barro (2011) is also somewhat negative about the multiplier effect. Agriculture Secretary Tom Vilsack said that a $1 payment of food stamps generates $1.84 in the economy in terms of economic activity. According to what Barro calls regular economics, however, additional transfer incomes to individuals with earnings below designated levels motivate less work. In addition, tax revenues to finance transfer programs discourage the work effort of taxpayers and business investment because of declining after-tax profits.

EMPIRICAL FINDINGS ON THE FISCAL POLICY

Empirical findings on the effect of tax cuts on the national economy are somewhat bifurcated. Gale and Potter (2002) conducted simulations to analyze the economic impact of the 2001 Economic Growth and Tax Relief Reconciliation Act (P.L. 107–16, the George Bush tax cut). They first showed how the Bush tax cut might affect the formation of public savings. Their simulations indicated that cumulative public savings (i.e., primarily governmental savings) would decline by about 1.58 percent of GDP by 2011. Since the tax cut would induce higher private savings, as predictable from Classical approaches, the cumulative national savings (= private savings + public savings) would decline by about 1.09 percent. When the decline was translated into the national output, the Bush tax cut was set to reduce GDP by about 0.3 percent in 2011. The simulations conducted by Gale and Potter generally confirm that tax cuts would cause crowding out of capital formation. Obviously, their study was conducted from the perspective of Classical theory. The analysis of the Bush tax cut from the perspective of Keynesian views also confirmed the crowding-out effect (Auerbach 2002; Bosworth 2012, 95–104; Gale and Potter 2002). Woods (2011, 51) shows some historical evidence against Keynesian governmental stimulations. During the depression of 1920–21, the unemployment rate was 12.4 percent and production declined by 17 percent. But from 1920 and 1922, the federal government cut its budget in half and reduced the national debt by one-third during the 1920s. By the late summer of 1921, the economy was on its way to recovery.

However, other studies report somewhat different results. Auten, Carroll, and Gee (2008) empirically investigated the impact of two tax cuts made during the Bush era: the Economic Growth and Tax Relief Reconciliation Act of 2001 and the Jobs and Growth Tax Relief Reconciliation Act of 2003. Their empirical studies showed that a 1 percent change in the net-of-tax share, measured as one minus the combined federal and state marginal income tax rate, was associated with about a 0.47 percent increase in taxable income: Tax cuts increase taxable income. Elmendorf et al. (2008) indicated that if all other behavioral responses of economic units were accounted for, income after the Bush tax cut would rise about 2 percent or more.

Romer and Romer (2010) provided a much more provocative and interesting finding on the effect of tax changes on economic outputs. Endogenous tax changes, which took place because government spending was changing or to offset other factors that might affect economic outputs in the near future, are likely to be correlated with other developments that affect economic outputs. Romer and Romer contend that the endogenous tax changes are not adequate observations to analyze the pure output effects of tax changes. In contrast, there are different categories of tax changes. Examples include tax changes to deal with an ongoing or inherited budget deficit; and to achieve a long-run fiscal goal such as higher normal growth, enhanced fairness, or a smaller government. These tax changes are motivated by past philosophy and beliefs about fairness. As a result, they are less likely to be systematically related to other factors that affect outputs in the short or medium run. These tax changes are called exogenous changes. Romer and Romer used legislated tax changes between 1945 and 2007 and identified exogenous tax changes. They ran a two-variable vector autoregression (VAR) that economists and public finance scholars have recently been using more often: Two variables are logged output (the chain-type quantity index for GDP) and the exogenous tax changes. Empirical findings show that an exogenous tax increase by 1 percent of GDP reduces GDP by about 3 percent over the next three-year period. The estimated fiscal impact of exogenous tax changes is larger than that from the changes in cyclically adjusted revenues that are often caused by nonlegislated factors or all legislated tax changes. Of various types of exogenous tax changes, those motivated by a desire to reduce an ongoing or inherited deficit have much weaker effects on GDP than ones taken for long-run reasons. Similar findings were observed in other countries. In highly taxed France, for instance, people worked about seven-tenths of the American work week. In the early 1970s, American tax rates were much higher and, as expected, the French worked more than the Americans. The finding holds true for countries as different as Japan, Chile, and Italy (Furchtgott-Roth 2012; Romer and Romer 2012).

MINIMIZING GOVERNMENTAL INTERVENTION

ELIMINATE FANNIE MAE AND FREDDIE MAC

In stark contrast to the supporters for enhanced governmental interventions, Woods (2009, 2011) argues that the increased credit supply is the main cause of all the economic turbulence. While he discusses how to curtail the role of the Fed, he also presents very insightful observations on inflation. In addition to the economic meaning of inflation that might cause resource misallocations as discussed in the previous chapter, inflation has some significant political implications as well. Inflation deprives individual consumers of the opportunity to enjoy cheaper commodities when overall productivity grows. In addition, when new monies are circulated into the economy, politically favored entities such as banks or firms with government contracts receive them first. At this moment, inflation has not yet hit the entire economy, so banks and firms can purchase economic commodities at previous price levels. By the time average people receive the new monies from the Fed through higher wages or lower borrowing costs, the commodity prices will already have gone up. The purchasing power of their monies will be diluted long before the new monies could reach them. When an individual buys an apple, he or she does so with the proceeds previously produced. In contrast, when monies are circulated out of thin air, not from previous production, the entities spending new monies are just taking goods or services without producing anything themselves (Woods 2009, 122–24). To remedy the boom-bust cycle and more detrimental inflation caused by artificial money injection, Woods suggests that federally established mortgage lenders Fannie Mae and Freddie Mac be abolished, the authority of the Fed be substantially reduced, and its policy implementation be transparent to taxpayers (Paul 2011; Schiff and Downes 2009; Woods 2009, 149–52).

ABANDON THE TOO-BIG-TO-FAIL MENTALITY

Throughout the financial crisis, we have been told that some firms are "too big to fail" (TBTF). Lenders have consistently believed that the firms are under government protection through bailout programs. With artificially cheap credits, TBTF firms were able to attract capital and to borrow even from the most conservative private investment firms, thanks partly to government protection. The largest banks were especially able to borrow from the Fed at much lower rates than smaller banks. Fannie and Freddie knew that they were TBTF (Woods 2009, 52–53). In contrast, Woods lists fundamental reasons why we should let failing companies fail. Without market discipline, large firms are likely to adopt risky strategies, riding on government protection. Resources are diverted from genuinely wealth-generating activities to bailed-out firms. Resources are distributed to the least skilled and deserving. TBTF firms fell in moral hazard so that they can be thrust into government protection. Allowing large firms to fail will encourage market participants toward savings-based rather than debt-based financing. Therefore, the federal government should stop all attempts to save the TBTFs (Huntsman 2011; Stern and Feldman 2009; Taylor 2012; Woods 2011, 52–54; 2009, 31–35).

CONTROL GOVERNMENTAL WASTE

Similarly, Woods (2009, 2011) asserts that governmental "nonproductive" spending and waste should be eliminated immediately (Laffer and Moore 2010). Woods (2009,

105–96) asserts that if war spending increases a country's wealth (based on Keynesian stimulus spending), there is a good suggestion for the United States and Japan. Each should build thousands of warships and meet in the middle of the Pacific. Then, they can sink all their ships. At that point, the two economies might have produced a substantial amount of national wealth by devoting labor, steel, and countless other production inputs à la Keynesian stimulus. Woods (2011, 106–10) also employs numerous examples of governmental waste, especially defense spending (Sherman and Meeropol 2013, 346–47). Boeing got a no-risk $30 billion contract from the Air Force. The Air Force leased refurbished 767 passenger jets to use as refueling tankers. The jets were not the best fit for the purpose, and the Air Force did not need any more fuel tankers. More than that, it would have been cheaper to purchase new planes than to lease them from Boeing. The idea was originated at a meeting with Boeing executives and Darlene Druyun, then deputy assistant secretary of the Air Force; Major General Paul Essex, head of the Air Force Global Reach Program; and Air Force Secretary James Roche. In 2003, Druyun was appointed to direct Boeing's missile defense division. Until she went to jail for finalizing the tanker deal, the public did not know such deals were going on.

OTHER POLICY SUGGESTIONS

There are numerous other suggestions to address the current crisis in the U.S. economy. Reich (2010) suggested more progressive taxes to reduce income inequality. He also supports more unemployment benefits and welfare benefits for the lower-class members. More health and education spending for the middle class will help them with health expenses and better train them for new jobs. All these would stimulate the economy (269–71). His suggestions target both income equality and fiscal stimulus. Others suggest that governmental regulations should be radically reduced and the overall productivity of the U.S. economy should be regained (Nothhaft 2011; Nothhaft and Kline 2011; Wiedermer, Wiedermer, and Spitzer 2011). The Fed recently revived its 1961 version of the so-called Operation Twist. The Fed will buy more longer-term Treasury securities and sell an equal amount of shorter-term securities. The former generally carries higher interest rates, so purchasing more of them is expected to further reduce interest rates, with the increased money supply in the longer-term Treasury securities market. Empirical findings, however, do not strongly support this expectation (Robb 2011; Sommer 2011; Wessel 2011).

The previous chapter introduced Minsky's financial instability hypothesis. Minsky assumed that the financial institutional arrangements would amplify the naturally cyclical process of growth. Each financial commitment supports other commitments when the financial institutional arrangements are growing. In contrast, any default on financial commitments undermines other commitments when the financial arrangements are declining. Mehrling (1999, 142) observes, "Minsky thus saw a natural role for government, as lender-of-last resort to ensure a lower bound on downward fluctuation in times of crisis, and as regulator during more peaceful times to identify and correct imbalances before they pose a threat to the system." In this sense, one might think Minsky's approaches are more Keynesian in that governmental intervention is more warranted.

The structural Keynesian approach introduced in the previous chapter clarified some structural factors in the national economy that are the main causes of economic instability. A corollary of the structural approach is that economic crises can be remedied by structural adjustments such as pursuing full employment, a social democratic government agenda in place of the neoliberal antigovernment sentiment, a solidarity-based labor market policy instead of neoliberal labor market flexibility, and replacing corporate global competition with managed globalization (Palley 2010, 2012). This approach is also closer to Keynesian solutions in terms of necessitating governmental intervention.

The Hidden Dimension in Macroeconomic Policies: Politics

Despite all the pros and cons over various policy suggestions, there is one thing that both researchers and practitioners keep in mind: politics. Republicans regularly beat up on Ben Bernanke and the Fed. Texas Governor Rick Perry even went so far as to label the Fed's recent initiative to expand the money supply as close to treasonous. Democrats also press the Fed too much. Massachusetts Congressman Barney Frank recently proposed stripping the regional presidents of the Federal Reserve banks of their FOMC votes. He further suggested that they be replaced by presidential appointees subject to Senate confirmation. All these political measures will make the Fed a weak creature of Washington (Mishkin 2011). The twelve-member House-Senate joint committee, evenly divided between Republicans and Democrats, failed again to reach an agreement on deficit-reduction plans. Their divide once again was as clear as their traditional party lines. This shows that political hurdles for deficit control measures are closely linked to fiscal or monetary policies. Since the measures are linked to the national fiscal policy, this example evidences that macroeconomic policies are strongly bounded by political conflicts whether they are correct steps or not (Hook and Boles 2011).

Chapter Summary

- **Tendency Toward Governmental Intervention**

Governmental intervention in the private market system has dominated the debate over macroeconomic policies.

(1) Supporters of fiscal policies recommend that the federal government enhance regulation over the previously less-regulated sector, the shadow banking systems. They also suggest that governmental credit injection into the market be much bigger and broader.

(2) Supply-side economists and politicians suggest that tax cuts will induce more savings because after-tax income will increase. This will lower interest rates and boost business investments. Politicians have suggested replacing the federal income tax schedule with flat taxes at much lower rates to boost the national economy.

(3) Critiques contend that the short-term stimulative effect of fiscal policies might be offset by the medium- and long-term fiscal burden. Empirical findings are also somewhat bifurcated on the impact of the policies on the national economy.

• **Minimizing Governmental Intervention**

Other scholars propose minimizing governmental intervention.

(1) Since the increased circulation of cheap credits by the Fed is the main culprit for resource misallocation, Fannie and Freddie should be eliminated, and the role of the Fed should be substantially reduced.

(2) Some believe that some business firms are too big to fail (TBTF) because if they fail, the national economy will also suffer. Critics contend that they are too risky to be kept alive.

(3) Governmental spending does not necessarily stimulate the national economy. In particular, governmental waste has nothing to do with economic growth.

(4) There are numerous other suggestions. Governmental spending should target the lower- and middle-class members. This measure will achieve both income equality and fiscal stimulus. The so-called Operation Twist suggests that the Fed buy more longer-term Treasury securities so that more money can be injected into the market for the securities and lower their interest rates, which tend to be higher than those of shorter-term securities. Minsky's financial instability hypothesis calls for a role of government in protecting against financial market instability. Structural Keynesian economists call for pursuing full employment, a social democratic government agenda, a solidarity-based labor market policy, and managed globalization.

• **The Hidden Dimension in Macroeconomic Policies: Politics**

Both Republicans and Democrats have maintained their own party positions with respect to the acceptable level of federal deficits. Partisan preferences have frequently overwhelmed macroeconomic fiscal and monetary policies.

25 | Congressional Macrobudgeting

As with the top-down budget control over agency budget requests in the executive budgeting system introduced in Chapter 1 in Part I, the U.S. Congress has also developed numerous procedural mechanisms to control committee budget proposals through centralized budget targets. Whenever the sum total of committee budget proposals exceeds predetermined budget totals, the centralized control mechanisms are invoked, a process called congressional macrobudgeting. This chapter investigates the following issues:

- Why Congressional Macrobudgeting Again?
- Tools of Congressional Macrobudgeting
- Challenges: Why Does Congressional Macrobudgeting Not Work?
- Prospect of Congressional Macrobudgeting

WHY CONGRESSIONAL MACROBUDGETING AGAIN?

Budget scholars describe the current national budget process as the "unraveling" of budget processes (Rubin 2007). The central budget-control mechanisms in the Budget Enforcement Act (BEA) of 1990, such as enveloped sequestration and PAYGO, were repealed in 2002. As a result, the congressional budget process has defaulted back to the 1974 Congressional Budget and Impoundment Control Act (CBA). Since 2002, budget resolutions have seldom been agreed upon on time. (Details of these procedures are introduced below.) Although there might be various causes for federal budget deficits (Kettl 2003), scholars assert that the virtual collapse of congressional budget processes, especially congressional macrobudgeting, is partially attributable to the record-high federal deficits in recent years. Therefore, reforms of budget processes or reiterations of congressional macrobudgeting are emphasized again as a way to control federal deficits (Meyers 2009; Rubin 2007).

Despite the question of the effectiveness of congressional macrobudgeting tools for controlling federal deficits, the top-down macrobudgeting tools have been continually revived in the national budget process. In response to the rapidly growing federal debt after the financial market collapse in 2008, a bipartisan committee was formed to control federal debt by at least $1.2 trillion over the next ten years and to develop these deficit-control measures by November 2011. The Budget Control Act (BCA) of 2011 stipulated that if all measures fail, across-the-board cuts would be imposed on discretionary spending (Fessenden et al. 2011; Gosling and Eisner 2013, 208–11). The BCA of 2011 obviously revived the mechanism provided by the previous congressional macrobudgeting tools. Federal spending in particular has grown rapidly in recent years. Although across-the-board cuts are inferior to rationally setting spending priorities (e.g., analyzing budget proposals case by case to generate the most efficient budget formats), they have been suggested as budget control tools over and over again (Gramm and Solon 2011).

TOOLS OF CONGRESSIONAL MACROBUDGETING

The various tools of congressional macrobudgeting can be divided into three main sets of control mechanisms: budget resolutions and budget reconciliations, across-the-board sequestration, and PAYGO sequestration.

BUDGET RESOLUTIONS AND BUDGET RECONCILIATIONS

Among many provisions, budget resolution and reconciliation procedures were key macrobudgeting tools to control the federal budget. At the very beginning of the congressional budget-review process, budget resolutions set targets for aggregate totals in four main areas: total revenues, total new budget authority and outlays, the deficit or surplus, and the debt limit. Section 302 (a) of the Congressional Budget and Impoundment Control Act of 1974 directs the House and Senate Budget Committees to allocate spending totals in budget resolutions among the various House and Senate committees. (Chapter 2 in Part I provides more details about budget committees.) After appropriations committees receive their spending allocations, they subdivide them among their subcommittees in a section 302 (b) report. According to section 311 of the Congressional Budget Act, points of order will be raised against measures that exceed the budget totals in budget resolutions (Center on Budget and Policy Priorities 2010; Keith 2004, 4–12; 2008, 12–20; Keith and Schick 2003, 23–84; Saturno 2004, 3–5; 2008, 4–9; Schick 2007, 52–83, 118–61).

If Congress wants to keep revenue and direct spending under existing laws within the budget totals in budget resolutions, reconciliation instructions must first be included in budget resolutions. Based on section 310 of the Congressional Budget Act, which specifies the reconciliation procedure, the budget committees can bundle multiple legislations that exceed the total budget target into a single piece of legislation (Keith 2008, 25–27; Keith and Schick 2003, 23–46; LeLoup 1977, 126–51; Schick 2007, 118–61).

ACROSS-THE-BOARD SEQUESTRATION IN GRAMM-RUDMAN-HOLLINGS

During the early 1980s when the federal deficits were rapidly growing, politicians agreed on establishing one of the most draconian budget-control procedures ever, the

Gramm-Rudman-Hollings Balanced Budget and Emergency Deficit Control Act of 1985, known as GRH. GRH included a provision of across-the-board sequestration that was revived in the Budget Control Act of 2011. It also targeted the year 1991 for zero deficits. In addition, Congress required that the president issue a sequestration order based on Office of Management and Budget (OMB) baseline projections (Gosling 2009, 156–60; Havens 1986; LeLoup, Graham, and Barwick 1987; Primo 2007, 105–22).

PAYGO Sequestration in the Budget Enforcement Act (BEA)

Around 1990, federal deficits were growing again and the national economy was declining. In response to a budgetary stalemate between political leaders caused by the budget and economic conditions, the Budget Enforcement Act (BEA) was enacted in 1990. While the focus of GRH was on deficit reduction, the BEA targeted spending control. It also attempted to minimize the possibility of general, across-the-board sequestration and divided discretionary budgets into defense, domestic, and international packages with spending caps set for each (i.e., enveloped sequestration). Removal of the general sequestration and separation of spending into enveloped targets were supposed to allow the Senate and House Appropriations Committees to do their work without apprehension that it would be blocked by economic or technical factors beyond their control (Doyle and McCaffery 1991).

More importantly, the BEA added the new provision of PAYGO: "The statutory PAYGO procedure, in effect from 1991 to 2002, mandated that new legislation increasing direct spending or reducing revenues be fully offset so that the deficit was not increased or the surplus diminished" (Schick 2007, 58). The PAYGO procedure did not require offsetting adjustments when spending increases or decreases resulted from the operation of existing laws, such as the number of beneficiaries of Medicare. However, the PAYGO procedure still tightly linked new direct spending measures to entitlement spending based on permanent law. For instance, the procedure required that an increase in direct spending be offset by reductions in other direct spending programs that might be existing entitlement programs, by revenue increases, or both (Keith 2008, 19; Primo 2007, 105–22). In this sense, the PAYGO procedure put new entitlement programs "into a zero sum relationship with existing entitlement programs" (Doyle 1996, 68). Measures violating the PAYGO procedure were subject to a sequester for across-the-board cuts, which the president would issue based on a sequestration report prepared by the OMB (Schick 2007, 58).

Challenges: Why Does Congressional Macrobudgeting Not Work?

Despite various mechanisms of congressional macrobudgeting, budget scholars have contended that such macrobudget procedures are likely to get bypassed due to political manipulation (White 2009). Sequestration provisions in Gramm-Rudman-Hollings (GRH) of 1985 exempted many entitlement programs (Havens 1986; LeLoup, Graham, and Barwick 1987), which made the sequestration mechanism *dead at birth*.

Whenever budget participants felt the need to bypass or revise such macrobudgetary tools, congressional macrobudget processes could not control hidden political or policy preferences of budget claimants. This is especially true in Congress, where it is extremely difficult to impose strong institutional rules upon equally empowered, fragmented, decentralized legislators and committees (Cogan, Murris, and Schick 1994; LeLoup 1977, 1980; LeLoup and Shull 2003; Schick 1980, 2007). These challenges are presented in more detail below.

DEAD AT BIRTH

Among many reasons, congressional macrobudget tools were mostly born not to survive. Many entitlement programs were exempted, as is clearest in the case of GRH. Half of the budget reduction was to come from defense programs, while the other half would come from everything else. However, many entitlement programs, such as the Social Security cash benefit programs, interest on debt, other welfare subsidies, and trust fund programs, were completely exempt from the GRH process, as were certain prior legal government obligations (Havens 1986). Even without considering the draconian constraints that proved to be politically unsustainable (Posner 2009), only 20 percent of governmental outlays ultimately became subject to the across-the-board sequestration in GRH (LeLoup, Graham, and Barwick 1987).

A PAYGO sequester in the BEA would be triggered by new entitlement programs that were not offset either by revenue increases or by cuts in existing entitlement spending. However, the only noticeable change in the BEA from GRH was that Medicare payments to providers could be cut by up to 4 percent from 2 percent (Doyle 1996). Many direct spending programs, such as entitlement programs and those approved by authorizing legislation, were also exempt from PAYGO sequestration. For instance, PAYGO was not triggered when a change in spending or tax revenues occurred pursuant to existing law, as noted above. A sequester would not be triggered if expenditures rose due to inflation or if revenues fell because of a weak economy (Schick 2007, 58). Social Security benefits, federal deposit insurance commitments, and emergency direct spending and revenue legislations were completely exempted from the PAYGO sequester (Keith 2008, 19). Also, reconciliation procedures could not be used for legislative changes in Social Security (Keith 2008, 25–27). The Budget Control Act of 2011 also exempted Social Security and other safety net programs from the sequestration. The cut to Medicare was capped at 2 percent (Palmer and Penner 2012). These failures in statutory designs rendered most of the congressional macrobudget tools virtually dead at birth.

DYSFUNCTIONAL BUDGET IMPLEMENTATION

Congressional macrobudget tools were further weakened even as they were being implemented. Doyle (1996) succinctly indicated a potential limitation of reconciliation in relation to the GRH sequester. When reconciliation bills were kept longer in committees, a GRH sequester tended to be triggered to cut discretionary spending more frequently. Thus, tax increases and entitlement spending cuts (e.g., nondiscretionary budget items) were more likely to be protected from deficit control. This means that the entire burden of deficit reduction was placed on discretionary spending. "Under such circumstances, reconciliation delayed was reconciliation denied" (Doyle 1996, 66).

In addition, congressional budget priorities reflected in functional allocations in budget resolutions do not match the structure of appropriations committees. Budget resolutions were supposed to provide guidelines for mandatory and discretionary subtotals for each of nineteen budget functions. However, appropriations committees make actual budget allocations based on information from about twelve appropriations subcommittees (Meyers 2009). Numerous other budgetary gimmicks were used as ways around budget targets. The president and Congress disregarded the firewall between discretionary and mandatory spending, which the BEA stipulated. Congress and the president scored reductions in mandatory spending based on the PAYGO sequester as offsets to boost discretionary spending (Rubin 2007; Schick 2007, 74–76). It is also notable that congressional macrobudget tools turned otherwise effective guardians (i.e., appropriations committees) into claimants, with the creation of budget committees that appeared to be an ultimate budget control mechanism to appropriations committee members. In other words, appropriations committees were less vigilant about controlling budgets because they believed that budget committees would do the job of policing unnecessary budget increases (Schick 1980).

IMPACT OF THE NATIONAL ECONOMY

Third, governmental budgets are highly swayed by the performance of the national economy. In particular, a growing economy is likely to lead to a budget surplus. One important question is whether budget spending caps were effective as budget constraints in times of budget surplus (McCaffery 1996; Rubin 2007; Schick 2007, 129–53). When there was a surplus, reconciliation was used as a primary legislative vehicle for tax cuts (Schick 2007, 142–47). When more resources were available, budget committees had directed the Congressional Budget Office (CBO) to accept OMB assumptions with rosier economic forecasts, in what is known as directed scoring (Posner 2009; Rubin 2003, 109; Schick 2007, 75). In addition, with an emerging surplus, the pure meaning of PAYGO changed. As long as legislations did not raise deficits in the "general" fund, points of order allowed non–revenue-neutral legislation (White 2009). Thus, external economic environments changed the meaning of budget control.

POLITICS

Finally, one common thread penetrates all three key reasons. Budget processes are not immune to politics. When numbers forecasting is needed, there is a greater possibility for political influence (Schick 2007, 66). Republicans tend to prefer dynamic scoring, as shown in the Reagan administration's tax cuts. They believe that tax cuts would stimulate the economy, which would ultimately increase tax revenues. Increased tax revenues might reduce deficits and, thus, budget decision makers need not to be too stringent in imposing congressional macrotools. In contrast, Democrats might be more concerned about their immediate impacts on revenues and so prefer static scoring that tends to focus on the deficit increase that tax cuts might immediately cause (Rubin 2003, 100–105).

Budget resolutions are highly politicized, with budget committees and budget resolutions strongly reflecting partisan issues and lines. "Some years the resolution made it through only because enough members felt that having a congressional budget was better than not having one" (Schick 2007, 141). Without political support, PAYGO might not have been effective either, as shown in President Bill Clinton's skillful usage of it against Republican demands for tax cuts (Schick 2007). Most of all, macrobudget policies are a reflection of various political claimants. If the main budget actors did not agree on the budget targets set by congressional macrobudget tools, such targets were defunct at birth and dysfunctional for budget implementation (Cogan, Murris, and Schick 1994; LeLoup 1977, 1980; LeLoup and Shull 2003; Schick 1980, 2007; Wildavsky and Caiden 2004).

PROSPECT OF CONGRESSIONAL MACROBUDGETING

Historically, when there is a call for fiscal austerity, top-down budget control tools tend to be invoked. Total spending in 2013 would be 32 percent more than what was projected by the CBO in January 2007. Even after adjusting for inflation, real nondefense discretionary spending would increase by 7.6 percent, and real defense discretionary spending would be up by 13 percent. With increasing federal spending came another call for fiscal austerity. The 2011 Budget Control Act revived the across-the-board cuts, as noted above (Gramm and Solon 2011). Whether the measures can successfully control federal deficits is open to question if we account for the previous experiences introduced in this chapter.

CHAPTER SUMMARY

- **Congressional Macrobudgeting Tools**

As a way of controlling record-high federal deficits, scholars and practitioners have resorted once again to the so-called congressional macrobudgeting tools. The latest example is the Budget Control Act of 2011, which stipulates across-the-board cuts in discretionary spending in case all budget control measures fail to curb the federal deficits.

- **Tools of Congressional Macrobudgeting**

Budget resolutions set congressional targets for total revenues, total new budget authority and outlays, deficits or surpluses, and debt limits. Budget reconciliations set targets for revenue and direct spending under existing laws.

• The Budget Enforcement Act of 1990

The Budget Enforcement Act of 1990 imposed enveloped sequestration on defense, domestic, and international discretionary spending. The PAYGO procedure in the act mandated that new legislation increasing direct spending or reducing revenues be deficit neutral.

• Challenges: Why Does Congressional Macrobudgeting Not Work?

There were various challenges to the successful implementation of congressional macrobudgeting.

(1) Many programs, such as entitlement programs, were exempted from sequestration procedures, so macrobudgeting tools were dead at birth. In addition, the burden of congressional macrobudget tools was placed mostly on discretionary spending.

(2) When the economy was growing, congressional macrobudget tools were used to cut taxes. Political factors oftentimes dominated these tools.

26 | Mechanics of Debt Management

The previous chapters in Part VI showed that debt has been used as a tool of fiscal and monetary policies by the federal government. According to Keynesian macroeconomic theories, debt-financed governmental expenditures are supposed to stimulate the national economy. In contrast, state and local governments are more likely to borrow monies by issuing municipal bonds to finance various capital projects when general fund tax revenues are not sufficient for launching projects. This chapter introduces specific mechanics of issuing municipal bonds. Readers can easily apply the mechanics of municipal bonds to Treasury securities issued by the federal government as well. This chapter focuses on the following topics:

- What Are Bonds? How Do They Work?
- Main Participants in Bond Issuance
- Different Bond Structures
- Factors Affecting Borrowing Costs: Competitive vs. Negotiated Bond Sales
- Other Factors Affecting Borrowing Costs

WHAT ARE BONDS? HOW DO THEY WORK?

STRUCTURE OF BONDS

Bonds are promissory notes the principal of which borrowers of money will pay back by a certain date. The principal is the total amount owed to lenders. As explained in Chapter 11 in Part II on cost-benefit analysis, whenever borrowers borrow monies (i.e., sell or issue bonds), they have to pay fees for using lenders' monies. The fees are interest on the outstanding principal. Until readers get familiar with the mechanics of bond management, coupon payment will be used instead of interest, although coupon payment is a somewhat outdated concept. Coupon payment refers to the fees for using lenders' monies because the coupon portion of bonds will specify how much borrowers should pay lenders as compensation. Borrowers have to periodically pay a percentage (or coupon rate) of the principal amount they borrowed and must pay back the principal by a certain date. This is referred to as the maturity of bonds (California Debt and Investment Advisory Commission 2005, 2006; Finkler 2010, 230).

An easy way to understand what bonds are and how they work is to show the structure of a typical term bond. Table 26.1 illustrates the structure of a term bond with a principal amount of $10,000 and a coupon rate of 5 percent, which matures in ten years. The principal amount of $10,000 is what borrowers (i.e., issuers of bonds) borrow from lenders (i.e., purchasers of bonds or investors in the bond instruments). The amount is called face value or par value. Face value simply means that borrowers must pay back, in this case, $10,000 in year ten when this term bond matures. In the column titled Principal Outstanding in Table 26.1, $10,000 will be recorded as the money owed to lenders or purchasers of this term bond over the time period until maturity. While borrowers will pay back this outstanding principal once in year ten, they also periodically pay fees for using lenders' monies, called coupon payments. In Table 26.1, the annual coupon payment will be $500 (= 5% × $10,000).

BOND PRICE

Can borrowers or issuers/sellers of this term bond receive $10,000 in cash when they issue or sell this term bond? The answer is: It depends. As illustrated later in this chapter, various factors affect how much borrowers can receive in cash when issuing this term bond. However, there is a standard way of estimating how much borrowers can receive in cash. This cash amount is called bond proceeds or the bond price of this term bond as opposed to the par or face value (California Debt and Investment Advisory Commission 2005, 7; Mikesell 2011, 641–43). As readers will recall from Chapter 11 in Part II, the money that you have in your pocket right now has higher value than the same amount of money you could have in the future. This concept is called time value of money. So future dollars should be converted to present values using an adequate discount rate. The going market interest rate is often used as a proxy for the discount rate.

In Table 26.1, the discount rate is assumed at 9 percent. Therefore, the present value of $500, which lenders will get back in year ten, will be only $211 (= $500 / (1 + 0.09)^{10}$). Readers can compute the present values of all periodic coupon payments using relevant numbers of years. For instance, the present value of $500 in year four will be $354 (= $500 / (1 + 0.09)^{4}$). Similarly, the present value of the principal to be paid back in year ten will be $4,224 (= $10,000 / (1 + 0.09)^{10}$). The sum of the streams of the present values of future periodic coupon payments and the present value of the principal is $7,433. This $7,433 is called "bond price," and is obviously different from the par value of $10,000. The practical meaning of the bond price is that borrowers can only receive $7,433 when they sell this term bond. Thus, the bond price denotes bond proceeds.

Why does this happen? The discount rate proxied by the going market interest rate of 9 percent means that potential lenders might earn higher earnings if they invest their monies in other interest-bearing instruments. In other words, the lenders who might feel this term bond carrying a 5 percent coupon rate less attractive than other interest-bearing instruments are less likely to demand this term bond. Whenever demand for a

Table 26.1

Term Bond Structure (in dollars)

Year	Coupon payment	Principal outstanding	Annual sinking fund deposit	Sinking fund balance (SF)	SF1	SF2	SF3	SF4	SF5	SF6	SF7	SF8	SF9	SF10
1	500	10,000	658	658	658									
2	500	10,000	658	1,376	717	658								
3	500	10,000	658	2,158	782	717	658							
4	500	10,000	658	3,010	852	782	717	658						
5	500	10,000	658	3,939	929	852	782	717	658					
6	500	10,000	658	4,952	1,013	929	852	782	717	658				
7	500	10,000	658	6,056	1,104	1,013	929	852	782	717	658			
8	500	10,000	658	7,259	1,203	1,104	1,013	929	852	782	717	658		
9	500	10,000	658	8,570	1,312	1,203	1,104	1,013	929	852	782	717	658	
10	500	10,000	658	10,000	1,430	1,312	1,203	1,104	1,013	929	852	782	717	658

Par value = 10,000   Coupon rate = 5%

Discount rate = 9%   Bond price = 7,433

Note: Assume that the going market interest rate is used as the discount rate.

certain economic commodity is low, its price goes down. This is why the actual bond price of this term bond is less than its par value. In other words, borrowers should accept $7,433 while they must pay back $10,000 in year ten because this term bond is not as attractive as other investment instruments. The difference between the bond price and the par value, in this case $2,567, is called a bond discount. If the coupon rate were higher than the discount rate or going market interest, this term bond might be more attractive than other investment instruments. In that case, borrowers could sell this term bond at a much higher bond price. The difference between the bond price and the par value is called a bond premium (California Debt and Investment Advisory Commission 2005, 7; Finkler 2010, 232).

BOND RETIREMENT

When borrowers issue bonds, they typically save a certain portion of the par value or principal into a sinking fund. Most municipal borrowers have debt-retirement sinking fund accounts. As shown in Table 26.1, borrowers can save $658 annually into a sinking fund. In year one, they can save $658, which will grow at a compounding growth rate to $1,430 (= $658 \times (1 + 0.09)^9)^1$ in year ten. They can save $658 in the sinking fund in year two and so on. The schedules of saving into the sinking fund are shown in columns SF1 through SF10. If readers sum up all streams of sinking fund deposits as of year ten, the total sum will be $10,000 that the borrowers will receive in year ten to pay back the principal. Readers can use the PMT function in Excel (= PMT (0.09, 10, , -10,000,)) to get $658.

MAIN PARTICIPANTS IN BOND ISSUANCE

Successful bond issuance needs highly coordinated efforts of various participants.

BOND ISSUER: BORROWER

Borrowers borrow monies by issuing bonds. When public entities issue bonds, the interest is often exempt from federal and state income taxes. The Internal Revenue Service (IRS) code allows tax-exempt status to bonds issued by states, counties, cities, and school districts. These bonds are widely known as municipal bonds (California Debt and Investment Advisory Commission 2005, 9, 27; 2006, 2–5). Since the federal income tax exempts interest income earned on municipal bonds, municipal bond issuers have been successfully borrowing at lower interest costs. At the same time, however, tax-exempt municipal bonds need to pay higher interest to investors in lower tax brackets since they might not be as tempted to buy tax-exempts as those in higher tax brackets. Thus, a CBO study indicates that a one dollar federal tax-exempt subsidy is matched by only 80 cents cost savings in municipal borrowing. For these reasons, other types of municipal bonds have been more frequently issued since the 2008 financial market crisis. Build America Bonds (BABs) are a part of the American Recovery and Reinvestment Act of 2009, and were designed to stimulate infrastructure and development spending at the subnational level. Municipalities may issue as many taxable BABs as they want and receive either a direct subsidy of as much as 35 percent of BAB issuance or provide the subsidy directly to investors in the form of tax credits. In sum, the patterns of municipal bond issuance have dramatically changed since 2008 (Martell and Kravchuk 2012; Rassell and Kravchuk 2013).

In 2009, state and local governments sold BABs as up to 16 percent of total municipal bond issuance. In 2010, BABs sold by governmental entities constituted over 27 percent of the entire long-term municipal bond market (Luby 2012). Luby compared the estimated bond yields and borrowing costs that underwriters (see below for what underwriters do) prepared for bond transactions that the State of Ohio planned in 2010. BABs were expected to achieve interest-cost savings ranging from 36 to 90 basis points. Even after accounting for underwriting fees and underwriter takedown, BABs carried much lower borrowing costs. Other studies conducted by the U.S. Department of the Treasury and scholars reported similar cost savings from BABs for state and local governments. Luby further estimated the impact of BABs on federal budget costs, accounting for multiple federal budget costing variables. Some of his major findings indicate that adjusting issuance growth and program years only modestly affect federal budget costs. If BABs further stimulate the overall bond issuance, including taxable bonds, then federal budget costs increase somewhat, but still the increase is small compared to the total federal budget. The intermediate and long-term budget break-even rate for federal budget costs is somewhere between 30 and 32 percent of federal subsidy rates. Below about 30 percent of this rate, federal budget costs are negative (i.e., cost savings), even when issuance grows or length of BAB programs in effect increases. Overall, BABs save borrowing costs compared with traditional tax-exempt municipal bonds.

INVESTOR: LENDER

There are roughly three classes of investors: individuals, mutual funds, and financial institutions such as commercial banks and insurance companies. When any of them purchases bonds issued by borrowers, they are lending their monies to them. One common characteristic among the investors is that they are likely to be in a fairly high federal income tax bracket, so they benefit from the tax-exempt status (California Debt and Investment Advisory Commission 2005, 9; 2006, 24–26). As noted above, municipal governments have relied more on BABs since 2008. Since BABs are not tax exempt, they are more attractive to investors who do not pay federal taxes, such as pension funds, corporations, and foreign nationals (Luby 2012; Martell and Kravchuk 2012).

BOND COUNSEL

Bond counsel is an attorney, firm of attorneys, or group of firms that provide the legal opinions on bond issuance. Bond counsel confirms whether issued bonds are valid and their interests are exempt from federal and state income taxes (California Debt and Investment Advisory Commission 2005, 9; 2006, 5–8).

FINANCIAL ADVISER

A financial adviser is a professional consultant, such as a consulting firm, an investment banking firm, or a commercial bank, which advises bond issuers in formulating and implementing a debt-financing plan. The role of the financial adviser depends on the financial sophistication and workload capacity of bond issuers (California Debt and Investment Advisory Commission 2005, 9; 2006, 8–10).

UNDERWRITER

Underwriters are intermediaries between bond issuers and investors who purchase whole bond issues directly from bond issuers and resell them to investors. The profit they earn during the process is called the spread. The spread normally reflects four separate components. The management fee covers the cost incurred from developing and executing the bond issuance package. The underwriting fee compensates underwriters for the risk of buying the whole bond issue. The takedown represents the discount at which the members of the underwriting syndicate purchase or take down bonds from the overall underwriting account. Bond issuers also reimburse physical costs in the course of the bond sale by underwriters (California Debt and Investment Advisory Commission 2005, 9–10, 22–23; 2006, 10–15).

CREDIT RATING AGENCIES

Credit rating agencies assess the capacity of bond issuers to make all coupon and principal payments to investors. Investors generally use the bond ratings made by credit rating agencies to determine the repayment risk associated with bond issues. As noted below, the bond ratings significantly influence borrowing costs of bond issuers (California Debt and Investment Advisory Commission 2005, 10; 2006, 15–21). In 1975, the Securities and Exchange Commission (SEC) designated some credit rating agencies as nationally recognized statistical rating organizations (NRSRO), which decreased competition among rating agencies. In addition, the issuer-pay business model induced bond issuers to pursue compromising credit ratings. Investment banks and hedge fund managers became more willing to shop for desirable ratings. Overall, the institutional changes produced less reliable credit ratings (Collins forthcoming; Martell and Kravchuk 2012).

TRUSTEES

Trustees actually carry out the administrative duties required under bond documents. Their duties include establishing accounts related to bond issuance, maintaining a list of bond holders, paying principals and interests on bond issuance, and representing bondholders in the event of default (California Debt and Investment Advisory Commission 2005, 10; 2006, 21–22).

DIFFERENT BOND STRUCTURES

Earlier in this chapter, readers learned about the structure of a typical term bond. In practice, however, serial bonds are more frequently issued. Steiss (2003, 255–72) succinctly illustrates major structures of serial bonds. The topics introduced in this section are highly technical and generally discussed in financial management text-books. Considering the recent development in financial market credit programs, especially since the 2008 financial market crisis, however, readers need to understand the fundamental mechanisms of typical serial bonds. Later on, readers will find it much easier to analyze even financial derivatives once they learn the nuts and bolts of bond mechanisms.

STRAIGHT SERIAL BOND

The main difference between term bonds and serial bonds is that parts of the principals in serial bonds have different maturities. Issuers of serial bonds have to pay back parts of principals at different time periods until maturity: The parts of the principals have different maturities. Table 26.2 illustrates typical structures of serial bonds.

The upper panel in Table 26.2 shows the structure of a straight serial bond. Assume that the issuer of a serial bond borrowed $10,000. At the beginning of year one, the outstanding principal is therefore $10,000. If the coupon rate of this straight serial bond is 5 percent, the issuer is supposed to pay $500 (= 5% × $10,000) by the end of year one. The issuer will also pay back a part of the principal by the end of year one. Under a straight serial bond structure, the issuer will annually pay an equal portion of the principal, $10,000, which will be $1,000 per year. In year one, the total annual debt service amount will be $1,500 (= $500 + $1,000). At the beginning of year two, the outstanding principal is $9,000 because the issuer pays back $1,000 by the end of year one. The coupon payment for year two, 5 percent of $9,000, is $450 but the issuer pays back the same, equal payment of the principal ($1,000). This process will be repeated until maturity. If the going market interest, which is used as the discount rate, is 9 percent, then the bond price for this straight serial bond is $8,408. Once again, the bond price is less than the par value of $10,000 because the issuer offered a coupon rate that is less than the going market interest.

ANNUITY SERIAL BONDS

The lower panel in Table 26.2 shows a different form of serial bond. Under this annuity serial bond structure, the issuer is supposed to pay an equal periodic payment of "annual debt service" similar to typical mortgage amortization schedules. The bond issuer makes an equal periodic debt service payment of $1,295 at the borrowing cost of 5 percent (i.e., the coupon rate in this case). Readers can compute the equal payment of $1,295 by using an Excel function: = PMT (0.05, 10, −10,000, ,). The issuer of this serial bond is supposed to make an equal periodic payment of $1,295 at the end of each year until maturity in year ten.

The equal periodic payment is the sum of the annual coupon payment ($500 = 5% × $10,000) and the annual payment of the principal ($795 = $1.295 − $500) for year

Table 26.2

Serial Bond Structure (in dollars)

Straight Serial Bond Structure

Year	Principal outstanding	Coupon payment	Principal payment	Annual debt service
1	10,000	500	1,000	1,500
2	9,000	450	1,000	1,450
3	8,000	400	1,000	1,400
4	7,000	350	1,000	1,350
5	6,000	300	1,000	1,300
6	5,000	250	1,000	1,250
7	4,000	200	1,000	1,200
8	3,000	150	1,000	1,150
9	2,000	100	1,000	1,100
10	1,000	50	1,000	1,050
Total		**2,750**	**10,000**	**12,750**
		Coupon rate = 5%	Bond price = 8,408	

Annuity Serial Bond Structure

Year	Principal outstanding	Coupon payment	Principal payment	Annual debt service
1	10,000	500	795	1,295
2	9,205	460	835	1,295
3	8,370	419	877	1,295
4	7,494	375	920	1,295
5	6,573	329	966	1,295
6	5,607	280	1,015	1,295
7	4,592	230	1,065	1,295
8	3,527	176	1,119	1,295
9	2,408	120	1,175	1,295
10	1,233	62	1,233	1,295
Total		**2,950**	**10,000**	**12,950**
		Coupon rate = 5%	Bond price = 8,311	

Note: The discount rate is 9 percent.

one. Since the issuer pays back $795 by the end of year one, the beginning outstanding principal in year two is $9,205 (= $10,000 − $795). The coupon payment for the outstanding principal for year two is $460 (= 5% × $9,205), and the principal to be paid back is $835 (= $1,295 − $460). Again, the sum of the two payments in year two is still $1,295, similar to typical mortgage amortization schedules. In this case, the bond issuer makes gradually larger periodic principal payments. If the going market interest is 9 percent, the bond price of this annuity serial bond is $8,311. This makes intuitive sense because the coupon rate is smaller than the market interest.

STEPPED COUPON SERIAL BONDS

Table 26.3 illustrates the structure of a stepped coupon serial bond. In the financial market investors or lenders are highly likely to feel less secure with loans with longer maturities. Therefore, they tend to demand higher coupon rates for the loans with

Table 26.3

Stepped Coupon Serial Bond Structure (in dollars)

Year	Annual principal payment	Floating coupon rate (%)	Coupon pmt Y1	Coupon pmt Y2	Coupon pmt Y3	Coupon pmt Y4	Coupon pmt Y5	Coupon pmt Y6	Coupon pmt Y7	Annual debt service
1	3,000	3	90							3,508
2	2,000	4	80	80						2,418
3	1,500	5	75	75	75					1,838
4	875	6	53	53	53	53				1,138
5	875	7	61	61	61	61	61			1,085
6	875	8	70	70	70	70	70	70		1,024
7	875	9	79	79	79	79	79	79	79	954
Total	**10,000**		**508**	**418**	**338**	**263**	**210**	**149**	**79**	**11,884**
				Bond price = 9,315						

Note: The discount rate is 9 percent.

longer maturities. Under a stepped coupon serial bond, the issuer is supposed to pay back the principal of $10,000 according to the principal payment schedule shown under the second column in Table 26.3, Annual Principal Payment.

One noticeable difference in Table 26.3 from Table 26.1 and Table 26.2 is that coupon rates are gradually increasing for later years. This schedule is called a floating coupon rate. In year one, the issuer has to pay 3 percent of the outstanding principal for year one, $3,000, which is $90. In year one, the issuer also has to pay 4 percent ($80 as coupon payment) of the principal amount ($2,000) to be paid back in two years. Similarly, the issuer has to make all coupon payments for the outstanding principals in year one. The sum of the coupon payments is $508. The total annual debt service for year one (shown under the last column, Annual Debt Service) is $3,508 (= $3,000 + $508). In year two, a portion of the principal, $3,000, is already paid back. This means that the issuer does not have to make a coupon payment for the portion. The issuer makes coupon payments for all remaining outstanding principals. The sum of coupon payments for year two is $418 and the annual debt service is $2,418 (= $2,000 + $418). This process is repeated until maturity. The bond price for this annuity serial bond is $9,315, which is much closer to the par value of $10,000. This also makes intuitive sense because coupon rates for later years are closer to the market interest rate of 9 percent.

NET INTEREST COST (NIC) AND TRUE INTEREST COST (TIC)

One lingering question, especially with the stepped coupon rate is: What is the borrowing cost? In Table 26.3, readers can guess that the borrowing cost might be somewhere between 3 percent and 9 percent. There are two methods of computing the borrowing cost: net interest cost (NIC) and true interest cost (TIC) (Finkler 2010, 233–35). Table 26.4 illustrates how we can compute NIC and TIC.

NIC is the sum of all coupon payments divided by the sum of bond year dollars. Table 26.4, featuring the same stepped coupon serial bond shown in Table 26.3, pres-

Table 26.4

Net Interest Cost and True Interest Cost (in dollars)

Year	Principal payment	Coupon payment	Annual debt service	Bond year dollars
1	3,000	508	3,508	10,000
2	2,000	418	2,418	7,000
3	1,500	338	1,838	5,000
4	875	263	1,138	3,500
5	875	210	1,085	2,625
6	875	149	1,024	1,750
7	875	79	954	875
Sum	**10,000**	**1,963**	**11,963**	**30,750**
	NIC = 6.38%		TIC = 6.27%	

ents an outstanding principal of $10,000 at the beginning of year one. At the beginning of year two, the outstanding principal is $7,000 because the issuer pays back $3,000 at the end of year one. This process is repeated until maturity in year ten. Then, bond year dollars for all seven years are summed up (column titled Bond Year Dollars). The column Coupon Payment shows annual coupon payments shown in Table 26.3. The sum of annual coupon payments divided by the sum of bond year dollars is 6.38 percent (= $1,963 / $30,750). The rate, 6.38 percent, is called the NIC.

In contrast, TIC accounts for all payments until maturity, including periodic coupon and principal payments. The column, Annual Debt Service, shows the periodic payments. TIC then computes the discount rate at which the present value of the annual debt service equals the par value of $10,000 (if we can assume that the issuer sold the bond at par value). TIC is more frequently used in the financial market, although the difference between the two methods is very small, as shown in Table 26.4.

FACTORS AFFECTING BORROWING COSTS: COMPETITIVE VS. NEGOTIATED BOND SALES

As discussed above, when the going market interest rate is higher than coupon rates specified in issued bonds, the bonds are less attractive. To make them more attractive, bond issuers tend to raise their coupon rates. Thus, higher market interest rates are likely to raise borrowing costs (Robbins and Kim 2003). However, multiple other factors affect the borrowing costs. This section first shows how different methods of selling bonds affect the borrowing costs.

COMPETITIVE SALES OF BONDS VS. NEGOTIATED SALES OF BONDS

Under a competitive sale, underwriters bid to purchase bonds and those proposing the lowest interest-rate cost win the bid. Bond issuers structure the bond sales, sometimes with the help of financial advisers. After underwriters purchase the entire bond issues, they resell them to investors. Under a negotiated sale, underwriters are chosen by bond issuers before issuing bonds. The interest costs and all specific details of the offering are determined by agreement between underwriters and issuers. If the bond sales are large enough, several underwriters form a syndicate to collectively purchase the bonds. Under a negotiated sale, issuers place underwriters in a monopsony, or a single-buyer position, for their bond sales (Peng and Brucato 2003; Robbins and Kim 2003; Simonsen, Robbins, and Helgerson 2001).

The literature generally suggests that competitive sales result in lower borrowing costs than do negotiated sales. In addition, the magnitude of interest-cost savings gets larger as the number of bids increases. Despite the empirical findings, most bond sales since 1970 have been made through negotiated sales. In 1970, 83 percent of the dollar volume of all municipal bond sales was made through competitive sales. By 1984, only 46 percent were sold competitively. In 1994, only about 20 percent of new bond sales were competitively sold (Simonsen, Robbins, and Helgerson 2001). During recent years, however, scholars and practitioners have exchanged different views on the cost advantages from the competitive sale of bonds.

WHICH METHOD OF BOND SALES SAVES BORROWING COSTS?

In general, information asymmetry exists between bond issuers and investors. There are five causes for such information asymmetry: type of securities, credit rating, issue purpose, issue frequency, and issue size (Peng and Brucato 2003). The logic of information asymmetry indicates that issuers know more about the riskiness of their bonds than investors do. When there is information asymmetry, investors tend to view unknown information as unfavorable and disadvantageous to them. As a result, bonds are viewed as riskier, and increased riskiness translates into higher borrowing costs (Robbins and Simonsen 2007).

Under a negotiated sale, underwriters are responsible for most of bond origination in addition to risk bearing and distribution. Thus, negotiated underwriters have more time to familiarize themselves with bond issuance through a thorough certification of bond-related information, also known as due diligence (Peng and Brucato 2003). Under this situation, the certification process leads underwriters to have a better understanding of issuers. This certification process will ease investors' concerns. Therefore, issuers experiencing the greatest information asymmetry will opt for negotiated sales to obtain the underwriter certification. Overall, this assumption means that issuers rationally choose the bond sale type that they expect will achieve the lowest borrowing costs. Scholars have asserted that this kind of selection bias should be controlled for in order to accurately measure the impacts of bond sale types on borrowing costs: Selection bias (i.e., bond issuers intentionally choose one bond sale type over other types) might have its impact on borrowing costs separate from the bond sale type (Robbins and Simonsen 2007).

Leonard (1996) found that there was no difference in borrowing costs between competitive and negotiated bond sales when selection bias was controlled for. After correcting for the selection bias, Peng and Brucato (2003) found a small interest-cost saving for high-quality General Obligation (GO) bonds competitively sold and a larger cost saving for low-quality bonds. However, they cautioned that there were only a few competitive sales for low-quality bonds. Kriz (2003) analyzed 521 state

GO bonds sold from 1990 to 1997. After correcting for the selection bias, he found that negotiated bond sales achieved interest-cost savings compared with competitive sales. However, Robbins and Simonsen (2007) reported a different finding. They used more recent data covering all local GO bonds sold from 2004 to 2005 in Missouri municipalities. After correcting for the selection bias, they found that competitive sales achieve significant borrowing cost savings. Guzman and Moldogaziev (2012) investigated whether the purposes of bond issuance affect borrowing costs. They analyzed true interest costs (TIC) of 3,695 municipal debt issues in California from 2000 to 2007. In all cases, negotiated sales face significantly higher borrowing costs, after correcting the self-selection bias. This issue seems to be a continuing future research topic.

OTHER FACTORS AFFECTING BORROWING COSTS

Numerous other factors influence borrowing costs. More experienced bond issuers are likely to generate interest-cost savings. When issuers had more experience in bond issuance measured in terms of the number of bond issues counted over a multiple-year period, borrowing costs decreased. In general, more frequent sales of bonds are expected to save borrowing costs. Bond experts advocated sales of identical bonds at intervals of not less than six months. A contrasting view indicates that infrequent issuers in relatively smaller jurisdictions gained interest-cost savings. In particular, infrequent bond issuers borrowing less than half a million dollars or borrowing substantially large amount of dollars saved the most. Higher credit ratings are also associated with lower borrowing costs. When years to final maturity of bonds are fewer, borrowing costs tend to be lower. Borrowing costs continue declining up to a certain amount of bond issuance but increase beyond a certain point (Hildreth 1993; Robbins and Kim 2003).

Small municipalities experience disadvantages when marketing their bonds. They usually sell a small number of bond issues, incur higher bond-marketing costs, and have limited information for bond dealers and buyers. They also have difficulty affording quality legal counsel and financial advisers. In contrast, larger governments issue bonds more frequently and have more experience that demonstrably reduces borrowing costs. They also possess resident expertise and debt management capacity. Larger governments benefit from their relationships with various market actors. In order to assist smaller municipalities, ten states established bond banks from the 1970s to the early 1990s. Bond banks pool bonds issued by smaller municipalities in order to achieve economies of scale. Bond bank issues have greater marketability, carry enhanced bond credit ratings, save underwriting costs, and attract more bond bidders. When bond banks assume some costs of bond issuance, smaller municipalities benefit from additional cost savings. Robbins and Kim (2003), using data on bond bank issuance in selected states in 1999, found that bond banks achieve significant borrowing cost savings. Some state governments have been using State Infrastructure Bank (SIB) programs, the purpose of which is somewhat similar to that of bond banks (Ryu 2006, 2007). Yusuf, O'Connell, Hackbart, and Liu (2010) found that SIB programs enable loans with lower borrowing costs than those of typical municipal bonds.

Small communities do not have the financial management capacity in terms of skilled staff and resources to keep a large and sophisticated financial management function. In such communities, generalists with less technical training are likely to manage financial activities. Therefore, population size is sometimes expected to measure a local jurisdiction's complexity, the size and professional skills of its financial staff, and the quality and quantity of financial information provided to investors and credit rating agencies. Based on local government GO bonds sold from 1994 to 1997 in Oregon, Simonsen, Robbins, and Helgerson (2001) found that population size is significantly and negatively related to true interest costs. They also found that the total value of bond issues is negatively related, but its squared value is positively related. This is some evidence for scale economies.

Some scholars found that institutional and fiscal conditions facing bond issuers affect borrowing costs. Using new state GO bonds issued between 1990 and 1997, Johnson and Kriz (2005; see also Yusuf et al., 2013) investigated the impacts of institutional conditions on borrowing costs. Expenditure limits and balanced budget requirements might reduce competition over scarce resources and thus mitigate principal-agent problems. Empirical findings indicate that expenditure limits and balanced budget requirements increased credit ratings of bond issuers. Since debt restrictions might constrain governmental flexibility, debt restrictions decreased credit ratings. Credit ratings generally reduced true interest costs of the new state GO bonds. In contrast, revenue limits directly (rather than through credit ratings) affect borrowing costs. Revenue limits might constrain the revenue raising power and fiscal flexibility of bond-issuing governments. Therefore, revenue limits increased the true interest cost. In a similar vein, Benson and Marks (2007) analyzed competitively sold, uninsured GO bonds from 1999 to 2000 in twenty-nine states. When states had a structural surplus, their borrowing costs were lower than those for the states with structural deficits.

As noted above, Guzman and Moldogaziev (2012) investigated whether there are cost differentials across bonds issued for different purposes. Bond issues for development and housing purposes, which are perceived as riskier, face significantly higher borrowing costs than those issued for public facilities or utility. Bond issues for utilities and environmental facilities face significantly lower borrowing costs. The authors also investigated different borrowing costs across different portfolio qualities. For triple-A-rated bond issues, the issues for utilities, environmental facilities, health care, and other purposes face much lower borrowing costs. For below triple-A-rated issues, bond issues for development face higher borrowing costs. For unrated bond issues, borrowing costs decrease for the issues for utilities, K–12 education, and higher education but increase for housing.

CHAPTER SUMMARY

- **Structure of Bonds**

Bonds are promissory notes on which borrowers will pay principals (specified as par value) by a maturity date and periodic coupon payments. Term bonds are the most typical form of bonds.

- **Bond Price**

Bond price generally denotes the amount of funds issuers can borrow when issuing bonds. Bond price tends to differ from the par value of bonds. Going market interest rates are used as discount rates to compute the bond price. When coupon rates of bonds are higher than the going market interest rates, bonds are more attractive to loaners and can sell at higher bond prices and vice versa.

- **Bond Borrowers**

Borrowers often save certain portions of principals in debt-retirement sinking funds. The monies sitting in the funds will accrue some interest earnings. All balances in the funds at the maturity of bonds will be used to retire the bonds.

- **Main Participants in Bond Issuance**

There are various participants in bond issuance.

(1) Institutional borrowers usually have tax-exempt status. Individuals, mutual funds, and financial institutions are typical lenders. Since 2008, new patterns in the municipal bond market have emerged.

(2) Bond counsels provide legal opinions over bond issuance. Financial advisers counsel borrowers in formulating and implementing debt-financing plans.

(3) Underwriters are intermediaries between bond issuers and investors. They purchase whole bond issues from bond issuers and resell them to investors.

(4) Credit rating agencies assess the capacity of bond issuers to make coupon payments and pay back principals.

(5) Trustees carry out the administrative duties required under bond documents.

- **Serial Bonds**

Serial bonds are more frequently used than term bonds in practice. Parts of principals in serial bonds have different maturities. Issuers of serial bonds have to pay back parts of principals at different time periods. Straight serial bonds, annuity serial bonds, and stepped coupon serial bonds are typical examples of serial bonds.

- **Net Interest Cost and True Interest Cost**

There are two methods of computing borrowing costs for stepped coupon serial bonds: Net Interest Cost (NIC) and True Interest Cost (TIC). TIC is more frequently used in the financial market.

- **Factors Affecting Borrowing Costs**

Multiple factors affect borrowing costs.

(1) Under competitive bond sales, underwriters proposing the lowest interest costs win the bid. Under negotiated sales, bond issuers choose underwriters before issuing bonds. The literature generally suggests that competitive bonds sales tend to result in lower borrowing costs than negotiated bond sales. Recent findings are bifurcated on the impact of sales types on borrowing costs.

(2) The experience of bond issuers, frequency and size of bond issuance, and credit ratings of bonds affect borrowing costs. Bond banks also significantly influence bor-

rowing costs. Larger communities tend to have lower borrowing costs. Sometimes borrowing costs also differ, depending on the purposes of bond issuance.

(3) Institutional and fiscal conditions also affect borrowing costs. Revenue and expenditure limits, balanced budget requirements, and budget surplus/deficits influence borrowing costs.

NOTE

1. Just assume that borrowers deposit $658 at the end of year one. Then, there are nine years until the end of year ten.

PART VII

NEW APPROACHES TO BUDGET AND FINANCE

27 | Emerging Topics

This chapter introduces topics of budgeting and finance, which have recently reappeared, emerged, or drawn our attention for theory building. The following three topics are discussed:

- Participatory Budgeting
- Behavioral Public Finance and Economics
- Collaborative Budgeting

PARTICIPATORY BUDGETING

Chapters 1 and 2 in Part I introduced executive and legislative budget systems in the United States. As illustrated, the two systems originated from the critical debate on budget reforms during the late 1800s and the early 1900s. There were two streams of reform traditions. Taft conservatives believed that inequity in a society is inevitable. They felt that the best elected officials were to act based on their own judgments, not on popular demands. In contrast, Progressive reformers believed that even elected officials should be under direct popular control. Progressive reformers favored expansionary, activist government with trust in the public and its representatives. Their focus on cost-effectiveness contrasted starkly with the Taft conservatives' focus on cost saving and efficiency. Taft conservatives contended that the Progressive reformers' support for the initiative, the referendum, the recall of judicial decisions, and direct primaries would result in the extinction of competition. Taft conservatives believed in the desirability of a governing elite and were suspicious of legislative bodies that might give in to public desires. These ideas have crystallized in the executive budget movement (Rubin 1994).

At virtually all levels of government in the United States, executive budgeting systems have dominated. Recently, however, budget practitioners and scholars have called for measures to enhance transparency and accountability that the Progressive reformers proposed more than a century ago. How do public representatives define their democratic responsibilities? What are the opportunities and limitations in participatory budgeting processes? Achieving democratic values in budget processes has garnered heightened attention again (Ebdon and Franklin 2006; Rossmann and Shanahan 2012).

WHY IS PARTICIPATORY BUDGETING NEEDED AGAIN?

Through participatory budgeting, citizens deliberate and negotiate over resource distribution. It also helps promote transparency and reduce government inefficiencies and corruption. Participatory budgeting allows individuals with low incomes and low levels of education to participate in choices of how government resources are allocated. In this regard, it improves government performance by enhancing institutional rules that induce citizens to engage more actively in public policy debates. It also enhances the quality of democracy by encouraging citizens to participate in open public debates and to increase their knowledge of budget issues (Wampler 2007, 21–22).

In a similar vein, Moynihan (2007, 56–58) suggests four arguments for participation: postmodern discourse theory, disillusionment with bureaucracy, the search for a democratic ideal, and the need for participation in developing countries. According to the postmodern argument, increased individual mobility, weakening of traditional family ties, and erosion of traditional values have resulted in a societal change that necessitates greater demand for access to information. The monopolistic and centralized control of public information by the traditional government bureaucracies could not provide needed information to citizens. The logic of disillusionment with bureaucracy emphasizes that participatory budgeting has been suggested as a way to expedite the search for more democratic collective decision-making mechanisms that can send signals to government. Public participation functions as an external check on bureaucracies. Recent proposals for participatory budgeting stress that even bureaucrats and elected officials who are part of the representative bureaucracy are not necessarily trustworthy. The search for the democratic ideal through the process of public deliberation generates benefits for a society as well as individuals by nurturing democratic legitimacy and a deliberative political culture. The need for participatory budgeting is particularly important because it increases transparency and social justice in developing countries.

PARTICIPATORY BUDGETING IN PRACTICE

During recent decades, the most notable participatory budgeting was first implemented around 1990, in twelve Brazilian cities. By 2005 participatory budgeting had spread to more than 300 local governments worldwide. Participatory budgeting opens up obscure budget decision-making processes to ordinary citizens so they, along with their governments, can discuss taxation and spending decisions. Since democratic reestablishment in 1985, Brazilian politics has been characterized by traditional patronage practices, exclusion of underrepresented social classes, and corruption. Participatory budgeting was suggested as a way to improve policy outcomes and Brazilian democracy. In 1989 in one Brazilian municipality, participatory budgeting attempted to give larger shares of public spending to poorer citizens and neighborhoods. In 1989 and 1990, about 1,000 citizens took part in the participatory budgeting process. By 1992, the number of participants had jumped to about 8,000, and after 1992, it increased to more than 20,000 a year (Wampler 2007, 23–24).

The case of citizen summits in Washington, DC, illustrates the potential of participatory budgeting in strategic planning and budgeting. In 1999, a series of citizen summits were created to involve citizens in the planning and budget process. The Office of Neighborhood Action was established to coordinate citizen participation. Nearly 3,000 citizens participated in the summits, and inputs from the summit meetings significantly shaped the city budget format and the allocation of resources. Each city department asked for resources to implement strategic issues raised at the summit meetings (Moynihan 2007, 68–70). Numerous other forms of participatory budgeting were implemented in countries in Europe, Latin America, Africa, and Asia (Shah 2007).

STRUCTURES AND BENEFITS OF PARTICIPATORY BUDGETING

A typical structure of participatory budgeting process indicates that citizen participants are the main budget decision makers. As Wampler (2007, Figure 1.1) shows, there are multiple (in this case, two) regional meetings where citizens participate. Participants in the regional meetings make the most important budget decisions, and a municipal budget council collects and coordinates proposals from the regional meetings. The municipal budget council makes a final budget proposal. During the entire budget process, the municipal government provides the regional meetings with technical and administrative support while citizen participants make final budget decisions. For instance, citizen participants analyze financial information and discuss priorities for the municipality. They debate proposed public policies and public works, and visit proposed public works projects. They vote on the policies and public works and elect representatives from the regional meetings to the municipal budget council. They approve technical plans and monitor the implementation of public policies and works. The municipal government in most cases provides only technical and administrative support, such as initial cost estimates for proposed public works (Wampler 2007, 29–32).

Participatory budgeting processes are supposed to bring a variety of benefits to the jurisdiction. They improve efficiency, accountability, and decentralization. Higher levels of participation empower citizens and allocate more resources to low-income districts. Citizens are more educated about proposed public projects and financial information (Ebdon and Franklin 2006; Wampler 2007, 27–28).

BEHAVIORAL PUBLIC FINANCE AND ECONOMICS

Models of market and governmental fiscal decisions are based on rational and self-interested individuals who attempt to maximize their satisfaction in the private sector as workers, consumers, and investors and in the public sector as citizen-voters. Behavioral economics or finance has recently challenged this assumption. Much indebted to psychology and sociology, behavioral economics investigates how individuals actually make fiscal choices. In particular, it pays specific attention to two aspects: motivation and cognition. Motivation is about why individuals make certain fiscal choices. Behavioral economics more broadly defines motivation by investigating the well-being of others as well as self-interest maximization. Individuals are frequently less self-interested and more altruistic. Cognition is the dimension on how individuals obtain and process relevant information. Individuals do not have perfect perception of options and policies. This is especially the case when the options are complex. Individuals do not have enough time for processing all the information they have, so they cannot include all policy options in their choice set. This observation is known as bounded rationality, according to Herbert Simon (Ulbrich 2011, 12).

Ulbrich (2011, 215) illustrates examples supporting behavioral economics. The assumption of self-interested individuals predicts that individual taxpayers might attempt to reduce their tax burdens by overstating tax breaks and understating taxable income. For instance, federal income tax payers might overstate noncorporate business expenses or charitable contributions to maximize their tax breaks. As federal income tax compliance declines, however, the tax burden will be shifted to fewer honest taxpayers. In the end, the honest taxpayers might resent the lower tax burden levied on the noncompliant taxpayers. There is a strong, culturally utilitarian norm in support of tax compliance. Many Americans pay their income taxes in response to the norms as much as from fear of penalties.

Congdon, Kling, and Mullainathan (2012, 1–13) use three more specific examples—health insurance, taxes, and externalities—to illustrate how psychological factors reshape the core concepts in public finance. According to the traditional public finance framework, people are expected to conduct a simple cost-benefit analysis of health insurance benefits. When patients feel very good, they might skip a medical dose because they believe taking the medicine might not be worth it. Some other patients might skip a dose because its medical benefits might not be salient right now. Therefore, the psychic cost-benefit analysis might be different from the traditional economic cost-benefit analysis introduced in Chapter 11 in Part II.

According to traditional, standard public finance, taxing low-elasticity products is desirable because it minimizes deadweight loss in what is known as the Ramsey rule, as introduced in Chapter 18 in Part IV. According to behavioral economics, tax analysis is more complicated. A study indicates that consumers may fail to accurately perceive the sales tax burden when they purchase consumer goods. Thus, this taxation looks similar to taxing nonsalient products, and therefore governments might be able to raise revenues without distorting behavior. Furthermore, there are two polar cases in consumer responses when they find their actual income decreases by the tax payment. They might reduce expenditures on all other goods by the tax amount. In this case, the nonsalient tax becomes similar to a nondistorting lump-sum tax. Therefore, the Ramsey rule cannot be directly applied to this condition. In other cases, consumers might make more-specific choices, such as specifically reducing their spending on grocery purchases. Or they will simply save less without changing their consumption. In sum, the effects of reduced tax salience must account for all changes in consumers' demand decisions.

Standard public finance indicates that taxation imposed over negative externality—

for example, carbon emissions—will restore social efficiency as introduced in Chapter 11 in Part II. However, psychological studies show that social comparisons can modify individual behavior more effectively than does taxation. One study, for instance, reported that when a utility company continuously sends a report showing how much electricity a customer used compared to his or her neighbors, the individual tends to reduce electricity consumption by about 2 percent. This implies that a nudge, in this case social comparison reporting, significantly affected energy consumption. It further implies that consumers might not choose optimal levels of energy consumption even with an efficiency-restoring carbon tax.

Congdon, Kling, and Mullainathan (2012, 17–20; see also Baddeley 2013) succinctly summarize key dimensions of behavioral finance and economics in three fundamental concepts: imperfect optimization, bounded self-control, and nonstandard preferences.

IMPERFECT OPTIMIZATION

Behavioral economics assumes that individuals fail to maximize their own welfare and their choices tend to be inconsistent. This concept has three subconcepts: limited attention, limited computational capacity, and biased reasoning. Due to individual cognitive-capacity limits, people are likely to pay attention to limited sets of environmental stimuli. When a certain information input is more salient, they tend to be more attentive to it. When individuals are directed to pay attention to one part of the environmental stimuli, they fail to notice even unusual informational inputs. When they face choices with no dominant alternatives, they simply avoid or defer their decisions. Individuals' subjective valuation of alternatives is often inconsistent. They frequently misunderstand average costs of products and their marginal costs. Mental accounting is different from conventional financial accounting in that individuals often focus on a certain aspect of financial measures. For instance, individuals tend to spend more frivolously what they regard to be won, or tax incentives such as child tax credits. Finally, individual choices are often blocked by uncertainty of events to take place. They are limited by motivational biases: Individuals tend to be overconfident about their capacities, for instance (Baddeley 2013, 106–16, 144–46; Congdon, Kling, and Mullainathan 2012, 20–27).

BOUNDED SELF-CONTROL

Even when individuals can maximize their utilities, they have difficulty realizing their interests. Forces such as temptation and procrastination are real phenomena that affect individual choices. Unlike standard economic assumptions, individuals cannot exert self-control in fully implementing rational choices. Examples of such behavioral barriers are procrastination and temptation, channel factors, state and affect, and addiction. Procrastination and temptation are main reasons for the gap between individual intention and action. Channel factors reveal, surprisingly, that only minor barriers or inducements can steer individuals toward or away from their individual choices. State and affect means that individual capacity to exert self-control highly depends on the state of decision-makers, such as stress, cognitive load, and hunger, when they are making their decisions. Addiction obviously might prohibit individuals from exerting self-control (Baddeley 2013, 128–209; Congdon, Kling, and Mullainathan 2012, 28–32).

Nonstandard Preferences

Individual preferences tend to change with changes in status. Individuals frequently hold other-regarding preferences. Standard economic assumptions indicate that individuals make their choices based on the end result. In contrast, behavioral economics contends that how individuals value an outcome depends on the path taken to achieve it. Reference-dependent preferences include endowment effect, loss aversion, and status quo bias. Endowment effect denotes that owners of some goods, in general, are more likely to value those goods highly and less willing to give up what they perceive they own. Individuals tend to value loss more significantly than gains. They also tend to stick to what they have currently. According to other-regarding preferences, individuals make their choices based on altruism, fairness, social norms, and interpersonal preferences, unlike the assumption of self-interested individuals in standard economic theories (Baddeley 2013, 116–18; Congdon, Kling, and Mullainathan 2012, 33–39).

Implications of Behavioral Finance and Economics on Governmental Policy

Congdon, Kling, and Mullainathan (2012, 9–13) contend that tools and concepts of behavioral economics will offer benefits in crafting governmental policies. Perceived prices, rather than actual prices, will drive consumers' behavior. Nudges have social effects. Automatically enrolling seniors in low-cost plans in Medicare Part D might protect them from mistakes. However, from a perspective of behavioral finance, allowing seniors to make mistakes can make it possible to pool the common risks and attendant policies. The social welfare function has some psychological effects. Social Security clearly conveys a message that saving more is preferable to consumption. Moral hazard explains unintended behavioral responses, but sometimes the latter can better be explained by psychological factors. For instance, procrastination may explain unemployment. Procrastination in filing for welfare programs, rather than their screening procedures, might better explain why people fail to participate in the programs. Governmental policies attending to these different behavioral dimensions might be more effective.

Chapter 23 in Part VI introduced differences between Classical and Keynesian approaches to macroeconomic activities. According to Classical views, individuals and firms have the capacity to rationally analyze economic conditions. Hence, for instance, the labor market will always be at its equilibrium. In contrast, Keynesians suggest that individuals and firms cannot be perfectly rational. Some nonrational, especially psychological, factors might keep them from making rational choices, as introduced in Chapter 23. Keynesian fundamental psychological laws include: the propensity to consume, liquidity preferences, and expectations of returns from investment. Thus, Keynesian approaches have already incorporated the effect of human psychology in explaining macroeconomic activities (Baddeley 2012, 232–54). The framework of behavioral finance and economics, therefore, will provide researchers with tools to explain what could not be explained with standard economic theories based on rationality or optimality or even the concept of bounded rationality (Congdon, Kling, and Mullainathan 2012, 32–33). However, there are still some caveats. As readers might have noticed, the concepts of bounded rationality or disproportionate information processing introduced in Part III presented frameworks very similar to what behavioral finance and economics suggest. The crucial difference between the concepts and behavioral finance might be the fact that the latter pays more attention to the "limits or barriers" to rational choice than the former does.

COLLABORATIVE BUDGETING

Collaboration or network management has recently been one of the most frequently discussed topics in the field of public administration. As collaboration has necessitated development of an accountability and performance framework different from the conventional politics-administration dichotomy, it has also called for developing new budget frameworks for emerging networks. However, readers should be keenly aware that managerial collaboration among various public organizations does not necessarily mean an equal level of resource sharing. Only a paucity of budget scholars has attempted to develop preliminary budget frameworks that might be relevant for resource allocation under networked service delivery. In Part II, readers learned about performance-based budgeting (PBB) systems. One of the most significant challenges was the so-called attribution issue. There will almost always be contested credit-claiming games over who achieved what and thus who should be rewarded in terms of increased resources or budgets. Scholars and practitioners have consistently recommended activity-based costing (ABC) methods to address attribution issues, but even such advanced resource-allocation attempts fall far short of silencing conflicts, especially when stakeholders come to actual money-allocation decisions. Probably, the attribution challenge would be much more pronounced if multiple organizations collaborated on the same public programs. Thus, the purpose of introducing collaborative budgeting is not to endorse it as an established budget theory agenda yet, but to call for "scholarly collaboration" on deciding whether collaborative budgeting issues are as real as various managerial attempts for collaboration popular in the field of public management. Only to the extent to which collaborative budgeting is real will we need to identify systematic patterns of collaborative budget processes and decisions that are markedly different from those under single organizations or jurisdictions.

COLLABORATION: STRUCTURE AND FUNCTION

Public sector organizations have been engaged in cross-sector collaboration to share information and resources to jointly achieve what they cannot achieve alone (Bryson, Crosby, and Stone 2006; Provan and Kenis 2008). Five key dimensions are implied in the definition of collaboration: governance, administration, organizational autonomy, mutuality, and norms. One way or the other, each of the five dimensions will affect the effectiveness of an entire network's performance or relationships among the participants in those networks (Thompson, Perry, and Miller 2008, 98–102). Networks have been proposed to bring about enhanced learning, more efficient use of resources, increased capacity to address complex problems, greater competitiveness, and better services for clients. In particular, public problems are getting more complex, and resources are getting scarce. Governments have turned to external partners for help. Overall, public managers have been encouraged to be more facilitators and coordinators than direct service providers. Partnering with other public and nonprofit organizations is supposed to increase efficiency, innovativeness, flexibility, and enhanced community ties, which will result in more effective program performance. In the absence of effective management, the costs of managing partnerships might outweigh the benefits (Graddy and Chen 2009, 53–54; Provan and Kenis 2008).

According to Provan and Kenis (2008), there are three types of networks. First, a form of shared participant governance, participant-governed networks, is highly decentralized, and partners collectively make decisions and manage network activities. All network members are interacting on a relatively equal power basis and are responsible for managing internal network relationships and external relations with external stakeholders. This form can be developed either formally through regular meetings or informally through ongoing but uncoordinated interorganizational efforts. Second, a single lead participating member may coordinate all major network-level activities and decisions, acting as a lead organization. Network governance is highly centralized and brokered. The lead organization may be emergent from the members themselves or may be externally mandated. Third, a separate network administrative organization (NAO), which does not provide its own services, can be set up for the specific purpose of governing the network and its activities. The network is externally governed, with an NAO established, through mandate or by members themselves. "Government run NAOs are generally set up when the network first forms, to stimulate its growth through targeted funding and/or network facilitation and to ensure that network goals are met" (Provan and Kenis 2008, 236).

As Bryson, Crosby, and Stone (2006) imply, networks are likely to develop from more participant-governed networks to either lead organization-governed networks or NAO-governed ones. In addition, key predictors of effectiveness of networks governance forms differ across each of the three types of networks. For instance, high-density trust and high-goal consensus among network participants are indispensable for participant-governed networks because the networks generally lack consensual basis for collaboration. In contrast, as the number of partners under shared governance increases, full and active face-to-face interactions are harder to achieve. Partners are likely to ignore critical network issues or spend a lot of time coordinating across multiple organizations. The problem of network complexity will be aggravated when partners are geographically dispersed and cannot easily meet with each other (Bryson, Crosby, and Stone 2006, 238). The problem can be somewhat addressed by centralizing network governance activities around a lead organization or NAO. Similarly, when network participants face high-interdependence task requirements that need complex skills that individual participants do not possess, lead organizations or NAO forms will be more effective (Provan and Kenis 2008).

What are the implications of the key aspects of collaborative network management on budgeting processes?

IMPLICATIONS OF COLLABORATION ON BUDGETING PROCESSES

Mitchell and Thurmaier (2011) offer some preliminary but important answers to the above question. Due to increased collaboration between public organizations, individual organizations need to adjust their budgetary and financial management systems to address accountability, transparency, and performance concerns associated with network participation. In addition, with the development of network settings, scholars have to understand how network-level budgeting functions.

Budgeting for collaboration is unique in four dimensions. First, there are competing interests within networks. If network participants and network goals are not aligned, conflicts might develop. The collaborative function of budgeting must be viewed through two lenses. It must account for participant calculation of benefits from network participation, and the network process must provide resources in a manner consistent with participant expectations. Second, networks raise unique accountability challenges. A fundamental issue for networked collaboration is that external service providers add another complex link to the democratic accountability chain. Network participation of the service providers therefore might generate the dysfunctions featured by principal-agent theory. Elected officials in networks should carefully review the terms of collaborative participation, establish identifiable performance and cost targets, and review performance of the network participants. In that case, accountability in networked services might be enhanced. More specifically, if collaborative agreement is reported in budget documents, accountability can be bolstered. In addition, resource sharing itself will foster interdependence and mutual accountability. Trust built through networks can also reduce transaction costs that might function as barriers to accountability.

Third, network-based costing raises a question typically found in activity-based costing (see Chapter 12 in Part II for more details of activity-based costing). Network participant organizations devote substantial amounts of personnel, time, and materials to collaborative network activities. It is imperative for future research to find out how to identify the resources devoted to collaborative network activities and to adequately allocate them to specific parts or cost objects within networks. Finally, the lack of institutional norms found in entrenched governmental budget processes, such as incrementalism, ironically might enable networks to implement efficient resource allocation methods. For instance, the Newark Downtown District successfully implemented performance-based budgeting for a public network. This was possible due to the lack of budget inertia found in incrementalism.

Mitchell and Thurmaier's (2011) framework on collaborative budgeting is one of the earliest attempts to explain budgetary implications from networked service delivery. What we further need is to identify whether and how scholars and practitioners can develop more specific dimensions in Mitchell and Thurmaier's framework. For example, Provan and Kenis (2008) suggested three types of network forms with different connotations on the four dimensions of trust, number of participants, shared vision, and need for technical capacities. It is very likely that Mitchell and Thurmaier's framework might apply to the three network types quite differently over the four dimensions.

CHAPTER SUMMARY

- **Participatory Budgeting**

Participatory budgeting has recently reappeared in public budget processes. It allows individuals with low incomes and less formal education to more actively participate in governmental resource allocation processes. It improves efficiency, accountability, and decentralization.

Participatory budgeting was first implemented around 1990, in twelve Brazilian cities. By 2005, participatory budgeting had spread to more than 300 local governments worldwide.

Under a typical participatory budgeting process, participants in regional meetings make most important budget decisions, and a municipal budget council collects and coordinates proposals from the regional meetings. The municipal budget council, not executive agencies, makes a final budget proposal.

- **Four Perspectives of Participatory Budgeting**

Scholars have supported participatory budgeting from four perspectives: postmodern discourse theory, disillusionment with bureaucracy, the search for a democratic ideal, and the need for participation in developing countries.

- **Behavioral Public Finance and Economics**

Behavioral economics or finance has recently challenged the assumption of self-interested individuals and rationality in market and governmental fiscal choices. Behavioral finance suggests that individuals are not always self-interested. In addition, human decision makers are limited in their information-processing capacity, in what is known as bounded rationality.

- **Frameworks for Behavior Finance**

Behavioral finance provides frameworks more comprehensive than bounded rationality.

(1) Imperfect optimization means that individual choices are constrained by limited attention, limited computation capacity, and biased reasoning.

(2) Bounded self-control denotes that even when individuals can maximize their utilities, there are likely to be gaps between choices and their implementation.

(3) Nonstandard preferences, such as reference-dependent preferences and other-regarding preferences, further block rational choices of individuals.

- **Collaboration: Structure and Function**

Public sector organizations have been more engaged in cross-sector collaboration sharing information and resources to jointly achieve what they cannot achieve alone. Networks have been proposed to bring about enhanced learning, more efficient use of resources, increased capacity to address complex problems, greater competitiveness, and better services for clients.

There are three types of networks: participant-governed networks, lead organization–governed networks, and NAO-governed networks. The effectiveness of each type of network depends on the level of trust, number of network participants, goal consensus, and need for special network-level competencies.

- **Implications of Collaboration on Budgeting Processes**

Budgeting for collaboration is unique because: (1) There are multiple competing interests within a collaborative network; (2) the accountability issue with a bureaucracy is altered when external service providers deliver public services; (3) activity-based costing is not just an internal management tool but determines levels of resource sharing in the network; and (4) the lack of institutional norms develops unique budgetary opportunities for network participants.

References

Abney, Glenn, and Thomas P. Lauth. 1985. "The Line-Item Veto in the States: An Instrument for Fiscal Restraint or an Instrument for Partisanship?" *Public Administration Review* 45, no. 3: 372–77.

———. 1997. "The Item Veto and Fiscal Responsibility." *Journal of Politics* 59, no. 3: 882–92.

———. 1998. "The End of Executive Dominance in State Appropriations." *Public Administration Review* 58, no. 5: 388–94.

———. 2002. "Gubernatorial Use of the Item Veto for Narrative Deletion." *Public Administration Review* 62, no. 4: 492–503.

Abrams, Burton A., and William R. Dougan. 1986. "The Effects of Constitutional Restraints on Governmental Spending." *Public Choice* 49: 101–16.

Alt, James E., and Robert C. Lowry. 1994. "Divided Government, Fiscal Institutions, and Budget Deficits: Evidence from the States." *American Political Science Review* 88, no. 4: 811–28.

———. 2000. "A Dynamic Model of State Budget Outcomes Under Divided Partisan Government." *Journal of Politics* 62, no. 4: 1035–69.

Anderson, John E. 2012. *Public Finance*. 2d ed. Mason, OH: South-Western, Cengage Learning.

Anderson, Sarah, and Laurel Harbridge. 2010. "Incrementalism in Appropriations: Small Aggregation, Big Changes." *Public Administration Review* 70, no. 3: 464–74.

Auerbach, Alan J. 2002. "The Bush Tax Cut and National Saving." *National Tax Journal* 55, no. 3: 387–407.

Auten, Gerald, Robert Carroll, and Geoffrey Gee. 2008. "The 2001 and 2003 Tax Rate Reductions: An Overview and Estimate of the Taxable Income Response." *National Tax Journal* 61, no. 3: 345–64.

Avant, Gayle R. 1993. Book review: "The Budget-Maximizing Bureaucrat: Appraisals and Evidence." *Journal of Politics* 55, no. 3: 824–27.

Axelrod, Donald. 1989. *A Budget Quartet: Critical Policy and Management Issues*. New York: St. Martin's Press.

Baddeley, Michelle. 2013. *Behavioural Economics and Finance*. New York: Routledge.

Bae, Sang-Seok, and Richard C. Feiock. 2004. "The Flypaper Effect Revisited: Intergovernmental Grants and Local Governance." *International Journal of Public Administration* 27, no. 8–9: 577–96.

Bae, Suho, Seong-gin Moon, and Changhoon Jung. 2012. "Economic Effects of State-Level Tax and Expenditure Limitations." *Public Administration Review* 72, no. 5: 649–58.

Baicker, Katherine. 2001. *Extensive or Intensive Generosity? The Price and Income Effects of Federal Grants*. National Bureau of Economic Research Working Paper no. 8384, July. Cambridge, MA: NBER.

Bailey, John J., and Robert J. O'Connor. 1975. "Operationalizing Incrementalism: Measuring the Muddles." *Public Administration Review* 35, no. 1: 60–66.

Bardach, Eugene. 2012. *A Practical Guide for Policy Analysis: The Eightfold Path to More Effective Problem Solving*, 4d ed. Thousand Oaks, CA: SAGE CQ Press.

Barr, James L., and Otto A. Davis. 1966. "An Elementary Political and Economic Theory of the Expenditures of Local Governments." *Southern Economic Journal* 33, no. 2: 149–65.

Barro, Robert J. 1989. "The Neoclassical Approach to Fiscal Policy." In *Modern Business Cycle Theory*, ed. Robert J. Barro, 178–235. Boston: Harvard University Press.

———. 2011. "Keynesian Economics vs. Regular Economics." *Wall Street Journal*, August 24.

Bartik, Timothy J. 1989. "Small Business Start-Ups in the United States: Estimates of the Effects of Characteristics of States." *Southern Economic Journal* 55, no. 4: 1004–18.

Baumgartner, Frank R., and Bryan D. Jones. 1993. *Agendas and Instability in American Politics*. Chicago: University of Chicago Press.

———. 2009. *Agendas and Instability in American Politics*. 2d ed. Chicago: University of Chicago Press.

Barzelay, Michael, and Fred Thompson. 2006. "Responsibility Budgeting at the Air Force Material Command." *Public Administration Review* 66, no. 1: 127–38.

Beam, Adam. 2011. "SC Agencies' Budgets Dwindling." Herald, August 29. www.heraldonline.com/2011/08/29/3324737_state-agencies-budgets-dwindling.html.

Becker, Gary S. 1983. "A Theory of Competition Among Pressure Groups for Political Influence." *Quarterly Journal of Economics* 98, no. 3: 371–400.

Benson, Earl D., and Barry R. Marks. 2007. "Structural Deficits and State Borrowing Costs." *Public Budgeting and Finance* 27, no. 3: 1–18.

Bergstrom, Theodore C., and Robert P. Goodman. 1973. "Private Demands for Public Goods." *American Economic Review* 63, no. 3: 280–96.

Berkman, Michael B., and Christopher Reenock. 2004. "Incremental Consolidation and Comprehensive Reorganization of American State Executive Branches." *American Journal of Political Science* 48, no. 4: 796–812.

Berry, William D. 1990. "The Confusing Case of Budgetary Incrementalism: Too Many Meanings for a Single Concept." *Journal of Politics* 52: 167–96.

Bertelli, Anthony Michael. 2004. "Strategy and Accountability: Structural Reform Litigation and Public Management." *Public Administration Review* 64, no. 1: 28–42.

Blais, André, and Stéphanie Dion, ed. 1991. *The Budget-Maximizing Bureaucrat: Appraisals and Evidence*. Pittsburgh: University of Pittsburgh Press.

Bland, Robert L., and Wes Clarke. 2007. "Texas: The Use of Performance Data in Budgeting and Management." In *Budgeting in the States: Institutions, Processes, and Politics*, ed. Edward J. Clynch and Thomas P. Lauth, 277–92. Westport, CT: Praeger.

Block, Walter E. 2010. "A Critical Look at *The Calculus of Consent*." *Georgetown Journal of Law and Public Policy* 8, no. 2: 433–50.

Boadway, Robin W., and David E. Wildasin. 1984. *Public Sector Economics*, 2d ed. Boston: Little, Brown and Company.

Boardman, Anthony, David H. Greenberg, Aidan R. Vining, and David L. Weimer. 2006. *Cost-Benefit Analysis: Concepts and Practice*, 3d ed. Upper Saddle River, NJ: Pearson Prentice Hall.

———. 2011. *Cost-Benefit Analysis: Concepts and Practice*, 4th ed. Boston: Pearson Prentice Hall.

Borcherding, Thomas E., and Robert T. Deacon. 1972. "The Demand for the Services of Non-Federal Governments." *American Economic Review* 62, no. 5: 891–901.

Bosworth, Barry P. 2012. *The Decline in Saving*. Washington, DC: Brookings Institution Press.

Bosworth, Barry, and Gary Burtless. 1992. "Effects of Tax Reform on Labor Supply, Investment, and Saving." *Journal of Economic Perspectives* 6, no. 1: 3–25.

Bourdeaux, Carolyn. 2008. "The Problem with Programs: Multiple Perspectives on Program Structures in Program-Based Performance-Oriented Budgets." *Public Budgeting and Finance* 28, no. 2: 20–47.

Boushey, Graeme. 2010. *Policy Diffusion Dynamics in America*. New York: Cambridge University Press.

———. 2012. "Punctuated Equilibrium Theory and the Diffusion of Innovations." *Policy Studies Journal* 40, no. 1: 127–46.

Bowling, Cynthia. J., Chunglae Cho, and Deil S. Wright. 2004. "Establishing a Continuum from Minimizing to Maximizing Bureaucrats: State Agency Head Preferences for Governmental Expansion—A Typology of Administrator Growth Postures, 1964–98." *Public Administration Review* 64, no. 4: 489–99.

Bowling, Cynthia J., and Margaret R. Ferguson. 2001. "Divided Government, Interest Representation, and Policy Differences: Competing Explanations of Gridlock in the Fifty States." *Journal of Politics* 63, no. 1: 182–206.

Boyne, George, Rachel Ashworth, and Martin Powell. 2000. "Testing the Limits of Incrementalism: An Empirical Analysis of Expenditure Decisions by English Local Authorities, 1981–1996." *Public Administration Review* 78, no. 1: 51–73.

Bravin, Jess. 2012. "Court Says Inmate Can't Sue for Injury." *Wall Street Journal*, January 11, A.2.

Breunig, Christian. 2011. "Reduction, Stasis, and Expansion of Budgets in Advanced Democracies." *Comparative Political Science* 44, no. 8: 1060–88.

Breunig, Christian, and Chris Koski. 2006. "Punctuated Equilibria and Budgets in the American States." *Policy Studies Journal* 34, no. 3: 363–79.

———. 2009. "Punctuated Budgets and Governors' Institutional Powers." *American Politics Research* 37, no. 6: 1116–38.

———. 2012. "The Tortoise or the Hare? Incrementalism, Punctuations, and Their Consequences." *Policy Studies Journal* 40, no. 1: 45–67.

Breunig, Christian, Chris Koski, and Peter B. Mortensen. 2010. "Stability and Punctuations in Public Spending: A Comparative Study of Budget Functions." *Journal of Public Administration Research and Theory* 20, no. 3: 703–22.

Briffault, Richard. 1996. *Balancing Acts: The Reality Behind State Balanced Budget Requirements.* New York: Twentieth Century Fund Press.

Brown, Richard E., Mark J. Myring, and Cadillac G. Gard. 1999. "Activity-Based Costing in Government: Possibilities and Pitfalls." *Public Budgeting and Finance* 19, no. 2: 3–21.

Brunori, David. 2007. *Local Tax Policy: A Federalist Perspective*, 2d ed. Washington, DC: Urban Institute Press.

———. 2011. *State Tax Policy: A Political Perspective*, 3d ed. Washington, DC: Urban Institute Press.

Bryson, J.M., B.C. Crosby, and M.M. Stone. 2006. "The Design and Implementation of Cross-Sector Collaborations: Propositions from the Literature." *Public Administration Review* 66 (Supplement): 44–55.

Buchanan, James M., and Gordon Tullock. 1962. *The Calculus of Consent.* Ann Arbor: University of Michigan Press.

Burton, Maureen, and Bruce Brown. 2009. *The Financial System and the Economy*, 5d ed. Armonk, NY: M.E. Sharpe.

Buss, Terry F. 2001. "The Effect of State Tax Incentives on Economic Growth and Firm Location Decisions: An Overview of the Literature." *Economic Development Quarterly* 15, no. 1: 90–105.

Caiden, Naomi. 2010. "Challenges Confronting Contemporary Public Budgeting: Retrospectives/Prospectives from Allen Schick." *Public Administration Review* 70, no. 2: 203–10.

California Debt and Investment Advisory Commission. 2005. *California Debt Issuance Primer Handbook.* CDIAC 05–06. Sacramento: California Debt and Investment Advisory Commission.

———. 2006. *California Debt Issuance Primer.* CDIAC 06–04. Sacramento: California Debt and Investment Advisory Commission.

Casas-Pardo, José, and Miguel Puchades-Navarro. 2001. "A Critical Comment on Niskanen's Model." *Public Choice* 107, nos. 1–2: 147–67.

Censky, Annaly. 2010. "QE2: Fed Pulls the Trigger." CNNMoney.com http://money.cnn.com/2010/11/03/news/economy/fed_decision/index.htm (accessed March 1, 2011).

Center on Budget and Policy Priorities. 2010. *Introduction to the Federal Budget Process.* Washington, DC: Center on Budget and Policy Priorities.

Chad, Cotti, and Mark Skidmore. 2010. "The Impact of State Government Subsidies and Tax Credits in an Emerging Industry: Ethanol Production, 1980–2007." *Southern Economic Journal* 76, no. 4: 1076–93.

Chaddock, Gail Russell. 2011. "Absent a Super Committee, Now Who'll Lean on Congress to Cut US Deficit?" *Christian Science Monitor*, November 29.

Chapman, Jeffrey, and Evgenia Gorina. 2012. "Effects of the Form of Government and Property Tax Limits on Local Finance in the Context of Revenue and Expenditure Simultaneity." *Public Budgeting and Finance* 32, no. 4: 19–45.

Chen, Yu-Che, and Kurt Thurmaier. 2008. "Advancing E-Government: Financing Challenges and Opportunities." *Public Administration Review* 68, no. 3: 537–48.

Chernick, Howard. 1979. "An Economic Model of the Distribution of Project Grants." In *Fiscal Federalism and Grants-in-Aid*, ed. Peter Mieszkowski and William Oakland, 81–103. Washington, DC: Urban Institute Press.

———. 1998. "Fiscal Effects of Block Grants for the Needy: An Interpretation of the Evidence." *International Tax and Public Finance* 5, no. 2: 205–33.

———. 2000. "Federal Grants and Social Welfare Spending: Do State Responses Matter?" *National Tax Journal* 53, no. 1: 143–52.

Clarke, Wes. 1997. "Budget Requests and Agency Head Selection Methods." *Political Research Quarterly* 50, no. 2: 301–16.

———. 1998. "Divided Government and Budget Conflict in the U.S. States." *Legislative Studies Quarterly* 23, no. 1: 5–22.

Clynch, Edward J. 2003. "Do Program Budgets and Performance Indicators Influence Budget Allocations? An Assessment of Mississippi Budgeting." In *Case Studies in Public Budgeting and Financial Management*, 2d ed., ed. Aman Khan and W. Bartley Hildreth, 93–114. New York: Marcel Dekker.

———. 2007. "Mississippi: Changing Gubernatorial-Legislative Dynamics in Budget Decision Making." In *Budgeting in the States: Institutions, Processes, and Politics*, ed. Edward J. Clynch and Thomas P. Lauth, 257–76. Westport, CT: Praeger.

Cogan, John F. 1994. "The Dispersion of Spending Authority and Federal Budget Deficit." In *The Budget Puzzle: Understanding Federal Spending*, ed. John F. Cogan, Timothy J. Murris, and Allen Schick, 16–40. Stanford, CA: Stanford University Press.

Cogan, John F., Timothy J. Murris, and Allen Schick, eds. 1994. *The Budget Puzzle: Understanding Federal Spending.* Stanford, CA: Stanford University Press.

Cokins, Gary. 2006. *Activity-Based Cost Management in Government*, 2d ed. Vienna, VA: Management Concepts.

Coleman, John J. 1999. "Unified Government, Divided Government, and Party Responsiveness." *American Political Science Review* 93, no. 4: 821–35.

Collins, Brian. (Forthcoming). "Credit and Credibility: State Government Bond Ratings, 1975–2002." *American Review of Public Administration.*

Conant, James K. 2007. "Virginia: Expenditure Increases, Tax Cuts, and Budget Deficits." In *Budgeting in the States: Institutions, Processes, and Politics*, ed. Edward J. Clynch and Thomas P. Lauth, 213–34. Westport, CT: Praeger.

Congdon, William, Jeffrey R. Kling, and Sendhil Mullainathan. 2012. *Policy and Choice: Public Finance Through the Lens of Behavioral Economics.* Washington, DC: Brookings Institution Press.

Congleton, Roger D. 2012. "Growing Up with *The Calculus of Consent*." *Public Choice* 152, nos. 3–4: 273–78.

Congleton, Roger D., and Randall W. Bennett. 1995. "On the Political Economy of State Highway Expenditures: Some Evidence of the Relative Performance of Alternative Public Choice Models." *Public Choice* 84, nos. 1–2: 1–24.

Cope, Glen Hahn. 1991. "Texas: Legislative Budgeting in a Post-Oil-Boom Economy." In *Governors, Legislatures, and Budgets: Diversity Across the American States*, ed. Edward J. Clynch and Thomas P. Lauth, 115–24. New York: Greenwood Press.

Cornia, Gary C., David L. Sjoquist, and Lawrence C. Walters. 2004. "Sales and Use Tax Simplification and Voluntary Compliance." *Public Budgeting and Finance* 24, no. 1: 1–31.

Cornia, Gary C., and Charles L. Usher. 1981. "The Institutionalization of Incrementalism in Municipal Budgeting." *Southern Review of Public Administration* 5, no. 1: 73–89.

Council of State Governments. 2012. *Book of the States*. Lexington, KY: Council of State Governments.

Courant, Paul, Edward Gramlich, and Daniel Rubinfeld. 1979. "The Stimulative Effects of Intergovernmental Grants: Or Why Money Sticks Where It Hits." In *Fiscal Federalism and Grants-in-Aid*, ed. Peter Mieszkowski and William Oakland, 5–21. Washington, DC: Urban Institute.

Crecine, John P. 1967. "A Computer Simulation Model of Municipal Budgeting." *Management Science* 13, no. 11: 786–815.

Crecine, John P. 1969. *Governmental Problem-Solving: A Computer Simulation of Municipal Budgeting*. Chicago: Rand McNally.

Cullis, John, and Philip Jones. 2009. *Public Finance and Public Choice: Analytical Perspectives*, 3d ed. New York: Oxford University Press.

Dalenberg, Douglas R., and Mark D. Partridge. 1995. "The Effects of Taxes, Expenditures, and Public Infrastructure on Metropolitan Area Employment." *Journal of Regional Science* 35, no. 4: 617–40.

Davis, Otto A., M. A. Dempster, and Aaron Wildavsky. 1966. "A Theory of the Budgetary Process." *American Political Science Review* 60, no. 3: 529–47.

———. 1974. "Towards a Predictive Theory of Government Expenditure: US Domestic Appropriations." *British Journal of Political Science* 4: 419–52.

Dezhbakhsh, Hashem, Soumaya M. Tohamy, and Peter H. Aranson. 2003. "A New Approach for Testing Budgetary Incrementalism." *Journal of Politics* 65, no. 2: 532–58.

Dolan, Julie. 2002. "The Budget-Maximizing Bureaucrat? Empirical Evidence from the Senior Executive Service." *Public Administration Review* 62, no. 1: 42–50.

Dometrius, Nelson C., and Deil S. Wright. 2010. "Governors, Legislatures, and State Budgets Across Time." *Political Research Quarterly* 63, no. 4: 783–95.

Donahue, Amy K., Mark D. Robbins, and Bill Simonsen. 2008. "Taxes, Time, and Support for Security." *Public Budgeting and Finance* 28, no. 2: 69–86.

Douglas, James W., and Roger E. Hartley. 2011. "The Fly Ball Effect: A Theoretical Framework for Understanding the Impacts of Short-Term Seed Grants." *Public Budgeting and Finance* 31, no. 4: 74–92.

Doyle, Richard. 1996. "Congress, the Deficit, and Budget Reconciliation." *Public Budgeting and Finance* 16, no. 4: 59–81.

Doyle, Richard, and Jerry McCaffery. 1991. "The Budget Enforcement Act of 1990: The Path to No Fault Budgeting." *Public Budgeting and Finance* 11, no. 1: 25–40.

Draper, Frank D., and Bernard T. Pitsvada. 1981. "ZBB–Looking Back After Ten Years." *Public Administration Review* 41, no. 1: 76–83.

Duncombe, Sydney H., and Richard Kinney. 1991. "Idaho: Process and Politics in Gem State Budgeting." In *Governors, Legislatures, and Budgets: Diversity Across the American States*, ed. Edward J. Clynch and Thomas P. Lauth, 63–70. New York: Greenwood Press.

Duncombe, William. 1996. "Public Expenditure Research: What Have We Learned?" *Public Budgeting and Finance* 16, no. 2: 26–58.

Duncombe, William D., and Jeffrey D. Straussman. 1993. "The Impact of Courts on the Decision to Expand Jail Capacity." *Administration and Society* 25, no. 3: 267–92.

Duncombe, William, and John Yinger. 1998. "School Finance Reform: Aid Formulas and Equity Objectives." *National Tax Journal* 51, no. 2: 239–62.

————. 2009. "State Education Aid, Student Performance, and School District Efficiency in New York State." Paper presented at the annual meeting of the Association for Budget and Financial Management, Washington, DC, September.

Dunn, William N. 2012. *Public Policy Analysis*, 5th ed. Upper Saddle River, NJ: Pearson.

Easterling, Nelson C. 2003. "Performance Budgeting in Florida: To Muddle or Not to Muddle, That Is the Question." In *Case Studies in Public Budgeting and Financial Management*, 2d ed., ed. Aman Khan and W. Bartley Hildreth, 115–26. New York: Marcel Dekker.

Ebdon, Carol, and Aimee L. Franklin. 2006. "Citizen Participation in Budgeting Theory." *Public Administration Review* 66, no. 3: 437–47.

Ellig, Jerry, Maurice McTigue, and Henry Wray. 2011. *Government Performance and Results: An Evaluation of GPRA's First Decade*. Boca Raton, FL: Taylor & Francis.

Elmendorf, Douglas W., Jason Furman, William G. Gale, and Benjamin H. Harris. 2008. "Distributional Effects of the 2001 and 2003 Tax Cuts: How Do Financing and Behavioral Responses Matter?" *National Tax Journal* 61, no. 3: 365–80.

Emshwiller, John R., and Gary Fields. 2011. "Suit Claims Prisoners Are Mistreated." *Wall Street Journal*, December 19.

Endersby, James W., and Michael J. Towle. 1997. "Effects of Constitutional and Political Controls on State Expenditures." *Publius: The Journal of Federalism* 27, no. 1: 83–98.

Esterling, Kevin. 2004. *The Political Economy of Expertise*. Ann Arbor: University of Michigan Press.

Evans, Kelly. 2011. "The Outlook: Bank–Run Risk in the Shadows." *Wall Street Journal*, December 5, A. 4.

Evans, William N., Sheila E. Murray, and Robert M. Schwab. 1997. "Schoolhouses, Courthouses, and Statehouses After Serrano." *Journal of Policy Analysis and Management* 16, no. 1: 10–31.

————. 1999. "The Impact of Court-Mandated School Finance Reform." In *Equity and Adequacy in Education Finance: Issues and Perspectives*, ed. Helen F. Ladd, Rosemary Chalk, and Janet S. Hansen, 72–98. Washington, DC: National Academy Press.

Eyler, Robert. 2010. *Money and Banking: An International Text*. New York: Routledge.

Feldstein, Martin. 1975. "Wealth Neutrality and Local Choice in Public Education." *American Economic Review* 61, no. 1: 75–89.

Fernandez, Raquel, and Richard Rogerson. 2001. "The Determinants of Public Education Expenditures: Longer-Run Evidence from the States." *Journal of Education Finance* 27, no. 1: 567–84.

Fessenden, Ford, Haeyoun Park, Alicia Parlapiano, Archie Tse, and Lisa Waananen. 2011. "The Plans for Reducing the Deficit." *New York Times*, October 27. www.nytimes.com/interactive/2011/07/22/us/politics/20110722-comparing-deficit-reduction-plans.html (accessed November 14, 2011).

Fifulco, Robert, William Duncombe, Beverly Bunch, Mark Robbins, and William Simonsen. 2012. "Debt and Deception: How States Avoid Making Hard Fiscal Decisions." *Public Administration Review* 72, no. 5: 659–67.

Filimon, Radu, Thomas Romer, and Howard Rosenthal. 1982. "Asymmetric Information and Agenda Control: The Bases of Monopoly Power in Public Spending." *Journal of Public Economics* 17, no. 1: 51–70.

Finkler, Steven A. 2010. *Financial Management for Public, Health, and Not-for-Profit Organizations*, 3d ed. Upper Saddle River, NJ: Prentice Hall.

Finkler, Steven A., Robert M. Purtell, Thad D. Calabrese, and Daniel L. Smith. 2013. *Financial Management for Public, Health, and Not-for-Profit Organizations*, 4th ed. Upper Saddle River, NJ: Pearson Education.

Fiorina, Morris P. 2003. *Divided Government*, 2d ed. New York: Longman.

Fisher, Patrick. 2009. *The Politics of Taxing and Spending*. Boulder, CO: Lynne Rienner.

Fisher, Ronald C. 2007. *State and Local Public Finance*, 3d ed. Mason, OH: Thompson Higher Education.

Forrester, John P. 2001. "Public Choice Theory and Public Budgeting: Implications for the Greedy Bureaucrat." In *Evolving Theories of Public Budgeting*, ed. John R. Bartle, 101–24. Bingley, UK: Emerald Group.

Forrester, John P., and Rebecca Hendrick. 2003. "Transition to Outcome-Based Budgeting: The Case of Missouri's Department of Revenue and Milwaukee, Wisconsin." In *Case Studies in Public Budgeting and Financial Management*, 2d ed., ed. Aman Khan and W. Bartley Hildreth, 173–94. New York: Marcel Dekker.

Forsythe, Dall W. 1997. *Memos to the Governor: An Introduction to State Budgeting*. Washington, DC: Georgetown University Press.

Forte, Francesco. 2012. "From *The Calculus of Consent* to Public Choice and to Public Economics in a Public Choice Approach." *Public Choice* 152, nos. 3–4: 285–88.

Frisco, V., and O. J. Stalebrink. 2008. "Congressional Use of the Program Assessment Rating Tool." *Public Budgeting and Finance* 28, no. 2: 1–19.

Fry, Brian R., and Jos C. N. Raadschelders. 2008. *Mastering Public Administration: From Max Weber to Dwight Waldo*, 2d ed. Washington, DC: CQ Press.

Furchtgott-Roth, Diana. 2012. "The Case for Supply-Side Tax Cuts: The Evidence Shows that Economic Growth Results." marketwatch.com, August 17. www.marketwatch.com/story/the-case-for-supply-side-tax-cuts-2012-08-16.

Galbraith, James K. 1987–1988. Book review: *Stabilizing an Unstable Economy: A Twentieth Century Fund Report* by Hyman P. Minsky. *Political Science Quarterly* 102, no. 4: 722–23.

Gale, William G., and Samara R. Potter. 2002. "An Economic Evaluation of the Economic Growth and Tax Relief Reconciliation Act of 2001." *National Tax Journal* 55, no. 1: 133–86.

Gamkhar, Shama. 2000. "Is the Response of State and Local Highway Spending Symmetric to Increases and Decreases in Federal Highway Grants?" *Public Finance Review* 28, no. 1: 3–25.

———. 2002. *Federal Intergovernmental Grants and the States: Managing Devolution*. Northampton, MA: Edward Elgar.

Garlino, Gerald A., and Edwin S. Mills. 1987. "The Determinants of County Growth." *Journal of Regional Science* 27, no. 1: 39–54.

Gilmour, John B. 2006. *Implementing OMB's Program Assessment Rating Tool (PART): Meeting the Challenges of Integrating Budget and Performance*. Washington, DC: IBM Center for the Business of Government.

Gilmour, John B., and David E. Lewis. 2006. "Does Performance Budgeting Work? An Examination of the Office of Management and Budget's PART Scores." *Public Administration Review* 66, no. 5: 742–52.

Gist, John R. 1982. "'Stability' and 'Competition' in Budgetary Theory." *American Political Science Review* 76, no. 4: 859–72.

Goel, R.K., and M.A. Nelson. 2003. "Use or Abuse of Highway Tax Revenues? An Economic Analysis of Highway Spending." *Applied Economics Letters* 10, no. 13: 813–19.

Gomez-Ibanez, Jose A., Robert A. Leone, and Stephen A. O'Connell. 1983. "Restraining Auto Imports: Does Anyone Win?" *Journal of Policy Analysis and Management* 2, no. 2: 196–219.

Goodman, Doug. 2007. "Determinants of Perceived Gubernatorial Budgetary Influence Among State Executive Budget Analysts and Legislative Fiscal Analysts." *Political Research Quarterly* 60, no. 1: 43–54.

Gosling, James J. 1986. "Wisconsin Item-Veto Lessons." *Public Administration Review* 46, no. 4: 292–300.

———. 2009. *Budgetary Politics in American Governments*, 5th ed. New York: Taylor & Francis.

Gosling, James J., and Marc Allen Eisner. 2013. *Economics, Politics, and American Public Policy*, 2d ed. Armonk, NY: M.E. Sharpe.

Graddy, Elizabeth A., and Bin Chen. 2009. "Partner Selection and the Effectiveness of Interorganizational Collaborations." In *The Collaborative Public Manager*, ed. Lisa Blomgren Bingham and Rosemary O'Leary, 53–69. Washington, DC: Georgetown University Press.

Graham, Cole Blease, Jr. 2007. "South Carolina: Executive Budgeting Brings a Stronger Gubernatorial Voice to the Table." In *Budgeting in the States: Institutions, Processes, and Politics*, ed. Edward J. Clynch and Thomas P. Lauth, 189–212. Westport, CT: Praeger.

Gramlich, Edward M. 1990. *A Guide to Benefit-Cost Analysis*, 2d ed. Englewood Cliffs, NJ: Prentice Hall.

Gramlich, Edward M., and Daniel L. Rubinfeld. 1982. "Microestimation of Public Spending Demand Functions and Tests of the Tiebout and Median-Voter Hypothesis." *Journal of Political Economy* 90, no. 3: 536–60.

Gramm, Phil, and Mike Solon. 2011. "The Budget Sequester's Silver Lining." *Wall Street Journal*, November 18, A. 15.

Gravelle, Jane G. 1992. "Equity Effects of the Tax Reform Act of 1986." *Journal of Economic Perspectives* 6, no. 1: 27–44.

Green, Mark T., and Fred Thompson. 2001. "Organizational Process Models of Budgeting." In *Evolving Theories of Public Budgeting*, ed. John R. Bartle, 55–81. Bingley, UK: Emerald Group.

Greenberg, David, and Andreas Cebulla. 2008. "The Cost-Effectiveness of Welfare-to-Work Programs: A Meta-Analysis." *Public Budgeting and Finance* 28, no. 2: 112–45.

Grimley, Brynn. 2011. "Budget Dominates Debate between North Kitsap Commissioner Candidates." Kitsap Sun, August 23. www.kitsapsun.com/news/2011/aug/23/budget-dominates-debate-between-north-kitsap/#axzz2ae7GN4mt.

Grizzle, Cleopatra. 2011. "For Better or For Worse: Reassessing the Impact of Tax and Expenditure Limitations on State Expenditures." *Journal of Public Budgeting, Accounting, and Financial Management* 23, no. 1: 94–116.

Guo, Hai, 2011. "The Effects of Tax and Expenditure Limit on State Discretionary Tax Adjustment." *Journal of Public Budgeting, Accounting, and Financial Management* 23, no. 1: 69–93.

Guzman, Tatyana, and Temirlan Moldogaziev. 2012. "Which Bonds Are More Expensive? The Cost Differentials by Debt Issue Purpose and the Method of Sale: An Empirical Analysis." *Public Budgeting and Finance* 32, no. 3: 79–101.

Hall, Steve, and Adam Garn. 2012. "'Remote Seller' Battle Just Getting Started." *CPAnswers*, May 14. Dublin, OH: Ohio Society of CPAs. www.ohioscpa.com/publications/news/2012/05/14/-remote-seller-battle-just-getting-started (accessed October 2, 2012).

Hamilton, Bruce W. 1976. "Capitalization of Intrajurisdictional Differences in Local Tax Prices." *American Economic Review* 66, no. 5: 743–53.

———. 1983. "The Flypaper Effect and Other Anomalies." *Journal of Public Economics* 22: 347–62.

Hanson, Andrew. 2009. "Local Employment, Poverty, and Property Value Effects of Geographically Targeted Tax Incentives: An Instrumental Variables Approach." *Regional Science and Urban Economics* 39, no. 6: 721–31.

Hanson, Andrew, and Shawn Rohlin. 2011. "Do Location-Based Tax Incentives Attract New Business Establishments?" *Journal of Regional Science* 51, no. 3: 427–49.

Harriman, Linda, and Jeffrey D. Straussman. 1983. "Do Judges Determine Budget Decisions? Federal Court Decision in Prison Reform and State Spending for Corrections." *Public Administration Review* 43, no. 4: 343–51.

Havens, Harry S. 1986. "Gramm-Rudman-Hollings: Origins and Implementation." *Public Budgeting and Finance* 6, no. 4: 4–24.

Hawkins, Robert B., Jr. 1990. *1988 State Fiscal Capacity and Effort*. Information Report M–170, August. Washington, DC: Advisory Commission on Intergovernmental Relations.

Heinrich, Carolyn J. 2012. "How Credible Is the Evidence, and Does It Matter? An Analysis of the Program Assessment Rating Tool." *Public Administration Review* 72, no. 1: 123–34.

Helms, Jay L. 1985. "The Effect of State and Local Taxes on Growth." *Review of Economics and Statistics* 67, no. 4: 574–82.

Hendrick, Rebecca M. 2011. *Managing the Fiscal Metropolis: The Financial Policies, Practices, and Health of Suburban Municipalities*. Washington, DC: Georgetown University Press.

Heniff, Bill, Jr. 2010. *Entitlements and Appropriated Entitlements in the Federal Budget Process*. CRS Report for Congress, RS20129, November 26.Washington, DC: Congressional Research Service.

Hicks, Michael J., and Michael LaFaive. 2011. "The Influence of Targeted Economic Development Tax Incentives on County Economic Growth: Evidence from Michigan's MEGA Credits." *Economic Development Quarterly* 25, no. 2: 193–205.

Hildreth, Bartley W. 1993. "State and Local Governments as Borrowers: Strategic Choices and the Capital Market." *Public Administration Review* 53, no. 1: 41–49.

Hines, James R., Jr., and Richard H. Thaler. 1995. "Anomalies: The Flypaper Effect." *Journal of Economic Perspectives* 9, no. 4: 217–26.

Ho, Alfred. 2007. "The Governance Challenges of the Government Performance and Results Act." *Public Performance and Management Review* 30, no. 3: 369–97.

———. 2011. "PBB in American Local Governments: It's More Than a Management Tool." *Public Administration Review* 71, no. 3: 391–401.

Holcombe, Randall G. 1980. "An Empirical Test of the Median Voter Model." *Economic Inquiry* 18: 260–74.

———. 1989. "The Median Voter Model in Public Choice Theory." *Public Choice* 61, no. 2: 115–25.

———. 2005. "Government Growth in the Twenty-First Century." *Public Choice* 124, nos. 1–2: 95–114.

Holtz-Eakin, Douglas. 1988. "The Line Item Veto and Public Sector Budgets." *Journal of Public Economics* 36: 269–92.

Hook, Janet, and Corey Boles. 2011. "Taxes Sink a Deficit Proposal." *Wall Street Journal*, October 27.

Horngren, Charles T., Srikant M. Datar, and Madhav Rajan. 2012. *Cost Accounting: A Managerial Emphasis*, 14th ed. Upper Saddle River, NJ: Prentice Hall.

Hou, Yilin, and William Duncombe. 2008. "State Saving Behavior: Effects of Two Fiscal and Budgetary Institutions." *Public Budgeting and Finance* 28, no. 3: 48–67.

Hou, Yilin, Robin S. Lunsford, Katy C. Sides, and Kelsey A. Jones. 2011. "State Performance-Based Budgeting in Boom and Bust Years: An Analytical Framework and Survey of the States." *Public Administration Review* 71, no. 3: 370–88.

Hou, Yilin, and Daniel L. Smith. 2006. "A Framework for Understanding State Balanced Budget Requirement Systems: Reexamining Distinctive Features and an Operational Definition." *Public Budgeting and Finance* 26, no. 3: 22–45.

———. 2010. "Informal Norms as a Bridge between Formal Rules and Outcomes of Government Financial Operations: Evidence from State Balanced Budget Requirements." *Journal of Public Administration Research and Theory* 20, no. 3: 655–78.

Huntsman, Jon. 2011. "'Too Big to Fail' Is Simply Too Big." Wall Street Journal, October 19. http://online.wsj.com/article/SB10001424052970204346104576635033336992122.html (accessed October 19, 2011).

Hyman, David N. 1986. *Modern Microeconomics: Analysis and Applications*, 3d ed. Homewood, IL: IRWIN.

———. 2011. *Public Finance: A Contemporary Application of Theory and Policy*, 10th ed. Mason, OH: South-Western, Cengage Learning.

Inman, Robert. 1979. "The Fiscal Performance of Local Governments: An Interpretative Review." In *Current Issues in Urban Economics*, ed. Peter Mieszkowski and Mahlon Straszheim, 270–321. Baltimore: Johns Hopkins University Press.

———. 2008. "The Flypaper Effect." NBER Working Paper no. 14579, December. Cambridge, MA: National Bureau of Economic Research.

Jacob, Benoy, and Rebecca Hendrick. 2013. "Assessing the Financial Condition of Local Governments: What Is Financial Condition and How Is It Measured." In *Handbook of Local Government Fiscal Health*, ed. Helisse Levine, Jonathan B. Justice, and Eric A. Scorsone, 11–41. Burlington, MA: Jones & Bartlett Learning.

Johnson, Craig L., and Kenneth A. Kriz. 2005. "Fiscal Institutions, Credit Ratings, and Borrowing Costs." *Public Budgeting and Finance* 25, no. 1: 84–103.

Jones, Bryan D. 2003. "Bounded Rationality and Political Science: Lessons from Public Administration and Public Policy." *Journal of Public Administration Research and Theory* 13, no. 4: 395–412.

Jones, Bryan D., and Frank R. Baumgartner. 2005a. "A Model of Choice for Public Policy." *Journal of Public Administration Research and Theory* 15, no. 3: 325–51.

———. 2005b. *The Politics of Attention*. Chicago: University of Chicago Press.

Jones, Bryan D., Frank R. Baumgartner, and James L. True. 1998. "Policy Punctuations: U.S. Budget Authority, 1947–1995." *Journal of Politics* 60, no. 1: 1–33.

Jones, Bryan D., Tracy Sulkin, and Heather A. Larsen. 2003. "Policy Punctuations in American Political Institutions." *American Political Science Review* 97, no. 1: 151–69.

Jordan, Meagan. 2003. "Punctuations and Agendas: A New Look at Local Government Budget Expenditures." *Journal of Policy Analysis and Management* 22, no. 3: 345–60.

Jordan, Meagan M., and Merl M. Hackbart. 1999. "Performance Budgeting and Performance Funding in the States: A Status Assessment." *Public Budgeting and Finance* 19, no. 1: 68–88.

Joyce, Philip G. 2008. "Linking Performance and Budgeting: Opportunities for Federal Executives." In *Performance Management and Budgeting: How Government Can Learn from Experience*, ed. F. Stevens Redburn, Robert J. Shea, and Terry F. Buss, 49–66. Armonk, NY: M.E. Sharpe.

———. 2011. "The Obama Administration and PBB: Building on the Legacy of Federal Performance-Informed Budgeting?" *Public Administration Review* 71, no. 3: 356–67.

Joyce, Philip G., and Scott Pattison. 2010. "Public Budgeting in 2020: Return to Equilibrium, or Continued Mismatch Between Demands and Resources?" *Public Administration Review* 70, Supplement 1: S24–S32.

Kamlet, Mark S., and David C. Mowery. 1980. "The Budgetary Base in Federal Resource Allocation." *American Journal of Political Science* 24, no. 4: 804–21.

Kaplan, Robert S., and Robin Cooper. 1997. *Cost and Effect: Using Integrated Cost Systems to Drive Profitability and Performance*. Boston: Harvard Business Review Press.

Kasdin, Stuart. 2010. "Reinventing Reforms: How to Improve Program Management Using Performance Measures. Really." *Public Budgeting and Finance* 30, no. 3: 51–78.

Kearns, Paula S., and John R. Bartle. 2001. "The Median Voter Model in Public Budgeting Research." In *Evolving Theories of Public Budgeting*, ed. John R. Bartle, 83–100. Bingley, UK: Emerald Group.

Keith, Robert. 2004. *The "Deeming Resolution": A Budget Enforcement Tool*. Washington, DC: Congressional Research Service.

———. 2008. *Introduction to the Federal Budget Process*. Washington, DC: Congressional Research Service.

Keith, Robert, and Allen Schick. 2003. *The Federal Budget Process*. New York: Nova Science.

Kelly, Janet M., and William C. Rivenbark. 2008. "Budget Theory in Local Government: The Process-Outcome Conundrum." *Journal of Public Budgeting, Accounting, and Financial Management* 20, no. 4: 457–81.

———. 2011. *Performance Budgeting for State and Local Government*, 2d ed. Armonk, NY: M.E. Sharpe.

Kelman, Steven. 1981. "Cost-Benefit Analysis: An Ethical Critique." *Regulation* (January–February): 33–40.

Kettl, Donald F. 2003. *Deficit Politics: The Search for Balance in American Politics*, 2d ed. New York: Longman.

———. 2007. *System Under Stress: Homeland Security and American Politics*, 2d ed. Washington, DC: CQ Press.

Key, V.O., Jr. 1940. "The Lack of a Budgetary Theory." *American Political Science Review* 34, no. 6: 1137–44.

Kiefer, Donald., Robert Carroll, Janet Holtzblatt, Allen Lerman, Janet McCubbin, David Richardson, and Jerry Tempalski. 2002. "The Economic Growth and Tax Relief Reconciliation Act of 2001: Overview and Assessment of Effects on Taxpayers." *National Tax Journal* 55, no. 1: 89–117.

Kiewiet, Roderick D. 1991. "Bureaucrats and Budgetary Outcomes: Quantitative Analyses." In *The Budget-Maximizing Bureaucrat: Appraisals and Evidence*, ed. André Blais and Stéphanie Dion, 143–73. Pittsburgh: University of Pittsburgh Press.

King, David Neden. 1984. *Fiscal Tiers: The Economics of Multi-Level Government*. London: Allen & Unwin.

Kioko, Sharon N. 2011. "Structure of State-Level Tax and Expenditure Limits." *Public Budgeting and Finance* 31, no. 2: 43–78.

Knight, Brian. 2002. "Endogenous Federal Grants and Crowd-Out of State Government Spending: Theory and Evidence from the Federal Highway Aid Program." *American Economic Review* 92, no. 1: 71–92.

Koehler, Frank, and B. J. Reed. 2003. "Target-Based Budgeting in Lincoln County." In *Case Studies in Public Budgeting and Financial Management*, 2d ed., ed. Aman Khan and W. Bartley Hildreth, 145–54. New York: Marcel Dekker.

Krause, George A. 2000. "Partisan and Ideological Sources of Fiscal Deficits in the United States." *American Journal of Political Science* 44, no. 3: 541–59.

Kriz, Kenneth A. 2003. "Comparative Costs of Negotiated Versus Competitive Bond Sales: New Evidence from State General Obligation Bonds." *Quarterly Review of Economics and Finance* 43, no. 2: 191–211.

Krugman, Paul. 2009. *The Return of Depression Economics and the Crisis of 2008*. New York: W.W. Norton.

Krugman, Paul, and Robin Wells. 2006. *Macroeconomics*. New York: Worth.

———. 2009. *Macroeconomics*, 2d ed. New York: Worth.

———. 2013. *Macroeconomics*, 3d ed. New York: Worth.

Ladd, Helen F., and John Yinger. 1989. *America's Ailing Cities, Fiscal Health and the Design of Urban Policy*. Baltimore: Johns Hopkins University Press.

———. 1994. "The Case for Equalizing Aid." *National Tax Journal* 47, no. 1: 223–35.

Laffer, Arthur. 2011a. How to Fight Black Unemployment. *Wall Street Journal*, September 12, A. 19.

———. 2011b. "Cain's Stimulating '9–9–9' Tax Reform." *Wall Street Journal*, October 19, A. 15.

Laffer, Arthur B., and Stephen Moore. 2010. *Return to Prosperity: How America Can Regain Its Economic Superpower Status*. New York: Threshold Editions.

Lauth, Thomas P. 1978. "Zero-Base Budgeting in Georgia State Government: Myth and Reality." *Public Administration Review* 38, no. 5: 420–30.

Lauth, Thomas P., and Catherine C. Reese. 2006. "The Line-Item Veto in Georgia: Fiscal Restraint or Inter-Branch Politics?" *Public Budgeting and Finance* 26, no. 2: 1–19.

Lauth, Thomas P., and Stephen C. Rieck. 1979. "Modifications in Georgia Zero-Base Budgeting Procedures: 1973–1980." *Midwest Review of Public Administration* 13 (December): 225–38.

Lee, Robert D., Jr. 2000. "State Item-Veto Legal Issues in the 1990s." *Public Budgeting and Finance* 20, no. 2: 49–73.

Lee, Robert D., Jr., Ronald W. Johnson, and Philip G. Joyce. 2013. *Public Budgeting Systems*, 9th ed. Burlington, MA: Jones & Bartlett.

LeLoup, L.T. 1977. *Budgetary Politics: Dollars, Deficits, Decisions*. Brunswick, OH: King's Court Communications.

———. 1978. "The Myth of Incrementalism: Analytical Choices in Budgetary Theory." *Polity* 10, no. 4: 488–509.

———. 1980. *The Fiscal Congress: Legislative Control of the Budget.* Westport, CT: Greenwood Press.

LeLoup, Lance, Barbara Luck Graham, and Stacey Barwick. 1987. "Deficit Politics and Constitutional Government: The Impact of Gramm-Rudman-Hollings." *Public Budgeting and Finance* 7, no. 1: 83–103.

LeLoup, Lance T., and William B. Moreland. 1978. "Agency Strategies and Executive Review: The Hidden Politics of Budgeting." *Public Administration Review* 38, no. 3: 232–39.

LeLoup, Lance, and Steven A. Shull. 2003. *The President and Congress: Collaboration and Combat in National Policymaking,* 2d ed. New York: Longman.

Leonard, Paul. 1996. "An Empirical Analysis of Competitive Bid and Negotiated Offerings of Municipal Bonds." *Municipal Finance Journal* 17, no. 1: 37–67.

Lewis, Carol W., and W. Bartley Hildreth. 2013. *Budgeting: Politics and Power,* 2d ed. New York: Oxford University Press.

Lewis, Verne B. 1952. "Toward a Theory of Budgeting." *Public Administration Review* 12, no. 1: 42–54.

———. 1988. "Reflections on Budget Systems." *Public Budgeting and Finance* 8, no. 1: 4–19.

Lindblom, Charles E. 1959. "The Science of 'Muddling Through.'" *Public Administration Review* 19: 79–88.

———. 1979. "Still Muddling, Not Yet Through." *Public Administration Review* 39, no. 6: 517–26.

Lowrey, Annie. 2013. "Tax Code May Be the Most Progressive Since 1979." New York Times, January 4. www.nytimes.com/2013/01/05/business/after-fiscal-deal-tax-code-may-be-most-progressive-since-1979.html?_r=0 (accessed January 5, 2013).

Luby, Martin J. 2012. "Federal Intervention in the Municipal Bond Market: The Effectiveness of the Build America Bond Program and Its Implications on Federal and Subnational Budgeting." *Public Budgeting and Finance* 32, no. 4: 46–70.

Lynn, Lawrence E., Jr. 1991. "The Budget-Maximizing Bureaucrats: Is There a Case?" In *The Budget-Maximizing Bureaucrat: Appraisals and Evidence,* ed. André Blais and Stéphanie Dion, 59–83. Pittsburgh: University of Pittsburgh Press.

Maher, Craig S., and Steven C. Deller. 2013. "Measuring the Impacts of TELs on Municipal Financial Conditions." In *Handbook of Local Government Fiscal Health,* ed. Helisse Levine, Jonathan B. Justice, and Eric A. Scorsone, 405–29. Burlington, MA: Jones & Bartlett.

Mankiw, Gregory N. 2013. *Macroeconomics,* 8th ed. New York: Worth.

Martell, Christine R., and Robert S. Kravchuk. 2012. "The Liquidity Crisis: The 2007–2009 Market Impacts on Municipal Securities." *Public Administration Review* 72, no. 5: 668–77.

Maux, Benoît. 2009. "Governmental Behavior in Representative Democracy: A Synthesis of the Theoretical Literature." *Public Choice* 141, nos. 3–4: 447–65.

Mayhew, David R. 1991. *Divided We Govern: Party Control, Lawmaking, and Investigations, 1946–1990.* New Haven, CT: Yale University Press.

McCaffery, Jerry L. 1991. "California: Changing Demographics and Executive Dominance." In *Governors, Legislatures, and Budgets: Diversity Across the American States,* ed. Edward J. Clynch and Thomas P. Lauth, 7–16. New York: Greenwood Press.

———. 1996. "On Budget Reform." *Policy Sciences* 29, no. 3: 235–46.

———. 2007. "California: Revenues Scarcity, Incremental Solutions, the Rise of Citizen Initiatives, and the Decline of Trust." In *Budgeting in the States: Institutions, Processes, and Politics,* ed. Edward J. Clynch and Thomas P. Lauth, 9–32. Westport, CT: Praeger.

McCubbins, Mathew D., and Ellen Moule. 2010. "Making Mountains of Debt Out of Molehills: The Pro-Cyclical Implications of Tax and Expenditure Limitations." *National Tax Journal* 63, no. 3: 603–21.

McCulley, Paul. 2009. *Global Central Focus: The Shadow Banking System and Hyman Minsky's Economic Journey.* Newport Beach, CA: PIMCO.

McIntyre, Robert S., and Michael J. McIntyre. 1999. "Fixing the 'Marriage Penalty' Problem." *Valparaiso University Law Review* 33, no. 3: 907–46.

McKinney, Jerome B. 2003. "Implementing and Managing Zero-Based Budgeting." In *Case Studies in Public Budgeting and Financial Management*, 2d ed., ed. Aman Khan and W. Bartley Hildreth, 127–44. New York: Marcel Dekker.

McKinnon, John D. 2011. "Flat Tax Seen as Savings Booster." *Wall Street Journal*, October 21, A. 5.

Mead, Dean Michael. 2013. "The Development of External Financial Reporting and Its Relationship to the Assessment of Fiscal Health and Stress." In *Handbook of Local Government Fiscal Health*, ed. Helisse Levine, Jonathan B. Justice, and Eric A. Scorsone, 77–124. Burlington, MA: Jones & Bartlett.

Mehrling, Perry. 1999. "The Vision of Hyman P. Minsky." *Journal of Economic Behavior and Organization* 39, no. 2: 129–58.

Melkers, Julia E., and Katherine G. Willoughby. 1998. "The State of the States: Performance-Based Budgeting Requirements in 47 out of 50." *Public Administration Review* 58, no. 1: 66–73.

Meltzer, Allan H. 2011. "Four Reasons Keynesians Keep Getting It Wrong." *Wall Street Journal*, October 28, A. 17.

Merrifield, John. 1991. "The Institutional and Political Factors Which Influence Taxation." *Public Choice* 69: 295–310.

———. 2000. "State Government Expenditure Determinants and Tax Revenue Determinants Revisited." *Public Choice* 102: 25–50.

Meyers, Roy T. 1996. *Strategic Budgeting*. Ann Arbor: University of Michigan Press.

———. 2009. "The 'Ball of Confusion' in Federal Budgeting: A Shadow Agenda for Deliberative Reform of the Budget Process." *Public Administration Review* 69, no. 2: 211–23.

Meyers, Roy T., and Irene S. Rubin. 2011. "The Executive Budget in the Federal Government: The First Century and Beyond." *Public Administration Review* 71, no. 3: 334–44.

Mikesell, John. 2007. "Changing State Fiscal Capacity and Tax Effort in an Era of Devolving Government, 1981–2003." *Publius: The Journal of Federalism* 37, no. 4: 532–50.

———. 2011. *Fiscal Administration: Analysis and Applications for the Public Sector*, 8th ed. Boston: Wadsworth.

———. 2012. "State Tax Policy and State Sales Taxes: What Tax Expenditure Budgets Tell Us About Sales Taxes." *American Review of Public Administration* 42, no. 2: 131–51.

Miller, Gary J., and Terry M. Moe. 1983. "Bureaucrats, Legislators, and the Size of Government." *American Political Science Review* 77, no. 2: 297–322.

Miller, Gerald J., Donijo Robbins, and Jaeduk Keum. 2011. "Conventional Budgeting with Targets, Incentives, and Performance." In *Government Budgeting and Financial Management in Practice: Logics to Make Sense of Ambiguity*, ed. Gerald J. Miller, 123–48. Boca Raton, FL: Taylor & Francis.

Minsky, Hyman. 1982. *Can "It" Happen Again? Essays on Instability and Finance*. Armonk, NY: M.E. Sharpe.

———. 1986. *Stabilizing an Unstable Economy*. New Haven: Yale University Press.

———. 1993. "On the Non-Neutrality of Money." *Quarterly Review* 18, no. 1: 77–82.

Mirrlees, James, Stuart Adam, Tim Besley, Richard Blundell, Stephen Bon, Robert Chote, Malcolm Gammie, Paul Johnson, Gareth Myles, and James Poterba. 2012. "The Mirrlees Review: A Proposal for Systematic Tax Reform." *National Tax Journal* 65, no. 3: 655–84.

Mishkin, Frederic S. 2011. "Politicians Are Threatening the Fed's Independence." *Wall Street Journal*, September 29.

Mitchell, David, and Kurt Thurmaier. 2011. *Toward a Theory of Budgeting for Collaboration*. Paper presented at the annual meeting of the Public Management Research Association, Syracuse, NY, June.

Mosher, Frederick C., and Max O. Stephenson Jr. 1982. "The Office of Management and Budget in a Changing Scene." *Public Budgeting and Finance* 2, no. 4: 23–41.

Moynihan, Donald P. 2007. "Citizen Participation in Budgeting: Prospects for Developing Countries." In *Participatory Budgeting*, ed. Anwar Shah, 21–55. Washington, DC: World Bank.

———. 2008. *The Dynamics of Performance Management: Constructing Information and Reform*. Washington, DC: Georgetown University Press.

Moynihan, Donald P., and Stéphane Lavertu. 2012. "Does Involvement in Performance Management Routines Encourage Performance Information Use? Evaluating GPRA and PART." *Public Administration Review* 72, no. 4: 592–602.

Mueller, Dennis C., and Peter Murrell. 1986. "Interest Groups and the Size of Government." *Public Choice* 48, no. 2: 125–45.

Mueller, Dennis C., and Thomas Stratmann. 2003. "The Economic Effects of Democratic Participation." *Journal of Public Economics* 87, nos. 9–10: 2129–55.

Mullins, Daniel R. 2010. "Fiscal Limitations on Local Choice: The Imposition and Effects of Local Government Tax and Expenditure Limitations." In *State and Local Fiscal Policy: Thinking Outside the Box?* ed. Sally Wallace, 201–65. Northampton, MA: Edward Elgar.

Mullins, Daniel. R., and Philip G. Joyce. 1996. "Tax and Expenditure Limitations and State and Local Fiscal Structure: An Empirical Assessment." *Public Budgeting and Finance* 16, no. 1: 75–101.

Mullins, Daniel R, and Bruce A. Wallin. 2004. "Tax and Expenditure Limitations: Introduction and Overview." *Public Budgeting and Finance* 24, no. 4: 2–15.

Mullins, Daniel R., and Kurt C. Zorn. 1999. "Is Activity-Based Costing Up to the Challenge When It Comes to Privatization of Local Government Services?" *Public Budgeting and Finance* 19, no. 2: 37–58.

Munley, Vincent G. 1984. "Has the Median Voter Found a Ballot Box that He Can Control?" *Economic Inquiry* 22: 323–36.

Natchez, Peter B., and Irwin C. Bupp. 1973. "Policy and Priority in the Budgetary Process." *American Political Science Review* 67, no. 3: 951–63.

National Association of State Budget Officers (NASBO). 2008. *Budget Processes in the States*. Washington, DC: National Association of State Budget Officers.

Niskanen, William, Jr. 1971. *Bureaucracy and Representative Government*. Chicago: Aldine.

———. 1991. "A Reflection on Bureaucracy and Representative Government." In *The Budget-Maximizing Bureaucrat: Appraisal and Evidence*, ed. A. Blais and S. Dion, 13–31. Pittsburgh: University of Pittsburgh Press.

———. 1994. *Bureaucracy and Public Economics*. Brookfield, VT: Edward Elgar.

———. 2003. *Autocratic, Democratic, and Optimal Government: Fiscal Choices and Economic Outcomes*. Cheltenham, UK: Edward Elgar.

Noonan, Douglas S. 2007. "Fiscal Pressures, Institutional Context, and Constituents: A Dynamic Model of States' Arts Agency Appropriations." *Journal of Cultural Economics* 31, no. 4: 293–310.

Norquist, Grover. 2013. "U.S. Senate Will Soon Vote on Bill to Impose State Taxation of Internet Sales." Huffington Post, March 21. www.huffingtonpost.com/grover-norquist/us-senate-will-soon-vote-_b_2925139.html (accessed March 21, 2013).

Nothhaft, Henry R. 2011. "A Labor Day Message for President Obama." *Wall Street Journal*, September 3–4.

Nothhaft, Henry R., and David Kline. 2011. *Great Again: Revitalizing America's Entrepreneurial Leadership*. Boston: Harvard Business Review Press.

Oates, Wallace E. 1972. *Fiscal Federalism*. New York: Harcourt Brace-Jovanovich.

———. 1979. "Lump-Sum Intergovernmental Grants Have Price Effects." In *Fiscal Federalism and Grants-in-Aid*, ed. Peter Mieszkowski and William Oakland, 23–30. Washington, DC: Urban Institute.

———. 1999. "An Essay on Fiscal Federalism." *Journal of Economic Literature* 37, no. 3: 1120–49.

———. 2008. "On the Evolution of Fiscal Federalism: Theory and Institutions." *National Tax Journal* 61, no. 2: 313–34.

O'Leary, Rosemary. 1989. "The Impact of Federal Court Decisions on the Policies and Administration of the United States Environmental Protection Agency." *Administrative Law Review* 41, no. 4: 549–72.

O'Leary, Rosemary, and Charles R. Wise. 1991. "Public Managers, Judges, and Legislators: Redefining the 'New Partnership.'" *Public Administration Review* 51, no. 4: 316–27.

Olsson, Ola. 2012. *Essentials of Advanced Macroeconomic Theory*. New York: Routledge.

Palley, Thomas. 2002. "Why Inflation Targeting Is Not Enough: Monetary Policy in the Presence of Financial Exuberance." Unpublished mimeo.

———. 2010. "The Limits of Minsky's Financial Instability Hypothesis as an Explanation of the Crisis." *Monthly Review: An Independent Socialist Magazine* 61, no. 11: 28–43.

———. 2012. *From Financial Crisis to Stagnation: The Destruction of Shared Prosperity and the Role of Economics*. New York: Cambridge University Press.

Palmer, John L., and Rudolph G. Penner. 2012. "The Hard Road to Fiscal Responsibility." *Public Budgeting and Finance* 32, no. 3: 4–31.

Papke, Leslie E. 1991. "Interstate Business Tax Differentials and New Firm Location: Evidence from Panel Data." *Journal of Public Economics* 45, no. 1 (June): 47–68.

Paul, Ron. 2011. "Blame the Fed for the Financial Crisis." *Wall Street Journal*, October 20, A. 17.

Peng, Jun, and Peter F. Brucato Jr. 2003. "Another Look at the Effect of Method of Sale on the Interest Cost in the Municipal Bond Market—A Certification Model." *Public Budgeting and Finance* 23, no. 1: 73–95.

Perry, Rick. 2011. "My Tax and Spending Reform Plan." *Wall Street Journal*, October 25. A. 19.

Peterson, Wallace C., and Paul S. Estenson. 1996. *Income, Employment, Economic Growth*, 8th ed. New York: W.W. Norton.

Plaut, Thomas R., and Joseph E. Pluta. 1983. "Business Climate, Taxes and Expenditures, and State Industrial Growth in the United States." *Southern Economic Journal* 50, no. 1: 99–119.

Plumer, Brad. 2012. "QE3: What Is Quantitative Easing? And Will It Help the Economy?" Washington Post, September 13. www.washingtonpost.com/blogs/wonkblog/wp/2012/09/13/qe3-what-is-quantitative-easing-and-will-it-help-the-economy/ (accessed September 13, 2012).

Poister, Theodore H., and Gregory Streib. 1999. "Performance Measurement in Municipal Government: Assessing the State of the Practice." *Public Administration Review* 59, no. 4: 325–35.

Posner, Paul L. 2009. "Budget Process Reform: Waiting for Godot." *Public Administration Review* 69, no. 2: 233–44.

Posner, Paul L., and Denise M. Fantone. 2008. "Performance Budgeting: Prospects for Sustainability." In *Performance Management and Budgeting: How Government Can Learn from Experience*, ed. F. Stevens Redburn, Robert J. Shea, and Terry F. Buss, 92–113. Armonk, NY: M.E. Sharpe.

Poterba, James M. 1994. "State Responses to Fiscal Crises: The Effects of Budgetary Institutions and Politics." *Journal of Political Economy* 102, no. 4: 799–821.

———. 1995a. "Balanced Budget Rules and Fiscal Policy: Evidence from the States." *National Tax Journal* 48: 329–36.

———. 1995b. "Capital Budgets, Borrowing Rules, and State Capital Spending." *Journal of Public Economics* 56: 165–87.

———. 1996. "Budget Institutions and Fiscal Policy in the U.S. States." *American Economic Review* 86: 395–400.

———. 1997. "Demographic Structure and the Political Economy of Public Education." *Journal of Policy Analysis and Management* 16, no. 1: 48–66.

———. 2011. Introduction: "Economic Analysis of Tax Expenditures." *National Tax Journal* 64, no. 2 (Part 2): 451–58.

Poterba, James M., and Kim S. Rueben. 2001. "Fiscal News, State Budget Rules, and Tax-Exempt Bond Yields." *Journal of Urban Economics* 50, no. 37: 537–62.

Primo, David M. 2007. *Rules and Restraint: Government Spending and the Design of Institutions*. Chicago: University of Chicago Press.

Provan, K.G., and P. Kenis. 2008. "Modes of Network Governance: Structure, Management, and Effectiveness." *Journal of Public Administration Research and Theory* 18, no. 2: 229–52.

Pyhrr, Peter A. 1970. "Zero-Base Budgeting." *Harvard Business Review* 48, no. 6: 111–21.

———. 1977. "The Zero-Base Approach to Government Budgeting." *Public Administration Review* 37, no. 1: 1–8.

Rafuse, Robert W., Jr. 1990. *Representative Expenditures: Addressing the Neglected Dimension of Fiscal Capacity*. Information Report M–174. Washington, DC: Advisory Commission on Intergovernmental Relations.

Rassel, Gary R., and Robert S. Kravchuk. 2013. "Good Debt, Gone Bad: The 2007–2009 Crisis in Municipal Debt Markets." In *Handbook of Local Government Fiscal Health*, ed. Helisse Levine, Jonathan B. Justice, and Eric A. Scorsone, 505–33. Burlington, MA: Jones & Bartlett.

Rebell, Michael A. 2002. "Educational Adequacy, Democracy, and the Courts." In *Achieving High Educational Standards for All*, ed. Timothy Ready, Christopher Edley Jr., and Catherine E. Snow, 218–67. Washington, DC: National Academy Press.

Reddick, Christopher G. 2003. "Testing Rival Theories of Budgetary Decision-Making in the United States." *Financial Accountability and Management* 19, no. 4: 315–39.

Reese, Catherine C. 1997. "The Line-Item Veto in Practice in Ten Southern States." *Public Administration Review* 57, no. 6: 510–16.

Reich, Robert B. 2010. *Aftershock: The Next Economy and America's Future*. New York: Alfred A. Knopf.

Reschovsky, Andrew. 1994. "Fiscal Equalization and School Finance." *National Tax Journal* 47, no. 1: 209–21.

Rhoads, Steven E. 1999. *The Economist's View of the World*. New York: Cambridge University Press.

Ribar, David C., and Mark O. Wilhelm. 1999. "The Demand for Welfare Generosity." *Review of Economics and Statistics* 81, no. 1: 96–108.

Robb, Greg. 2011. "Fed Decides on $400 Billion Bond Swap." Marketwatch.com, September 21. www.marketwatch.com/story/fed-decides-on-400-billion-bond-swap-2011-09-21 (accessed September 21, 2011).

Robbins, Mark D., and Daehwan Kim. 2003. "Do State Bond Banks Have Cost Advantages for Municipal Bond Issuance?" *Public Budgeting and Finance* 23, no. 3: 92–108.

Robbins, Mark D., and Bill Simonsen. 2007. "Competition and Selection in Municipal Bond Sales: Evidence from Missouri." *Public Budgeting and Finance* 27, no. 2: 88–103.

Robbins, Mark, Bill Simonsen, and Barry Feldman. 2008. "Citizens and Resource Allocation: Improving Decision Making with Interactive Web-Based Citizen Participation." *Public Administration Review* 68, no. 3: 564–75.

Robinson, Marc, and Jim Brumby. 2005. *Does Performance Budgeting Work? An Analytical Review of the Empirical Literature*. IMF Working Paper WP/05/210. Washington, DC: International Monetary Fund.

Robinson, Scott E. 2004. "Punctuated Equilibrium, Bureaucratization, and Budgetary Changes in Schools." *Policy Studies Journal* 32, no. 1: 25–39.

Robinson, Scott E., Floun'say Caver, Kenneth J. Meier, and Laurence J. O'Toole. 2007. "Explaining Policy Punctuations: Bureaucratization and Budget Change." *American Journal of Political Science* 51, no. 1: 140–50.

Rogers, James R. 2005. "The Impact of Divided Government on Legislative Production." *Public Choice* 123, nos. 1–2: 217–33.

Romer, Christina D., and David H. Romer. 2010. "The Macroeconomic Effects of Tax Changes: Estimates Based on a New Measure of Fiscal Shocks." *American Economic Review* 100, no. 3: 763–801.

Romer, Thomas, and Howard Rosenthal. 1979a. "Bureaucrats Versus Voters: On the Political Economy of Resource Allocation by Direct Democracy." *Quarterly Journal of Economics* 93, no. 4: 563–87.

————. 1979b. "The Elusive Median Voter." *Journal of Public Economics* 12: 143–70.

————. 1982. "Median Voters or Budget Maximizers: Evidence from School Expenditure Referenda." *Economic Inquiry* 20: 556–78.

Rosen, Harvey S., and Ted Gayer. 2010. *Public Finance*, 10th ed. New York: McGraw-Hill.

Rosenthal, Alan. 1998. *The Decline of Representative Democracy: Process, Participation, and Power in State Legislatures*. Washington, DC: CQ Press.

————. 2004. *Heavy Lifting: The Job of the American Legislature*. Washington, DC: CQ Press.

Rossmann, Doralyn, and Elizabeth A. Shanahan. 2012. "Defining and Achieving Normative Democratic Values in Participatory Budgeting Processes." *Public Administration Review* 72, no. 1: 56–66.

Roubini, Nouriel, and Stephen Mihm. 2010. *Crisis Economics*. New York: Penguin Press.

Rowley, Charles. 1984. "The Relevance of the Median Voter Theorem." *Journal of Institutional and Theoretical Economics* 140: 104–26.

Rubin, Irene S. 1991. "Budgeting for Our Times: Target Base Budgeting." *Public Budgeting and Finance* 11, no. 3: 5–14.

————. 1994. "Early Budget Reformers: Democracy, Efficiency, and Budget Reforms." *American Review of Public Administration* 24, no. 3: 229–52.

————. 1998. *Class, Tax, and Power: Municipal Budgeting in the United States*. Chatham, NJ: Chatham House.

————. 2003. *Balancing the Federal Budget: Eating the Seed Corn or Trimming the Herds?* New York: Chatham House.

————. 2007. "The Great Unraveling: Federal Budgeting, 1998–2006." *Public Administration Review* 67, no. 4: 608–17.

————. 2010. *The Politics of Public Budgeting: Getting and Spending, Borrowing and Balancing*, 6th ed. Washington, DC: CQ Press.

Ryu, Jay E. 2006. "Fiscal Impact of an Innovative Highway Financing Alternative on State Highway Expenditures: The Case of Federal Assistance Funds in the State Infrastructure Bank (SIB) Programs." *Public Works Management and Policy* 11, no. 1: 33–48.

————. 2007. "Federal Highway Assistance Funds in the State Infrastructure Bank (SIB) Programs: Mechanisms, Merits, and Modifications." *Public Budgeting and Finance* 27, no. 4: 43–65.

————. 2009. "Exploring the Factors for Budget Stability and Punctuations: A Preliminary Analysis of State Government Sub-Functional Expenditures." *Policy Studies Journal* 37, no. 3: 457–73.

————. 2011a. *Bounded Bureaucracy and the Budgetary Process in the United States*. Brunswick, NJ: Transaction Publishers.

————. 2011b. "Legislative Professionalism and Budget Punctuations in State Government Sub-Functional Expenditures." *Public Budgeting and Finance* 31, no. 2: 22–42.

Ryu, Jay E., Cynthia J. Bowling, Chunglae Cho, and Deil S. Wright. 2007. "Effects of Administrators' Aspirations, Political Principals' Priorities, and Interest Groups' Influence on State Agency Budget Requests." *Public Budgeting and Finance* 27, no. 2: 22–49.

————. 2008. "Exploring Explanations of State Agency Budgets: Institutional Budget Actors or Exogenous Environment?" *Public Budgeting and Finance* 28, no. 3: 23–47.

Samuelson, Paul A. 1954. "The Pure Theory of Public Expenditure." *Review of Economics and Statistics* 36, no. 4: 387–89.

————. 1955. "Diagrammatic Exposition of a Theory of Public Expenditure." *Review of Economics and Statistics* 37, no. 4: 350–56.

Saturno, James V. 2004. *The Congressional Budget Process: A Brief Overview*. Washington, DC: Congressional Research Service.

————. 2008. *Points of Order in the Congressional Budget Process*. Washington, DC: Congressional Research Service.

Schick, Allen. 1966. "The Road to PPB: The Stages of Budget Reform." *Public Administration Review* 26, no. 4: 243–58.

————. 1980. *Congress and Money: Budgeting, Spending and Taxing*. Washington, DC: Urban

————. 1983. "Incremental Budgeting in a Decremental Age." *Policy Sciences* 16, no. 1: 1–25.

————. 2007. *The Federal Budget: Politics, Policy, Process*, 3d ed. Washington, DC: Brookings Institution Press.

————. 2009. "Budgeting for Fiscal Space." *OECD Journal on Budgeting* 9, no. 2: 1–18.

Schick, Allen, and Harry Hatry. 1982. "Zero Base Budgeting: The Manager's Budget." *Public Budgeting and Finance* 2, no. 1: 72–87.

Schiff, Peter D., and John Downes. 2009. *Crash Proof 2.0: How to Profit from the Economic Collapse.* Hoboken, NJ: John Wiley.

Schneider, Mark. 1989. "Intermunicipal Competition, Budget-Maximizing Bureaucrats, and the Level of Suburban Competition." *American Journal of Political Science* 33, no. 3: 612–28.

Schneider, Mark, and Byung Moon Ji. 1987. "The Flypaper Effect and Competition in the Local Market for Public Goods." *Public Choice* 54, no. 1: 27–39.

Shadbegian, Ronald J. 1996. "Do Tax and Expenditure Limitations Affect the Size and Growth of State Government?" *Contemporary Economic Policy* 14, no. 1: 22–35.

————. 1999. "The Effect of Tax and Expenditure Limitations on the Revenue Structure of Local Government, 1962–87." *National Tax Journal* 52, no. 2: 221–37.

————. 2003. "Did the Property Tax Revolt Affect Local Public Education? Evidence from Panel Data." *Public Finance Review* 31, no. 1: 91–121.

Sharkansky, Ira. 1968. "Agency Requests, Gubernatorial Support and Budget Success in State Legislature." *American Political Science Review* 62, no. 4: 1220–31.

Shah, Anwar, ed. 2007. *Participatory Budgeting*. Washington, DC: World Bank.

Sheffrin, Steven M. 2004. "State Budget Deficit Dynamics and the California Debacle." *Journal of Economic Perspectives* 18, no. 2: 205–26.

Sherman, Howard J., and Michael A. Meeropol. 2013. *Principles of Macroeconomics: Activist vs. Austerity Policies.* Armonk, NY: M.E. Sharpe.

Sigelman, Lee. 1986. "The Bureaucrat as Budget Maximizer: An Assumption Examined." *Public Budgeting and Finance* 6, no. 1: 50–59.

Simonsen, Bill, Mark D. Robbins, and Lee Helgerson. 2001. "The Influence of Jurisdiction Size and Sale Type on Municipal Bond Interest Rates: An Empirical Analysis." *Public Administration Review* 61, no. 6: 709–17.

Snell, Ron. 2010. *Zero-Base Budgeting in the States.* Washington, DC: National Conference of State Legislatures.

————. 2012. *NCSL Fiscal Brief: Zero-Base Budgeting in the States.* Washington, DC: National Conference of State Legislatures.

Snow, Douglas R., and Irene S. Rubin. 2006. "Illinois: Constitutional versus Negotiated Powers." In *Budgeting in the States: Institutions, Processes, and Politics*, ed. Edward J. Clynch and Thomas P. Lauth, 103–18. Westport, CT: Praeger.

Sommer, Jeff. 2011. "Let's Twist Again, Like We Did in '61." New York Times, September 10. www. nytimes.com/2011/09/11/your-money/federal-reserve-considers-a-revival-of-operation-twist.html (accessed September 10, 2011).

Sonnier, Blaise M. 2010. "An Analysis of Colorado's Notice and Reporting Requirements for Internet and Remote Sales." *Journal of State Taxation* 28, no. 6: 23–59.

Sonnier, Blaise M., and Sharon S. Lassar. 2012. "State Taxation of Remote and Internet Sales: Congressional Options on the Table." *Journal of State Taxation* 31, no. 1: 19–26.

Stalebrink, Odd J., and Velda Frisco. 2011. "PART in Retrospect: An Examination of Legislators' Attitude Toward PART." *Public Budgeting and Finance* 31, no. 2: 1–21.

Stallmann, Judith I., and Steven Deller. 2011. "State Tax and Expenditure Limitations, Business Climate, and Economic Performance." *Public Budgeting and Finance* 31, no. 4: 109–35.

Stanford, Karen A. 1992. "State Budget Deliberations: Do Legislators Have a Strategy?" *Public Administration Review* 52, no. 1: 16–26.

St. Clair, Travis. 2012. "The Effect of Tax and Expenditure Limitations on Revenue Volatility: Evidence from Colorado." *Public Budgeting and Finance* 32, no. 3: 61–78.

Steinhauer, Jennifer S., and Robert Pear. 2011. "House Set to Vote Down Payroll Tax Cut Extension." New York Times, December 19. www.nytimes.com/2011/12/20/us/politics/house-set-to-vote-down-payroll-tax-cut-extension.html?adxnnl=1&pagewanted=all&adxnnlx=1375297508-exFATnwJek-BHSKOtXKZ/Vw (accessed December 19, 2011).

Steiss, Alan Walter. 2003. "Procedures for Programming and Financing Capital Improvements." In *Case Studies in Public Budgeting and Financial Management*, 2d ed., ed. Aman Khan and W. Bartley Hildreth, 255–72. New York: Marcel Dekker.

Stern, Gary H., and Ron J. Feldman. 2009. *Too Big to Fail: The Hazards of Bank Bailouts.* Washington, DC: Brookings Institution Press.

Stokey, Edith, and Richard Zeckhauser. 1978. *A Primer for Policy Analysis.* New York: Norton.

Stotsky, Janet G. 1991. "State Fiscal Responses to Federal Government Grants." *Growth and Change* 22, no. 3: 17–31.

Straussman, Jeffrey D. 1986. "Courts and Public Purse Strings: Have Portraits of Budgeting Missed Something?" *Public Administration Review* 46, no. 4: 345–51.

———. 1988. "Rights-Based Budgeting." In *New Directions in Budget Theory*, ed. Irene S. Rubin, 100–23. Albany: State University of New York Press.

Straussman, Jeffrey D., and Kurt Thurmaier. 1989. "Budgeting Rights: The Case of Jail Litigation." *Public Budgeting and Finance* 9, no. 2: 30–42.

Suranovic, Steven. 1997. "Why Economists Should Study Fairness." *Challenge* 40, no. 5: 109–24.

Swain, John W., and C. Jeff Hartley Jr. 2001. "Incrementalism: Old but Good?" In *Evolving Theories of Public Budgeting*, ed. John R. Bartle, 11–27. Bingley, UK: Emerald Group.

Swain, John W., and B.J. Reed. 2010. *Budgeting for Public Managers.* Armonk, NY: M.E. Sharpe.

Taggart, William A. 1989. "Redefining the Power of the Federal Judiciary: The Impact of Court-Ordered Prison Reform on State Expenditures for Corrections." *Law and Society Review* 23, no. 2: 241–72.

Tanglao, Leezel, and Z. Byron Wolf. 2010. "What the Tax Cut Extension Means for You." abcnews.go.com, December 17. http://abcnews.go.com/print?id=12423601 (accessed March 1, 2011).

Tannenwald, Robert. 1998. "Come the Devolution, Will States Be Able to Respond?" *New England Economic Review* (May–June): 53–73.

———. 1999. "Fiscal Disparity Among the States Revisited." *New England Economic Review* (July–August): 3–25.

———. 2002. "Interstate Fiscal Disparity in 1997." *New England Economic Review* (Third Quarter): 17–33.

Tarr, David G., and Morris E. Morkre. 1984. *Aggregate Costs to the United States of Tariffs and Quotas on Imports: General Tariff Cuts and Removal of Quotas on Automobiles, Steel, Sugar, and Textiles.* Washington, DC: Bureau of Economics Staff Report to the Federal Trade Commission, 54–74.

Taylor, John B. 2012. *First Principles: Five Keys to Restoring America's Prosperity.* New York: W.W. Norton.

Texas Governor's Office of Budget and Planning. 2003. "Strategic Planning and Budgeting in the "New Texas": Putting Service Efforts and Accomplishments to Work." In *Case Studies in Public Budgeting and Financial Management*, 2d ed., ed. Aman Khan and W. Bartley Hildreth, 155–72. New York: Marcel Dekker.

Thompson, Ann Marie, James L. Perry, and Theodore K. Miller. 2008. "Linking Collaboration Processes and Outcomes: Foundations for Advancing Empirical Theory." In *Big Ideas in Collaborative Public Management*, ed. Lisa Blomgren Bingham and Rosemary O'Leary, 97–120. Armonk, NY: M.E. Sharpe.

Thompson, Fred. 2007. "The Political Economy of Public Administration." In *Handbook of Public Administration*, ed. Jack Rabin, W. Bartley Hildreth, and Gerald J. Miller, 1063–93. Boca Raton, FL: Taylor & Francis.

Thompson, Joel A. 1987. "Agency Request, Gubernatorial Support, and Budget Success in State Legislature Revisited." *Journal of Politics* 49, no. 3: 756–79.

Thurmier, Kurt, and Katherine Willoughby. 2001. "Windows of Opportunity: Toward a Multiple Rationalities Model of Budgeting." In *Evolving Theories of Public Budgeting*, ed. John R. Bartle, 29–54. Bingley, UK: Emerald Group.

Tiebout, Charles M. 1956. "A Pure Theory of Local Expenditures." *Journal of Political Economy* 64, no. 5: 416–24.

"Times Topics: Financial Regulatory Reform." 2010. New York Times, November 4. http://topics. nytimes.com/topics/reference/timestopics/subjects/c/credit_crisis/financial_regulatory_reform/ index.html.

Trimidas, George, and Stanley L. Winer. 2005. "The Political Economy of Government Size." *European Journal of Political Economy* 21, no. 3: 643–66.

Turnbull, Geoffrey K., and Peter M. Mitias. 1999. "The Median Voter Model Across Levels of Government." *Public Choice* 99, nos. 1–2: 119–38.

Ulbrich, Holley H. 2011. *Public Finance in Theory and Practice*, 2d ed. New York: Routledge.

U.S. Advisory Commission on Intergovernmental Relations (USACIR). 1990. *The Structure of State Aid to Elementary and Secondary Education*. Washington, DC: U.S. Advisory Commission on Intergovernmental Relations.

U.S. Congressional Budget Office. 2012a. *Economic Effects of Reducing the Fiscal Restraint That Is Scheduled to Occur in 2013*. Washington, DC: U.S. Congressional Budget Office.

———. 2012b. *Economic Effects of Policies Contributing to Fiscal Tightening in 2013*. Washington, DC: U.S. Congressional Budget Office.

U.S. Department of Commerce. 2010. *Fiscal Year 2010 Performance and Accountability Report*. Washington, DC: U.S. Department of Commerce.

U.S. General Accounting Office. 1997. *Performance Budgeting: Past Initiatives Offer Insights for GPRA Implementation*. GAO/AIMD-97-46. Washington, DC: General Accounting Office.

U.S. Government. 2012. Recovery.gov: Track the Money. www.recovery.gov/Pages/default.aspx (accessed November 5, 2012).

U.S. Government Accountability Office. 2005. *Understanding the Tax Reform Debate: Background, Criteria, & Questions*. GAO-05-1009SP, September 1. Washington, DC: Government Accountability Office.

Vining, Aidan R., and David L. Weimer. 1992. "Welfare Economics as the Foundation for Public Policy Analysis: Incomplete and Flawed but Nevertheless Desirable." *Journal of Socio-Economics* 21, no. 1: 25–37.

Wagner, Richard E. 2012a. "*The Calculus of Consent*: A Compass for My Professional Journey." *Public Choice* 152, nos. 3–4: 393–96.

———. 2012b. "The Institutional Framework for Shared Consumption: Deemphasizing Taxation in the Theory of Public Finance." *Public Finance and Management* 12, no. 1: 5–20.

Wampler, Brian. 2007. "A Guide to Participatory Budgeting." In *Participatory Budgeting*, ed. Anwar Shah, 21–55. Washington, DC: World Bank.

Wanat, John. 1974. "Bases of Budgetary Incrementalism." *American Political Science Review* 68, no. 3: 1221–28.

Wasylenko, Michael. 1997. "Taxation and Economic Development." *New England Economic Review* (March/April): 37–52.

Webb, Natalie F., Anke Richter, and Donald Bonsper. 2010. "Linking Defense Planning and Resource Decisions: A Return to Systems Thinking." *Defense and Security Analysis* 26, no. 4: 387–400.

Weimer, David L., and Aidan R. Vining. 2005. *Policy Analysis: Concepts and Practice*, 4th ed. Upper Saddle River, NJ: Pearson Prentice Hall.

————. 2011. *Policy Analysis: Concepts and Practice*, 5th ed. Upper Saddle River, NJ: Pearson Longman.

Weingast, Barry R. 2009. "Second Generation Fiscal Federalism: The Implications of Fiscal Incentives." *Journal of Urban Economics* 65, no. 3: 279–93.

Wessel, David. 2011. "Federal Reserve Considers Whether to Twist Again." *Wall Street Journal*, September 15, A. 5.

West, William F., Eric Lindquist, and Katrina N. Mosher-Howe. 2009. "NOAA's Resurrection of Program Budgeting: Déjà-Vu All Over Again?" *Public Administration Review* 69, no. 3: 435–47.

Wheelan, Charles. 2011. *Introduction to Public Policy*. New York: W.W. Norton.

Whicker, Marcia Lynn. 1991. "South Carolina: The Demise of Legislative Dominance?" In *Governors, Legislatures, and Budgets: Diversity Across the American States*, ed. Edward J. Clynch and Thomas P. Lauth, 137–48. New York: Greenwood Press.

White, Joseph. 2009. "What Not to Ask of Budget Processes: Lessons from George W. Bush's Years." *Public Administration Review* 69, no. 2: 224–32.

————. 2012. "Playing the Wrong PART: The Program Assessment Rating Tool and the Functions of the President's Budget." *Public Administration Review* 72, no. 1: 112–21.

Wiedermer, David, Robert A. Wiedermer, and Cindy Spitzer. 2011. *Aftershock: Protect Yourself and Profit in the Next Global Financial Meltdown*, 2d ed. Hoboken, NJ: John Wiley.

Wiedermer, John David, Robert A. Wiedermer, Cindy Spitzer, and Eric Janszen. 2006. *America's Bubble Economy*. Hoboken, NJ: John Wiley.

Wildavsky, Aaron. 1969. "Rescuing Policy Analysis from PPBS." *Public Administration Review* 29, no. 2: 189–202.

————. 2007. *Budgeting and Governing*. Piscataway, NJ: Transaction Publishers.

Wildavsky, Aaron, and Naomi Caiden. 2004. *The New Politics of the Budgetary Process*, 5th ed. New York: Pearson-Longman.

Williams, Alan. 1972. "Cost-Benefit Analysis: Bastard Science? And/or Insidious Poison in the Body Politick?" *Journal of Public Economics* 1, no. 2: 199–226.

Williams, David. 2011. "Tax Zombie That Refuses to Die; New Deal Levy for Rural Phones Has Outlived Its Purpose." Washington Times, August 19. www.washingtontimes.com/news/2011/aug/19/tax-zombie-that-refuses-to-die/ (accessed August 19, 2011).

Wood, Dan B. 1993. Book review: *The Budget-Maximizing Bureaucrat: Appraisals and Evidence*. *American Political Science Review* 87, no. 4: 1013–14.

Woods, Thomas E., Jr. 2009. *Meltdown: A Free-Market Look at Why the Stock Market Collapsed, the Economy Tanked, and Government Bailouts Will Make Things Worse*. Washington, DC: Regnery Publishing.

————. 2011. *Rollback: Repealing Big Government before the Coming Fiscal Collapse*. Washington, DC: Regnery Publishing.

Yusuf, Juita-Elena (Wie), Jacob Fowles, Cleopatra Grizzle, and Gao Liu. 2010. "State Fiscal Constraints on Local Government Borrowing: Effects on Scale and Cost." In *Handbook of Local Government Fiscal Health*, ed. Helisse Levine, Jonathan B. Justice, and Eric A. Scorsone, 77–124. Burlington, MA: Jones & Bartlett.

Yusuf, Juita-Elena, Lenahan O'Connell, Merl Hackbart, and Gao Liu. 2012. "State Infrastructure Banks and Borrowing Costs for Transportation Projects." *Public Finance Review* 38, no. 6: 682–709.

"Zero-Base Budgeting a Worthwhile Exercise: A Mindless Commitment to Continuity Can Hamper Efforts to Find a Better Way." 2011. Editorial, *Portland Press Herald*, August 26.

Index

About the Author

Jay Eungha Ryu is an associate professor of public policy and administration in the department of political science at Ohio University. He received a BA from Seoul National University in 1986, MPA degrees from Seoul National University (1988), and George Washington University (1998), and a PhD from the University of Georgia in 2003. He is the author of *Bounded Bureaucracy and the Budgetary Process in the United States* (2011). His work has been published in *Public Budgeting and Finance*, *Journal of Public Administration Research and Theory*, *American Review of Public Administration*, and *Policy Studies Journal*.

Ryu's main research agenda covers the political economy of public budget decisions. Budget decision makers intend to rationalize entire budget decision-making processes, but are restrained by their capacity limits and political institutions. Ryu attempts to explain this so-called mechanism of intended rationality. Scholars have applied economic frameworks to budget processes at various levels of the federal tier. Economic models present unique tools to quantify the level of taxation and spending and to identify numerically testable factors. Other scholars have tended to employ political approaches in explaining the processes. Political models provide for practical observations of information-rich stories to analyze the decisions. Ryu has been combining these two approaches to investigate how decisions on taxation and spending are made.

Ryu also has been investigating how revolving loan systems can stretch scarce financial resources needed for public infrastructure systems. State Infrastructure Bank (SIB) programs and similar national infrastructure bank programs have recently garnered national attention as alternatives to expedite construction of public infrastructure systems. Ryu also has focused on another research issue. He empirically tests whether performance-based budgeting (PBB) systems reallocate resources where they can be used most efficiently and effectively.

He has been practicing Kendo (Kumdo) for thirty-two years and is an avid soccer player.